Rhyming English Couplets

About the Author

Mulki Radhakrishna Shetty was born in India. He was educated in Bangalore and qualified as a physician from Madras University. He later studied in England, Canada and the United States, where he practiced Medical Oncology. In 2005 he authored two books "The Itinerant Indian" and "Encyclopaedia of Quotable Couplets" which found a place in the Limca Book of Records 2007. This was followed by two volumes of 'English Couplets' in 2007(Limca book of records 2008). This book is the fourth volume of **'English Couplets'** and took nearly seventeen months to write.

He now lives in Bangalore.

Rhyming English Couplets

M.R. SHETTY

PENTAGON PRESS

Rhyming English Couplets
by M.R. Shetty

First Published: 2009

© M.R. Shetty

ISBN 978-81-8274-361-8

All rights reserved. No part of this publication may be reproduced, stored in a retrieval system, or transmitted, in any form or by any means, electronic, mechanical, photocopying, recording, or otherwise, without first obtaining written permission of the copyright owner.

Published by
PENTAGON PRESS
206, Peacock Lane, Shahpur Jat, New Delhi-110049
Phones: 011-64706243, 26491568
Telefax: 011-26490600
email: rajan@pentagon-press.com
website: www.pentagon-press.com

Printed at Thomson Press, Faridabad.

Introduction

Two lines of verse that have rhyme and metre are called couplets. This book titled 'Rhyming English Couplets' is the fourth volume of 'English Couplets'.

The earliest known forms of couplets were in Chinese literature, 'Shi Jing' (10th Century B.C.). These were placed at the door steps during the Chinese new year. These were followed by couplets in 'Ramayana' (500-100 B.C.), 'Mahabharata' (200 B.C. to 200 A.D.) and In Tamil literature the Thirukkural' (200 BC-800 A.D.).

In the 10th century A.D. Ferdowsi the Persian Poet wrote the 'Shahanameh' which consisted of fifty thousand couplets. This was followed, by Chaucer (1343-1400) in English literature who wrote 'Canterbury Tales' in Couplet form. John Gower (1330-1408 A.D.) who wrote 34,000 couplets was followed by John Dyrden (1631-1700 A.D.), Jonathan Swift (1667-1745) and Alexander Pope (1688-1744).

In urdu literature Wali Deccani (1667-1707) and Ghalib (1797-1969) were very well known for their couplets.

A rhyme happens when two words sound the same but have dissimilar meaning and is often used in poetry and song. Example 'Rain-Spain'

Metre is the basic rhythmic structure of verse and is concerned with acoustics without relationship to meaning, example lub-dub' as in the heart beat.

Here are some examples of couplets from the literature.

> 'Don't gamble even if you win
> your gain is a bait to draw you in'
>
> *Thirukkural*

> 'Pain of love be sweeter far
> than all other pleasures are'
>
> *John Dryden*

Rhythm:

Rhythm and its movements are a natural expression of humans, as in the heart beat, pulse, sleep patterns and so on. Rhythm is also universal, as in movements of the earth around the sun, and other regular planetary movements.

Rhythm also has a role in human memory. Poetry is better remembered than prose, so is music, which is why children remember better when sung to, as in nursery rhymes.

Why do I write:

I write because the process is automatic, and it brings me peace of mind. The couplets write themselves. Also to experience the world in new and original ways and to explain it like it's never been said before.

> 'What oft' is thought
> but ne'er so well expres't
>
> *Alexander Pope* (1688-1744)

How I write:

> 'A thought becomes a word
> waiting to be heard
> couplets then alight
> from thoughts in full flight'.

What I write:

A variety of couplets that are axioms, aphorisms, proverbs, poetry and amusings. It is a dictionary with all of the above.

Introduction

"So many choices
to please the inner voices"

I will now discuss the neuroscience of poetry and music since they are closely related.

'Music resembles poetry, in each are numerous graces which no methods teach and which a master hand alone can reach'.

Alexander Pope (1688-1744)

A feature common to poetry and music is rhythm. Rhythm has acoustic properties which enable it to travel as sound waves to reach the human ear. The ear lobe directs the sound to the middle ear across the ear drum, which in turn causes vibrations of the fluid in the Innner ear. The Cochlea (snail shell) is an organ that converts sound vibrations into nerve impulses, which are carried to the brain by the auditory nerve. The Hippocampus (hippos 'horse' + kampos 'sea monster') is the center for memory (limbic system). Rhyme and rhythm are the tools in the magic we call memory. The hippocampus then goes about converting the rhythm of short term memory into permanent long term memory to be later stored in the cortex.

The process now switches to the nerve cell, of which there are billions, these talk to their neighbour cells through connections called synapses (a moat between nerve cells). A nerve cell can convert sound into electrical signals, which in turn gets converted to a chemical signal at the synapses of the nerve cell. The entry sound and word are stored at specific synaptic addresses in the brain in electro-chemical language.

The process of converting short term memory into permanent long term memory is complex, and is facilitated by its emotional content.

$$\text{Memory} = \text{Emotion} \times \text{rhyme} \times \text{rhythm}$$
$$(M = ER^2).$$

Rhythm stimulates multiple pulses of serotonin[1] (neurotransmitter) which produces growth of new synaptic connections. In addition there is increased release of glutamate (glue) that strengthens the synapse. A new enzyme molecule Protein Kinase MZeta[2] (memory storage molecule) also helps in strengthening the synapses and has a role in making memory permanent.

In Summary I have tried to explain how poetry and music[3,4] through rhyme and rhythm are able to make an indelible impact on the memory forming apparatus of the human brain. How through millions of years, humans have stored and disseminated thought via the oral tradition. Why emotion is an important component of the permanent memory storage process. How the brain is, and always was a plastic organ capable of growth well into old age, whose mysteries are being slowly unraveled, through the works of neuro-scientists around the world.

The couplets in this volume and previous volumes exemplifies this ability very well. To be able to retrieve stored memories of a lifetime and produce nearly sixty thousand couplets over a sixty month period, was one of the most joyful experiences of my life. I hope the readers will enjoy reading them as much as I have in writing them.

Rhythm thronged in his head, words jostled to be joined together, he was on the verge of a poem.

John Galsworthy (1867-1933) in 'To Let' (1921)

Bangalore **M.R. Shetty**

References:
1) Kandel ER 'In search of memory' Norton N.Y. 2006.
2) Rapid erasure of Long Term memory association in cortex by an inhibitor of "Protein Kinase MZeta" Research from SUNY Downstate Medical Center 'Science' August 2007.
3) Levitin D J, 'This is your brain on music' the science of a human obsession, Dutton Penguin Group NY 2006.
4) Sacks O'Musicophilia'. Tales of Music and the brain, Picador 2007.

Contents

Introduction	*v*
A	1
B	20
C	47
D	79
E	118
F	132
G	177
H	195
I	228
J	240
K	244
L	248
M	330
N	365
O	374
P	379
Q	423
R	425
S	447

T	511
U	554
V	559
W	564
Y	588
Z	589
Index	592

A

Abandon
> Abandon every perk
> if you need steady work

Abide
> When the law is on your side
> the opponents will abide

> Why won't he abide
> this demon inside

Ability
> Men of ability
> are the nobility

> No ability
> without responsibility

> No responsibility
> without ability

> They all have the ability
> to court infidelity

Able
> I don't think I am able
> to spin a lofty fable

> Through fact and fable
> to teach we are able

Abode
> A well crafted ode
> has its own abode

> From the tadpole to the toad
> is a change of abode

> In his abode
> a toad is a toad

> Middle of the road
> is no abode

> No abode for the toad
> the middle of the road

> The untrodden road
> is the best abode

Absconded
> Once we were fully bonded
> one of us just absconded

Absence
> Absence like a blotter
> removes the written matter

> He wrote his spoof
> in the absence of proof

*Absense makes us fonder
far beyond and yonder*

*Absense of scope
what happens to hope*

Absolutely
*Absolutely
she said very cutely*

Absorbed
*No second look
absorbed in her book*

Abstinence
*Makes sense
abstinence*

Abstruse
*What is the use
if the writing is abstruse*

*What's the use
of being abstruse*

Abuse
*Don't abuse your body
with daily rum and toddy*

*Silent abuse
down to his shoes*

*All is wrong with the world
where abuses are always hurled*

Accent
*Don't lament
her cut glass accent*

Acceptance
*Acceptance is a must
when the disgust is just*

Accidents
*Why do you bicker
accidents will occur*

Acclaim
*When acclaim does elude
don't yourself delude*

*Your only aim
must be acclaim*

Accomplished
*His accomplished best
was put to the test*

*It's an accomplished feat
if your work sells down the street*

Accumulate
*Some they accumulate riches
by having people in stitches*

Accuracy
*Resort to accuracy
to rid yourself of secrecy*

Accusations
*Accusations without proof
went through the roof*

Accused
*Without any reason
they accused him of treason*

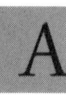

Accusing
> Don't let it linger
> the accusing finger

> Every accusing finger
> looking for a place to linger

> The accusing finger
> tends to linger

Ace
> If you leave him his space
> he will become an ace

Acerbic
> His acerbic tongue
> had him hung

Aces
> Those who hold the aces
> also have sad faces

Acquainting
> His way of acquainting
> was to fall in front of her fainting

Acres
> With a few acres around
> they slept in the middle very sound

Across
> Across my neighbours wall
> was a girl beautiful and tall

Act
> Clear up your act
> with a little bit of tact

Action
> Action is a kind
> of traction on the mind

> Back in action
> after three weeks in traction

> Every course of action
> has repentance as a fraction

> Let not your action
> succumb to distraction

> Wish is just a fraction
> of what is needed for action

> There is a lesser prize
> if your actions are not wise

Active
> Active in tussles
> their vocal muscles

Acumen
> What use is acumen
> without ink in the pen

Adam
> Adam and Eve they grapple
> about who owns the apple

> How to grapple
> with Adam and his apple

Addiction
> Addiction has a wing
> though not a good thing

> Addictions take to flight
> when no one is in sight

Addition
> In addition to will
> must have the skill

Adept
> He is adept
> who has spring in his step

Adjust
> Adjust your hat
> give full face of the bat

Adjusted
> He adjusted his briar
> and lit a matchstick fire

Admire
> Always admire
> a lovely attire

> I will never tire
> of the people I admire

> Of all the people I admire
> of her I will never tire

> She is admired much
> for her feathery touch

> The girl about town
> they admired her gown

Admiring
> They sat around the fire
> admiring their attire

Admonishment
> Admonishment was meant
> to be within the tent

Adorable
> Her most adorable feature
> was how she faced up to the future

Adoration
> Is it just adoration
> or infatuation

> Though worthy of adoration
> no need for coronation

Adrenal
> Nothing more final
> than a failing adrenal

Adult
> Until you join a cult
> you're no adult

Adultery
> Day or night
> adultery isn't right

> Yet to see adultery
> by climbing a tall tree

Adventure
> Adventure and fear
> uncomfortably near

> Adventure found
> adventure bound

> Adventure is at hand
> when you travel many a land

> Every new adventure
> starts as a venture

*He forgot his denture
on his nautical adventure*

*I won't need a denture
after this adventure*

*My final adventure
is to not lose my denture*

*My molar adventure
was restricted to denture*

*Verbal adventure
without losing your denture*

*Forests have a sound
where adventures abound*

Adversity

*Hand in the kitty
in adversity*

*How can I pity
all this adversity*

Advice

*Advice can be wrong
where it don't belong*

*Advice given with care
works less than given with scare*

*Best advice is twice
given to the unwise*

*Don't do it twice
when you give advice*

*Good advice
never comes twice*

*How to be nice
and still give advice*

*The casting dice
heeds no advice*

*When you have to make a choice
seek advice from inner voice*

Affable

*He was so affable
it was quite laughable*

Affair

*An affair to remember
the feeling of slumber*

*Madness has a flair
in mid-day affair*

*Monogamy gave him a scare
so he had an affair*

*Somersaulting in mid-air
is no mean affair*

*They swim as a pair
having an affair*

*In affairs of anguish
a tendency to languish*

Affection

*A moment spent in affection
was time for reflection*

*Show of affection
was love on reflection*

*True affection can be found
when love makes it around*

Affinity

*A banana peel
has affinity for the heel*

*Why is it that noses
have affinity for roses*

Affluent

*He may not be fluent
but is very affluent*

Afford

*Can't afford to bungle
your life in the concrete jungle*

*Can't afford to slip
where the iceberg has a tip*

*He can't afford to sneeze
while flying on the trapeze*

*On a cold winter day
cannot afford to stray*

Afloat

*Easy to gloat
after staying afloat*

Afraid

*Afraid to frown
lest he may lose his crown*

*Afraid to speak
he who is meek*

*Like two beans in a stalk
afraid to talk*

*Many a price was paid
for the times I was afraid*

Afternoon

*Let it come soon
the lazy summer afternoon*

*On a languid afternoon
there was no full moon*

*Afternoons in the summer
they listened to the drummer*

Afterthought

*Afterthought
is worse than naught*

Against

*Against the trend
she was a platonic friend*

Age

*Old age is a stage
reached by the final page*

*Age is a flood
that travels through the blood*

*Age say the wise
is too much of a price*

*All things will age
stage by stage*

*Come of age
become a sage*

*Don't lose your twinkle
to old age and wrinkle*

He evolved with age
from the jungle to the cage

He renounced being a sage
when dalliance came of age

He seemed to quietly age
when he didn't turn a page

In old age dead
if improperly fed

In old age he mellow
the song and dance fellow

In old age he sang
he would like to go out with a bang

In old age it pays
his prancing ways

In the small print of the page
that's where she writes her age

Men come of age
just before becoming a sage

My spine made a bend
as age caught up in the end

Never ask their age
said the bearded sage

Old age and doubt
together they caused gout

Old age as it whittles
let me stick to skittles

Old age can devour
the most fragrant of flower

Old age full of sorrow
from a declining bone marrow

Old age is a race
at a deathly pace

Old age is a time
to make rhythm and rhyme

Old age is a treasure
which the youth can never measure

Old age is here
but I have memories my dear

Old age is in the main
about agony and pain

Old age is reflected
in the mirror all unexpected

Old age is sublime
just a wrinkle in the face of time

Old age it dreads
the silvery white threads

Old age may be in fashion
but where is all the passion

Old age was meant
to be doubly bent

Stage by stage
we reach the golden age

Stand up and don't fall
when old age, gives you a call

Tells me my age
my creaking rib-cage

*We all must age
in life's only stage*

*We are not on the same page
but live in the same age*

*When the bones begin to melt
old age it gets felt*

*Will never age
the printed page*

*Written in every page
the torments of our age*

Aged

*The aged bird with wings
that flutter as she sings*

Aged

*The middle aged matron
turned out to be a patron*

Ageing

*Ageing and grey
nothing but pray*

*Though ageing and blind
she had a working mind*

Agent

*Have a good agent
if you wish to be cogent*

Ages

*Back to the middle ages
slowly and in stages*

*Can they be sages
children of all ages*

*It appears in stages
wisdom through the ages*

*What's between the pages
will last through the ages*

Aggression

*Aggression was meant
to throw them off the scent*

Aging

*He collects felines
and aging wines*

*He wasn't averse to upstaging
though he was aging*

*Though I am aging
I am more engaging*

Agony

*Oh the agony
of bringing up progeny*

*Why is it in the main
about agony and the pain*

Agreeing

*She tested his mettle
before agreeing to settle*

Agreement

*An agreement is meant
to be signed under the tent*

Aided

*Not without being aided
the pirates could have raided*

Ailing

> If she had been ailing
> from our duty all failing

Aim

> Aim high
> to reach for the sky

> Don't aim for the gullet
> when you think of the word bullet

> If you aim always to be meagre
> you will end up as a little leaguer

> When you bowl leg spin
> aim for the third pin

Aims

> Many they make claims
> about the height of their aims

Air

> Don't fall off the chair
> when something is in the air

> Up in the air
> he hit it for a pair

Alarming

> It takes a new morning
> to rid you of things alarming

> It was quite alarming
> when she found her own prince charming

> The fog finds it alarming
> that the sun came out in the morning

> Things became alarming
> once the cook gave a warming

Alcoholic

> Alcoholic drink
> can make your face pink

> Alcoholic quiver
> starts in the liver

Alien

> In an alien world
> all things are curled

Aligned

> He was maligned
> because his teeth were aligned

Alive

> Alive and well
> love can tell

> There is honey in this hive
> and a bee fully alive

> Thoughts come alive
> nine to five

Alley

> Let's get pally
> at the bowling alley

Aloft

> The balloon is aloft
> all bets are off

Alone

> Are we ever alone
> deep down to the bone

> Better left alone
> the dog and his bone

A

*Dog with a bone
must be left alone*

*He couldn't go there alone
so he sent his clone*

*He is never alone
who talks to his clone*

*How could she have known
she would end up all alone*

*How to be alone
in your comfort zone*

*I am in a zone
just leave me alone*

*It just feels right
to be alone at night*

*Leave me alone
said the bee to the drone*

*Once you atone
do it alone*

*She became very alone
when she lost her drone*

*She got up and went
I became alone in my tent*

*They pick a bone
when you are quiet and alone*

*When I am alone
need her voice on the phone*

*When she feels alone
I have flowers to atone*

Alpha

*Alpha and Omega
they both did yoga*

Alphabet

*Birds in their coop
drink alphabet soup*

Already

*He doesn't need a tool
who already is a fool*

Alter

*How can you alter
our steps that at night falter*

Always

*Always consider giving
Once you make a good living*

*Always in my eye
only you why*

*Always keep it near
both tobacco and beer*

*Always when I think
it is her wearing mink*

*It's not always the beer
but he acts a little queer*

Amaze

*Fix your gaze
on things that amaze*

*Things that amaze
are in his suitcase*

*What distance does to the gaze
it never ceases to amaze*

Amazed

*I am always amazed
why he is unfazed*

Amazing

*The sunset is amazing
with flames that flicker blazing*

Ambition

*Caught up in ambition
without a hint of fruition*

*Raw face of ambition
accomplished in a mission*

*Striving ambition
is a paramount condition*

*He was ambitions beyond caring
and careless beyond daring*

Ambitious

*He who is ambitious
can turn vicious*

Amends

*Distance makes amends
for the disquiet among friends*

Amiable

*Amiable and able
he was always at the table*

Amuse

*Author must choose
a lie that will amuse*

*How to amuse
the alskan moose*

*They amuse each other
with a tickle of the feather*

Anaconda

*What has it to gain
the anaconda in the main*

Ancestors

*Ancestors in attendance
produced good descendents*

*Some of my ancestors
must have been jesters*

Anchor

*I dropped anchor
found a cure for my canker*

Anchored

*Anchored to my mind
she was one of a kind*

Anew

*Everything we do
gets repeated anew*

Angel

*Let us taste this wine
my angel divine*

*Many an angel will call
upon them whom tragedy befall*

*You are my angel asleep
when dreams come out to peep*

Angels have wings
that are flightful things

How can the angels fly
with the wings of a butterfly

If angels they had sisters
they wouldn't be called misters

The angels in your life
that ease your daily strife

Wonder it takes to wing
the angels when they sing

Angelic

Angelic themes
the stuff of dreams

Anger

Anger has taught
us what we must not

Anger once swallowed
makes the person hallowed

Can he live longer
he who is slow to anger

He looked back in anger
became weaker but not stronger

Head becomes stronger
if you get rid of anger

Manage your anger
when in a cliffhanger

Angles

Untold angles
when semantics tangle

Angry

He took an angry stand
when he couldn't understand

When angry birds speak
they turn the other cheek

When the angry ocean speaks
many a big boat it leaks

Annoyance

An inexact science
cause of annoyance

Annoyance as a duty
has its own beauty

Answer

The answer I was waiting
forever needed painting

Answers will come
to the beating of the drum

The answers are found
in a world of sound

Answering

Dilemmas need answering
without any wavering

Anxiety

Anxiety and scares
for the seal between two bears

Anything

Anything goes
under the nose

Anytime

Anytime it is possible
if you put it in a crucible

Ape

Don't be an ape
cut the red tape

How he took shape
man the naked ape

All sizes and shapes
they came the apes

Appeal

Eternal appeal
without much spiel

Every spoke has a wheel
that is its appeal

Fish they appeal
to the performing seal

Men of steel
have shining appeal

Appeal

Under your nose they steal
and we have no appeal

Unsullied appeal
has a special feel

Where is the appeal
for the tiger to consider me his meal

Why appeal
if there is no repeal

Appealing

Can't be appealing
a love without meaning

Feeling that is appealing
is worthwhile to be stealing

Guilt is a feeling
not very appealing

How can I be appealing
when my head is reeling

How can you edit a feeling
that is so appealing

It's all very appealing
when the meaning keeps revealing

Mans search for meaning
to women very appealing

Onion needs peeling
until it becomes appealing

Sound, word, and meaning
each equally appealing

To some very appealing
the very thought of stealing

Why is it so appealing
something so revealing

Appease

How to appease
the virulence of the bees

Appetite

Appetite cannot be whet
by any amount of debt

Appetites he fights
on days and lonesome nights

Appetites they are fed
by the things that are said

The dinner gong struck long
and their appetites were strong

There are appetites to quell
if you wish to live well

Applause

As the curtain it draws
there is a deafening applause

Apple

Don't know why
she is the apple of my eye

He bit into the apple
when he had a snake to grapple

Appliance

Modern appliance
for self reliance

Appreciate

Make it a lasting duty
to appreciate natures beauty

Make it your duty
to appreciate beauty

They appreciate the joke
the ordinary folk

Will they appreciate you
the more you do

You must appreciate
those who negotiate

Approach

It is best to reproach
with a gentle approach

Approval

Approval of the clans
not needed for my plans

Approve

I have things to prove
for her to approve

Aptitude

Need a special aptitude
to enjoy your solitude

Arabia

Arabia has oil
deep down into the soil

Arabian

How can we dine
without Arabian wine

I cannot dine
without Arabian wine

Arched

Clothes all starched
and back fully arched

He was a parched male
with an arched tail

Arctic
will the arctic tern
ever return

Argument
An argument avoided
can leave them divided

An argument isn't done
until it is won

His argument was bent
whatever it meant

Arguments of length
will lose their strength

With arguments he is able
to spin a pretty fable

Army
He joined the army
where the climate is balmy

Aroma
Aroma isn't far
if there is coffee in the bar

Arrange
How to arrange the hours
to fit in the showers

How to arrange
things that don't change

Where we had arranged to meet
she quickly came up the street

Nothing really changes
it just re-arranges

Arrival
A new arrival
soon found his rival

Arrived
He arrived in good time
with her to dance and dine

Arrogance
Arrogance on the whole
is bad for the soul

Arrogant
What a thing to say
in such an arrogant way

Arrow
He may be a straight arrow
but he missed the sparrow

Is it the arrow at all
when the sparrow takes a fall

Little arrows everywhere
not a sparrow in the air

Arteries
Popping at eateries
puffing up his arteries

Roads like arteries clogged
drivers all day they slogged

Ashamed
Ashamed of being poor
there is no cure

Why are we ashamed
when love it is claimed

A

Ashore
What came ashore
is the stuff of lore

Ask
Don't ask me how
I did it then and now

Let me ask the drummer
to play for her this summer

Asked
Where have you been
asked the king of his queen

Asleep
Many an ocean will keep
the fish that is fast asleep

When the world is asleep
you have many hours to keep

Asphalt
Every grain of salt
must mix with asphalt

Assault
Don't just speak
just assault the peak

Scattergun assaults
will not correct faults

Assess
Assess as such
without saying much

Assurances
Assurances
are not insurances

Astray
He was led astray
by his ashtray

Once they have gone astray
just sit down and pray

Ate
Who ate my muffin
hasn't heard of coffin

With well oiled legs
he ate hard boiled eggs

Atonement
Go to cantonment
to seek atonement

When things need atonement
go to the cantonment

Attached
They should have been attached
being so closely matched

Attachment
Their attachment was Sapphic
and all too graphic

Attack
A virulent attack
he made on every fact

Stay ahead of the pack
before they attack

He attacks
with imagined facts

Attention
For attention she vies
with flickering eyes

Attentive
She placed her attentive eye
on slightly older men why

She reads it out loud
to the attentive crowd

Attire
Aphorism and satire
wearing well tailored attire

Baptism by fire
gives you a golden attire

Before it gets to your attire
get the kettle out of the fire

Before you write satire
wear proper attire

Divine fire
is their inner attire

Each new satire
wearing a different attire

Every new attire
is the product of desire

Every single attire
a product of her desire

He is cool in a fire
with dapper attire

In fitting attire
he was spitting fire

Inner fire
needs a new attire

Rekindle her fire
with a new attire

Straits dire
without attire

Wear new attire
act out your desire

When you walk the flaming fire
wear proper attire

Attired
Newly attired
is the brain re-wired

Newly attired
the mind re -wired

The way he was attired
he was fired

We are attired
the way we are wired

Attitude
Whatever the latitude
devil may care attitude

A piece of single gratitude
made her change her attitude

Bad attitude
equals ingratitude

Given lots of latitude
he had to change his attitude

Latitude is an attitude
for people with no fortitude

Learn to measure attitude
by the amount of ingratitude

No gratitude
just attitude

Parents who give latitude
get children with attitude

Servitude
is attitude

To change your attitude
you must have fortitude

Attitudes can cure
many diseases for sure

Attracted

It wasn't his tie
that attracted her eye

Attraction

Every addition
has its attraction

Kids have attraction
when driven to distraction

Main distraction
laws of attraction

The magnet has attraction
for the Iron and its fraction

Many distractions
have special attractions

Once the attractions fade
look for a tree with shade

There are no fractions
in fatal attractions

Warring factions
have their attractions

Attracts

Sound of the sonnet
attracts many a gannet

Attributes

Many tributes
have good attributes

Audience

The audience for our cares
they show up unawares

Author

Book tells the author
why do you bother

Authority

Where it is vested
authority can be tested

Autocrat

Every autocrat
slowly he gets fat

Autumn

Not without sieves
autumn leaves

The autumn came too soon
but where is the moon

Where does it go at noon
the autumn moon

Avenge

To avenge is a wish
for a plateful of fish

Averse

Wolf in sheep's clothing
is averse to any loathing

Avid

To food he is avid
his gut becomes gravid

Avoiding

He cannot go avoiding
when it is time to be voiding

Awake

How to stay awake
when mistakes take the cake

Keep awake
for loves sake

Keep awake
for nonsense's sake

Awaken

How to awaken
a heart that is broken

Aware

We must be aware
that life is wear and tear

Awareness

Awareness that is passive
can be submissive

Away

What will they say
if you go away

Awe

She was in awe
of what in him she saw

Awesome

Every perfect blossom
makes the fragrance quite awesome

Place awesome
but cowboy lonesome

Awful

Couldn't have bean crisper
this awful whisper

Tighten boot lace
we're in an awful place

Awhile

Let it last awhile
your all encouraging smile

Let me live awhile
for life is so fragile

Let us sail awhile
on the blue nile

Awkward

In an awkward manner
he held up the banner

In every awkward pause
there is a stealthy because

B

Babies

*Babies burp
sparrows chirp*

*Babies they long
for many a quiet song*

*Babies when they smile
warm your heart for a while*

Baby

*The baby isn't keen
to keep the bed sheets clean*

Bachelor

*Bachelor at heart
survives on tart*

Back

*Turn your back
when you get flak*

*With back to the wall
he made a phone call*

Backed

*He backed into a car
and saw many a star*

Backroom

*The backroom boys
they bring their own toys*

Bad

*Don't say things bad
if you have nothing to add*

*How can he be bad
who is well clad*

*Like a bad apple
they show up in a grapple*

*Most of our lands
are in bad hands*

*Once he turns bad
he can be had*

Badly

*Give it to her gladly
what I don't need badly*

Baiting

*Does he need baiting
who is clown in waiting*

*With coffee she was waiting
which seemed a bit like baiting*

Baked
> Some they try to float
> the half baked anecdote

Bakes
> They are all on the make
> while she bakes the cake

Balance
> We make them into heroes
> whose bank balance has many zeroes

Balanced
> With a balanced hand
> he divided the land

Balancing
> The great balancing act
> must be done with tact

Bald
> Easy to scald
> his head who is bald

Ball
> At every port of call
> he went and had a ball

Ballot
> Ballot is a box
> watched by a fox

Ban
> How to ban
> foods in the can

Banana
> Ice cream with split banana
> for the man from Copacabana

Band
> Playing at the band stand
> is a very compulsive hand

Bandit
> If you can't stand it
> go become a bandit

Banished
> The banished queen
> was never again seen

Bank
> Before the markets tank
> head for the bank

Barber
> The barber made it brisker
> the long and flowing whisker

Bare
> Down to his bare bones
> in the tombstones

Barefoot
> Barefoot through the fields
> where Rice bushels were yields

Bargain
> A good bargain
> to be good again

> If you bargain with the rain
> what is there to gain

Bark
> Don't let the dog bark
> when you embark

I must embark
before the dog it bark

Barn

A well spun yarn
best told in the barn

Barter

He will barter
all things but his garter

Bash

There cannot be a bash
without food to stash

Bats

Bats with open wing
from the ceiling they swing

Batsmen

The batsmen they play
front foot all day

Battle

Battle for the riches
not without hitches

Don't go forth to battle
brandishing just a rattle

It's a constant battle
between the cow and the rattle

Tie up your cattle
before going to battle

When you go off to battle
leave behind your rattle

Battlefields

Battlefields they yield
a bloody field

Battles

Battles of the mind
one of a kind

Bay

Do they have a say
the fisher folk out in the bay

Beached

Beached whales
tell no tales

Beaks

They attended to their beaks
parrots with red cheeks

Beamer

He who bowls a beamer
has to be a seamer

Beaming

From smile to beaming
each of a different meaning

Make your own meaning
when words come at you beaming

Beans

Hold on to your jeans
and spill the beans

Not the type it seems
to spill all the beans

Rhyming English Couplets

Beard

> With a beard like a goat
> he must be a turncoat

Bearded

> The bearded goat
> got the sympathy vote

> They came out of the den
> the bearded men

Beast

> Beauty went to the feast
> but couldn't find the beast

> Both man and beast
> upon each other they feast

> Nature of the beast
> best seen at the feast

Beat

> Horses feet
> they trot to a beat

Beats

> He beats around the bush
> to save himself a blush

> What is this thing
> that beats everything

Beautiful

> A place for a fling
> beautiful Darjeeling

> All beautiful and dainty
> she came upon a bounty

> Beautiful as Neptune
> she passed by me in June

> Beautiful red flowers
> they open up to the showers

> Every beautiful flower
> requires a rainshower

> For each beautiful sound
> a new memory is found

> Her footsteps he has found
> make a beautiful sound

> How beautiful art thou
> from toe tips to the brow

> How can I be blind
> to her beautiful mind

> Makes a beautiful lace
> with each fiber in place

> My most beautiful line
> awaits a sip of wine

> Nothing will be
> as beautiful as thee

> Only a rose can think
> in a beautiful shade of pink

> Such a beautiful setting
> is no place for fretting

> The beautiful flower bed
> filled with roses all red

> The beautiful glimmer
> of the stars in the summer

Beauty

*The peacock will flail
his beautiful tail*

*Why was I so blind
to her beautiful mind*

*A thing of beauty
does its duty*

*Beauty and fame though fleeting
people flock to them greeting*

*Beauty casts a spell
with a voice of sweet smell*

*Beauty isn't revealed
to the heart that is concealed*

*Beauty like no other
in the face of my mother*

*Beauty of the country
must be guarded by the sentry*

*Beauty we must share
that is found everywhere*

*Beauty will find a reason
to return fresh each season*

*Don't look away
when beauty comes your way*

*Eyes have a duty
to unearth all her beauty*

*Her beauty it haunted
him whose love she wanted*

*Her beauty talks
from the way she walks*

*How long will it keep
beauty that is skin deep*

*If love becomes a duty
it loses its beauty*

*Such beauty lay in her eye
that many a goblin would die*

*The beauty in the rose
best discovered by the nose*

Bed

*Nothing much to be said
about the stranger in my bed*

Bee

*Many a bee has fed
upon the rose red*

*Wherever the nose dives
there are bee hives*

Bee-hive

*Bee-hive for the drone
is a comfort zone*

*Under the bee-hive he sat
where they both had a spat*

Beer

*He is full of beer and chips
way down to his hips*

*When it comes to beer
he has no peer*

Before

*Before you pose
check out your nose*

Rhyming English Couplets

Beginning

*From the beginning of time
love was always divine*

*In the beginning there was a letter
whose message you mustn't fritter*

*Since the beginning of time
there was sugar and then lime*

*The shape of things to come
are beginning to hum*

Begs

*The farmer he begs
the ducks to lay eggs*

Behave

*After a close shave
he learned to behave*

*He learned to behave
after a close shave*

*Learn to behave
with twelve foot waves*

*She rolled her eyes to the sky
and said why you behave so why*

*The reason they behave badly
you gave them permission gladly*

Behaved

*She ranted and raved
till he behaved*

Behaves

*He only behaves
who has close shaves*

*In all my close shaves
my fate it behaves*

*With slyness and shy
the fox he behaves why*

Behaving

*In the morning when I am shaving
is the only time for behaving*

Behaviour

*Bad behaviour cured
happiness assured*

*Bad behaviour
let it be your saviour*

*Behaviour of nations
comes in many permutations*

*Good behaviour
can be your saviour*

*Decent behaviour
your only saviour*

*Good behaviour
only saviour*

*Good behaviour
your only saviour*

*His behaviour he mended
after he was upended*

*How can it make her glad
when his behaviour becomes bad*

*How to decode
behaviour on the road*

B

*Mans behaviour and desire
needs a new attire*

*Once fed on toddy
his behaviour becomes shoddy*

*Once they are confronted
their behaviour gets blunted*

*Some day bound to crash
if behaviour is all rash*

*You will not meet your saviour
with negative behaviour*

*Your only saviour
change of behaviour*

Behind

*Behind closed doors
they settle scores*

*Behind every nook
a man reading a book*

*Behind the clouds why
there is gold in the sky*

Behold

*Something to behold
both briskly and bold*

Beholden

*I am beholden
to moments once golden*

B **Beholder**

*Eye of the beholder
beauty is I told her*

*Good thing I told her
it's in the eye of the beholder*

*In the eye of the beholder
beauty is I told her*

Belief

*Have self belief
and get out of grief*

*Self belief
brings relief*

Believe

*Known to few
that I believe in you*

Belittle

*Little by little
he began to belittle*

Belong

*How I long
to be where I belong*

*How I really long
to be where we belong*

Belonging

*It's about longing
and forever belonging*

*I had two inner longings
that became belongings*

Bend

*Don't bend to the wind
until you reach sindh*

Rhyming English Couplets

*I will bend you to my will
if you just stand still*

*Road without a bend
where will it end*

Bended

*With a bended knee
he performs the flea*

Beneath

*Don't marry beneath
lest you lose your teeth*

Benefits

*Benefit of the clout
will clear the doubt*

Berated

*Underrated
and berated*

Beside

*With a cautionary rider
he sat down beside her*

Best

*A bird does her best
to feed chicks in the nest*

*A day to rest
will serve you best*

*A little bird in the nest
sits on eggs and does its best*

*A teapot is best
with a little tempest*

*Be your best
when put to the test*

*Best to bend the twig
before it becomes big*

*Do your best
for your guest*

*East and West
each think they are the best*

*He says it best
when earnesty is a test*

*He thinks he is best
from the hair on his chest*

*How many eggs in the nest
will turn out to be the best*

*In flood and the rain
best to take the train*

*Injury is best
treated by rest*

*Inside his nest
he is at his best*

*Last one to rest
the mother who is best*

*Once we are put to rest
for the world it is best*

*Pen and pad is best
to put you to the test*

*Pick what is best
and leave the rest*

B

*Put it to the test
your will to be the best*

*She said with zest
I will do my best*

*Show off your best
when you feather your nest*

*Some things are done
best on the run*

*The best way to cure vice
is to put it on ice*

*The cripples own crutches
are his best riches*

*They went to a place where gibbons
looked their best with pink ribbons*

*To be in repose
is the best pose*

*To lie down is best
for an hour filled with rest*

*Truculence is at best
used as a test*

*Voters will attest
politicians are not the best*

*When help gets its turn
it is best to return*

*You can be the best
if you don't lose your zest*

Bet

*Don't take a bet
with the man you have never met*

*I'll take a bet
he knows nothing yet*

*I'll take a bet
there will be fish in this net*

*I'll take a bet
what you see is what you get*

*The numerate they met
and calculated their bet*

*They took a bet
once the stage was set*

Betray

*His mischief made him stray
to paths that led to betray*

*Hope and pray
she don't betray*

Betrayal

*Betrayal came first
of love and its trust*

Betrayed

*Because he strayed
him she betrayed*

Better

*Better to give
not long to live*

*Better to keep mum
when the accountant does the sum*

*Better to keep mum
when you find cadmium*

*Better to meet the baker
before I meet the maker*

*Better to think
before kick meets kick*

*Couldn't have said it better
down to the last letter*

*I took it out of the shelf
the better half of myself*

*Things can be said better
even to the last letter*

*To better its daily selling
story must be improved by the telling*

*Which side of the wall
is it better to fall*

*Who condescends better
down to the last letter*

Between

*Between her and me
can we vanquish the sea*

*Between lawn mowing
she tended to her sowing*

*Between them was a moat
the tiger and the goat*

Beware

*Beware of your fury
directed at the jury*

*Beware of your mind
it can trick you blind*

Beyond

*Beyond the coconut trees
the moon and the soft breeze*

*Beyond the seven seas
where there are hives without bees*

Bidding

*Do my bidding
finish your pudding*

Big

*Gout it brings woe
to many a big toe*

*His head was too big
for the size of his wig*

Binding

*Don't go abiding
with what's not binding*

Biography

*Reading biography
was a bit stuffy*

Bird

*A little bird said
I will chirp until fed*

*Somethings are meant to be
said the bird to the bee*

*Birds are at their best
when they build their nest*

*Birds as they sing
they flap their wing*

B

*Birds of a feather
in bad weather*

*In the Isle of mull
all the birds are gull*

*Said one fish to the other
we are birds of a feather*

*The birds in the morning gloat
with a sweet voice from their throat*

Birth

*Before my birth
no worries about girth*

*Birth of a notion
without pill or potion*

*Every new birth
is the product of mirth*

*Expand your girth
before you give birth*

*From birth we are schooled
that at night we are cooled*

*I didn't worry about girth
before my birth*

*Place of my birth
heaven on earth*

*Some are inclined to mirth
from the moment of their birth*

*We are all of equal birth
not by weight or girth*

*Who gave it birth
this planet called the earth*

*Why give birth
when sadness fills the earth*

Birthday

*On my birthday I sit
in front of the candles lit*

Bit

*Bit by bit
it became a hit*

Bites

*He bites his nails
and wags their tails*

Biting

*Biting on red cherry
she waited for the ferry*

Bitter

*All things taste bitter
when you miss a sitter*

*How can they be bitter
the pigs in a litter*

*I had never tasted bitter
until I met this critter*

Bitterness

*Let them loot
the bitterness in the fruit*

Blackboard

*Blackboard and chalk
will make the teacher talk*

Rhyming English Couplets

Blame

*Blame your inner voices
for some of your choices*

*Don't blame your brain
if you go against the grain*

*Don't lend your name
you might get the blame*

*Good people take the blame
for other peoples shame*

*Have enough people to blame
is the name of the game*

*He who is lame
always gets the blame*

*No credit no blame
just keep my name*

*The only way to blame
is to call them by another name*

*The tongue that gets the blame
must hang out in shame*

*Who is to blame for the blunder
when love is split asunder*

Bland

*Nothing seems bland
when there is cash at hand*

Blank

*He campaigned on a plank
that was altogether blank*

Bleach

*He turned bleach
when chased by a leech*

Bleary

*Bleary eyed they came
the morning after the game*

Bled

*Many a man has bled
for gold silver and lead*

*The summer heat it bled
all the ice from the sled*

Bleed

*Every man will plead
he is capable of bleed*

*He kneels down to plead
with the leech not to bleed*

*Leeches will go and plead
with god who is next to bleed*

*Many a leech will bleed
however much you plead*

*Oh rubber tree
how you bleed for me*

*Small errors can bleed
by planting a poor seed*

Blend

*Has its own blend
coffee in the end*

Blending
> Into the sunset blending
> the day seems to be ending

Bless
> Only a penny can bless
> the forever penniless

Blessed
> A child to be blessed
> must be caressed

> Anyone could have guessed
> that he was fully blessed

> Can he be considered blessed
> who is totally dispossessed

> Equally blessed
> the fairest and the foulest

> Thanksgiving was blessed
> by the turkey well dressed

> You might have guessed
> from the heavens we were blessed

Blessing
> She gave her blessing
> to the salad dressing

> Count your blessings
> and gods caressings

> Count your blessings
> and her caressings

> Disguised blessings
> gods caressings

> Rain gods blessings
> are little caressings

> Surrounded by blessings
> and salad dressings

Blind
> A journey into the mind
> to things that I was totally blind

> Blind as a bat
> sleepy as a cat

> Common sense can be blind
> to the smartest mind

> Darker turn of the mind
> has a way of being blind

> Don't be blind
> to the landscapes of the mind

> Don't be blind
> to the thoughts that cross your mind

> Even for the blind
> it is a state of mind

> Even the blind
> can read your mind

> How can I be blind
> to all that's on my mind

> If it does things to your mind
> the reader isn't blind

> It says a lot
> who has no blind spot

> People who are blind
> have a musical mind

Rhyming English Couplets

*Seek and you shall find
though you may be blind*

*Some things are blind
to every state of mind*

*The curtains make us blind
to the windows of the mind*

*The listener is not blind
so don't go speak your mind*

*They had to be blind
to the corners in the mind*

*This thing called mind
oh so blind*

*To his failing she was blind
pretending to be kind*

*To many things blind
man and his mind*

*Was the tortoise blind
when he fell behind*

*We are mostly blind
to our sub conscious mind*

*When matters clog the mind
reality goes blind*

*Which one is blind
is it the brain or the mind*

*Why was I so blind
she was one of a kind*

Blinded

*Completely he was blinded
by being single minded*

Blindfold

*My blindfold is on
but where has sleep gone*

Blinding

*The blinding light
of head lights at night*

Blindness

*Blindness is a thing
that can be afflicting*

*Blindness is best
put to the test*

Blinds

*Through the window blinds
I could read their minds*

Blink

*A blink is just a blink
there is reason to think*

*Couldn't get a wink
of sleep without a blink*

*He found it in a blink
the missing link*

*He made her blink
with a coat made of mink*

*How to stop and think
without a single blink*

*In the blink of an eye
she was gone know not why*

*She would wink when he blink
and blink when he wink*

*The sun will sink
into the ocean in a blink*

Blinking

*Blinking makes it go
thinking makes it slow*

*He thinks when he is blinking
no one else is looking*

Bliss

*All soaked in bliss
a moment such as this*

*Bliss such as this
how could we miss*

*How did I miss
bliss such as this*

*I gave it a miss
and missed out on bliss*

*If nirvana is bliss
what is all this*

*Images such as this
can only lead to bliss*

*It all came down to this
one moment of bliss*

*What else is this
other than bliss*

*When things go amiss
it eats into bliss*

Blood

*A form of blood letting
this thing called betting*

*Bad blood from the past
whose shadows are cast*

*Blood out of bone
water out of stone*

*Her cruel words they fell with thud
on the floor with a pool of blood*

*However fine the setting
there will be blood letting*

*My blood became a flood
seeing the tiger in the mud*

*Rush of blood
happens in a flood*

*Said the leech to the leech
there is blood on the beach*

*Sharks can smell blood
even in a flood*

*Some they hold fort
where there is blood in every sport*

*The blood stayed cold
until the painting was sold*

*To get blood off his hands
he traveled many lands*

*Vampire thinks it is good
that blood takes the place of food*

*We are an imperfect lot
prone to blood clot*

Blooded

*He was so red blooded
tears they never flooded*

Bloodshed

> Bloodshed it is said
> is conceived in the head

Bloody

> The aftermath was bloody
> and the repair work was shoddy

Bloom

> Every flower must bloom
> to lift the cloud of gloom

> Found it hard to bloom
> when she fell upon gloom

> How can the leaves bloom
> under the autumn moon

> Let it not bloom
> your imperial gloom

> She made room
> for every seasons bloom

> The rose lost its bloom
> as the clouds gathered up gloom

> They lift the gloom
> flowers in full bloom

> We were half way to the moon
> when our love began to bloom

> When faced with gloom
> he grew flowers that bloom

Blossom

> Bees they hover
> after blossom shower

> Every blossom needs a branch
> and she her own ranch

> Every branch has a blossom
> whose fragrance is quite awesome

> Every spring blossom
> was quite simply awesome

> There was a blossom in every branch
> so they bought the ranch

Blossomed

> Like a newly blossomed lilly
> she frolicked around the filly

> The plant needed a shower
> before it blossomed a flower

Blot

> There is no way to blot
> away the ink spot

Blow

> If you don't know it
> you might still blow it

Blows

> The mouse came to blows
> with the elephant and his nose

Blue

> Before you turn blue
> put it behind you

> Bolt from the blue
> it doesn't bring a clue

Bluff

*Is it just bluff
or will you show the stuff*

Blunder

*Biggest blunder
was to surrender*

*Go and hide under
when you make a blunder*

*His first major blunder
was trying to sell his plunder*

*Mans biggest blunder
is the way he plunder*

*Prone to commit blunder
without sense of wonder*

*Those who plunder
make huge blunder*

*Too much thunder
start of blunder*

*Trying to steal the thunder
he made a tactical blunder*

*Was it right to plunder
or was it just a blunder*

*When two sides blunder
each other they plunder*

Blurred

*The tear once it occurred
the writing became blurred*

Body

*Body full of toddy
became very shoddy*

*Each other they trail
head body and tail*

Bold

*Act bold
strike gold*

*All are not bold
who sparkle like gold*

*He is bold
who knows when to fold*

*He needs to be bold
to swim in the arctic cold*

*He says it pays
his bold and brash ways*

*He who is bold
walks away with gold*

*How can I be bold
when she has on me a hold*

*I have options
in bold captions*

*In the mountain cold
how to be bold*

*Only the bold can go far
even in a cold war*

*Only the bold
survive the cold*

Seemingly bold
to be out in the cold

The young we are told
are easily bold

Thinking that is bold
can turn things into gold

Bolder

Eye of the beholder
daily it got bolder

Now and then
work with bolder men

So he told her
to get a bit bolder

Some they get bolder
as they get older

Bolt

Bolt from the blue
comes without a clue

Bolt from the blue
leaves no clue

Bonding

Better to be bonding
than to be absconding

Bone

She had a bone to pick
without the use of stick

To condemn or condone
he who holds on to his bone

Book

A book well read
is digested it is said

Book becomes a hit
with things special in it

Even a new look
couldn't sell the book

He sat all day whining
at the book signing

I just put it on the shelf
the book writes itself

Pages can't be turned
once the book is burned

The book it had
a jacket well clad

Write a book about your beat
and be ready to take the heat

Between books and talks
take long walks

Books just get written
by people who are smitten

Books must make us think
without allowing a blink

Books write themselves
as if written by elves

Boom

Every new boom
needs elbow room

Border

Across the border
use mail order

Mayhem and murder
across the border

Bore

You will surely bore them
if you try to ignore them

Bored

The bull got bored
after the matador was gored

Boredom

Boredom is a sage
staring at the page

Boredom it can last
so get rid of it fast

Boredom it is said
must also be fed

Boredom needs a balm
like breeze from the palm

Boredom will win
say the kith and kin

Boring

Two boring people
sat atop the steeple

Born

A new born is a treasure
beyond all measure

A new one will be born
once the moose loses his horn

A new summer is born
after the one that has gone

Born as a cute pair
the cubs of a Polar Bear

Born to be kind
every innocent mind

Born to be wild
destiny's child

Dogs bark at me on the road
why was I born a toad

He lived atop cape horn
where tall ocean waves are born

In middle age wild
the new born child

Many a sheep is born
with a ram horn

On an early winter morn
a baby sheep was born

Out of the suns rays born
many a sunlit morn

Some are born to good taste
and others to parental haste

Some they wish to be seen
as if they were born very mean

Some to the world are born
who are totally stubborn

*The penguins they keep hatching
chicks that are born all matching*

*Through the thicket and the thorn
a beautiful rose is born*

*With a single knee cap
was born this chap*

Borrow

*Borrow from him if you can
to decipher the man*

*Borrow steal or beg
must have his daily peg*

*How can I borrow
your love from to-morrow*

*In parting do not borrow
if not enough for to-morrow*

*Once you decide to settle
borrow neighbours kettle*

*People of high rank
don't borrow from the bank*

Borrowed

*Every borrowed penny
adds up to many*

*He did his gig
with a borrowed wig*

Borrower

*Borrower or lender
who is the offender*

Bother

*Why bother
the absent father*

Bottom

*Can't get any badder
than the bottom of the ladder*

Bought

*He bought his own Abbey
and gave up being a cabby*

Boulder

*His tail felt like a boulder
when he threw it over his shoulder*

*She handed him a shoulder
when his head felt like a boulder*

Bouncer

*The bouncer kept climbing
while he was imbibing*

Bound

*Where are they bound
the hare and the hound*

Boundless

*Boundless hate
make it wait*

Bowler

*The bowler he made his case
at a disconcerting pace*

Brain

*A brain newly wired
is well attired*

A brain re-wired
is newly attired

Brain doctor in the end
with many minds to mend

Brain is in the main
seat of all pain

From the storm to the rain
all happens in the brain

Go fix your brain
before it begins to rain

Her brain was drawn
to his brawn

How to mend
the brain in the end

How to train
the runaway brain

How to train
this limbic brain

How to train
this vagabond brain

In his brain there is a worm
that makes others squirm

In the brain you will find
the working of the mind

In the morning walk
when the brain begins to talk

Look inside your brain
there is a runaway train

Much to gain
who changes his brain

Rebuild your brain
in new terrain

Say something good
that is brain food

That the brain has no feeling
is quite revealing

The brain fever bird
makes itself heard

The brain it tingles
when I write jingles

The brain must be stupid
to fall for such lipid

The brain started firing
with brand new wiring

The brain won't let you
forget what is new

They knew he was wise
with a brain that size

Uncontrolled brain
is runaway train

Brand

All that matters in brand
is cocktail in hand

Upgrade the brand
to make a Rand

Brandish
*They brandish their brands
with money in their hands*

Brands
*Foreign brands
in many lands*

Brave
*Even the brave must face
the final resting place*

*He knelt beside her grave
pretending to be brave*

*How can he be brave
who is this side of the grave*

*How to be brave
with one foot in the grave*

*To return from beyond the grave
have to be more than a little brave*

Bravely
*Bravely he went into the blizzard
thinking he was a wizard*

Bravery
*Bravery of the foal
in the racetrack is the goal*

Braves
*The seagull braves
the wind and the waves*

Bread
*At the bakers I must stop
stale bread to swap*

*Break bread and drink wine
with stories as we dine*

*For daily bread they fight
who are of less than humble plight*

*Give us our daily dread
even if we don't have bread*

Break
*He is cunning as a fox
and can break into locks*

Breakdown
*Men who breakdown
must wear a gown*

Breath
*Don't hold your breath
it might affect your health*

*Half my breath it takes
every move she makes*

*Let me get my breath
to rejuvenate my health*

*With every labored breath
the whale renews her health*

Breathe
*He who holds his tongue
must still breathe with his lung*

Breaths
*A few breaths I must save
so I reach safely to the grave*

Breed

*A friend in need
is a rare breed*

*Breed breed breed
too many mouths to feed*

*They were a special breed
out of a special seed*

*We are all said to lead
a life more than just to breed*

Breeder

*A prolific breeder
cannot be a reader*

Breeding

*Fine breeding
slowly receding*

*Good breeding
is easy reading*

*Grounds for breeding
starts with feeding*

Breeds

*There is no grid
that breeds the hybrid*

Breeze

*Close your eyes and pray
in the calm breeze of the day*

*Life will cease
in the cold winter breeze*

*Pollen laden breeze
started the sneeze*

*The breeze through my hair
when spring is in the air*

*The pollen in the breeze
brought on the sneeze*

*The trees they waft
a breeze sure and soft*

*There was a gentleness in the breeze
which was good for my wheeze*

*Where the palm trees sway
from the breeze that comes their way*

Brevity

*Brevity plays host
when least is most*

Brew

*The brew and its aroma
Can wake you up from a coma*

Brewed

*Fill the cup
once it is brewed up*

Bribes

*Bribes are just token
eaten just like bacon*

Bride

*The bride he chose
was a stylish english rose*

Bridge

*Better to count your penny
if there is a bridge too many*

*Bridge from the past
to a future that is vast*

*Bridges must be built
with concrete on silt*

*Some of the bridges we cross
are full of slippery moss*

Brief

*Even her brief glance
it deserves a chance*

*How to make the tears brief
teach me oh lotus leaf*

*Let it be brief
when you feed the thief*

*Make it brief
the expression of grief*

*Men in brief
make a girls grief*

*The barber made it brief
the long hair and its grief*

Briefcase

*To make good case
carry a briefcase*

Bright

*Bright as a button
without being a glutton*

*The fireplace burns bright
all through the night*

*The moon all bright and stark
at whom the wolves they bark*

*The moonlight bright
their mighty delight*

*The sun shines bright
through the moon and its light*

*Tired of burning bright
the sun it eases into the night*

*With full and bright eyes
his demeanor she spies*

*With less light at night
how are the stars so bright*

Brighten

*Chances don't brighten
once the noose it tightens*

Brightened

*Her letter it brightened
him more than it frightened*

Brightest

*She latched on to it why
the brightest star in the sky*

Brightness

*The sun will never stray
fills brightness to my day*

*There is brightness like no other
than the light thrown by the mother*

Brilliant

*Brilliant and ebullient
for the reader it was meant*

*He was brilliant and blinding
as his bat started unwinding*

Brisker
>His walk it turned brisker
>as he twisted his whisker

Brittle
>If you choose something brittle
>you could lose more than a little

>You will be called brittles
>if you fall like skittles

Broke
>She broke off their ties
>with fire in her eyes

Broken
>Of broken ties
>spoke the cloud in her eyes

Brook
>In the shade by the brook
>they sat down to look

Broom
>He was just another broom
>sharing her room

>How can I sweep with a broom
>without ruining my plume

>How to clean the room
>with one sweep of the broom

>In the corner was a broom
>waiting to clean the room

Brother
>Said the one to the other
>why can't both we be brother

Brought
>Can it be brought to fruition
>without any tuition

>Of all the things sold
>none brought in the gold

Browser
>The button on the browser
>doesn't bother your trouser

Brunch
>I have a hunch
>we will meet at the brunch

Brunette
>She fell in his net
>the blue eyed brunette

Brute
>In Eden there was a brute
>who did not wear a suite

Bubbles
>Bubbles from a brook
>deserve a second look

Buck
>With a little bit of pluck
>make extra buck

Bud
>Nip it in the bud
>before it turns to mud

>Nip it in the bud
>let it fall with a thud

Buddies
*One of them muddies
the water for the buddies*

Budding
*Each budding flower
needs rain shower*

Buddy
*He sits in his study
with the pen as his buddy*

Budged
*How much ever she nudged
he couldn't be budged*

Build
*How to build a cupola
without a single lola*

Bullet
*Said the gun to the bullet
you are only a pellet*

*The bullet missed his head
but he fell down dead*

Bully
*Just because he can
he is a bully of a man*

Bumper
*Bumper sticker
will make you snicker*

Bumpy
*It is no front row seat
the bumpy side of the street*

Bungle
*How much more bungle
than law of the jungle*

Burden
*As such
burden too much*

*How to sift
through burden or gift*

*They bear their own burden
both king and the warden*

*We can never be certain
to bear our own burden*

*Will ease many a burden
the final curtain*

*I have been gifted
by the burdens lifted*

Buried
*All buried in books
that filled corners and nooks*

*Buried deep in the past
hidden treasures very vast*

*They wake up in your sleep
some things buried deep*

Burn
*Calories left to burn
when they come out of the turn*

*Fires that burn brightly
are like people who are sprightly*

*If you miss the turn
in hell you will burn*

*The arctic tern
needs calories to burn*

*Without money to burn
she didn't know where to turn*

*Burns in my feet
from the searing heat*

Burning

*A lamp burning with oil
day and night as we toil*

Burst

*How to burst into song
when your voice is not strong*

*How to burst the bleb
when desire becomes a web*

*If you lilt enough long
you will burst into song*

Business

*The business of rumour
carries no humour*

Busters

*They come in clusters
these chart busters*

Busy

*Too busy spinning verses
to fill his monthly purses*

*Too busy to talk
but not busy to walk*

Butterflies

*Butterflies in a hurry
in flightful flurry*

*Butterflies in the field
looking for flowers to feed*

*Butterflies it bring
the tulips in the spring*

*Butterflies they fly
when you try to touch them why*

*Don't go catching
butterflies before they are a hatching*

*When you are away
my butterflies they stay*

Butterfly

*A butterfly will never be
humming like a bee*

*Butterfly wings
are one of those things*

*She simply fluttered by
the spotted butterfly*

Buy

*Where does he buy his hat
the aristocrat*

Buzz

*From words that fit tighter
came the buzz from the writer*

*The buzz will slip
if the bee has a lisp*

Bye

*One last eye
before the good-bye*

C

Cage

> Once the bird had spoken
> the cage it flew open

Caged

> Caged bird has wings
> is that why she sings

Calamity

> Every calamity
> wiped out by jollity

> He who has vanity
> cannot see calamity

> In the face of calamity
> how to keep sanity

> In times of calamity
> it's time for amity

> They resorted to amity
> in the face of calamity

> To avert calamity
> is a duty to humanity

> Wounded vanity
> close to calamity

Calcium

> Calcium is known
> to fire up the bone

Calendar

> The calendar it turned to may
> the month that would make us pay

Calling

> We all have a calling
> some quite appalling

Callous

> He who is callous
> brings us no solace

Calm

> All is not calm
> from the gathering storm

> As if on balm
> he kept his calm

> I need no balm
> when the ocean is calm

> No better balm
> than a loved ones calm

*She looked a calm creature
with a bright future*

*The calm after the storm
is the sailors' balm*

Calmer

*She made her choice
with a calmer voice*

Camp

*The lady with the lamp
lit up the camp*

Campfire

*The evening must be fair
to the campfire and the pair*

Campus

*Campus book
with a new look*

Can

*Just because you can
don't do the can can*

Candle

*Light a candle
when it is too tough to handle*

Canister

*No need to ask the barrister
to open a routine canister*

Canoe

*The canoe I will paddle
while you put up the saddle*

Cantering

*She took to cantering
after all the bantering*

Capacious

*Capacious and crisp
but soft as a wisp*

Capacity

*Capacity to blurt
out things that hurt*

Captivating

*Captivating and brisk
her story was told with risk*

Capture

*There was so much to capture
of the uninhibited rapture*

*He spun a fair tale
about how he captured a whale*

*Her images once captured
had him all enraptured*

*Once he was captured
he was enraptured*

*Defies logic
how he captures the magic*

Care

*A turban worn with care
will never leave your head bare*

*Do I really care
be it rabbit or a hare*

*If you have time to spare
do a lawn care*

*It makes sense
to take care of the pence*

*Need someone to care
for the love I have to share*

*Once it takes to the air
words we must use with care*

*They don't care for warning
even if it is alarming*

*Use it with care
for scissors are a pair*

*Where have you been little elf
take care of yourself*

*Why do we care
what to-morrow will lay bare*

*With a long and distant stare
she told him she doesn't care*

*With his usual care
he snipped his mustache of hair*

*You will find it where
there is tender loving care*

Career

*A career will not float
if it is a leaking boat*

*Choose a career
where you have no peer*

*How to choose
a career without noose*

Careful

*Careful what you wish
also where you fish*

*If you tangle with a bear
be careful of your hair*

*Wherever you put your feet
be careful on the street*

Carefully

*However carefully you tread
you might meet with dread*

*Listen very carefully
love is never silly*

*Words carefully planted
grow up straight and not slanted*

Careless

*Food he spies
with careless eyes*

*Freudian slips
through careless lips*

*From careless ways
he caused delays*

*He was careless in his ways
towards the end of his days*

*Him she spies
with careless eyes*

*Many a spider has caught
the fly in careless thought*

*Others can put you on hold
from your careless tongue I am told*

Price he pays
for his careless ways

Carelessly

A bird carelessly resting
when she should be nesting

Carelessly hurled
their designs for the world

Cares

I live just on pears
with very little cares

Caress

I have pawns to caress
making my moves in chess

Caressings

Her gentle caressings
came without dressings

Caring

People who are caring
do things that are daring

Carnival

The carnival is over
let's more to dover

Carousers

They were both carousers
in white flannel trousers

Carry

Carry a big basket
when you go to the market

They carry their only bundle
on wheels that slowly trundle

When you go to the hills
carry your pills

Cars

One billion cars
can't go fars

Case

After I made my case
it was that look on her face

He made his case
with a nose on his face

How to make your case
without losing face

Make your case
to make it a better place

Cash

Cash it will link
two men in a blink

He didn't have enough cash
to buy himself mish-mash

Castle

She played a hand
in his castle in the sand

Castles in the air
not good for welfare

Castles were built
on grounds of silt

Rhyming English Couplets

He will lose all his hair
who builds castles in the air

Look for it where
there are castles in the air

Need helping hand
for castles in the sand

Casual

They may look casual
business as usual

Cat

Who will bell the cat
asked the neck tie to the hat

Catch up

Even after they patch up
there was much to catch up

Cattle

Like cattle
in their afternoon prattle

Round up the cattle
on horse and saddle

Caught

As he went by
he caught her eye

Don't be caught
by flatter unsought

Don't be caught
by your blind spot

Don't get caught
when your score is naught

Don't get caught
with a loose knot

He was on a sticky wicket
and the ball was caught in a thicket

Lessons are taught
once they get caught

Whatever he has got
is what the fox has caught

Cause

As part of a larger cause
we must take pause

Cause of consternation
this levitation

Every cause
needs a because

When you step into a cause
make sure it's not jaws

Caves

They came out of the caves
the bearded knaves

Cease

He will cease to be blind
who understands their mind

Hummingbirds cease their hum
to the rains when they come

Red light at junction
I cease to function

Ceases
    He who ceases sinning
    is on the way to winning

Celebrate
    Much to celebrate
    if you are celibate

    They celebrated it in song
    so their love could live long

Celebration
    With due calibration
    it was time for celebration

Cement
    To stand on wet cement
    and make ludicrous comment

Center
    If the universe has a center
    Where is the door to enter

Century
    A century of turmoil
    all because of oil

Certain
    A certain kind of folk
    who don't eat egg yolk

Chalice
    When you go to Paris
    carry with you a chalice

Champagne
    Champagne bubbles
    to forget your troubles

    How can we dine
    without champagne wine

Chance
    Between the seagull and the eagle
    what chance has the beagle

    Don't let it be token
    the chance once taken

    Don't miss the chance
    to go to the dance

    Give it a chance
    the daylight dance

    Give it a chance
    the song and the dance

    Give it chance
    the quick glance

    Given half a chance
    he would ask her for a dance

    He took a chance
    she may be at the dance

    Here's your last chance
    to make her heart dance

    If it doesn't stand a chance
    at least give it a glance

    If you wait for things to glitter
    many a chance you will fritter

    Let's go to the dance
    if we get another chance

    Nothing was left to chance
    just a leg glance

*There is a small chance
she will give a momentary glance*

*True or false
give them a chance*

*Chances become slim
when you are favoured to win*

*Chances I must take
to keep myself awake*

*I'll take chances
to get her responses*

*They fritter away their chances
with unwelcome glances*

*Wasted chances
from the missed glances*

Change

*Change what is there
fair and square*

*Change your tune
it's the month of June*

Changing

*Every changing shadow
affects the lilies in the meadow*

Channels

*Men in flannels
need right channels*

Character

*Character by far
will shine like a star*

*Character gets its taint
from a lack of restraint*

*Character is a treasure
whose praise we must measure*

*He who has character
has that unknown factor*

*His main actor
was good character*

*When character is sliced
it gets quickly iced*

Charge

*Cannot move the barge
without anyone in charge*

Charger

*For life to become larger
some people need a charger*

Charitable

*I have yet to see a leech
be charitable in his speech*

*Only a few are able
to be charitable*

Charity

*Try to bring parity
with a little bit of charity*

Charm

*By the smoothness of her charm
many they came to harm*

*Candor and charm
together no harm*

Cool and calm
he acts out his charm

Exudes her charm
with grace and form

He used his charm
like a potent balm

Her bewitching charm
was true to form

Her charm was an ornament
that needed no comment

They twisted their arm
and turned on the charm

To seek it is the charm
of a more alluring form

Charmed

Not easily charmed
nor quickly alarmed

Charmer

He couldn't have been warmer
the eternal charmer

Charming

A charming young rival
announced his arrival

He was so charming
it was quite heart warming

Less than charming
but not alarming

Neither charming nor witty
what a pity

She has things to say
in her usual charming way

She was ever so charming
and always disarming

Charms

Centerpiece is charms
for love in all its forms

He took to telling yarns
to enhance his charms

He used his charms
without any qualms

Her charms lay in her past
through the years slowly lost

Sets off alarms
if you say farewell to charms

They went to the farms
and said farewell to charms

Chase

Eager to chase
he makes his case

He made an about face
and gave up the chase

Once the dog makes a case
it begins the chase

She gave him the chase
and he got a red face

When man he chases bliss
he forgets it is a miss

Chasing

Her mind kept racing
as the runners she was chasing

Chat

Let's have a chat
about the world being flat

Let's have a chat
about this and that

Chatter

Is it only chatter
or does it really matter

Keep up the chatter
about the things that matter

Let there be chatter
on your daily platter

Mad as a hatter
do with less chatter

Magpies that chatter
and eye-lids that batter

Much of the chatter
put into words that matter

Chattering

The chattering class
with buttons made of brass

Chatting

Chatting with the boys
about them new found toys

Cheap

He bought a cheap ticket
and went to watch cricket

Talk is cheap
when you walk in your sleep

They don't lose sleep
for what was bought cheap

Cheat

Husbands who cheat
feed them goats meat

Cheating

Cheating spouses
end up as mouses

It is not worth repeating
how people go on cheating

It's not worth repeating
which of them is cheating

Some believe in cheating
soon after the greeting

Cheats

He has yet to see the knife
who cheats on his wife

Checking

Don't go checking
who it is that's pecking

Cheeks

With razor sharp beaks
the parrot pecked at her cheeks

Cheer

*Cheer we must muster
to keep love and its luster*

*Go for the beer
when there is news to cheer*

*How to have good cheer
without bottle of beer*

*To bring good cheer
go for the beer*

Cheerful

*How to stay cheerful
without jug of beer full*

Cheers

*Earn your cheers
from your peers*

Chest

*The hermits chest
became the birds nest*

Chew

*Chew on that
what's under the hat*

*When work finds you
find tobacco to chew*

Chicken

*The chicken means a lot
to the cooking pot*

Chicks

*They come out of eggs
chicks with two legs*

Chide

*Don't chide as such
when it isn't very just*

Chiding

*Better a little chiding
than a big hiding*

*He needs a chiding
as to why he is hiding*

Child

*Grown ups if they knew
there is a child in them too*

*Her second child was wild
the first one was mild*

*The child is a part
of every mothers heart*

Childhood

*A child will never go thanking
for all the childhood spanking*

*Was a bit chancy
his childhood fancy*

Children

*Children have their spills
and grown ups their pills*

*The children all day
among the lilies they play*

Chilli

*He ate more than chilli
and became a hill Billy*

China

He met a little mynah
on his way to china

No one to talk to but the mynah
on the slow boat to china

Show me the way to china
he asked the little mynah

Slow boat to china
cannot stop at Regina

Chip

It better have a because
when you chip at a cause

Chirp

The day will be good in the morrow
with a new chirp of the sparrow

Chocolates

Chocolates and cheese
can they stop my wheeze

Choice

A sudden voice
that gives you no choice

Gave me no choice
my inner voice

Give them a choice
with a soft voice

He made his choice
in tune with his inner voice

How to make a choice
amidst all this noise

I give you no choice
said the inner voice

Make your choice
from the inner voices

My ears have a choice
of choosing their own voice

Once you give them a choice
they recover their voice

The sound of her voice
gives me no choice

They take away your voice
when they don't give you a choice

To listen is my choice
to her soft sweet voice

To listen to her voice
is my first choice

Birds have choices
for backyard voices

Choices are fed
to voices in the head

Choices become thin
when there are voices within

I have all the choices
offered by the inner voices

Some choices though easy
can make your gut queasy

The sum of all the choices
have their own voices

Cholera
>It broke out in Madeira
>this thing called Cholera

Choose
>He had to choose
>it was her or the booze

>Man can choose
>which animals to use

>Shake well before use
>if that's what you choose

>For her he chooses
>perfect little roses

Choosing
>Binge boozing
>not of my choosing

Chords
>She picks at the chords
>and there's music for the gods

Chore
>Doesn't feel like a chore
>to say it like never before

Chose
>I could never have chose
>better than her a rose

>The elephant she chose
>her nose over a hose

>To be led by the nose
>is what he chose

Chosen
>Until he was done
>he was the chosen one

Church
>Every humpty must fall
>over the church yard wall

>His only grouse
>that he was a church mouse

Churning
>Inside us each is a churning
>where lava it keeps burning

Cigarette
>The lungs get a hit
>when a cigarette is lit

>Cigarettes have been
>my smoke machine

Circumspect
>He became circumspect
>the stick insect

Circumstances
>Cast long glances
>at your circumstances

>Circumstances change
>once our lives re-arrange

City
>Every city has a hill
>where they hold hands and sit still

>Nitty gritti
>happens in the city

Civilization
*A civilization once wounded
let it not be hounded*

*Under the log why
new civilizations lie*

Civilized
*Civilized by oil
and by human toil*

Claimed
*Claimed it as my own
deep down to the bone*

*He claimed that his craft
slipped away in a raft*

Clairvoyant
*Pigmy or giant
both can be clairvoyant*

Clarity
*A writer must chase
both clarity and grace*

*Clarity and guile
adds much to style*

*Clarity begins in the home
and before you reach Nome*

*So much clarity
in immortality*

*There is no clarity
between perception and reality*

*With clarity and candor
he dished out slander*

Clash
*They dissipate in a flash
fireflies when they clash*

Class
*Do it with class
when you raise the glass*

Classes
*They lowered their glasses
at the upper classes*

Clause
*Make it a clause
escape without a pause*

Clawed
*He clawed his way back
into the attack*

Clean
*A clean white shirt
is it enough to chase a skirt*

*Clean them you must
books that gather dust*

*Ek-do-teen
never looked so clean*

*One bird to the other
let me clean your feather*

*There is a plan
to clean up the clan*

*Wipe the slate clean
so nothing can be seen*

Your chit may be clean
but where have you been

Cleanliness

Cleanliness is a hope
when we buy soap

Clear

A good bottle of beer
to make things clear

All things become clear
after bottle of beer

Each season makes it clear
they add up to a year

Cleft

All that was left
was his chin with a cleft

Clever

A clever line can be said
pulled out of the head

A clever line I knew
would make the meaning come true

A very clever vandal
avoids all the scandal

Be careful of your liver
the crocodile is very clever

Good news is clever
makes you wait forever

Have to be very clever
to make love last forever

He pulled out of his hat
clever lines to chat

It's now or never
is a line very clever

Now more than ever
be more than just clever

Oh what a clever lad
who had more than one dad

The clever are sometimes blind
to the people who to them are kind

The clever lines you say
are forever here to stay

When bee gets in the bonnet
think of a clever sonnet

Why can't we be clever
and make it last forever

Cleverly

Cleverly they have fed
me the voices in my head

Cleverness

Cleverness it seems
hatch new dreams

Clients

No clients to please
with wine chatter and cheese

Climbs

The spider climbs the rung
where the fish nets are hung

Clock
> With one eye on the clock
> the nurse she took stock

Clockface
> The clockface on the hour
> on top of the tower

Cloistered
> They both were meant
> to be cloistered in their tent

Clone
> Animals have known
> that man is a recent clone

Close
> Nothing has ever come close
> to watching her upturned nose

> As they inch closer
> she pinched him through his trouser

Closer
> Closer to nirvana
> those who go to Copacabana

Closet
> Empty the closet
> and open the faucet

Cloud
> Can speak very loud
> even a wisp of cloud

> There are times when the cloud
> through the rain it speaks loud

> Look up at the sky
> where the dark clouds lie

> The clouds they try
> to hide the blue roof of the sky

> Many a cloudy day
> can turn around if you pray

Cloven
> Under the thatched roof
> lay many a cloven hoof

Clover
> How to avoid the clover
> ask the lawn mower

Clown
> Don't let each other down
> the king and the clown

Cluck
> It can't be a duck
> if it says cluck cluck!

Clucked
> The turkey it clucked
> when a feather was plucked

Clue
> Children don't have a clue
> what parents go through

> I have no clue
> about this bolt from the blue

> The duck had no clue
> why the egg turned blue

*The parrot turned blue
why he had no clue*

*We don't have a clue
why the violets are blue*

Clutch

*In moments of clutch
use words that say much*

Coalfires

*Coalfires and squire
in their evening attire*

Coffin

*No such thing called laffin
when you go to buy a coffin*

Coherence

*Coherence is a kind
of picture of the mind*

Coiled

*Don't try and wake
the well coiled snake*

Coin

*Two sides of the coin
at the edge they join*

*The coins in the fountain
can they buy me a plantain*

Cold

*As we get old
feet get cold*

*Cold is a cold
whatever else you are told*

*She left him in the cold
in a move very bold*

*They shiver in the cold
both young and the old*

*Things must be told
before they turn cold*

Collection

*His collection was stellar
of wines in the cellar*

Collusion

*Messianic delusions
are in collusion*

*Two people in collusion
will find a solution*

*With the two in collusion
they reinforce their illusions*

Colour

*The tigers only gripe
is the colour of his stripe*

Colourful

*He had a roving eye
and a colourful tie*

*The gift was meant to trap
her heart with a colourful wrap*

Columbus

*If Columbus had used a bus
there wouldn't be all this fuss*

Combines
He combines words
like chirping birds

Come
How did they come to be
from the birds to the bee

Comedy
Comedy and satire
need separate attire

Comfort
Many an evening was spent
in the comfort of their tent

Comfortable
Comfortable in his skin
even though it is thin

Comical
Mostly comical
though metaphorical

Command
Endless demands
at their command

Commander
Commander in chief
should be commander in grief

Commas
Full stops and commas
have their own aromas

Comment
Why should I comment why
about the ointment and the fly

Her comments they did last
moments from the past

Commit
Before you commit
obtain a permit

It is better to mark time
before you commit the crime

Common
He always can
the common man

Our common foe
is the whitlow

They must go toe to toe
who have a common foe

Commotion
He rises without commotion
the sun beyond the ocean

Company
Depending on their company
words create a symphony

We relish it least
the company of a beast

Wholesome company
as good as symphony

Words that sound better
in the company of each other

You run the company
I will the symphony

Compared

All other fish they pale
compared to the whale

Compassion

Compassion is a part
of man from the start

Compassion needs to be fed
or daily we are dead

For mothers it is no fashion
their day to day compassion

Compassionate

He may be a trickster
the compassionate victor

Competent

Take a leaf
from the competent thief

Competition

Competition I loathe
if it is cut throat

Complain

Don't explain don't complain
if you miss the train

Let me make it plain
all they do is complain

The sea gulls make it plain
to the sailors who complain

When there is a feast
complain the least

Whoever the sailor he may be
mustn't complain about the sea

Complaint

Got to be a saint
never to lodge complaint

Complicated

Less complicated
once they were placated

They were a complicated lot
who populated each plot

Compliment

When you pay them a compliment
use the right implement

Composed

With his manners he posed
all well composed

Composition

Less imposition
from a short composition

Composure

The mind lacks composure
in indecent exposure

Compromise

There is a prize
in compromise

Compulsion
*Writing is a compulsion
that needs no propulsion*

Compulsive
*Does it need fodder
this compulsive disorder*

*He could be called compulsive
who is so impulsive*

Conceal
*Cannot conceal
the broken seal*

*He who conceals it better
will not get a stinging letter*

Conceit
*Closely deceit
follows conceit*

Concentrated
*Concentrated malice
is the poison in the chalice*

*He offered him a chalice
with concentrated malice*

Concept
*Every new concept
has its own precept*

Concerns
*When concerns reach the brim
don't act out your whim*

Concessions
*Give me concessions
I'll give you possessions*

*The concessions you make
will not take the cake*

Conclusion
*Conclusion foregone
for the lovelorn*

*Conclusions are foregone
once we are born*

*Conclusions must vary
with each delicious story*

Concrete
*There are enough people to bungle
in every concrete jungle*

Conditions
*No renditions
without conditions*

Confess
*Confess your sin
after peg of gin*

Confession
*Confession on the whole
is bad for the soul*

*Is there no lesson
learned by confession*

*True confession
needs no mansion*

*The best confessions
after transgressions*

Confessional
    Confessional parts
that include the warts

Confidence
    Built brick by brick
the confidence trick

    Confidence is his
who thinks ignorance is bliss

    Confidence will grow
with arrow and bow

Confident
    Be confident in doubt
and lift up your snout

Confines
    Let not there be lull
in the confines of your skull

Conflict
    Conflict resolution
not without collusion

    Conflicts in the land
have reached the heartland

    Don't sit and cry
until the conflicts die

    Puzzles to be solved
conflicts to be resolved

Conform
    It always pays
to conform to their ways

Confront
    Against my grain
to confront a train

    All other fish they pales
when they confront the whales

    Don't duck
confront your luck

    Giant or elf
confront yourself

Confronted
    Confronted by the bear
I had misread his stare

Confronting
    Confronting a trough
can be very tough

Confused
    Can easily be used
who are confused

Confusion
    All else is confusion
during blood transfusion

    Confusion can
confuse a man

    Confusion is a kind
memory of the mind

Conical
    He looks all comical
whose head is conical

Conquer

*Conquer solitude
with a golden attitude*

*He goes on a tear
to conquer despair*

*I would not have lived in vain
if I helped to conquer their pain*

*To conquer all the senses
rid yourself of pretenses*

*He who rests his hand
conquers many a land*

Conquest

*Conquest is best
after putting it to the test*

*To lose is to win
like the conquest of sin*

Conscience

*A conscience once broken
will not just be token*

*A good conscience will keep
your daily sound sleep*

*Conscience doesn't matter
when it is mind over chatter*

*Conscience filled with terror
from many a past error*

*Conscience is a wretch
for the ways it can stretch*

*Conscience is clear
I have no one to fear*

*Conscience is your witness
who can judge you and your fitness*

*Conscience must go to school
when the brain tries to rule*

*Conscience needs repair
if you wish to have affair*

*Conscience plays a hand
in keeping life bland*

*Conscience takes a beating
when it is over heating*

*Conscience took him there
when he had time to spare*

*Don't be a nuisance
I hinted at my conscience*

*His conscience it lay dead
upon wine and bread as he fed*

*His conscience it lies
free of human ties*

*His conscience turned cold
before he became bold*

*If conscience was a cat
the rat would tip his hat*

*In the conscience it dwell
both heaven and hell*

*In the hands of a fool
conscience is a tool*

*Tear up your conscience
and become a nuisance*

*Though he was well lettered
his conscience it was cluttered*

*When gin reaches its peak
conscience begins to leak*

*When his conscience took a puncture
he couldn't find the tincture*

*With his conscience on hold
he ventured to be bold*

*Let their consciences speak
until they become meek*

Conscious

*I am conscious of a ghost
to whom my mind plays host*

Consciousness

*Where the two minds meet
there is consciousness to greet*

Consequences

*Consequences are dire
once you start a fire*

*Consequences can be dire
for him who kindles a fire*

*Consequences dire
from the web of desire*

*Consequences vast
moments from the past*

*Fear and consequences
come in sequences*

*He who bites the apple
has consequences to grapple*

Considerable

*Commensurate with his girth
he was a man of considerable mirth*

Considers

*He who knows himself
considers himself an elf*

Consoling

*The river keeps rolling
with sounds that are consoling*

Constantly

*Constantly the pair
have love in repair*

*I am constantly fed
by the orchestra in my head*

Constitution

*I am for a good constitution
and a good institution*

Consume

*Easy to consume
her every perfume*

Consumption

*Built in assumption
for public consumption*

Contact

*Before you make a pact
make eye contact*

*Have contact
to interact*

*Use tact
with eye contact*

Contagious
*His contagious charm
protected him from harm*

Contemplate
*On a quiet and silent night
we contemplate our plight*

Contemplation
*Contemplation has proved
that judgment is improved*

Contender
*How to be a contender
if you're just a pretender*

Contentment
*Contentment in wealth
is good for health*

Contracts
*They covered their tracks
with big contracts*

Control
*Don't go on a stroll
without self control*

*His self control
took a stroll*

*Self control
make it your goal*

*To go on a stroll
without self control*

Controlled
*Hand in hand they strolled
both quiet and controlled*

Controversy
*Controversy it takes
to clean up the lakes*

*How to see
through controversy*

Convenient
*Convenient for sure
to be rich rather than poor*

Convention
*Many a great invention
defies all convention*

*Many an invention
against convention*

Converging
*Converging paths
of daily wraths*

Convert
*Hard to convert
the introvert*

Conveys
*The word it conveys
the image in many ways*

Convictions
*With fixed convictions
they stand for elections*

Convincing
*He gave a convincing talk
to join him and his flock*

Cook
>How can we cook meat
>in the kitchen with no heat

Cooking
>He was too good looking
>to do his own cooking

Cool
>He walked into a pool
>thinking it was cool

>How to stay cool
>not learned in school

>In the cool evening breeze
>she couldn't stop to sneeze

>To be late is cool
>but not for school

Corals
>Corals they blossom
>from the ocean bottom

Cordials
>The cordials in the shelf
>they couldn't reach the elf

Cornered
>How can it be benign
>the cornered canine

Corporate
>Corporate rage
>on every page

Correction
>Course correction
>new direction

>Course correction
>was a good selection

Corridors
>Corridors of the past
>memories that are vast

Corrosion
>Corrosion on the whole
>is bad for the soul

Corruption
>Widespread corruption
>is a widespread eruption

Cosmetic
>His most cosmetic part
>fell off the chart

Cost
>Cost thousand rupees
>and a few peas

Cosy
>Don't be cosy
>thinking it is rosy

Cottage
>Cottage in the hills
>where water runs the mills

Couch
>I have things to vouch
>once in the couch

Counted
>The tea leaves were counted
>on hot water then mounted

Counting

He lay there counting sheep
waiting for deep sleep

Country

A day in the country
with the landed and the gentry

Don't make this country
just for the landed gentry

Having served his country
he ended up with the gentry

Out of the window sill
my country this is still

To live in a country
where the land is for the gentry

Couple

Newly married couple
their love must be supple

Not always supple
relations between the couple

There is nothing that can't be fix
with a couple of tooth pix

Couples together
who admire each other

Couplets

Couplets don't know why
make the sparks fly

Couplets have time
for both rhythm and rhyme

Couplets I told her
in the eye of the beholder

Couplets may not have logic
but they retain their magic

Couplets that are sloppy
can also make me happy

Couplets they alight
from a thought in full flight

Couplets were heard
before the written word

Couplets will unfold
from the mind I am told

My day gets its tonic
from couplets that are laconic

She answered with her lips
with couplets and quips

Courage

Courage it will take
to be a fish in the lake

Courage must be ample
to set a good example

Courier

The fox can't use the furrier
as his only courier

Course

Keep them on course
reason and discourse

Coverage
They give a lot of coverage
for the person who is average

Coward
He is not coward
he does it for reward

Cowardice
Cowardice is nice
if it is against vice

Cowboy
The cowboy veneer
is without peer

Cozy
Baby kangaroos' couch
is her mothers cozy pouch

Something about his middle
cozy for the fiddle

Crab
Every hole in the sand
is crab land

Why would I brag
I'm only a crab

Crabs have a hand
making holes in the sand

The crabs they start feeding
as the waves they go receding

Cracked
After each sip
he cracked the whip

Usually cracked up to be
something we cannot see

Wasn't by me
what was cracked up to be

Craft
Craft of writing
don't make it writhing

Don't be daft
just master the craft

Cranes
They dance the cranes
to show off their manes

Crawl
The sun sand and the waves
they crawl into the caves

Creaking
Though creaking at the hinges
he would not stop his binges

Creaky
Makes a point
my creaky joint

Crease
Wear trousers with a crease
for fortunes to increase

Creative
Creative juices
need new fuses

Creative thinking
happens without blinking

Creatively

>Clothes that fit
>and creatively sit

Creativity

>Creativity has norms
>and marginal forms

>Creativity is a kind
>of exercise for the mind

>Creativity is a voice
>that gives me no choice

>Creativity on the whole
>is ingrained in the soul

>How to release
>creativity like a breeze

>Must be witty
>creativity

Creature

>Parrot is a creature
>that can foretell your future

>All creatures great and small
>they seem to enter the mall

>Some creatures of habit
>they just lob it

Credit

>Credit is best
>when given by the rest

>Got without merit
>lost without credit

Cricket

>Cricket was meant to be seen
>only on the village green

Cried

>People have cried
>because the fears have tried

Cries

>Mosquito cries
>when it sees dragon flies

Crime

>To be stuck is a crime
>in the warp of time

Crimes

>Tell tale signs
>of past crimes

>There were no crimes
>in more gracious times

Crisp

>Before they get crisp
>a baby's words have lisp

>He who has a lisp
>can't be very crisp

Crisper

>Say things crisper
>with half a whisper

Critically

>He makes a living
>by critically giving

Critics

Critics have sought
the thinker not the thought

Critics make me rumble
praise makes me humble

Critics they go fighting
about every piece of writing

Crocodile

How to cross rivers
where ever the crocodile shivers

I don't want to repeat
he has crocodile feet

The crocodile can eat your liver
if you don't know how to cross the river

Crocodiles will greet
with wide open teeth

Crossroads

Why so many toads
at the crossroads

Crowd

A portion of the crowd
vociferous and loud

Join the crowd
where everything is loud

In every crowded block
the ticking is from the clock

Crown

Below the crown is a king
and in his palm a farthing

Don't let him drown
the king who wears the crown

Every crown jewel
won after a long duel

He still eyes the crown
though about to drown

Save the crown
when about to drown

The queen with no frown
has a jewel in her crown

Cruel

Almost is a word
too cruel to be heard

If a person is too cruel
feed them a lot of gruel

Cruelty

Cruelty has no bounds
when it makes the rounds

Cruelty in the end
so hard to mend

Cruise

On a roll
on cruise control

Crushes

Teenage crushes
the ultimate rushes

Crutch

He went for his crutch
when he couldn't do much

Cry

*Don't ask why
when pretty girls they cry*

*Done in by
things that make you cry*

*For their mothers they why
little children cry*

*Inevitably why
death makes us cry*

*Nothing must make you cry
until the tears run dry*

*She could easily cry
without a single try*

*What men buy
can make you cry*

*Without having to try
it answers to a cry*

*Write why
if you can't make them cry*

Crying

*All spent from crying
when the times were really trying*

*Born to this earth crying
continues through to dying*

*No one was crying
as I lay there dying*

Cryptic

*He was always cryptic
from being dyspeptic*

Crystal

*Many a crystal ball
has led to downfall*

*The fish seem near
when it is crystal clear*

*To wash away your sin
use crystal clear gin*

Cue

*Please give me a cue
and I will do it for you*

*Rainbow is on cue
before the storm is due*

Cultivate

*Where can I find a balm
to cultivate inner calm*

Cultivates

*He cannot be blind
who cultivates his mind*

Cultivation

*Cultivation is the root
of the mind bearing fruit*

Culture

*Codes of their culture
guarded by the vulture*

*Vegetarian culture
not for the vulture*

Cunning

*Even though nose is running
don't forget to be cunning*

*He has a cunning nose
as long as a hose*

*Out of the Pandora's box
came a cunning little fox*

Cunningness

*Cunningness pays
in untold ways*

Cure

*A garden will cure
your worries for sure*

*Eat a lot of jelly
to cure melancholy*

*Find a cure for bore
it's never been done before*

*Find a cure it is said
for a cold in the head*

*Frivolity is the cure
when you have to endure*

*He who feigns gladness
will find a cure for madness*

*How to cure a structure
with Iodine and tincture*

*How to endure
when there is no cure*

*How to find a cure
for love that doesn't endure*

*How to find a cure
that will all day endure*

*Nothing like a sense of humour
to cure a fractured femur*

*Panacea or cure
gold has a lure*

*The cure for sanity
is a big calamity*

*There is a cure
for the insecure*

*There is a hitch
if a scratch doesn't cure the itch*

*There is a lure
to search for the cure*

*To cure your sciatica
go to Antarctica*

*Walking is a cure
more than talking pure*

*What use is oil
if it cannot cure this boil*

*Words from our lips
can cure hardships*

Cured

*He who is cured of vice
must quickly put it on ice*

*Layer by layer
he was cured by prayer*

Cures

*Dubious cures
have their lures*

Curiosity

*Curiosity aroused
only to be doused*

*Curiosity has no bounds
when it makes the rounds*

*Curiosity killed the rat
in one second flat*

*Curiosity shines
through inquisitive minds*

*If your curiosity needs quelling
just listen to what he is telling*

*My curiosity needs curing
these objects so alluring*

Curl

*My neighbour was a girl
who caressed her curl*

Currency

*Grooming gets relevancy
when it is the sole currency*

Current

*Current events
discussed in tents*

Curse

*Curse on the purse
gets bad to worse*

*He rid himself of curse
by emptying his purse*

*His reply was terse
without a hint of curse*

*That and worse
result of a curse*

*The camel he felt worse
when he confronted his curse*

*They fritter away the curse
of a fully laden purse*

*This form of verse
can rid you of curse*

*Usually for the worse
when blessed by a curse*

Cursed

*He is cursed
who loves himself first*

*He who is cursed
has a temper that is nursed*

*His lips became pursed
whenever he cursed*

*Whoever blinks first
need not be cursed*

Curses

*Curses and quips
with pursed lips*

*Muttering curses
about empty purses*

Curtain

*Better to be certain
before you raise the curtain*

*Nothing is certain
what is behind the curtain*

*The final curtain
can't be more certain*

*The final curtain
is it really certain*

*All curtains will drop
when there are no ways to stop*

Curve

*Every tail has a curve
and a purpose to serve*

*He can spin a good tale
about the curve in his tail*

Custom

*A custom once breached
cannot be re-reached*

*The customs of our times
have no rhythm or rhymes*

Customer

*Customer has might
for he is always right*

Cute

*The pianist was cute
but the listener was a brute*

Cynical

*Cynical gesture
followed by adventure*

D

Dad

*The only one I had
he who was my dad*

Dagger

*Cloak and dagger
increased his swagger*

*He wears a dagger
and walks with a swagger*

Daily

*Daily we must be fed
sweet music to the head*

*He daily hits the pillow
after good day with the willow*

*He munched at crisp wafers
as he read his daily papers*

*How to look for beauty
in daily domestic duty*

*Miller for the mill
needs a daily refill*

*My daily fix
is a bag of trail mix*

*My daily sip
of juicy gossip*

*Our daily turmoil
is in need of oil*

*Pig is the token
for your daily bacon*

*The sun keeps forgetting
that it daily should be setting*

*They have their daily toil
who are closer to the soil*

*To seek and to find
from our daily grind*

Dame

*The hunchback he came
from Notre dame*

Dance

*Anybody can dance
given the chance*

*He who pays the piper
shall not dance to the viper*

Meditative stance
after the dance

Dancing

Dancing to every tune
under the august moon

Danger

Danger is when
you walk into the den

Instrument of danger
e-mail from a stranger

There are no perks
where danger lurks

Dangerous

Always carry a cushion
on a dangerous mission

Daily it becomes wide
the dangerous divide

They are the dangerous kind
who can undermine your mind

Dangers

Out there in the sea
are dangers for you and me

The dangers in the deck
of every shipwreck

Dare

Don't you dare
offend the bear

Let them spare
ideas that dare

You'll find the answer there
where no one else will dare

Dares

He who dares
meets the snares

Daring

The bull is daring
with nostrils flaring

Though he was high and daring
In love careful and caring

Dark

Dark clouds they loom
where there is death and gloom

Dark side of the moon
where men and women swoon

How dark will it get
after the sun has set

In the corners dark
of minds take a walk

Lurking in the dark
from a missing spark

No use going stark
in a place that is all dark

Too many things to hide
in his dark side

Darker

His darker side
has its own tide

Darkest

The bell rings at the tower
from day light to the darkest hour

Darkness

Darkness can be lit
by a candle that is fit

Darkness gets its meaning
when bright light shows up beaming

Even the darkness reacts
to doctored facts

How can you tell light
without the darkness of the night

How would you know it is night
if darkness had no light

In darkness the mice
chew on cheese partly slice

So much solace
in dusk and darkness

Darling

My darling daughter
so much sought after

The caged starling
is a darling

Date

Met her at the gate
on my first date

Daughter

Many a good daughter
is most sought after

Dawn

Each and every night
has dawn in its sight

From dawn to dusk
they undo the husk

From dusk to dawn
the race is on

How to mow the lawn
from the evening to the dawn

She waits for the dawn
the flying swan

The sun as it breaks out of the dawn
the tiger it stretches to yawn

The sun it was drawn
to an earlier dawn

To get a move on
just wake up to the dawn

Wake up to the dawn
with one big yawn

Day

All day we toiled
once the wheels were oiled

Day and night haunted
by the one I really wanted

Day or night
try to get it right

If I had my way
I'd be adam any day

Put on your hat
you have all day to bat

With each passing day
it gets further away

Daydreams

Daydreams are schemes
without any themes

Daylight

No daylight to cart
darkness is smart

Until we get it right
daylight will remain night

Days

After a hard days toil
I watch the pot boil

How many days
have you strayed from your ways

Daytime

Daytime came how
after a night filled with love

Dead

Better to be dead
than the things that were said

Full speed ahead
if you wish to be dead

Genius it is said
happens after you are dead

He caught the twinkle in her eye
to come back from the dead why

He could be dead
who doesn't fix his head

I am not dead
I have music in the head

Improperly fed
the goose went dead

In sleep they are dead
the voices in your head

It's a dead heat
say the men on the beat

Many times we are dead
in life it is said

Matters came to a head
just before he was dead

Music isn't dead
I have a jukebox in my head

Must the ego be fed
until we are dead

No mouth to be fed
once I am dead

Not much was said
after he was found dead

On the tombstone it said
why do you lie here dead

Rumours were being fed
while naming the dead

The brain must be fed
until we are dead

*The cows they cannot be fed
from leaves that are once dead*

*The devil is never dead
he is constantly being fed*

*The issue is dead
unless revived and fed*

*There is an orchestra in my head
which says music isn't dead*

*There is nothing to be fed
once the ego is dead*

*They don't leave your head
until you are dead*

*They don't stay in the head
thoughts once we are dead*

*Though old in the head
the brain ain't dead*

*To get out of it dead
make war it is said*

*Unless forever fed
without love I am dead*

*Unless it is fed
romance will be dead*

*Until the mosquito is dead
there is a sound in my head*

*Until they lost their head
they weren't considered dead*

*Vanity must be fed
until we are dead*

*With her smile she fed
before he went dead*

*Your lucky day she said
is when you wake up dead*

Deadliest

*The deadliest sin
makes love thin*

Deadline

*If you cross the red line
there will be a deadline*

Deadlines

*Deadlines must be met
when you wish to place a bet*

*Deadlines
for headlines*

Deadly

*After one deadly sting
the bee takes to wing*

*He is deadly serious
and says things curious*

*When the cocktail becomes deadly
everything becomes a medley*

Deaf

*If you are deaf in the ear
a pistol can make it clear*

Deal

*After a big meal
they sat down to deal*

*Easy to deal
the full meal*

*He is all iron and steel
and master of the deal*

*How to deal
with the banana peel*

*Make a deal
if you fall for the spiel*

*No big deal
to slip on a peel*

*The first to make a deal
last to sit for a meal*

*They cut a deal
over whiskey and meal*

*This so called deal
is slippery as the eel*

*What's the big deal
said the polar bear to the seal*

*When you make a bad deal
have nerves of steel*

Dealing

*Children have to be dealing
with parents without feelings*

*Continue dealings
without hard feelings*

Dealt

*Body blows dealt
without being felt*

Dear

*Walk beside me my dear
until the path becomes clear*

Death

*A slow death it dies
the well painted lies*

*At his death bed he was told
It was just a common cold*

*Battlefields must yield
to death in the field*

*Before death gets its turn
I have time to burn*

*Between birth and death
where did it go health*

*Birth and death have found
that eternity is around*

*Can't do your sums
once death it comes*

*Circle of death
must be tread in stealth*

*Death and me became parted
when I became faint hearted*

*Death as such
isn't thought of much*

*Death brings a tear
to loved ones who are near*

*Death brings out the tears
and some of our fears*

*Death brings relief
only to your grief*

*Death brings relief
to all the assembled grief*

*Death can be kind
to those who don't mind*

*Death can ruin your health
together with your wealth*

*Death can slowly creep
when you are fast asleep*

*Death comes in stealth
and ruins your health*

*Death comes quicker
soaked in liquor*

*Death comes uninvited
like a ball that is flighted*

*Death doesn't keep score
as to how many are at the door*

*Death happens in a blink
with no time to think*

*Death has a future
if the surgeon can't find a suture*

*Death has no fear
captures man and deer*

*Death has resolved
that problems will be solved*

*Death if you please
after the wine and cheese*

*Death in a cage
where the animals they age*

*Death is a thief
beyond belief*

*Death is expensive
so he became pensive*

*Death is forever
but life is never*

*Death is in the main
about the fear of pain*

*Death is no prize
for your deeds say the wise*

*Death is no surprise
for it cannot happen twice*

*Death is not a curse
when life it burdens the purse*

*Death is very clever
it can live forever*

*Death is very skilled
it comes without being willed*

*Death is well
in both heaven and hell*

*Death it comes offering
that much less suffering*

*Death it comes slowly
to both the high and the lowly*

*Death it slowly lumbered
to the days that were numbered*

Death it stalks like a shadow
to the graveyard in the meadow

Death it surrounds
while making its rounds

Death it will clinch
my final inch

Death keeps baiting
while we are waiting

Death let it be brief
the bringer of relief

Death makes it better
down to the last letter

Death makes it clear
it is a partner in fear

Death makes its case
in a very private place

Death makes its case
staring you in the face

Death makes its case
to the mosquitoes as they pace

Death makes its case
with a fatal embrace

Death must sit
in the graveyard pit

Death picked up pace
with one fatal embrace

Death please wait
for my leap of faith

Death will cure
many things for sure

Death will live forever
in life give up never

Death with all its power
above everything it will tower

Don't ask the spider why
death stalks the fly

Duty it will not shirk
once death begins its work

Escape death we can never
however much we are clever

Every final breath
could only mean death

Far or near
death strikes fear

He parted with his wealth
before his impending death

her concerns must be met
how much ever close to death

How can a mortal see
that death keeps waiting for me

How can death be a foe
when it includes your big toe

How is health
between birth and death

I woke up to a different dawn
following the death of swan

Rhyming English Couplets

*In death he wishes to pose
in one final repose*

*In death I wish to be hurled
to a bold and better world*

*Less is the fear
when death is near*

*Like the moth to the flame
death when it came*

*Mans finest hour
Death bed or the tower*

*No need to sing a verse
for death may not be a curse*

*One day it will call
death for us all*

*Our death I hope will be kind
to those whom we leave behind*

*People they choose death
by ignoring their health*

*Sing yourself to health
or sting yourself to death*

*Slow death
bad for health*

*Someone has been lying
that it was death defying*

*The vultures then feast
upon the death of a beast*

*Upon death it makes a start
the embalmers art*

*Upon death we become a ghost
or so it is with most*

*We have to go miles
before death upon us smiles*

*When death comes our way
no one it can sway*

*When death it does stare
there is much to despair*

*When death meets 'I'
don't ask why*

*Why is death certain
after the final curtain*

Deathbed

*On his deathbed
he and his love were wed*

Deathly

*Deathly stalk
is vulture talk*

*The whisky went into his liver
and caused him a deathly shiver*

Deaths

*Beyond deaths door
heaven will give us more*

*Deaths unfair notice
wasn't the best poultice*

Debate

*The hens don't debate
about how to incubate*

D

Debt

*Couldn't repay debt
so he sat down and wept*

*Debt is owed heavily
to the mother of the family*

*From a mountain of debt
he quickly leapt*

*How to select
what debt to collect*

*In a cold sweat
thinking of his debt*

*Many a person has slept
with love as a debt*

*No way out
of debt and gout*

*The debt remained
from promises made*

*Where can it be kept
this karmic debt*

Debts

*Countless debts
from being inept*

Decaffeinated

*He was decaffeinated
and ill-fated*

Deceit

*Many a mans conceit
is proper self deceit*

*Men of deceit
never ask for receipt*

*Petulant in deceit
he never gave a receipt*

Deceive

*Hard to perceive
why they flatter to deceive*

December

*On early December mornings
breakfast in bed are longings*

Deception

*Debris of deception
gets good reception*

*He who resorts to deception
gets a cold reception*

*It is called deception
when deceit gets a reception*

*Self deception has a way
of making you part of a play*

*Why is it that deception
always gets a reception*

Decided

*Once they decided to dine
he went and bought the wine*

*They decided to go
to a spot in Mexico*

Decision

*Decision made in haste
ends up as poor taste*

*Decisions of late
I have left it to fate*

*Once facts take hold
make decisions all bold*

*While lounging in the shade
decisions were made*

Declined

*Dined and wined
but vice declined*

Declining

*In declining health
all you need is wealth*

Decorate

*Even the tattered tomes
they decorate our homes*

*They decorate the night
angels in their flight*

Decry

*They will decry
those who don't try*

Dedication

*Dedication is ample
when it is through a temple*

Deed

*Before every deed
make sure there is a need*

*Do a good deed
feed oats to the steed*

*Every deed must be fed
by a word it is said*

*Once the deed is done
just drop your gun*

*The start is for the steed
important as the deed*

*Through deed and word
silently heard*

*To expiate is a need
far greater than the deed*

*Until the deed is done
have them on the run*

*Word action and deed
upon each other they feed*

Deeds

*Deeds with the bat
can bell many a cat*

*Good deeds are the seeds
that the future it needs*

*Unmounted steeds
not ready for deeds*

*Unspoken deeds
make you sweat beads*

Deep

*Deep down in the well
many frogs they dwell*

*Deep in his vagrant heart
there is a soft part*

*Deep in the desert the wind
blows all the way to Sindh*

*Deep in the ocean blue
the shipwreck left a clue*

*Deep inside the cloud
is a thunderbolt very loud*

*Deep into the past
for memories that last*

*His place is set in stone
deep down to his bone*

*How deep is your slumber
when there is falling lumber*

*How hard it is to keep
beauty that is skin deep*

*In the deep arctic night
where polar bears play and fight*

*Into the forest deep
they stray the black sheep*

*Once you dig deep
he has the intelligence of a sheep*

*With a twist of his tail
he plunged deep the whale*

Deeper

*They have a deeper self
both giant and the elf*

Defanged

*Must be defanged
or be hanged*

Defeat

*Even in defeat
they show their teeth*

*He was in defeat
all teeth on two feet*

*How to face defeat
with flat feet*

*No mean feet
to accept defeat*

*Wonders you will meet
when you accept defeat*

Defeated

*Defeated and spent
with his back all bent*

*It must not be repeated
that the war left us defeated*

*What he said when defeated
could not be repeated*

Defeating

*A tryst that is fleeting
is self defeating*

Defeatist

*Every defeatist
he waves a fist*

Defence

*No defence
against such offence*

*Self defence
is no offence*

*She let her defences fall
and dropped her parasol*

Defend

*How to defend
your commitment to the end*

*Not easy to defend
wars that never end*

Defensive

*No defensive thought
whenever he is caught*

Defies

*He who defies
has jaundice in his eyes*

Defined

*Words combined
so a new world is defined*

Defy

*Who could defy
the look in her eye*

Degenerate

*Degenerate culture
of the inveterate vulture*

Delicate

*More delicate than a flower
only love can devour*

Delight

*A candle will delight
love when it needs light*

*A surging delight
at other peoples plight*

*Better delight her
if you are a writer*

*Caribous plight
hunters delight*

*Circles of delight
the sea birds in flight*

*Day and night
he plants words that delight*

*Day or night
instant delight*

*Every juicy bite
of the apple is delight*

*Every serpent must bite
to relive its delight*

*He took to the space flight
with the bounding pulse of delight*

*Like a candle in the night
that gives me much delight*

*Many authors write
just to delight*

*No need for light
all we need is delight*

*Not much delight
in always being right*

*On the wings of delight
they spent the night*

*Ribbons of light
causing waves of delight*

*She showed her delight
when he switched on the light*

*Snowstorms at night
a skiers delight*

*So much delight
when butterflies alight*

*Such a delight
when love takes to flight*

*The devastation and plight
caused by the weeds in delight*

*The moon shining with delight
showed her full face to the night*

*The moon would delight
in the softness of the night*

*The seagulls show delight
on an endless winter flight*

*They moaned at their plight
though it was all delight*

*Though endless is the night
it continues to delight*

*To the ear is delight
the songs of the night*

*Wasps in flight
seeking delight*

*When love is right
it is heavenly delight*

*Words will throw light
at the face of delight*

Delightful

*Every delightful line
must bide its time*

Delightfully

*He was always meant
to be delightfully absent*

Delighting

*How to go delighting
about bad writing*

Delights

*The heady delights
of Arabian nights*

*The seagulls in delights
on endless winter nights*

Deluded

*The two who are deluded
must have colluded*

Delving

*Don't go delving
into things over whelming*

Demand

*There is a demand in lands
for skillful hands*

*Their demands will calm
if you grease their palm*

Demanding

*Ever so demanding
lack of understanding*

Demon

*A demon once trapped
can be unwrapped*

*Demon of doubt
is losing his clout*

*The demon within
makes the resistance thin*

*There is a demon in my chest
who I understand best*

*There was a demon in the city
who evoked no pity*

*His demons came in the way
of what he wanted to-day*

*I have demons to slay
and no time for play*

Den

*Cannot be into zen
without being in a den*

*He will get out when
the bear is in the den*

Denial

*Self denial
must be kept in a vial*

Deny

*She would never deny
her unsparing eye*

*They tend to deny
what they see with the naked eye*

Denying

*There is no denying
that life is death defying*

Depending

*Depending on how they were feted
some get very elated*

*He loses his reason
depending on the season*

*Things will always be said
depending on what they are fed*

Depends

*Depends on what is fed
from the time you get out of bed*

*Depends on what you pick
as your own yardstick*

*How green is your grass
depends on the amount of moss*

Deployed

*Deployed with skill
his message was shrill*

Depressed

*Can't get depressed
when joy is expressed*

*The silently oppressed
can be depressed*

Depression

*Depression is creeping
if you are all day sleeping*

Depths

In the depths of the ocean blue
lie pearls that girls love too

In the depths of the wood
where the tiger hunts for food

Derail

About to derail
my body thin and frail

Describe

Good to have mirth
when you describe your girth

Desert

All the way to sindh
the sound of the desert wind

Camel is the brand
in desert land

Deserve

All things smitten
deserve to be written

I may be a seedling
I don't deserve the needling

Deserves no pity
Mediocrity

He deserves no pity
who meets serendipity

Deserving

They think they are deserving
and say things all self serving

Designer

Every day at the diner
I met a young designer

Designs

Mans reckless designs
cause all the crimes

Designs

They have their designs
who have gold in their eyes

Desire

At first there was desire
then came the fire

Change into new attire
when you find hearts desire

Desire and it's pains
are the only remains

Desire burns out
without any doubt

Desire can be stilled
by the strong willed

Desire is like a fire
that will never retire

Desire will stay
if you wish it away

Driven by desire
need things to acquire

Every new attire
is a product of desire

*Every shared desire
as if echoed in the choir*

*Fading desire
where is thy fire*

*How to aspire
without desire*

*How to retire
with object of desire*

*However big the fire
subdue your desire*

*I'd rather fulfill your desire
than face up to your ire*

*It fills your cup
when desire is up*

*Newly felt desire
how to go and acquire*

*Once you voice your desire
let him strike for fire*

*Send a wire
to transcend desire*

*Set it afire
your whiff of desire*

*She was struck by his desire
to set her heart on fire*

*Showroom attire
object of desire*

*Stoked by the fire
many a desire*

*The chase is still on
until all desire is gone*

*The desire is strong
to do things though wrong*

*The torments of desire
how to douse the fire*

*The web of desire
is the spiders attire*

*There is no attire
like unquenched desire*

*They go headlong
whose desire is strong*

*To desire he is wed
like a serpent to its head*

*To linger is not a desire
with finger in the fire*

*To set your feelings on fire
chase every desire*

*Tongue that spits fire
beyond the limits of desire*

*Treat each desire
like a new attire*

*Try not to quell
their desire to excel*

*unfulfilled desire
needs new attire*

*When desire becomes blush
there is a blood rush*

*When will there be fire
in this dormant desire*

Desired

*Some people are wired
to be the most desired*

Desires

*Best place to keep
desires fully asleep*

*Burning desires
like the fires*

*Cut out your desires
for diamonds and sapphires*

*Desires are too strong
even when they are wrong*

*Desires became strong
when you know it is wrong*

*Desires it has taught
more than it is not*

*Desires like thief alight
by candle light*

*Desires must now
be curbed and how*

*Desires once depleted
he thinks he is cheated*

*Desires will purge
when you fight the urge*

*Don't grumble
if your desires are humble*

*Fulfilled desires
don't quench the fires*

*He who desires more
constantly keeps score*

*How to keep score
when desires are more*

*How to quench the fires
of unwanted desires*

*My desire it lies
within her Spanish eyes*

*Put out the fires
of worldly desires*

*Secret desires
come in varied attires*

*Some they acquires
beastly desires*

*Their desires were fed
upto the time they were dead*

*They continue to haunt
the new desires that I want*

*They dance to her desires
with enchanting satires*

*They have in them least
desires of the beast*

*They need new attires
the new found desires*

*When desires reach a peak
the will must be made weak*

*With each glance she desires
to stoke love and its fires*

Desolation

*It is no consolation
that heaven is desolation*

Despair

*A synapse in despair
needs quick repair*

*Despair can hurt you
more than any virtue*

*Despair must not be fed
until we are dead*

*Don't despair
stick to flair*

*He who is an heir
lives in despair*

*Hope can repair
every despair*

*How to repair
this state of despair*

*Men of despair
in need of repair*

*No need to despair
the loss was only hair*

Desperation

*Desperation it breeds
from unhealthy seeds*

Despise

*Do not despise your girth
you are the only one on earth*

Despite

*Despite a broken wing
she can still sing*

*Despite a lisp
his words came out crisp*

*Despite all the wine
he walked a straight line*

*Tomorrow will come
despite the hum drum*

*Why does she wear a frown
despite the jewels in her crown*

Destinies

*Separately they went
as their destinies had meant*

Destiny

*The destiny of many
depends on a penny*

*With destiny in your hands
travel distant lands*

Destroy

*Ill will can
destroy a man*

Destruction

*Destruction by greed
is mans perpetual need*

How to ration
the politics of destruction

Destructive

Don't let it peak
your destructive streak

Don't sharpen the beak
of your destructive streak

Don't take a peak
at mans' destructive streak

Every destructive streak
lodged in her beak

His destructive side
unspoken pride

Detached

A meaning once attached
can never be detached

Fangs detached
can be re-attached

Detached

Once the egg is hatched
the hen becomes detached

Detail

A certain detail
she notices without fail

No need to detail
the peacocks tail

Detest

Can't keep abreast
of things you detest

Don't detest
putting them to the test

Develop

Let them not develop legs
these rotten eggs

Men who bite their nails
will soon develop tails

Developed

Almost down to the wire
we developed a flat tyre

Devices

Best left to his devices
he and his vices

Devil

He had abuses to choose
the devil after the booze

How to level
with the cunning devil

Keep your head level
before you tempt the devil

The angels feel the heat
when the devil is on the beat

The devil feels well
wherever he dwell

The devil is never dead
alive and well in your head

The devil plays his tune
mostly in June

*The devil will leave you things
that will make your heart sings*

*The devil within
is forging sin*

*Alone in hell
where the devils dwell*

*Unhook the claws
from the devils paws*

Devoted

*Husband most devoted
he was summarily voted*

*Many a page
devoted to bondage*

Devotion

*Devotion to his work
is his only perk*

*There is no lotion
for mutual devotion*

*Where can I buy the lotion
for single minded devotion*

*Worthy of her devotion
man in full motion*

Devour

*A beast can devour
at the height of his power*

*After a shower
food to devour*

*Before the bees devour
there is sweet taste in the flower*

*In a single idle hour
how much can you devour*

*In one well planned hour
opponents to devour*

*Many a serpent will devour
even an innocent flower*

*Many bottles to devour
in just one Idle hour*

*To smell the sweet flower
before the bees they devour*

Devouring

*After devouring the fishes
who cleans the dishes*

*Bees go devouring
all things that are flowering*

Dew

*No one else but you
like the morning dew*

*What ever their hue
the flowers get their dew*

Dialogue

*Many hours to log
in the process of dialogue*

*Many hours we must log
in the cause of dialogue*

Diamond

*Brought herself to wing
the diamond in her ring*

*The jewel on many a head
is the diamond it is said*

*When you shop for diamonds
take with you some almonds*

Dictatorships

*Dictatorships can slip
way down to the hip*

Die

*A great place to die
where they won't notice or cry*

*A little I die
when I swat a fly*

*Best not to try
when it is do or die*

*Better to die
than to live a lie*

*Daily we must try
something new till we die*

*Do so many have to die
before they question why*

*Don't cry
till you grow old and die*

*Don't know why
marriages they die*

*Every daylight it must die
in the evening of the sky*

*Every minute I die
when I don't see you why*

*Everyday I die
a little bit why*

*Finger in every pie
until the day I die*

*Fire fighters die
without saying good – bye*

*Go hide or die
when she looks you in the eye*

*He is prepared to die
who doesn't question why*

*He thought he would die
from the glare of her accusing eye*

*He was prepared to die
once love caught his eye*

*He will die young
who is high strung*

*Hold your head high
till the day you die*

*However hard we try
someday we will die*

*I don't plan to cry
even when I die*

*I think I will die
if she doesn't come by*

*It wouldn't be a lie
to say many times we die*

*My inward eye
can it ever die*

No need to cry
till the day you die

No need to cry
we are all going to die

Once before you die
tell a single lie

Peacefully why
some refuse to die

People think he die
when he wink with both eye

Someday I must die
and relinquish all ties

The die was cast
for tendencies of the past

The landed and the gentry
would they die for the country

The lilies they die
once the pond it runs dry

The universe it fits in why
into my brain till I die

Till the day he die
she caught his eye

To live is to die
everyday why

To the home in the sky
where we really die

Until I die
you are the star of my eye

Wait till I die
before you begin to cry

Wars are fought why
so the undeserving can die

When looked in the eye
he would rather die

When shame it fills the sky
is it better to live or to die

Wit and wisdom why
when all are going to die

Without a tear to cry
when some of us we die

Would all the fish die
if the oceans they run dry

Would you rather die
or tell a white lie

Writings they can die
faced with the public eye

Died

After a fling
he died in a sling

Envy and pride
in me both have died

He died in his shoe laces
on cold mountain faces

He woke up and cried
when the funeral it died

I almost died
eating things all fried

D

*Many a time I have lied
that the evil thoughts have died*

Dies

*He who dies for a cause
says it is because*

*He who dies in shame
has lost more than a name*

*He who dies of fright
usually does it at night*

*No family ties
for those who dies*

*Until he dies
he has wandering eyes*

Diet

*A diet full of beans
to live within your means*

*Both of us we diet
in candle light and quiet*

*He fed his pet poodle
a diet full of noodle*

*Put it on a diet
to make your mind quiet*

*To improve collective memory
a diet based on celery*

Differences

*Differences you must settle
over coffee in the kettle*

Different

*Different only in name
but we are all still the same*

Difficult

*A very difficult task
to make a rhyme that will last*

Dignity

*Dignity and fortitude
laced with good attitude*

*Let dignity be his
on a day such as this*

Digression

*A simple digression
became a transgression*

Dim

*It would be considered dim
to teach a duck to swim*

Dine

*How better to dine
than with good red wine*

*How can I dine
without your summer wine*

Diner

*He who is a whiner
can't eat at the diner*

Dinner

*For dinner at the tent
wear your favourite scent*

Dinosaurs
When Dinosaurs quibble
the earth worms wriggle

Diplomacy
To deep diplomacy on course
do we need force

Dire
She put out his fire
when he was in straits dire

Dirty
Every new broom
needs a dirty room

Disagreements
Disagreements and fights
that ruin many nights

Disappear
Buy things too dear
and money will disappear

Disappears at noon
the man in the moon

Disappears into the night
the sun all shining and bright

Disappointly
She looked at the sky
disappointingly why

Disarray
It's time to pray
while in disarray

Disaster
In trying to avoid disaster
they got into trouble faster

Nothing arrives any faster
than unheralded disaster

Nothing grows faster
than a disaster

Nothing moves faster
than ecological disaster

They both blurted
that disaster was skirted

Who will reach there faster
towards magic or disaster

Discard
Hard to discard
message from the bard

With just one look
the devil discards the book

Discipline
Discipline say the sages
don't pay the wages

Discipline your senses
without pretenses

To bring discipline to thought
just undo the knot

Where have you been
my discipline

Discomfort
> Discomfort she carried
> that was long time buried

Discontent
> Discontent was meant
> with good intent

Discounted
> Stand up and be counted
> until you are discounted

Discoveries
> Discoveries were made
> by sitting in the shade

> New discoveries were made
> when they held hands in the shade

Discreet
> Be discreet
> on wet concrete

Discrete
> Made me discrete and kind
> the concrete in my mind

Disease
> A disease half cured
> and the rest endured

Disgrace
> Carry it out with grace
> your moments of disgrace

Disgrace
> Disgrace keeps pace
> with the whole human race

Disguise
> Blessings have a guise
> that they try and disguise

> How to disguise
> your love say the wise

> How to disguise
> your thoughts say the wise

> They disguise your thoughts
> these blood clots

> He quickly wises
> upto his disguises

Disgust
> Her source of disgust
> was upon him thrust

Dish
> Cats make a dish
> out of rats and the fish

> Don't smell the fish
> before it hits the dish

> He would want his dish
> full of salmon fish

> There is a little fish
> that eats larvae for a dish

Dishonesty
> Dishonesty stays
> with you always

Dismount
> Make it count
> before you dismount

Disorder

A compulsive disorder
to put the mind in order

In a world of disorder
where there is no border

Disown

My choices are my own
while others I disown

Dispelling

Many an author has fought
dispelling unsavory thought

Display

A careless display
of the streaks of grey

The beginning of pangs
when he displays his fangs

Dissensions

Afraid of questions
and dissensions

Dissent

Not much dissent
by the hunted pheasant

The baby has started his ascent
said the doctor in dissent

Dissenting

One dissenting voice
completely changed our choice

Dissolve

Some day as we evolve
will the planets they dissolve

Distance

A century is a distance
can be recalled in an instance

Before the birds fly
into the distance in the sky

Can't last the distance
in each and every instance

Distances are high
where twinkle stars lie

Distance enhances beauty
but don't forget your duty

Distance in the end
is a loves' best friend

Into the distance why
in the morning sun they fly

Into the distance why
the birds at dusk they fly

Though the distances were many
they only charged a penny

Distant

At dusk they fly
into the distant sky

Every distant star
twinkles from afar

*In the far distant past
when they roamed the lands vast*

*On a distant and remote day
they held hands in Bombay*

*Songs from the distant drum
and guitar strings to strum*

*The past sounded better
while reading her distant letter*

*You can see the distant star
better than me by far*

Distinct

*His lexical choice
has a distinct voice*

*There is a distinct layer
between the seer and the sayer*

Distortions

*A lens from the past
whose distortions can last*

Distraction

*Distraction is ripe
when it involves hype*

*Don't be a distraction
in the thick of the action*

*Driven to distraction
by impulsive action*

*Every course of action
must rid you of distraction*

*From thought to action
let there be no distraction*

*He is a man of action
without any distraction*

*Men prone to action
don't like distraction*

*Put words into action
without any distraction*

*There is no distraction
at the epicenter of action*

*All my distractions
were love and its attractions*

*Gentlemen of style
prone to distractions and guile*

*So many distractions
I look to things in fractions*

Distress

*How to address
both stress and distress*

*How to express
personal distress*

*Learning in distress
is the true meaning of stress*

*Life is filled with stress
and a bit of distress*

*Man in distress
thinks mistress*

*When in distress
call up the seamstress*

Distressed
*He who is obsessed
is never distressed*

Distribute
*They distribute the blame
when the excuse is lame*

Disturbed
*Don't wish to be disturbed
or my passions curbed*

*How can it be curbed
the mind disturbed*

*The cat it purred
at being disturbed*

Disturbing
*Wrong things blurting
even so disturbing*

Divergent
*Every divergent mood
need not make you brood*

Diverted
*Her diverted eyes
brought stress to their ties*

Divide
*The big divide
of time and tide*

Dividends
*Dividends are forever
like diamonds are never*

Divine
*Coffee feels divine
when it is Arabian wine*

*Divine right for things
not just for kings*

*Don't try to counter
this divine encounter*

*Every crowd pleasing line
was made to sound divine*

*It feels divine
when vengeance is mine*

*Not good to dine
when vinegar feels divine*

*Oh so divine
this Arabian wine*

*Only one is divine
between vinegar and wine*

*She looked divine
before I had the wine*

*To make love divine
add a tincture of wine*

*Youth it is divine
like sweet red wine*

*Nothing more diviner
than a two-liner at the diner*

Divorce
*Divorce is alive and well
for marriages that go through hell*

*Divorce is of use
as the ultimate abuse*

*Divorce would be easy
if it didn't make you queezy*

*Don't use force
get divorce*

Dog

*The dog has his day
and the frog croaks away*

*Dogs have a go
at neighbours ego*

*What's a walk in the park
without dogs that bark*

Domain

*An island is in the main
my exclusive domain*

Donate

*It sends a big shiver
when they ask to donate your liver*

Donations

*Communities must treasure
donations in every measure*

Done

*Done in by the weather
many a birds feather*

Doubt

*Banish all doubt
he is really stout*

*Benefit of the doubt
to the person with gout*

*Coax it out
and clear the doubt*

*Coax the meaning out
when you have doubt*

*Combustion comes out
when in self doubt*

*Doubt dispelled
forever expelled*

*Each morning I step out
into a mountain of doubt*

*First come out
and clear the doubt*

*Fishhooks and doubt
don't go fishing without*

*Give in to stout
like benefit of the doubt*

*Go figure it out
and clear the doubt*

*He did me out
whatever there was of doubt*

*He wore himself out
trying to clear the doubt*

*How to be without
pimples and doubt*

*I can do without
dead ends and doubt*

Rhyming English Couplets

Lingering doubt
reduced his clout

Once found out
it clears the doubt

Once more though I doubt
you I cannot do without

Once nightmares run out
so it does doubt

Once you figure it out
what happens to doubt

Pin pricks of doubt
messages that shout

Place to clear all doubt
is the top of the mount

The reason is in doubt
for a big turnout

There is no doubt
that man is without

Though he may be devout
there will be lingering doubt

To clear all the doubt
coax the meaning out

To clear the doubt
coax the truth out

Too much self doubt
was the cause of his gout

What was left out
cleared all the doubt

When in doubt
do without

When in doubt
figure it out

When there is doubt
the volleys they go out

When you make room for doubt
you will end up being without

I am never without
a million doubts

It all evens out
without any doubts

When doubts begin to creep
nothing left but to weep

Doubted

They never really doubted
that conditions could be flouted

Down

Down to earth soon
the man in the moon

He put down the tea
on the table by his knee

Down

Let them not sneer
just hold down the beer

Down

Way down south
where the fountain has a mouth

D

*Way down to his toes
it reached down his nose*

Dragon

*Breathing fire it was him
the dragon who went for a swim*

*Don't try to tag on
to a Komodo dragon*

*Every dragon slain
will ease the pain*

*Load the wagon
and dance with the dragon*

*When the dragon breathes fire
the consequences are dire*

*Food by the wagons
in the world of the dragons*

Drain

*Going down the drain
doesn't require a train*

*Rain is rain
until it hits the drain*

Drained

*I had myself trained
not to be drained*

Drank

*He drank from the fountain
after he moved the mountain*

Drawn

*Make it long drawn
the unstifled yawn*

*No swords were drawn
since it was all about brawn*

*The grandmaster had drawn
the white pawn*

Dreads

*He who dreads the grey
can't have much to say*

Dream

*A childs little dream
towards ice cream*

*A layer of cream
that shattered my dream*

*A long forgotten dream
strawberry's and cream*

*A mid summer stream
where I sit and dream*

*A recurring dream
with a similar theme*

*A sleep walkers dream
is to reach for the ice cream*

*All they do is dream
up a new scheme*

*Anyone can dream
about poppy and cream*

*By the shores I sit and dream
of the soft and purling stream*

*By the soft and purling stream
on the shores I sit and dream*

Rhyming English Couplets

*Don't care a fig
just dream big*

*Every failed dream
they joined the same team*

*Forever I must keep
my dream time and sleep*

*Hatch up a scheme
in search of a dream*

*How can I miss
a dream such as this*

*How real it did seem
when I woke up from a dream*

*I dream of sunlight
in the darkness of the night*

*I had a Wimbledon dream
about strawberries and cream*

*In my esteem
she was lovely as a dream*

*It was all part of a scheme
to enter into her dream*

*Let it be your dream
to go against the stream*

*Like the oft recurring dream
of the patented scheme*

*Nothing to rue
once dream comes true*

*Once you swallow your dream
all you can do is scream*

*Salmon chase their dream
swimming up stream*

*Salmon they dream
of swimming upstream*

*She woke up from her dream
not knowing whether to scream*

*Stop to drink at the stream
when you are chasing a dream*

*Strawberrys and cream
fill many a dream*

*Such a good team
we were in this dream*

*The dream it came true
when its time was due*

*The easy flowing stream
by which I sit and dream*

*The horses they dream
being switched in mid-stream*

*The impossible dream
is gods little scheme*

*The stranger in my dream
who wasn't on my team*

*They offer you a dream
that makes you scream*

*They sat beside the stream
counting every dream*

*To dream big
wear a wig*

D

To make it possible
dream the impossible

We sit and dream
by the shadow on the stream

What kind of dream is this
that the cobra has forgotten his kiss

When I dream of things
its like angels fluttering their wings

. Who usurps your dream
drop him from the team

Dreamer

A salesman is a dreamer
more than a schemer

He was a day dreamer
who found love in a steamer

Dreamless

After every dreamless sleep
must I wake up and weep

Many a dreamless night
didn't always feel right

Dreams

About her it seems
my warm summer dreams

All dreams come true
once you imbibe the brew

Built by men of dreams
palaces and themes

Day dreams can mean
she was not to be seen

Day dreams it seems
are more than ice creams

Don't stop to cry
dreams when they die

Dreams are kept away
in the bright light of the day

Dreams have schemes
written on my reams

Dreams have shapes
even for the apes

Dreams have ties
to their past lives

Dreams I have in sleep
can sometimes make me weep

Dreams it seems
have unending themes

Dreams make it clear
reality was at one time near

Dreams of greed
also have a seed

Dreams that take flight
when cast in a glamorous light

Dreams they alight
when you switch off the light

Dreams they start
with an honest heart

Everywhere she seems
is the girl of my dreams

Fill your dreams
with clever schemes

From high up in the sky
she stepped into my dreams why

From nowhere it seems
she came into my dreams

Fulfill your dreams
with unending schemes

Going to extremes
in your day dreams

I can't be bothered
by dreams poorly fathered

I don't have the means
to get the girl of my dreams

I dream of the south seas
where love fills my dreams

I have many schemes
dressed up as dreams

I have my schemes
for the planet of my dreams

In my dreams they roamed
the sins unatoned

Into my dreams they peep
while I am asleep

It is not common it seems
for hopes to become dreams

It is not the stuff of dreams
to live within your means

It's no time to cry
once the dreams run dry

Know not why
dreams must die

Life it seems
about unspoken dreams

Like yesterday it seems
our nostalgic dreams

Make room for your dreams
and fit them into schemes

Man of a thousand dreams
is full of many schemes

Many dreams were fed
by writing them it is said

Midnight dreams
of fearful screams

More beautiful it seems
a life lived off dreams

More so in dreams
love it seems

Mountains and streams
I cross them in my dreams

My best schemes
re-enacted in dreams

People have these dreams
or so it seems

People with big dreams
have their own schemes

D

*Pocket full of themes
and childhood dreams*

*Some of our dreams in youth
turned out to be uncouth*

*Sweet dreams and bliss
both hers and his*

*The price can be high
for dreams that reach the sky*

*They must be forgotten
dreams misbegotten*

*They rush to their dreams
with pre-planned schemes*

*They sell your dreams
clothed in schemes*

*To dreams we are prone
in the transition zone*

*Towards me she leans
to share with me her dreams*

*Turn your genes
into joyful dreams*

*We were quickly humbled
by dreams that tumbled*

*When I wake up from my sleep
I have dreams to keep*

*With my dreams I made a pact
that they come to me intact*

Dreamt

*He who dreamt big
lost his hair to wig*

Dreamy

*I make them irate
in a dreamy state*

*My dreamy eyes
ready for steamy ties*

*On dreamy starlit nights
lovers mull their plights*

Dressed

*Always dressed in white
and a belt buckled tight*

*I was all dressed up in a suit
when my labour bore fruit*

*She was all dressed in mink
and mine eyes they would not blink*

Dried

*When his pen was dried of ink
he took to taking drink*

Drink

*Don't drink from the chalice
if you have a background of malice*

*Drink is food
when you brood*

*Drink made him a man
from the tin can*

*Even without a drink
I was tickled pink*

*He shared a drink with a gypsy
that made them both tipsy*

Rhyming English Couplets

He would drop in for a drink
and make the host think

Many a drink will sing
as if born to be king

Never skipped a drink
nor slept a wink

Olives in your drink
tickles me all pink

Once her tail is up
she will drink from the cup

All drinks must pale
in the presence of ale

Drinks from fermentation
would be my recommendation

He always drinks most
when proposing a toast

He drinks to his host
and also to his ghost

Drinking

It's not the drinking
it's what happens to thinking

Drive

Have guts
drive them nuts

Drone

She found a drone
when she picked up the phone

What can you do for me
said the drone to the bee

What will be will be
said the drone to the queen bee

When she picked up the phone
the other end was a drone

You will not wake up a drone
if you wave a juicy bone

Drooped

Her eyelids they drooped
as the Ice – cream she scooped

Drop

Drop all this talk
go back to black board and chalk

Droplets

Droplets of water
on the stone pitter patter

Dropped

The onion was dropped
just before it was chopped

Drought

Drought is a pain
relieved by the rain

Drowned

She drowned all her fears
by wiping away her tears

Drum

If doldrums was a drum
I have a guitar to strum

Drumsticks

I get my kicks
with drumsticks

Drunk

He got drunk at sea
but it wasn't from tea

He was too drunk
to be called a monk

I had drunk my fill
of the cold air that was still

The drunk and his ghost
lean on the lamp post

They were drunk and reeling
down to the last drop of feeling

Drunkard

The drunkard he feels
his legs are on wheels

Drunken

Drunken brawls
and graffiti walls

Dry

He has a dry run
who walks in the sun

The lakes that went dry
in the Andes why

Ducklings

Ducklings feel fine
when the ducks are in line

Due

It only takes two
to give each one their due

So much to chew
if you give them their due

Put yourself in my shoes
and pay all my dues

Dull

How to mull
over something so dull

Many a dull day
moulded by the clay

Without her very dull
memories that I mull

Dumb

How can he be dumb
who has a right thumb

Dust

From dust to dust
we all must

Like a cloud of dust
the swarming locust

Our body it must
someday turn to dust

Dutiful

It's better to be dutiful
than very beautiful

Duty

I did my duty
for the blue eyed beauty

Our duty is to buoy
and not to annoy

Rhyming English Couplets

*To create thing of beauty
just do your duty*

Dwell

*A desert is well
where the Oases dwell*

*Does barbarism dwell
only in hell*

*Don't dwell
just read it well*

*Don't dwell
on books that don't sell*

*Let your imagination dwell
on things that make you feel swell*

*No place to dwell
this war is hell*

*The ocean gets its swell
from the full moon where it dwell*

Dweller

*Even a cave dweller
can write a best seller*

Dying

*Dying is giving
your life to the living*

*Dying to be heard
this mocking bird*

*He must be lying
who has no fear of dying*

*How to go on living
when love it keeps on dying*

*There is a hitch
to dying very rich*

*There is no denying
that living can be dying*

*They make you think you are dying
for your country they are lying*

*To stop him from lying
tell him he is dying*

*We slowly live for dying
without the need for crying*

*Who said I am dying
said he while denying*

D

E

Eager

Don't be eager
to drink bottle of vinegar

Eager to please
soft as the breeze

Eager to please
the mice with the cheese

He takes his eager leaps
and thinks it is for keeps

Eagle

To look the eagle in the eye
without having to fly

Way up in the sky
where the eagles fly high

Where fish eagles stop
at many a tree top

Eagles

Where the fish eagles
focused on the beagles

Early

Early in the morn
when sunshine is born

Everything starts too early
even the hurly burly

Ears

Music to the ears
until the meaning clears

Earth

At the earth they gazed
angels in heaven unfazed

Down to earth guy
from birth why

Earth wind and fire
stoke mans desire

Mother earth on a diet
the wind and the waves became quiet

On the earth below
where lovely rivers they flow

On this earth there is no glue
so love to the heavens it flew

Open up mother earth
I wish to hide my girth

Rhyming English Couplets

She turned a clear eye
from the earth to the sky

The earth and the sun
for people seeking fun

The earth has much to gain
from the torrential rain

The earth in the morning was clad
with a mist that made me glad

The earth is a fragile planet
that houses all and the gannet

The man in the moon
will be on earth soon

When the earth comes of age
the oceans will show their rage

Earthly

Embalmed in print
my earthly stint

Ease

Mice they come with ease
to where there is cheese

Easier

There is something we should know
it is easier in the snow

Easy

Both short and the tall
so easy to fall

Crocodiles and him
both easy in their skin

Easy for us to tell
who holds his bottle well

Not easy to decipher
the intentions of the viper

Once it gets into your head
not so easy to shed

Eat

She arrived in a flurry
to eat chicken curry

Eating

Many a table talk
happens while eating pork

The red beak of the parrot
is from eating too much carrot

Eats

You will become big
who eats like a pig

Eavesdropping

Don't go scoffing
at eavesdropping

Echo

The echo in my ear
from the drop of her tear

Economic

Why is there no length
for economic strength

Economies

Economies they trust
the upper curst

E

Economy
>Economy of thought
>cannot ever be taught

Ecstasy
>Without me
>where would ecstasy be

Ecstatic
>How to be ecstatic
>when things look static

Eden
>The garden of Eden will keep
>two lovers who fall asleep

>What's the use of Eden
>if it has no maiden

Effective
>How can it be effective
>if it ain't fictive

Efforts
>Don't have a clue
>why my efforts went blue

Egg
>The golden egg
>walked away on one leg

>When a bird lays an egg
>it drops between her leg

>First I saw the eggs
>then out came the legs

Ego
>Ego is a curse
>and strain on the purse

>Face it turned red
>when the ego was fed

Egret
>One egret to the other
>my feather is the better

Elaborate
>Man has a duty
>to elaborate on beauty

Elegance
>Elegance and poise
>with little or no noise

>Elegance and poise
>without much noise

>Elegance is a kind
>of measure of her mind

Elegant
>He kept describing the rose
>with quiet and elegant prose

Elegantly
>Elegantly done
>while on the run

Elephant
>She led him by the nose
>the elephant in repose

>Elephants begin to wonder
>about lightning and thunder

>Elephants they greet
>with trampling feet

Elf

>Even the little elf
>gets ahead of himself

Elope

>How can we elope
>when love is just a hope

>No way to elope
>down the slippery slope

Eloquence

>He makes his own bliss
>once eloquence is his

Else

>He had an alibi
>which no one else would buy

>No one else would buy
>his only alibi

Emotion

>All that emotion
>bred in commotion

>All this commotion
>is distilled emotion

>Direct link to emotion
>is music without commotion

>Emotion in commotion
>sets poetry in motion

>Emotion is no pretense
>when it is intense

>Every captured emotion
>served as balm and lotion

>He sold it as a lotion
>a full bottle of emotion

>How to make emotion
>without any commotion

>Negative emotion
>needs no promotion

>Not just a notion
>that love is emotion

>Poetry in motion
>is the product of emotion

>Self promotion
>is mostly emotion

>So much commotion
>music and emotion

>Take a stroll
>for emotion control

>That music is emotion
>is not just a notion

>There is no emotion
>without primordial lotion

>There must be a lotion
>for the blunted emotion

>Triggered enough emotion
>to cause a lot of commotion

>Words come out reeling
>from emotion and feeling

>Words finally sit
>how the emotion feels it's fit

Emotional

*Don't get there late
to the emotional state*

*How to make it last
without emotional cost*

*How to purge
this emotional surge*

Emotionally

*To make right into wrong
must be emotionally strong*

Emotions

*Deepest of emotions
cause of all commotions*

*Emotions are bunk
especially when you are drunk*

*Emotions come along
when love is strong*

*Emotions like a wave
thoughts they pave*

*Emotions need a tug
and an occasional hug*

*Emotions need lotions
to stop their commotions*

*Emotions running high
though she know not why*

*Emotions they keep dealing
with thoughts and feeling*

*Emotions will rule
the heart of a fool*

*How to train
emotions in the brain*

*Rub your emotions
with the right notions*

*When emotions run high
to calm down you must try*

*Words they evoke
emotions that choke*

Emperor

*The emperor he loathes
fashion in his clothes*

Empire

*After the empire
moves in the vampire*

*Cricket and its empire
needs a new umpire*

*Don't get crestfallen
all empires have fallen*

Empires

*Empires before they fall
see the writings on the wall*

*It wasn't just the frost
that empires were lost*

Employ

*Must daily employ
a trick and a ploy*

Emptily

*The forlorn in the face
stares emptily into space*

Rhyming English Couplets **123**

Empty

How much ever rivers there may be
they can all empty into the sea

———

Humpty Dumpty
my head is empty

———

When you feel testy
ask humpty empty

———

Enchanting

She was so enchanting
approaching her was quite daunting

———

Encouraged

Though encouraged by the feat
they stared at defeat

———

Encumbrance

Encumbrance can
be heavy upon a man

———

End

All eggs in a basket
end up in a casket

———

And when the end came
couldn't give love a name

———

Be quick to end it
but don't rebuke the pundit

———

Like gold in the end
you're best friend

———

Mockingbird in the end
loses many a friend

———

Once you lose your footing
you end up flat and sitting

———

She returned in the end
she had him to tend

———

The banana has a bend
but I love it no end

———

The best friend in the end
is the one who can offend

———

The mind in the end
is there for us to spend

———

The stranger in the bed
was a lizard in the end

———

They end their days
saying we have our ways

———

Till the end of time
he knows how to rhyme

———

When journey comes to an end
back ends up in a bend

———

Endearing

His talk was crisp
with an endearing lisp

———

How could he be endearing
when the heat all day was searing

———

Ending

Never a good ending
for a money lending

———

Endless

Let's take a walk
for endless talk

———

E

Ends

*Many a tongue slip
ends up as a quip*

*The circle never ends
if you fill it with friends*

Endurance

*Endurance is quiet
like a reducing diet*

Endure

*How to endure
a love so pure*

*How to endure
sadness without a cure*

Enemies

*Enemies have known
that he is an enemy of his own*

*Enemies no longer
their bond became stronger*

*Enemies plight
cause of delight*

*Enemies will be hatched
from allies who aren't matched*

*Enemies will rattle
if you win every battle*

*Know thy enemies mind
even if you are blind*

*No enemies to devour
when knowledge has power*

*With enemies he toyed
until they were destroyed*

Enemy

*Enemy within
commits all the sin*

*He can wear you out thin
the enemy within*

*The skull bone that is thin
lets the enemy in*

Energetic

*Always energetic
but never static*

Energies

*Energies I must sap
trying to bridge the gap*

Energy

*Energy is meant
to be properly spent*

Engagement

*Engagement of fools
against the rules*

Engaging

*Don't go engaging
when the hormones are raging*

Enjoy

*He brings her a rose
and they enjoy the repose*

Enraptured
So much joy captured
by her entrance all enraptured

Enslave
They learned to enslave
the minute they got out of the cave

Entail
Every little tail
what does it entail

Entertained
The red rag and the bull
entertained them to the full

Entertaining
How to get a ticket
to an entertaining form of cricket

Entice
Many a sweet word
can entice a herd

Enticing
Cake with no icing
is not at all enticing

Entrusted
She entrusted to his keeping
her love when he was sleeping

Envious
The envious must part
with this feeling of the heart

Epidemics
Epidemics they pick
the overtly sick

Episode
The episode was heard
from the messenger bird

Equality
Equality
is the way to parity

Equations
Equations changed
and re-arranged

Erase
How to erase a frown
with just half a crown

Erased
The proverbial phrase
can never be erased

Erotic
Through the nostrils consume
the erotic perfume

Error
Why is it that error
doesn't show up in the mirror

Escape
Has no form or shape
from death he cannot escape

I am out of shape
and no escape

Escape
The escape route
bore fruit

*The great escape
slowly took shape*

*They planned their escape
while chewing on grape*

*We have no choice
but to escape the noise*

*Wear worry beads
to escape from your deeds*

Escaped

*Though I was well caped
the meaning it escaped*

Especially

*He packs a big punch
especially after lunch*

Essence

*It is of the essence
she be aware of my presence*

Esteem

*Best to redeem
your self esteem*

*He renewed his esteem
as part of a scheme*

*Members of the team
held in high esteem*

*Self esteem
gained steam*

*Self esteem
not what it seem*

*Society has a scheme
to hold you in esteem*

*Whose esteem will you raise
if you seek anothers praise*

Eternal

*Eternal thing
when love takes to wing*

*Eternal youth
how far from the truth*

Eternity

*Eternity is the goal
of time on the whole*

*In eternity there is life
free of all strife*

Ethic

*They find it hard to stick
to a good work ethic*

Eve

*Eve she grapple
with adams apple*

Even

*Even the viper
followed the pied piper*

Evening

*Evening cup of tea
means peace and prosperity*

*The rays of the evening sun
when all the work was done*

Everlasting

Cannot be everlasting
this thing called fasting

Everlasting joy
needs no frosting why

Month of fasting
can't be everlasting

Everyone

Everyone can see
the plum in the tree

Everyone is weary
except when they are cheery

Everyone would rave
how good he looked in the grave

Everything

Everything divide by two
half will come to you

Everything happens for the good
said the woodpecker to the wood

Everything I do
is for both of us too

Everytime

Everytime I blossom
the feeling is quite awesome

Everytime you fall
get up and stand tall

Evidence

Evidence is ample
that you must set the example

Evidence is in the cranium
not in the geranium

Evidence is wafer thin
that love should be made into sin

Evidence must be strong
before calling someone wrong

The evidence is not strong
when right is made into wrong

The evidence was weighed
and the scene surveyed

They nod and grin
when evidence is thin

Evil

An evil cast of the eye
done by the devil why

Evil before it swoops
does its many loops

Evil has its roots
down to his boots

Evil is buoyed
when roof is destroyed

Evil thought must return
and wait for its turn

Good and evil are twins
one of the them usually wins

Just turn the page
when evil takes stage

*The evil eye once cast
has a tendency to last*

*When wealth goes off course
evil gets its source*

Evolution

*Every evolution
needn't be a revolution*

Examine

*Examine your head
if you feel weak in bed*

*To make a good pact
examine cold hard fact*

Example

*Some they will trample
at even a good example*

Exchange

*Better to sell your rat
in exchange for a cat*

*Can't exchange it for rice
pearl of a great price*

*Exchange your fears
for bottles of beers*

*Harsh exchange of words
is for the birds*

*Rid yourself of curse
in exchange for a purse*

*They exchange yarns
horses in the barns*

*Two people who stutter
exchanged words to the letter*

Exchanging

*Exchanging glances
start of romances*

Excited

*Don't get excited
until your work is cited*

Excitement

*Added counts
excitement mounts*

*Clothes are wearable
excitement unbearable*

*Daily dose of excitement
needs a little incitement*

Exciting

*The pages were so inviting
to a land all so exciting*

Excursions

*Excursions of the mind
even for the blind*

Excuse

*Does metric have a use
when we measure excuse*

*How to choose
a good excuse*

*How to choose
this lame excuse*

*Put it to good use
the lame excuse*

*Put it to use
the good excuse*

*She must quickly choose
any old excuse*

*What is the use
of a useless excuse*

*Wrong excused
is right abused*

Exercise

*Exercise your options
it said in large captions*

Expanses

*The great expanses of the sea
where many a sailor may be*

Expect

*He who climbs trees
must expect to meet bees*

*Walking down the street
who do you expect to meet*

*Your help will return
when you expect your turn*

Expectation

*Every expectation
ends in consternation*

*High expectation it is said
is to wake up from the dead*

*Expectations are meant
to end up in lament*

*Expectations grow
from three wishes in a row*

*Expectations high
end up as a sigh*

*Expectations run high
that we will live forever why*

*Expectations were high
that some of us won't die*

*Expectations
are life's temptations*

*I don't deny
expectations were high*

*When expectations are high
think of her only why*

*With expectations I burn
waiting for her return*

Expendable

*Is it commendable
for joy to be expendable*

Expended

*She expended her wrath
down his every path*

Expensive

*Carton of milk
expensive like silk*

*Expensive charters
through economic waters*

He became very pensive
when the goods became expensive

Experience

Every tiny tot
needs to experience a lot

Experience has taught
that it cannot be bought

Experience has taught
to distill your thought

Experience is a part
of love from the start

Experience is the center
to where we must all enter

Experience it how
to quickly say wow

Experience it twice
before learning say the wise

Experience must be told
in letters bright and bold

Experience said the mister
can turn out to be a twister

Experience when it flows
with word that glows

Experience will speak
to love at its peak

In experience is found
the most fertile ground

Let experience add
to the ones you've already had

The experience was vast
though he loved and lost

Experiences when they meet
can accomplish a great feat

Experiment

My experiment with words
like the chirping of the birds

Experimentation

Experimentation is for the youth
however uncouth

Explain

Don't ask me to explain
what is simple and plain

How to explain
something so plain

Let me make it plain
this is hard to explain

Make it plain
when you explain

No need to explain
something so plain

No need to explain
what is simple and plain

The more you explain
the less it becomes plain

Very hard to explain
in English simple and plain

Explaining
> Always complaining
> without explaining

Expression
> Self expression
> is an oral tradition

> Expressions that are coarse
> the cause of remorse

Extinct
> Without instincts
> man could be extinct

Extravagant
> Extravagant ways
> forever it stays

Extreme
> No other extreme sport
> than going from port to port

Eye
> How can I vie
> with his jaundiced eye

> Prose is for the eye
> don't ask why

> She had a quick eye
> for men with a slick tie

> What I saw with my eye
> enough to make you cry

> You have to be a beagle
> to look in the eye of the eagle

> You when first I eyed
> your hair it was fully dyed

Eyelids
> When your eyelids droop
> are you looking at the soup

Eyes
> His hands left his pocket
> but eyes remained in the socket

> My eyes were filled with wonder
> at both lightening and thunder

> When their two eyes they met
> they forget how to forget

Eylids
> Take your pick
> make eylids flick

F

Fable

>He spun a fable
>about a horse in the stable

>He who is able
>can spin a good fable

>It must be a fable
>that every peer is noble

>They spin each other a fable
>at the dining room table

Fabric

>Brick by brick
>a new fabric

Face

>Bickering heirs
>face to face in chairs

>Don't go for the melon
>with a face so sullen

>Face beware
>of grief and care

>Face needs paint
>without restraint

>From knitting too much lace
>came the wrinkle in her face

>Give it a face
>your personal space

>Good cheer makes its case
>if you have a smile on our face

>He cannot be a saint
>whose face needs paint

>He will someday face the urn
>who does you a bad turn

>Her face was made whole
>by a well placed mole

>His face looked glum
>inspite of eating plum

>How can we chase
>a god without a face

>I will face it when it comes
>with drumsticks and drums

>Let us sit and chat
>with the full face of the bat

Shaving makes its case
for the most lathered face

She covered it up with lace
one side of her face

Stick a mirror in his face
to make your case

The deep lines on her face
trying to make their case

There must be a link
why her face turned pink

Too strong a case
can blow up in your face

With a leonine face
he makes his case

With a sun drenched face
she made her case

Facial

Facial hues
hold many clues

Facility

They both preferred a facility
in the dark without electricity

Fact

Cause of all the friction
when fact is made into fiction

Fact and fiction
end as dereliction

Fact is fact
but use it with tact

He couldn't hide the fact
his was only an act

It is a well known fact
that the two of them had a pact

Many a pact
not based on fact

Say things with tact
after the fact

Don't let the facts
stand in the way of your acts

Facts get all twisted
if truth is not enlisted

Facts to figure
makes brain bigger

Facts will figure
when things get bigger

He must know all the facts
who thinks feels and acts

With facts fast and loose
he seemed to have no clues

Fade

Every flower will fade
in the sunshine or in the shade

Faded

Has long since faded
my reason to be jaded

Fading

In the fading evening light
the sun made room for the night

Wave that breaks and tumbles
the fading sound of rumbles

Where do you go at noon
the fading autumn moon

Fail

His horse it never fail
the rider though frail

How can it fail
this blackmail

Without fail
paper ships sail

You might fail
who trims his sail

You will stop getting mail
once you succeed to fail

Failed

The husband was nailed
because he failed

Failing

Failing health
crept up in stealth

His most noble failing
was to go sailing

If you have a failing liver
better sell your silver

He had his failings
and his derailings

Hide your failings
and your derailings

His own failings
caused his derailings

Fails

Don't prop the sails
once the wind fails

He who never fails
hasn't conquered the trails

Many a man will fall
who fails to listen at all

When all else fails
just set sail

Failure

Every failure is a gift
that eventually gives you a lift

Failure can be dire
way down to the wire

Failure is a learning
curve when you are yearning

To go from failure to fear
the way isn't clear

Faint

Don't call him a saint
he might just faint

It is hard to pick
a very faint nick

Who was the first to faint
the sinner or the saint

Fainted

Seeing the bear she fainted
the mermaid as she painted

Rhyming English Couplets

Faintest

>*Faintest breath of scandal
>blame it on the vandal*

Faintly

>*It may be though faintly
>he was rather saintly*

Fair

>*Was it fair
>to call it an affair*

Fairies

>*The fairies wave a wand
>to put enough fish in the pond*

>*To fairies they belong
>the magic in the wand*

Fairy

>*I have a favourite fairy
>whose name is just marry*

Faith

>*Burn the midnight oil
>with faith and toil*

>*Faith and toil
>burn midnight oil*

>*Faith and toil
>needs grease and oil*

>*Faith confirmed
>by love affirmed*

>*Faith has appeal
>and ability to heal*

>*Faith it leaps
>across the seven seas*

>*How can we leap
>into faith that is asleep*

Faithful

>*A book in the end
>is a faithful friend*

>*Faithful until death
>is good for health*

>*Faithful was he
>while out to sea*

>*Left to their own devices
>they would be faithful to their vices*

>*The river and its course
>faithful to its source*

Faithfully

>*Faithfully I leap
>into dreams in the my sleep*

Fake

>*The monster in the lake
>is it true or is it fake*

Fall

>*Don't fall short
>just play your part*

>*Short or tall
>one day they will fall*

>*Suddenly last fall
>she gave me a call*

*To wake up in the fall
and see the first snowfall*

*Where the ice is thin
easy to fall in*

Fallen

*Don't look sullen
if your heroes have fallen*

*Many a bee has fallen
for the yellow in the pollen*

Falling

*Falling lumber
had his number*

*The falling leaves have found
the softness of the ground*

*Through falling autumn leaves
we walked between the trees*

False

*False hope has scope
like ordinary dope*

*One false move
can break the groove*

Faltered

*When neurochemistry faltered
behaviour totally altered*

Fame

*A new facet of fame
was added to his name*

*All fame is fleeting
can take many a beating*

*Fame is fleeting
so said the greeting*

*He came up lame
looking for fame*

*That all fame is fleeting
is worth repeating*

*This thing called fame
from where did it came*

*Worth repeating
that fame is fleeting*

Familiar

*She threw the dog his bone
in an all too familiar tone*

Family

*Family needs to be fed
without losing your head*

*Like black flies
with family ties*

*Some they forbade
from the family trade*

Famine

*Food or famine
same for the vermin*

Famous

*Famous last words
mostly for the birds*

*Famous names
have their games*

Fanciful
> Many a fanciful theory
> ends up being dreary

Fancy
> Flight of fancy
> all too chancy

Fans
> Fans they keep wheeling
> from the high ceiling

Fantasies
> Fantasies came true
> out of the sky blue

> Fantasies laid bare
> if you have time to spare

Fantasy
> Fantasy has the power
> above all to tower

> No better ecstasy
> than to live in fantasy

> Of fantasy he was fond
> so he waved the magic wand

Far
> A drink to take him far
> he ordered from the bar

> He was never far
> from the side bar

> How far this weather will last
> once the rain came down so fast

> I will not be far
> from wherever you are

> Sound track of the sitar
> can transport you very far

> The hand in the jar
> has still to go far

> Though distances are far
> there is a twinkle in the star

> Wherever you are
> I am never too far

Fare
> Always carry spare
> money for the fare

Farewell
> Farewell my friend
> I am going round the bend

Farm
> Farm fresh eggs
> chicks with legs

Fashion
> Fashion ruled
> once the passions cooled

> Looking through fashions
> there lurk deep passions

> Weaker fashions are a kind
> mostly for the blind

Fast
> Adam he went on a fast
> but had to eat the apple very fast

*How can it last
if you say it too fast*

*Many a slip
done at a fast clip*

*Not so fast
just make it last*

Faster

*How to get faster
to the final chapter*

*How to get there faster
from servant to master*

*Up they soar faster
birds out of the water*

Fatal

*It is fatal to think
without pen and ink*

Fatal

*Once they were total
now they are fatal*

Fate

*A distance traveled far
is the fate of the fallen star*

*Be a master of your fate
without being irate*

*Better to be late
if sorrow is your fate*

*Better to be late
when others decide your fate*

*Don't be late
when fate opens the gate*

*Don't decide their fate
without much debate*

*Enemy at the gate
what is our fate*

*Even fate will tire
fulfilling his desire*

*Fate has been kind
to his state of mind*

*Fate makes it clear
to both sergeant and seer*

*Fate must have coined
a future all ruined*

*He cursed his fate
when love came late*

*He who is always late
missed his meeting with fate*

*Iceberg sealed the fate
of the ship of state*

*It's never too late
to re-do your fate*

*Let fate be kind
to happiness of the mind*

*Let fate be kind
to your state of mind*

*Minute too late
can seal your fate*

*Never be late
for your meeting with fate*

*Never too late
to confront your fate*

*Never too late
to search your fate*

*On our last date
she sealed our fate*

*Start with a blank slate
and re-write your fate*

*Start with a clean slate
before it seals your fate*

*The choice of fate
becomes your mate*

*The lotuses they ate
sealed their fate*

*The mule with his heel
your fate he can seal*

*Through heavenly gate
to an eternal fate*

*We end up in quicksand
fate when she deals a hand*

*Will seal its fate
the prolonged stale mate*

Fateful

*One fateful day in May
they both romped in the hay*

Fates

*War between states
can seal their fates*

Fault

*Fault confessed
becomes undressed*

*Generous to a fault
but rubs wound into salt*

*He is worth his salt
who is polite to a fault*

*He was full of salt
and polite to a fault*

*How can you fault
a pole that cannot vault*

*In a fault who is found
is guilty all round*

*Is it my fault
if you cannot pole vault*

*She explained my fault
with a somersault*

*The fault it lies in me
for all the world to see*

*The fault lies with me
if I cannot the meaning see*

*They rub wound into salt
when it is their fault*

*Those who find fault
rub wound into salt*

When wound meets salt
whose is it fault

Whose is it fault
if the ocean is all salt

Whose it is fault
if age is pepper and salt

Whose it is fault
when there isn't enough salt

All his faults
came out of the vaults

All mothers are slow
to find faults that they know

He bears his faults well
in a way that is hard to tell

He faults you till the end
the enemy not the friend

She swallows his faults
who has money in the vaults

Their faults in the end
can drive you round the bend

There are not enough vaults
to fill virtues and faults

Your faults they will know
both friend and foe

Favour

Don't forget a favour
lifelong try and savour

I did myself a favour
that I someday wish to savour

They will not let you savour
all the things you favour

He was in a hurry
had favours to curry

Once you refuse favours
someone else they savours

Fear

A girls biggest fear
his eyes will one day veer

A mind without fear
can see things clear

Abandon fear
welcome cheer

Anger and fear
are friends very near

Bad news I fear
more than the poison in the spear

Beauty engenders fear
why it is not clear

Crippling fear
mortgaged cheer

Endearment makes it clear
it is not based on fear

Enters through one ear
the truth that I fear

Every eye must fear
love when it comes very near

Every imagined fear
like a floating cloud must clear

Every man has a fear
he will one day face the spear

Every spotted deer
has only one fear

Fear and hate
are twins on a plate

Fear belongs
to both weak and the strong

Fear comes resembling
a non stop trembling

Fear is a phantom
magnified by the quantum

Fear is strong
that love can go wrong

Fear it brings
out the flapping wings

Fear it stays long
whose belief in god isn't strong

Fear makes it clear
don't live in fear

Fear makes it clear
its time to disappear

Fear makes it clear
life is very dear

Fear of a kind
will focus the mind

Fear of being called a sissy
he resorted to hypocrisy

Fear of life
full of strife

Fear of losing
is not of my choosing

Fear was uncovered
at being discovered

Fear when it grows
the mind it slows

Folly makes it clear
it was the product of fear

Forever they fear
there will be nothing to cheer

Got to fear most
the shifting goal post

Have no fear
mind will clear

He that stands tall
must fear the slightest fall

He who has no peer
has nothing to fear

He who has ten toes
need not fear any foes

How to hold back
this fear attack

*I have this fear
she will whisper in my ear*

*I live in fear
she will say good-bye dear*

*I want to make it clear
I fear her every tear*

*I will whisper you my fear
if you lend me your ear*

*It increases my fear
when the fleas are near*

*Incredible fear
that love will turn to tear*

*It was never very clear
why love engenders fear*

*Leaves have fear
that autumn is near*

*Life makes it clear
death is something to fear*

*Living in fear
of the dropping tear*

*Living in fear
the spotted deer*

*Make it clear
you won't live in fear*

*Many a blouse I fear
was stained with her tear*

*Many a fear it does choose
things that are of no use*

*Many a tear
has been cast out of fear*

*My biggest fear
no money for beer*

*My worst fear
a drop of her tear*

*No fear of bees
on the high seas*

*No need to fear tides
once you have seen the sides*

*No need to fear
when conscience is clear*

*Not from just fear
many a dripping tear*

*Nothing is as clear
as the phantom of fear*

*Nothing to fear
from the monks all austere*

*On my face when it settles
I fear the nettles*

*Once you exchange your fear
things will become clear*

*Our fear center
is a ready tormentor*

*Parrots fear to pose
because of the colour of their nose*

*Rid yourself of fear
by going to it very near*

*Sabre toothed cats
have a fear for rats*

*The fear, the flies
and the lies*

*The mind becomes clear
when fear is near*

*The spear made it clear
it can bring out a fear*

*The spotted deer is in fear
when the tiger slowly appear*

*There is fear in the den
to the furies of the pen*

*There is no fear
until you face a spear*

*Those who fear to love
have only love to fear*

*Those with weak knees
must fear the bees*

*To fear losing
is of ones own choosing*

*To live in constant fear
when the road to heaven isn't clear*

*To lose all fear
give the tiger some beer*

*To remove every tear
engendered by fear*

*Tortured by fear
nothing was clear*

*Whatever is your fear
it's time to make it clear*

*When fear comes your way
just run away*

*When flight follows fear
the path isn't clear*

*When nothing is clear
face up to fear*

*Where has my fear gone
now that it is nearly dawn*

*Will it tomorrow clear
this head full of fear*

*You have nothing to fear
I will not shed a tear*

Feared

*Her throat she cleared
and said much worse than feared*

*Little children they feared
his chestnut beard*

*Much worse than we feared
has to be endured*

Fearful

*Don't go to wars
if you are fearful of scars*

*Fearful of the price
she bought just a slice*

Fearless

*She who is an heiress
is totally fearless*

Fears

*Though old in years
he still harbours fears*

*All the past years
when fears bore the tears*

*Always have fears
of the listening ears*

*Away from his fears
he flew flapping his ears*

*Cares and fears
dripping tears*

*Death will forgive
he who fears to live*

*Deep rooted fears
about flying spears*

*Distant shores have ears
that's one of my fears*

*Don't drown your tears
with unfounded fears*

*Faces though glowing
untold fears flowing*

*Forget your fears
until the mind clears*

*Gypsy has no fears
when bankruptcy it nears*

*He added to her fears
or so it appears*

*He fears the skull and bone
for it might be his clone*

*He fears to take to bed
what goes on in his head*

*He who fears a scar
must not go to war*

*He who is bald
fears the slightest scald*

*He who is busy with fears
must make time for tears*

*I daily face my fears
some of which draw tears*

*I had my latent fears
but they didn't lead to tears*

*If you worship your fears
you will end up with tears*

*New fears
from the sunset years*

*Not in a thousand years
can I forget my fears*

*One way to drown your fears
is to quell your tears*

*Our worst fears
cause all the tears*

*She was captive of her fears
until the mind it clears*

*The mind has no fears
when the eye has no tears*

*There will be latent fears
until the mind clears*

Rhyming English Couplets

*They made up for their fears
by opening up their ears*

*Until my mind clears
of love and its fears*

*We have added to our fears
over a thousand years*

*What kind of fears
cause crocodile tears*

*When hair stands on end
I have fears to mend*

*Windows too have tears
and old age fears*

Fearsome

*He was fearsome and yellow
but his mood was mellow*

Feast

*All day I can feast
on suns rays from the east*

*All sides of the beast
can be had at the feast*

*Feast and fasting
both can't be lasting*

*How can a bird eat a beast
unless crow comes to feast*

*If you watch them feast
men are beast*

*In Eden there was a feast
when apples were found least*

*Last but not least
he ate at the feast*

*Not enough yeast
to call this a feast*

*There is no feast
without fish from the East*

*They all turned into beast
when beauty came to the feast*

*West or East
there are flies at the feast*

*Where is the feast
asked the beauty to the beast*

Feasting

*One of them is lasting
feasting and fasting*

Feather

*Before the hen ducks
at her feather she plucks*

*We know of each other
not like birds of a feather*

*With feather in her feet
she stepped into the suite*

*Eagles in flight
with their feathers woven tight*

Fed

*Bucket full of herrings
fed to the lemmings*

F

*He fed his filly
with water lilly*

*More will be said
once I am fed*

Feed

*Bookworms read
while they feed*

*Cooking is for the plate
to feed the palate*

*Don't feed your need
beyond your greed*

*Feed them cheese
for tranquility and peace*

*I always feed them yolk
who are my kinfolk*

*I feed my cravings
from life savings*

*The bookworms they feed
while alongside they read*

*The way to feed a filly
is with water lilly*

*When you feed the beast
make sure it is yeast*

*Words and deed
come back to feed*

Feeding

*The animal keeps running
feeding on cunning*

*The sparrows they chirp
and after feeding they burp*

*They resort to force feeding
despite our pleading*

Feel

*All through summer
she feel for the drummer*

*Are there more onions to peel
before I get the feel*

*Don't eat food
just to feel good*

*Every last reel
has an ending with a feel*

*His early morning saunter
made him feel a bit gaunter*

*It's what's in the head
that makes it feel like lead*

*She made so much of me
couldn't feel the sting of the bee*

*Some of the things we have done
makes us feel like none*

*The fires that we feel
are the products of zeal*

*There is something in the air
I can feel it in my hair*

*To chirp after a meal
and get the proper feel*

Rhyming English Couplets

*To hear feel and see
what is within me*

Feeling

*The feeling cannot be told
though written in letters all bold*

*A feeling once fixed
must not be jinxed*

*Can send your head reeling
that certain feeling*

*Can't fight this feeling
that is so appealing*

*Feeling is a gift
must not be held in thrift*

*Feeling is divine
from a well crafted line*

*For feeling they are meant
both music and the scent*

*He walked into this feeling
with his head all reeling*

*Her eyes they came home revealing
that there was little left of feeling*

*How can I hide
this feeling inside*

*How to fight off the flu
without feeling blue*

*I know the meaning
of this lonely feeling*

*I wish you wouldn't tempt
this feeling of contempt*

*If lampposts had feeling
drunks they would be kneeling*

*It takes you back to feeling
how love is felt kneeling*

*May not be appealing
the shape I give to feeling*

*Poetry is a feeling
that sets the mind reeling*

*She found that special feeling
as he proposed to her kneeling*

*The feeling never abated
about feeling a bit jaded*

*The in-depth feeling
of poetry reading*

*This feeling of strife
can be cut with a knife*

*This must be the feeling
that gives life its meaning*

*To change its shape is a leaning
that the moon keeps on feeling*

*To create a feeling
that is to her appealing*

*To give shape to feeling
in a way that is appealing*

*Wheeling and dealing
gives you good feeling*

When something is wrong
gut feeling gets strong

When the turkey says tutt
there is a feeling in the gut

Words take on meaning
and lovely feeling

All he did was moan
with feelings hard as stone

Can't find a clue
why feelings turn blue

Feelings as they surge
looking for words to purge

Feelings become grated
once overstated

Feelings come and go
and nothing left to show

Feelings come out stark
without me having to bark

Feelings distilled
into love instilled

Feelings fragile
if you are not agile

Feelings must be fed
like the daily loaf of bread

Feelings small or tall
a tear says it all

Feelings stirred
by vice incurred

Feelings that cave
into thought in a wave

Feelings they have taught
that love needs to be caught

Feelings they will trade
that's how they are made

Feelings true or false
how to tell them apart

Feelings will be dead
if thoughts they are not fed

Things can go wrong
when feelings are strong

He says things blatant
from feelings that are latent

I gave my feelings for free
for what you did to me

I have feelings too
may be more than you

Inner revealings
have their feelings

Inner revealings
my couplets have feelings

Inner revealings
with deep felt feelings

People make their dealings
in the absence of feelings

Put your feelings into paper
thick or thin as wafer

*The feelings become more
depending on the musical score*

*The words don't fit
the feelings where they sit*

*Their feelings they did vent
until their tongues became bent*

*Their feelings were lush
in the evening rush*

*There isn't a single scribe
who can my feelings describe*

*They both can be charming
when feelings are warming*

*They often hid
their feelings with a lid*

*Unless it is dead
feelings go to the head*

*Until feelings are spilled
we don't feel fulfilled*

*Use sound to make sense
of feelings very intense*

*When your feelings they get a form
love can kick up a storm*

*When feelings hit the ceiling
everything becomes revealing*

*When feelings they gush
their faces will blush*

Feels

*Nose feels good
when it smells food*

Feet

*You still need your feet
on easy street*

Feline

*He makes a beeline
for every feline*

*She looked at him twice
with feline eyes*

*There isn't a single feline
above the Arctic treeline*

Fell

*He fell over a log
and stepped on the frog*

Felt

*Where will it be felt
if I tighten my belt*

Fence

*Makes the thief tense
if strong is your fence*

Fences

*Barbed fences
their only defences*

Ferocious

*Ferocious and fierce
on the money purse*

F

Fetching

*Whatever she asked needed fetching
her eyes were so bewitching*

Feted

*Some they will sprint
to be feted in print*

Fever

*One bite from the beaver
enough to give me a fever*

*Saturday night fever
when will it leave her*

Few

*I am you
known to few*

*Known to few
you are what you do*

Fickle

*Don't be fickle
you will end up as pickle*

Fiction

*Fact and fiction
woven into diction*

*My writing through fiction
caused a lot of friction*

Fidelity

*Fidelity wears thin
faced with choices of sin*

*Marry a swan
and fidelity is gone*

Fidelity

*When will it be in
that fidelity is sin*

Fierce

*With an imagination fierce
he had thoughts to pierce*

Fight

*A fight with your mate
can seal your fate*

*Don't fight over a rifle
for a cause flimsy and trifle*

*Don't pick a fight
if you don't have the right*

*Don't put up a fight
if they can decide your plight*

*Fight we must
whose cause is just*

*He was toiling all night
spoiling for a fight*

*How to fight
off the sound bite*

*More heat than light
when two experts fight*

*Once you pick a fight
back it up with might*

*Some day they will fight
when the going gets tight*

*To get it right
have a dog in the fight*

Who is right
in a fight

Fighting

Don't keep fighting
put it in writing

Husband brings her a rose
but they end up fighting in prose

Fights

A dog will not fail
if he fights tooth and nail

We had our fights
and caterpillar nights

We've had our fights
and soothing nights

Fill

Fill their cup
who prop you up

Filled

Lake filled to the brim
when he jumped in to swim

Final

In one final rage
he turned the page

Financial

Who is to gain
from financial pain

Financially

What better cure
than financially secure

Find

Find something to rave
with one foot in the grave

Fine

Grapes that look fine
at each turn of the vine

I feel fine
though last in line

More than a fine feather
that can stand up to the weather

The reader feels fine
from many a fine line

This may be fine
not better than wine

Finger

A finger on his cap
and a hand on the tap

Wedged between his fingers
the smoking cigar lingers

Fingertips

From fingertips to lips
the cigarette it slips

Finish

Don't pull the rug
before I finish this jug

Start and the finish
do it without blemish

What more can we ask
once we finish the task

Finishing

Finishing touches
over mid-day lunches

Finite

It was finite at best
his mastery of jest

Fins

Dolphins have fins
and very smooth chins

Fire

Don't fire it a lot
your warring shot

Don't stoke the fire
of two peoples ire

Fire it hatches
when you strike the matches

How to douse
the fire in the house

Tell them to douse the fire
before it becomes a pyre

The big ball of fire
to the ocean it retire

The scorpion shows it's ire
with a sting full of fire

Where can I park my fire
without eliciting her ire

With irons in the fire
she sat playing the lyre

Fireflies

Fireflies that glow a little
in the evening light just brittle

Where do fireflies park
when the night is pitch dark

Fireproof

Don't goof
you're not fireproof

Fires

Fires are stoked
by the once provoked

Fires must be doused
wherever they are housed

No need to douse
coal fires in the house

Until the fires are slain
the winds they must remain

Fireside

They kept themselves warm
with a fireside yarn

Firmly

Trees can't move around
with roots firmly in the ground

With eyes firmly in the socket
he is the whole packet

First

Could end up as dust
the pawn that you moved first

*First he made paws
to which he added claws*

Fish

*Down the rolling river
the fish with their fins they shiver*

*Every fish hook
must have a new look*

*He is like a fish in a shoal
with a lofty goal*

*I have fish to fry
so don't sit and cry*

*The fish they float
under the flat bottomed boat*

*The fish they lay in a pouch
of the pelican in a couch*

*The fish they nibble
without a quibble*

*The pelican returns
with fish taking turns*

Fishing

*I like to skip school
when going fishing is cool*

Fist

*With his fist fully anchored
in a jug of tankard*

Fit

*Fit as a fiddle
down to his middle*

*Fit in the words tighter
to become a good writer*

*I am ready and fit
to listen to her wit*

*Whenever you see fit
come by me to sit*

Fitness

*If it is fitness you are after
exercise your laughter*

*On the whole
fitness plays a role*

Fitted

*The house is fully fitted
and the sweater fully knitted*

Fix

*We both were in a fix
in the summer of sixty six*

Flail

*A dog has nothing to flail
once you cut his tail*

*He who loses his tail
has nothing to flail*

Flail

*How does it flail
the elephant its tail*

Flair

*The birds with flair
fly up in the air*

Flak

*All the flak
behind my back*

*Don't give me flak
you will get it back*

*If you hold it back
they will give you flak*

Flake

*Each falling flake
filled snow into the lake*

Flame

*Be kind to your flame
it may be just a game*

*Blush gets its name
from the colour of the flame*

*Flies have been taught
that the flame is hot*

*Like a flame to the wick
somethings they will always stick*

*Must it have a name
that flickers like a flame*

*The candle gets its name
from the unflinching flame*

*The moths played a game
against the yellow flame*

*The righteous path
to the flame for the moth*

Flames

*Flames need a fan
for love when it can*

Flamingos

*Flamingos start slapping
their wings into flapping*

Flash

*If you flash the blade at the cherry
the slip fielder will be merry*

Flashed

*He flashed his tail
when she lifted her veil*

Flatter

*Better to flatter
to prolong the chatter*

*Each other they flatter
friends who natter*

*Surrounded by flatter
he was always ready for chatter*

Flattered

*At first he flattered
watered it down when it mattered*

*So easily flattered
when it really mattered*

Flattering

*He had a flattering tongue
all the way to his lung*

Flaunt

Of all the things I want
some things I wish to flaunt

Some they take pills
to flaunt their skills

Whatever it is they want
is just so that they can flaunt

Flavour

Some words I favour
to express loves flavour

Flawless

Once you are flawless
easy to be lawless

Flea

If every man were a flea
he could bite them all with glee

Not unlike the flea
he couldn't hide his glee

Fleece

How can he fleece
who is paid by the piece

Flicker

Flicker is a name
given to candle and its flame

Flickered

The waves flickered like silver
that was very hard to pilfer

Flight

Day or night
there is a buzz in its flight

Flight full things
birds with wings

Flight of fancy
got all chancy

For bats in flight
twilight is right

In flight they play
the geese in may

In hindsight he might
have taken the flight

Once the cranes take to flight
they fly through the night

Once you take to flight
no choice but to alight

Slowing down from their flight
the sandhill cranes they alight

Sparrows take to flight
at the smallest of plight

The flight of the cranes
through the window panes

The stars in the night
guide the birds in their flight

They slowed down their flight
to settle for the night

Wasps in flight
they seek the light

When faced with a boa
take next flight to Goa

Words woven tight
so thoughts may take to flight

Flightless

Broken wings
flightless things

Flightless bird
waiting to be heard

Flights

The flights are made to stall
when fog makes a call

Flighty

He was a bit flighty
thinking he is almighty

Flirt

Before you flirt with fate
have a clean slate

Flirting

Flirting gets a start
as a feeling from the heart

Float

Elephants can float
just like a boat

No need to gloat
when you can't swim or float

Floating

Floating duck
seeks food through muck

For each flap of the wings
the eagle all floating sings

He is master of his craft
who can build a floating raft

Flock

Homing pigeons they clock
many hours as a flock

Flora

How to siphon the aura
from fauna and the flora

Flounder

He will not flounder
who is an all rounder

Flourish

No one will flourish
without his daily nourish

Once you set sail
flourish or fail

Flower

A single little flower
stuck on her hair after shower

Every flower needs a vase
for its final phase

Has it wasted its thud
the flower bud in the mud

*In many a lost hour
there withered a flower*

*Like a flower in the garden
without a warden*

*Like a flower on the tree
this thing called poetry*

*Like the petals of the flower
that insects they devour*

*Many a fragrant flower
waiting for bees to devour*

*No flower is meant
to be without scent*

*Opens in the morning hour
the pond full of lotus flower*

*She lived the life of a flower
a new fragrance with each rain shower*

Flowering

*Flowering trees
home of the bees*

*Purple petals on the ground
where flowering trees abound*

Flowers

*Flowers from the fields
where butterflies got their yields*

*Flowers on which to feed
butterflies have a need*

*Flowers quite awesome
in the branches will blossom*

*Flowers they need gathering
before they go withering*

*Flowers were never meant
to be lacking in scent*

*It could be just the flowers
the forest after the showers*

*Pink flowers love noses
whether or not they are roses*

*Say it with flowers
roses have powers*

*So hard to tally
the flowers in the valley*

*The flowers and the leaves
with caterpillar sieves*

*The flowers he knew
were found at the kew*

*The flowers that fill
my window sill*

*The flowers withered and gone
but their scent it lingers on*

*The forest is in flames
with flowers without names*

*There is a valley beyond the towers
full of beautiful flowers*

*There is honey in the flowers
which many a bee devours*

Flowing

*He has a nose
for the flowing prose*

*The flowing river so soft
gently they row their craft*

*The river waters flowing
they reach the ocean slowing*

*The sound of flowing water
is not pitter patter*

Flows

*The hourglass has a band
through which flows the sand*

Flu

*They end up with the flu
once they say I do*

Fluorescent

*So loaded with scent
he became fluorescent*

Flushing

*All that was left was silt
after flushing out the guilt*

Fluster

*Don't fluster
if you lose your luster*

*They think they can fluster
who hide behind the bluster*

Flustered

*She became all flustered
when she couldn't find the mustard*

Flutter

*The pendulum swings
to the flutter of wings*

*The things that they mutter
caused all the flutter*

*With a flutter of his tail
the peacock set sail*

Fluttering

*The bee it stings
with fluttering wings*

Fly

*Birds in the distant sky
towards the sun they fly*

*Don't let them fly
the underlings why*

*Nimbly it is flung
at the fly the lizards tongue*

*The fly is quickly hung
by the flick of the lizards tongue*

*There is a fly in the bottle
pressing hard at the throttle*

Flycatcher

*Every bird watcher
looks for flycatcher*

*When they watched the watchers
they found only flycatchers*

Flying

*Flying is best
when it is to your nest*

*Without the parachute to go diving
is the closest thing to flying*

Rhyming English Couplets

Flytrap

> It closed with a flap
> the flytrap

Focus

> Focus it is said
> is about clearing the head

> He called off the horses
> to focus on other causes

> The focus in my eye
> ruined by a stye

Focused

> To be focused and beaming
> is not demeaning

Focussing

> Focussing is a kind
> of meditation of the mind

Foils

> Each others foils
> through their daily toils

Fold

> She fell into his fold
> when he gave her a band of gold

Folded

> He folded his sleeve
> and got ready to heave

Follow

> They follow each other
> One thing after the other

Fond

> Ducks in the pond
> of each other fond

> The fish may not be fond
> of all the things in the pond

Fonder

> She became of me fonder
> the more I looked beyond her

Fondly

> Fondly they talked
> holding hands as they walked

Fondness

> His fondness for pulses
> was governed by impulses

> There are some chaps
> who have fondness for laps

Food

> How to raise your brood
> without so much as food

> A fool and his folly
> always very jolly

> A fool can be wise
> if he doesn't speak twice

> Even a fool
> gets something out of school

> Fool and his folly
> together quite jolly

> He must re-tool
> who becomes a fool

He sits on a high stool
who thinks himself a fool

Only a fool
breaks his own rule

This man ain't no fool
though he hasn't been to school

Fooled

He couldn't easily be fooled
though he was unschooled

Foolish

He was flushed and schoolish
more so than foolish

How to give it a name
this foolish game

Little foolish games
do they have names

To be foolish is no risk
better than ruptured disc

Fools

Fools and wises
come in all sizes

Fools make conclusions
without good inclusions

Footprints

Footprints in the sand
where the sunset is very grand

They don't wait till the dawn
who leave footprints on the lawn

To walk the footprints of folly
thinking it will make you jolly

Footsteps

Footsteps in the fog
it was only the dog

Forbidden

Forbidden fruit to eat
more than a little sweet

Forbidden fruit why
after the devil caught his eye

Forbidden terrain
some parts of the brain

From the forbidden streams
comes love it seems

Guilt ridden
but is it forbidden

How to grapple
with the forbidden apple

How to loot
the forbidden fruit

Much of the loot
was the forbidden fruit

The apple though forbidden
from Adam it was not hidden

The best thing to loot
is the forbidden fruit

Force

Don't force me to act
remember we have a pact

*He veers off course
who is a spent force*

*Without the use of force
find a recourse*

Forced

*The bitter in every pill
forced against my will*

Forecast

*How long will it last
this forecast*

Forest

*He gave the tiger its name
and a forest flush with game*

Foretelling

*Give it some re-telling
without much foretelling*

Forever

*Could this last forever
no no never*

*Forever ain't enough
to tell you all the stuff*

*Forever they become a part
the intimacies of the heart*

*Men and their ways
forever it stays*

*No one else will do
forever it will be you*

*Nothing is forever
not even your liver*

*Once enchanted
forever haunted*

*Once it is never
but twice is forever*

*To live forever
have to be clever*

*To part from her never
mine she was forever*

*Will it take forever
for me to get clever*

Forfeited

*He was happily seated
with everything forfeited*

Forget

*Don't forget the cup
when you are tidying up*

*Don't forget your bacon
on your way to macon*

*Forget about your houses
if you leave your spouses*

*Forget your thrift
when you bring a gift*

*Just don't forget
there is always a yet*

*There is nothing left to bury
if you forget it in a hurry*

They forget about their feet
the two eyes when they meet

Forgetting

The leech keeps forgetting
that it is meant for blood letting

Forgive

Every plan has a sieve
not easy to forgive

Forgive the lot
or forget them not

Learning to forgive
is the best way to live

To forgive is fine
if you get to sip wine

Forgiveness

Forgiveness can bless
love that is a mess

Forgiveness gets a start
in the mothers heart

Forgiveness is in
and it is not a sin

Forgiveness is in
where have you been

Forgiveness is in
without being a sin

Forgiveness like gold
shines forever we are told

Forgiveness will win
against the thickest sin

However thin
forgiveness is in

Use it at will
the forgiveness pill

Whatever the season
forgiveness needs no reason

Forgiving

Whatever you do for a living
always be forgiving

Forgot

He forgot what he said
once he went to bed

He had an appointment
but forgot the ointment

He turned back from the grave
because he forgot to shave

I forgot the gift
and she was miffed

She forgot to lock
her jewel box

When the mouse ran up the clock
forgot to put on his sock

When the train stopped at Reading
he forgot to pick up his bedding

Forgotten

Forgotten fast
knowledge from the past

Loaned to a friend
forgotten in the end

Not forgotten fast
memories that last

Fork

Hand me that fork
I'd like to eat pork

Formal

Formal ties
weariness in the eyes

Fortitude

Even ineptitude
needs fortitude

Fortunate

I wish they knew
they are the fortunate few

The fortunate bit
our love was a hit

They get their due
the fortunate few

Fortune

A fortune once made
can put you in the shade

Fortune favours the fool
that is the only rule

Fortune filled the tower
while misfortune took a shower

Fortune made its case
in a fortuitous place

Has its own tune
good fortune

Some lose their socks
after fortune knocks

They learn to tune
into new found fortune

Fortunes of a fool
are his only tool

People come and stare
at fortunes laid bare

What was the cost
of fortunes made and lost

Forward

The little bird moved forward
with the knee bent all backward

Foul

Both foul and fair
in this affair

He whose heart is foul
has his face in a growl

His manner it is foul
like the unblinking owl

Prepare to growl
when you're mood is foul

The mouse it called foul
when confronted by the owl

F

*The nightingale and the owl
they ran each other foul*

*The tiger he did growl
at the owl whose mood was foul*

*The weather is foul
where the mountain lions growl*

*When pomp played foul
it evoked a growl*

Found

*Many things are found
by simply shopping around*

Fountain

*He found a fountain
at the top of the mountain*

Fours

*How to open doors
if you walk on all fours*

Fox

*Old fox
need not pull up his socks*

Fragile

*Be agile
relationships are fragile*

Fragrance

*Fills me at dusk
the fragrance of musk*

*For you only meant
the fragrance and the scent*

*Fragrance is for the nose
in quiet repose*

*Fragrance is lost by the hour
by the dying of the flower*

*Fragrance makes its case
through a pretty face*

*Fragrance of the petal
in the nostrils it settle*

*Fragrance of the pines
while we sip the wines*

*Fragrance that is caught
by pondering thought*

*Fragrance was awesome
when they went into blossom*

*I remembered for a mile
the fragrance of her smile*

*The cadence of his prose
has the fragrance of a rose*

*The cadence of your prose
has the fragrance of a rose*

*The flower it tells a story
of fragrance and its glory*

*The fragrance from it will fall
without the rose at my beck and call*

*Their fragrance went to my head
the flowers in the flower bed*

Rhyming English Couplets

Fragrant

*For her he chose
a pink fragrant rose*

*Rose is a rose
with a fragrant pose*

Frail

*His body may be frail
but the peacock is all tail*

*The frail they get hung
for their tail and tongue*

Frame

*A restful frame of mind
let it not fall behind*

*His frame may be small
but he stand very tall*

*The mosquito it can name
all parts of my frame*

Frangrance

*Frangrance makes its pose
from pink petals of the rose*

Fraudulent

*Mistake me not
you have fraudulent thought*

Freak

*He sharpens his beak
the control freak*

*The control freak
is never meek*

Freckled

*As and when he heckled
his face it became freckled*

Freckles

*If you have clean Knuckles
you won't get freckles*

Free

*A borrowing spree
can never be free*

*A leap from tree to tree
makes the fall very free*

*All the fruits are free
from the forbidden tree*

*All the fruits are free
plucked off the marriage tree*

*Bile it flows for free
from the biliary tree*

*Calorie free spree
is it ever free*

*Deep in our minds is a home
where we feel free to roam*

*Doesn't come free
the fruit of the tree*

*Empty and free
top of the family tree*

*Every free market
ends up in a basket*

F

*Free fall is free
after drinking spree*

*Free market is dead
once everyone is fed*

*Free speech
never out of reach*

*Further up the tree
where mangoes ripe for free*

*Go on a writing spree
all human thought is free*

*Hanging on a tree
the swinging comes free*

*He didn't know where to land
when she gave him a free hand*

*He dished out good byes for free
when he set out to sea*

*High up it is free
the fruit of the mango tree*

*High up on the tree
where the fruit is free*

*Holding hands is free
under the pipal tree*

*Honey won't be free
if you squeeze it out of the bee*

*If you free up your spleen
you will not be seen as mean*

*Insects are free
to circle the tree*

*It's that time of the year
of the free flowing beer*

*Land of the free
happens to be tree*

*Like the apple it must free
the worm within me*

*No citation is free
said the drone to the bee*

*Once the fetters fall
it becomes free for all*

*Oxygen will be free
if you plant a tree*

*People who are free
can live under the tree*

*Plucked off the tree
the cherry is for free*

*Poetry flows free
like leaves to a tree*

*Promote free speech
without being a leech*

*Risk is never free
when you jump from tree to tree*

*She sat where the shade was free
under the mango tree*

*The free spirit
must find a way to live it*

*The lighthouse by the sea
where the fresh wind is free*

Rhyming English Couplets

*The owl stays for free
in the old oak tree*

*The right to free speech
can become out of reach*

*The sailor feels free
when he is always at sea*

*They climb up the tree
yearning to breathe free*

*They come for free
leaves to a tree*

*Trying to break free
in a single spree*

*Under the chestnut tree
where the squirrels eat for free*

*Under the oak tree
the grass it grows free*

*Whatever it used to be
nostalgia is for free*

*Where the breeze that flows in free
under the banyan tree*

*Why is free speech
so much out of reach*

*Why is it free
fruit of the forbidden tree*

*Why oh speaking tree
your fruits are for free*

*Woodpecker is free
to dig a hole in the tree*

*Words from the bodhi tree
whose messages are free*

*You can chew for free
the leaves of the yew tree*

Freedom

*Don't grant it to the leech
freedom of speech*

*Don't preach to the leech
freedom of speech*

*Even the leech
has freedom of speech*

*Freedom and hope
reason to elope*

*Freedom is a wish
known only to the fish*

*Freedom is at hand
when you till your own land*

*Freedom is divine
when tasted with wine*

*Freedom is like a bird
waiting to be heard*

*Freedom must be fed
daily it is said*

*Freedom of expression
does it need repression*

*Freedom of expression
makes its own impression*

*Freedom of speech
is out of reach*

*Freedom of speech
not given to the leech*

*Freedom suppressed
can make you depressed*

*Freedom will come
only for some*

*I have freedom of speech
and people to preach*

*I need freedom struggle
from this snuggle*

*Not out of reach
freedom of speech*

*Sense of freedom is stored
and unleashed when you are bored*

*The apple gave freedom
to a man called Adam*

*We have freedom to dress
just to impress*

*What's the use
without freedom to choose*

*When you find your voice
it will be freedom of choice*

Freely

*Blood from his nose
it freely flows*

*The underwater snake
swims freely in the lake*

Freeze

*Let us not freeze
in this cold breeze*

French

*The French they say
Paris is gay*

Frenetic

*Wild goose chase
at a frenetic pace*

Frequently

*Frequently not heard
those who live by their word*

Fresh

*Gives you a choice
a fresh new voice*

*It is so fresh and vivid
it makes me quite livid*

*The fresh morning air
as it runs through her hair*

*The fresh ocean breeze
to rid me of sneeze*

*When you jump from a cliff
fresh air you get to whiff*

Friction

*Let there not be friction
when you speak your diction*

*Syntax and diction
smooth without friction*

Friend

*A book in the end
is your best friend*

*A friend in need
can make you bleed*

*A friend in the end
you can offend no end*

*Blow by blow
he made friend into foe*

*Cannot keep a friend
who marries in the end*

*Don't offend
even the fair weather friend*

*Friend into foe
if you step on his toe*

*He drives me round the bend
but he is still a friend*

*He is a friend
who doesn't need me in the end*

*Hold it up no end
the tail of a friend*

*I have coffee and sugar to lend
to the neighbour who is a friend*

*Mans best friend
is a hog in the end*

*My own best friend
is only in the end*

*No better friend than this
my favourite book that I miss*

*Only one true friend
at the seasons end*

*Seagull in the end
is the sailors only friend*

*Till the end
be a friend*

Friendless

*How to untie
his friendless eye*

*With a friendless summer all gone
the winters light has shone*

Friendly

*Don't agree fully
with the friendly bully*

*Friendly terms
hot with the worms*

*Friendly ties
make for good allies*

*He made the rat bite the cheese
with friendly ease*

*Ill will do not harbour
against your friendly neighbour*

*With a friendly wag of the tail
he and the dog set sail*

F

Friends

> Friends and foes
> they step on your toes

> Friends sail the ships
> to cement their friendships

> Friends till I die
> the camera and I

He made friends of his choosing
and went away boozing

> His tavernous friends
> drunk they ends

> Let us just be
> friends who drink tea

> Make amends
> and renew friends

> Make amends
> with your friends

Old friends like gold
don't collect mould

Pick your friends well
make sure they can spell

They are your friends
who make amends

Three friends and a goat
we tried to cross the moat

Try and make amends
if you still have friends

Friendship

> A friendship was saved
> once they both behaved

> Friendship became a fraction
> after every interaction

> Friendship in repair
> brought happiness to the pair

> Friendship in the end
> always on the mend

> Friendship is a blessing
> even without caressing

> Friendship is a breeze
> if you shake hands and squeeze

> Friendship is a gift
> that can give you a lift

> Friendship is a wand
> a wave can make it a bond

> Friendship we must savour
> and not consider it a favour

> Friendship will end
> if you doubt a friend

> Friendship will mend
> after the frown of a friend

> She tied a friendship band
> on his right hand

> Enmity will thrive
> if friendships don't survive

*Friendships are broken
that are just token*

*Friendships broken will gain
from the relief of all the pain*

*Friendships get better
when stated in a letter*

*Friendships in the end
constantly on the mend*

*Friendships need to bend
so as not to offend*

*Friendships we must never
so easily sever*

*Friendships will frost
once goodwill is lost*

*Good times will test
your friendships best*

*Gymnast and the czar
friendships can go far*

*Why do they sour
friendships by the hour*

Fright

*Day or night
poverty brings fright*

*Moonlight in the night
is a protection against fright*

Frightened

*As the coach approaches
it frightened away the roaches*

*She slipped on ice
and frightened the mice*

*They head butted the rams
and frightened all the clams*

Frisky

*How to get frisky
on a ten cent whiskey*

Frolicking

*Frolicking and picking
at each other picnicking*

*Frolicking and picking
at each other without nicking*

Front

*She was a front row girl
with hair in a beautiful curl*

Frosting

*The frosting on the cake
only for our sake*

Frown

*Dish out a frown
when they let you down*

*They will find a reason to frown
in the better part of town*

Frozen

*Frozen too soon
for ducks the lagoon*

Frugal

*He cannot be regal
who is all frugal*

He is so frugal
he must have been a seagull

Frugality

Lessons in frugality
have their own brutality

Fruit

A basket of fruit
was all he could loot

From the fruit tree
vitamin-C is free

The fruit of the water lilly
can make you feel silly

The heavy hanging fruit
ready for the loot

The lotus fruit was made
for memories to fade

The tree that bears fruit
must have deep root

Fruits of the loom
in their best bloom

Fruits of their toil
seen in every soil

I do not wish to belabour
the fruits of my labour

Like a grass without roots
that won't bear fruits

Once you face its fruits
nothing else suits

People they belabour
the fruits of your labour

Frustration

Frustration is a means
of shattering your dreams

He was all consternation
from self inflicted frustration

Fulfilled

A net full of fish
is a fulfilled wish

Fun

A bad deed is done
sometimes in jest and fun

A shepherd on the run
chases sheep for fun

A task well done
sometimes not fun

After all is said and done
let's just do it for fun

All it takes is one
person to spoil the fun

Begins the fun
once the day is done

Evil it has fun
in the mid-day sun

Forever there is fun
in my island in the sun

Fun isn't this anymore
and I cannot just keep the score

Fun on the quiet
is your best diet

Fun they poke
after rum and coke

Half the fun
is a job well done

Have fun
job done

Hemp is fun
better than none

Ice-cream is fun
in the hot afternoon sun

In the land of the mid night sun
all things are done in fun

In the long run
just have fun

Into the setting sun
the birds they fly for fun

It is no fun
for the nose to run

Just when I think I am done
starts all the fun

Learning should be fun
but not under the gun

Live a life of fun
in the glow of the sun

Make it a fun day
when you wake up on Sunday

Make it your dream for fun
that which cannot be done

Make of it fun
what needs to be done

No place for fun
with a loaded gun

Nobody should run
from things that spell fun

Not enough fun
under the sun

Not even for fun
will the dog bark at the sun

Not even in fun
nothing left to be done

Not even in fun
submit to none

November was fun
under the winter sun

On a scale of one
stupidity is fun

One liners that make you run
for the second time in fun

Romping isn't fun
in the late afternoon sun

Takes away the fun
love in the broiling sun

*The fun and the fizz
got by in a whizz*

*The shadow has fun
hiding from the sun*

*The things we wished for fun
so much better once done*

*There is much to be done
before it becomes fun*

*War is never fun
so something must be done*

*Where shall we run
for an evening of fun*

*With half the fun
the job was done*

Function

*Both form and function
cause of dysfunction*

*Form and function
of the synaptic junction*

*Serpents in the night
can function without light*

Funeral

*He made his case
with a funeral face*

*He was a live wire
down to the funeral pyre*

*The funeral pyre
is about me and not the fire*

*Funerals can be rather dry
if nobody comes there to cry*

Funny

*Funny lines
with musical rhymes*

*Meant to be funny
to make your days sunny*

*Sugar and honey
are names quite funny*

Furious

*Suddenly furious
always mysterious*

Furniture

*I wore out the furniture
reading all the literature*

Fury

*Duty of the jury
is to put out all the fury*

*Many a fury of sound
deep in the memory found*

Fuse

*He has a short fuse
and puts it to use*

*Men have short fuses
that sometimes have uses*

Fuss

*She danced without fuss
both slow and sinuous*

Them and us
makes for fuss

Future

Cannot be bought or sold
what the future may hold

Every past has a future
that is the law of nature

How to foretell
that the future will be well

I promised her a future
that both of us must nurture

In future I would refrain
from looking inside my brain

In my dreams of the future
the casino is a feature

It is good to nurture
plans for the future

Let go of the past
the future is very vast

Let it come by fast
a future that will last

Minus the future from the past
and make the present last

No future in this
give the past a miss

No past no future
just a meaningless creature

Once you meet your match
your future you can hatch

One more wound to suture
their lives without a future

Our future will remain
within the structure of the brain

Past is past
and the future is vast

Plough back the earnings
into future yearnings

So many ways to nurture
a child and his future

The Eagle has a future
being a mythical creature

The final suture
sealed his future

The future is bleak
for those who don't speak

The future is vast
what is past is past

The future is very vast
after you minus the past

The future it seem
is a distant dream

The future looked grim
though love filled to the brim

The future path is clear
however far or near

The past is what it had to be
the future is that we cannot see

The present make it last
future minus the past

Wait for the future
is like a tug on the suture

When I think of the future
I add one more suture

You are the feature
between the past and the future

G

Gadfly

>Gadfly is a pest
>who is doing his best

>The gadfly is best
>when acting like a pest

Gain

>Always something to gain
>though many a loss is pain

>Gain or loss
>depends on the toss

>Man has much to gain
>from the winds and the rain

>Much to gain
>by changing your brain

>Not much gain
>to re-live the pain

>Nothing to gain
>in the fast lane

>Short term gain
>long term pain

>If you see what remains
>you can count the gains

Gallop

>He wrote at a gallop
>while feeding on scallop

Gambling

>The gambling streak
>is meant for the weak

Game

>Game of deception
>gets good reception

>He who turns up lame
>must have played a good game

>More of the same
>you will lose the game

>Much of the same
>is the only game

>They give it no name
>the rules of the game

>Watch dogs of the game
>they need a different name

Whatever the name
it is just a game

They play mind games
that have no names

Why play games
and call each other names

Gander

One eyed gander
dished out slander

Gangrene

Gangrene I am told
when his foot turned cold

Gasping

He asked to comb his hair
while gasping for air

Gather

The ravens they rather
where the carcasses gather

Gathering

Does it portend harm
the gathering storm

Gaze

The male gaze
how to erase

Gears

Don't meet your peers
without shifting gears

Gender

Some say they are tender
folks of a different gender

Stick to your gender
without being an offender

Generally

Those who cry and tell
have generally lived well

Generosity

Generosity and sharing
can only be with caring

Generosity

Generosity is a skill
that needs a lot of will

Out of pity
Generosity

Gentle

Her speech was so gentle
that it was ornamental

In the gentle breeze they sigh
holding hands together why

One gentle touch
can mean so much

The gentle country squire
needs more land to acquire

Ways we must seek
to be gentle and meek

She gently mended a lock
and looked up at the clock

Germinate

Seeds will germinate how
without the use of the plough

Germination
Germination is a need
for love is just a seed

Germs
The tiniest of germs
can become the deadliest of worms

Gesture
A gesture with a touch
appreciated much

In a more than casual gesture
she invited him to adventure

Offending gesture
needs no tincture

Get
Left or right
just get it right

Ghost
A walking talking ghost
is what the ghost loves most

He acts like he is most
the invisible ghost

He met with her ghost
over tea and toast

It was not a ghost
the horse at the post

Many a ghost
loves marmalade on toast

Merely as a ghost
he stayed too long at his post

Oh ghost who talks
come with me for walks

Oh host who talks
to the ghost who walks

The horse at the post
was no more than a ghost

Giant
For both giant and elf
god is the higher self

From giant to elf
who knows himself

Giant or elf
believe in yourself

Giant or elf
get back to yourself

Giant or elf
master thyself

Giant waves must keep
their appointments in the deep

Gift
Gift of the river
was a cold shiver

Give him a lift
by deliverying a gift

He was tall and strapping
and came with gift wrapping

The best gift is a cloak
for the women folk

Gifted

*To give them a lift
give them a gift*

*A gifted mind
can never be blind*

*Country uplifted
by the young and the gifted*

Giggle

*I wish it were a giggle
and not a nasty niggle*

Gin

*Through thick and thin
he held on to his gin*

Girl

*Let us hear her sing
the girl in the valvet swing*

*The girl in the velvet swing
says ting-a-ling ling*

*The little girl was smitten
by the book about a kitten*

Girth

*How can there be mirth
while discussing your girth*

*Jollity and girth
are the object of mirth*

*What is it worth
if it doesn't add to girth*

Glad

*Once the bad is had
even the good feel glad*

*When the good feel so bad
why do the bad feel so glad*

*Why are they glad
doing things that are bad*

Gladder

*It made me so much gladder
when he was bit by the adder*

Glamour

*Why do people clamour
at the things that have glamour*

Glance

*Brought together by chance
they gave each other a glance*

*It put him in a trance
from her a single glance*

*Just a chance meeting
with a glance that was fleeting*

Glancing

*She cast a glancing eye
as he bit into the pie*

Gland

*Made him bland
when he lost his gland*

Glare

*In the glare of the setting sun
the ducks quack for fun*

Under the glare of lights
a little heart it fights

Glides

The sun it glides
behind the mountain and the tides

Glitter

All the glitter
can't make you fitter

All the glitz and glitter
they don't easily fritter

Glitter

If you don't get fitter
you will lose your glitter

So easy to fritter
hard earned glitter

There is a glitter
in the midst of all the litter

Glittering

The sun shines its rays
on the snow in glittering ways

Globe

In his ear lobe
he could hear the whole globe

Gloom

Even a single spoon
lost can bring about gloom

In my little room
she left me to my gloom

No name for gloom
on a floating balloon

Pecking each others plume
they overcome their gloom

The crowd in the room
was speaking about gloom

There were clouds of gloom
that over the skies where they loom

Glories

All those past glories
unfit as to-days stories

Glories to bask
is an endless task

Not enough glories to bask
for the man behind the mask

Past glories
old stories

So many glories
that have their own stories

Glorious

A glorious plight
to share in her delight

After the storm
a glorious calm

The moon is a glorious sight
to many a lovers delight

The mountain has spawn
this glorious flush of dawn

Glory

Basking in the glory
is a celebrities story

Glory and delight
of Eagles in flight

It's all about glory
told as nice story

Many a glory it will seem
like the pinnacle of a dream

Many a persons story
the hard road to glory

Reflected glory
same old story

The glory of our days
are numbered in many ways

The sun fades in glory
as evening tells its story

Glossies

News stand with glossies
and front page lassies

Glow

No one will ever know
how the glow worms glow

The ocean waters flow
to the evening sun and it's glow

The volcanic flow
with intense glow

The words they will glow
if you write what you know

Why would their cheeks glow
when the oxygen is low

The yellow rose it glows
beside her when it pose

Glowing

Out of the pen comes flowing
words that are glowing

Goal

Mind control
must be your goal

I set my own goals
for the four and twenty foals

God

All he does is nod
when I speak to god

Dear god do me a favour
that she and I can savour

Don't insist
god does exist

Don't make of it thrift
the god given gift

Every act of god
not without a nod

God accepts all offerings
that relieve you of sufferings

God almighty
why am I so flighty

God bless
who have nothing to confess

Rhyming English Couplets **183**

God did his best
man did the rest

God gave no reason
for the dry season

God gave us a neck
to receive many a peck

God gave us feeling
so we could pray to him kneeling

God given beauty
does its duty

God had his reasons
to create the four seasons

God had to be cheating
to make beauty so fleeting

God has a hand
in each grain of sand

God has a master plan
for every and each man

God has a plan
in the life of a man

God has his ways
in paradise he says

God he has a balm
to keep us all calm

God he has hurled
us into a hurrying world

God he lends a ear
from whom he wishes to hear

God he made a rose
beside the thorn to pose

God he offers us why
this sunshine covered sky

God he sets his sight
on making us do what is right

God is busy granting
his love that is enchanting

God is in his future
who worships always nature

God made his case
by giving me this space

God makes them pay
who lose their way

God played his hand
when we inhabited this land

God played his part
when the universe got its start

God plays a part
in the mysteries of the heart

God please grant me the time
to do tasks unfinished of mine

God reveals his mind
usually to the blind

God says it is wise
to live in paradise

God to the oceans gave
both water and the wave

G

God will bless
if you say it with less

God will have his way
if you don't stop to pray

God will not bless
if more becomes less

He was all very shaken
in the path god forsaken

How can he bowl wides
with the hand of god that guides

How can we define god
without him giving the nod

I am afraid to pose
with this god given nose

I wish you knew
god made me for you

If god had time to spare
he would be every where

If god is in heaven
can I meet him at eleven

In god we must
put all our trust

In the grand scheme of things
god never gave men wings

Lotus placed neat
at god and his feet

Must turn to god
he who is a sod

Oh dear god
let me come home to her nod

Oh my god
when will they give us the nod

Once god gives the nod
the canvas will be broad

Only god is the defender
of every and each offender

Please god please bless
me with a goddess

She was like no other
the fairy god mother

Some say he can
god shoe up as man

Thank god it is short
life from the very start

The god in me
prays to thee

The morning gets a nod
from the sun god

The way god talks
to me when I walks

There is a distant land
where god sows seeds with his hand

There is magic in your art
when god plays his part

To every will of god
man he must nod

*To put man to the test
god he knows best*

*We need a personal god
who gives us his nod*

Goddess

*It is the sailors wish to be
with the goddess of the sea*

*The goddess she lay
on the golden hay*

*There is a goddess in the sea
where the sailor wishes to be*

*When a goddess plays chess
just say god bless*

Godforsaken

*The path that was taken
was godforsaken*

Godless

*Don't be a fan
of the godless man*

Gods

*Abode of the gods
where good deeds get nods*

*Don't go messing
with gods every blessing*

*Every gods blessing
needs careful caressing*

*Gods best creation
is mans recreation*

*Gods best plan
was to make a clam*

*Gods honest truth
best told in the booth*

*Gods little blunder
is he I wonder*

*Gods only blunder
man the spineless wonder*

*Gods prescription
defies description*

*Gods will bless
whose needs are less*

*He is both father and man
fits well with gods plan*

*He who can do it all
answers to gods call*

*How to savour
gods little favour*

*Is he I wonder
gods little blunder*

*Lightning and thunder
gods little wonder*

*Moth reaches the flame
reciting gods name*

*Pain and suffering
is one of gods offering*

*The gods did they really
move about so freely*

Godsend
*All weather friend
is a godsend*

Gold
*Gold has a hold
on people we are told*

*Gold will remain gold
on the riverbed that is cold*

*He must be vain
who has gold in his chain*

*Not much use for gold
in horseshoe I am told*

*Not until it is sold
how good is this gold*

Golden
*Not much use
for this golden goose*

Good
*A library has good looks
that is stacked with good books*

*Good bye he said to toil
with exciting things on the boil*

*Good things you must choose
when you dish it out as news*

*The bad side of good
is too much food*

*To know it is good
nothing works like it should*

Goodness
*Evil can be chartered
once goodness is bartered*

*Goodness is a paint
used only by the saint*

*To nature and its goodness
we bestow our madness*

Goodwill
*Don't let it spill
our mutual goodwill*

Gorilla
*There was this gorilla
dancing on a flotilla*

Gorillas
*Gorillas they sleep
in the forests thick and deep*

Gossip
*Coconut juice to sip
listening to gossip*

*Moves at a fast clip
unfounded gossip*

Gossips
*Gossips and quips
come out of his lips*

Governess
*Please god please bless
me with a governess*

Rhyming English Couplets

Grab

*Grab his tail
before you fail*

*The eel it will wail
if you grab it by the tail*

Grace

*At your own pace
retain your grace*

*Don't question grace
even if out of place*

*Grace picks up pace
when she is all dressed in lace*

*He mustered all his grace
and eloquently made his case*

*Her movements filled with grace
love it picks up pace*

*How to keep pace
with divine grace*

*Is there another face
with so much grace*

*Lyrical grace
can it win a race*

*Make your case
or fall from grace*

*Sank without a trace
and without grace*

*Scorn in his face
melted her grace*

*She makes her case
with beauty and grace*

*There are moments of grace
in each and every face*

*There is still grace
in the one horse race*

*To walk away with grace
wear a tight shoe lace*

Graces

*From graces when they fall
they get wake up call*

*Untaught graces
can take you places*

Gracious

*Gracious in defeat
with dancing feet*

Graduated

*She slowly graduated
and became infatuated*

Graduation

*His graduation speech
was like an educated leech*

Grammar

*Grammar must be fed
to clever lines that are said*

*He who stammer
not above grammer*

Grand

No touch is so grand
as that of a baby's hand

Grandiose

Down to his toes
he was all grandiose

Granted

He raved and ranted
took things for granted

Grasp

Why did I choose a wasp
with so many things to grasp

Gratitude

Gratitude is nice
in both men and mice

Grave

At my grave do not weep
I am fast asleep

Don't forget to shave
while working towards the grave

Don't have to be brave
to be lowered into the grave

Don't try to save
yourself from the grave

He pulled out of the grave
because he hadn't had a shave

How can you be brave
with one foot in the grave

If you were so brave
why are you in the grave

It was a close shave
between the pulpit and the grave

Nothing to rave
on the way to the grave

Nothing to rave
one foot in the grave

The grave is best
for devils to rest

The place to be brave
the right side of the grave

The pompous and the brave
they also need a grave

Thousands who were brave
end up in the grave

Gravel

There is no gravel
in time travel

Graveled

The road all graveled
was the least traveled

Gravestone

I don't want my bone
under this gravestone

Gray

When the clouds turned gray
he spied the birds of prey

Rhyming English Couplets

Grease

How can it derail
once you grease the rail

Greasy

Must play its role
even the greasy pole

Great

Nothing so great
not enough to hate

Greed

Break neck speed
fuelled by greed

Greed is good
when your need is food

Greed is very clever
for it never lets you sever

How to feed
their insatiable greed

How to feed
your insatiable greed

However hard it tries
greed it never dies

In the service of greed
more than we need

In this hour of need
please bless me with greed

Just to feed your greed
things you don't need

Let not what you need
be dominated by greed

Of all the things we need
hold on to dear greed

Once we agreed
they upped their greed

Some feed their greed
by taking the lead

There is no seed
that can fulfill all greed

They feed and read
the worms out of greed

They fulfill their greed
with reckless speed

We must all take the lead
and withdraw from total greed

Where is the need
in the clutches of greed

Whose greed is greater than mine
must have been born a swine

Greedy

Service to the needy
but not to the greedy

Greek

Whenever he opens up to speak
all she thinks of is greek

G

Green

A day on the green
can make anyone lean

Cannot be seen
the grasshopper green

Don't be seen
chewing anything green

Greet

A vehicle it will greet
him who crosses the street

Each other they greet
Walking down the street

Each other they greet
with happiness in their feet

Each season they greet
with a dancing of the feet

Feet are meant to greet
and to think on our feet

First they greet
then turn on the heat

How nicely they greet
dogs when they see meat

How shall I greet
destiny when I meet

How to greet
one ever so sweet

Learn how to greet
natures treat

Mutteringly they greet
with stuttering feet

No one to greet
on one way street

On the shores they greet
the arrival of the fleet

Pretty ladies they greet
at the lamppost down the street

She came out to greet
with anklets on her feet

Stockholders will greet
a balance sheet neat

The earth will greet
both rain and sleet

The morning dew must greet
the bare soles of my feet

The wet grass it greet
the touch of my bare feet

There is magic in her feet
when she dances to greet

Thunder they greet
dark clouds when they meet

When the river crossed the street
floods they had to greet

With a touch of the feet
some people they greet

Yaks they greet
at fifteen thousand feet

Greeting
Don't accept them greeting
pleasures that are fleeting

Greetings
Many a yew tree
held out greetings for me

Greets
Each other they greets
once under the sheets

With high heels she greets
me on cobbled streets

Grew
He grew a long neck
so his parrot it could peck

The cast and the crew
everyday they grew

Grey
They returned to the fray
after they turned grey

Grief
All is not well
if grief gets a spell

Beyond the reef
is love without grief

Don't rubbish grief
it may strengthen your belief

Grief must be brief
so joy can bring relief

Grief on grief
doesn't bring relief

He turned a new leaf
and overturned his grief

He was told to sleep
when overcome with grief

How can there be grief
when you watch the lotus leaf

Just coming into grief
she was shaking like a leaf

Let every private grief
end up with relief

Let it be brief
your encounter with grief

Many a grief
ends in relief

On fallen leaf
writ was thy grief

Overcome with grief
she sought relief

The lotus leaf
can drown your grief

When grief came greeting
I dreaded the meeting

Grieves
It looks like the tree it grieves
when it sheds it's leaves

Grieving
> After the bereaving
> time for grieving

Grin
> Fat or thin
> bear and grin

Grinds
> He who grinds the wheel
> responsible for the meal

Grip
> I could feel his grip
> when I was ready to slip

> She was in the grip
> of a guilt trip

Gripe
> No need to gripe
> it is mostly hype

Gritty
> A village in a city
> where they care about nitty gritty

Groom
> Every groom
> fears the bedroom

> Give him room
> the shotgun groom

> Give them room
> enough to groom

Ground
> So short is the hound
> his belly it touches the ground

Group
> They dine as a group
> and slurp at the soup

Grouped
> Once they grouped
> the sea birds swooped

Grow
> Even a small twig
> can grow up to be big

> He called his beard she
> and said let it grow on me

> She refused to grow an inch
> the little red finch

Growing
> Grey streaks unknowing
> from her mane slowly growing

> Sense of doubt keeps growing
> though I think I am all knowing

Growl
> The tiger will growl
> when he sees a wild fowl

> They both could not growl
> the wild fowl nor the owl

Grown
> The wool it has grown
> on the sheep that I own

Growth

*Don't be a sloth
get dendrite growth*

*For your inner growth
talk to a sloth*

Grudge

*I will not bear any grudge
once decided by the judge*

*You're coffee will get colder
if you're a grudge holder*

*Once you harbour grudges
you lose your taste for fudges*

Gruel

*Love can be very cruel
and taste like bland gruel*

Guess

*More or less
for you to guess*

Guest

*Always feed your guest
even if it empties your nest*

*How to request
stuff from a guest*

*Choose your guests well
make sure they can spell*

Guidance

*Guidance is not far
when I see the northern star*

Guiding

*He traveled many a land
with her guiding hand*

Guilt

*Guilt it will stare
when you have affair*

*Guilt unproven
cawed the raven*

*He was guilt ridden by
doing things on the sly*

*Heavy with guilt
he pulled up the quilt*

*She brushed aside her hair
with no guilt in the air*

*So many they wilt
under the burden of guilt*

Guitar

*A guitar to strum
and chewing gum*

Gulf

*Gulf it wides
once you take sides*

*The gulf became wider
between the goat and the tiger*

Gunfight

*At noontime it will end
gunfight without end*

*Gunfight with a friend
will eventually end*

Gunslingers

> *Both gunslingers*
> *with itchy fingers*

Guts

> *For ifs and buts*
> *you don't need guts*

Guzzle

> *We have nothing to cheer*
> *so let's guzzle beer*

Guzzled

> *He guzzled his beer*
> *the man with the question mark ear*

Guzzling

> *He had no peer*
> *in guzzling beer*

Gym

> *How to become slim*
> *without going to the gym*

> *Sundays on a whim*
> *I go to the gym*

H

Habit

*Hat and the rabbit
just an old habit*

*A habit once uprooted
need not again be booted*

*A habit pays its due
to every little cue*

*Bad habit it stays
if you don't mend your ways*

*I have yet to see a rabbit
that has a weak habit*

*It's all part of a habit
to think he is still a rabbit*

*To go against the grain
is a habit of the brain*

*Bad habits
breed like rabbits*

*Could it be in your sleep
bad habits when they creep*

*Easy to announce
habits we need to denounce*

*Habits have assured
that happiness can be cured*

*Habits that take root
bear their own fruit*

*He needs to be feted
whose bad habits are uprooted*

*His habits ingrained
permanently remained*

*If you count all your habits
there wouldn't be enough Rabbits*

*Man must mend
his habits in the end*

*Old habits die hard
for the saint or the bard*

*Old habits die hard
just like shedding lard*

*Old habits die hard
said the preacher to the bard*

*Prince pauper or bard
old habits die hard*

*Rooted to the soil
with habits old they toil*

*Some have to be urged
to have their habits purged*

Hair

*Through her hair she ran
her fingers as fast as she can*

Half

*Don't scoff
at your better half*

*Half done work
object of smirk*

*Their eyes half met
as she served a let*

*Two half wits when they sit
become full bit by bit*

Halfway

*Must find a way
to meet them halfway*

Halves

*What else is it but
two halves of the same nut*

Hamlet

*He ended up in a hamlet
and ordered an omelette*

Hand

*Hand in hand they stroll
with a common goal*

*Where must it land
the glove in need of a hand*

*Down to the last letter
she can handle it better*

*Let us travel many lands
holding each others hands*

Handshake

*To whom is he beholden
though his handshake is golden*

Hang

*How to hang
out in penang*

Hanging

*Hanging drops
from mountain tops*

*The hanging bat
can never wear a hat*

Happening

*Why is it not
happening and hot*

Happiest

*Happiest man alive
can take a nose dive*

*Happiest moment of the day
when something clever I say*

Happiness

*Always for the good
happiness has stood*

For happiness to come
pick a guitar to strum

Happiness and strife
in the front end of life

Happiness can be clad
by the good and the bad

Happiness casts its spell
when you do something well

Happiness caught
no matter what

Happiness divided
can never be voided

Happiness elusive
for the angel reclusive

Happiness elusive
for the reclusive

Happiness in June
is to sing her a tune

Happiness is a condition
that defied all rendition

Happiness is a quest
pursued alone is best

Happiness is a secret
known only to the egret

Happiness is a state of mind
same for us and the blind

Happiness is an attire
that speaks to the hearts desire

Happiness is due
when you stand in a queue

Happiness is fed
by thought in the head

Happiness in the end
from a well chosen friend

Happiness is the fruit
of love and pursuit

Happiness is this
where nothing is remiss

Happiness it brings
to the soul that sings

Happiness it buys
family ties

Happiness it finds
the best of minds

Happiness it lies
where yes meets eyes

Happiness it shows
in a child when it snows

Happiness it will greet
her with dancing feet

Happiness once bleached
cannot again be reached

Happiness re-lived
tensions relieved

Happiness speaks
volumes when it leaks

*Happiness such as this
without you I would miss*

*Happiness takes time
without the help of wine*

*Happiness to them is kind
who have peace of mind*

*Happiness usually found
on dangerous ground*

*Happiness was meant
to be godsent*

*Happiness was sent
by the camel into the tent*

*He who is blind
can have happiness of mind*

*Her happiness was matched
by the eggs she hatched*

*In deep sorrow I learn
that happiness will get its turn*

*Purse strings are things
that happiness brings*

*Pursuit of happiness
not by sloppiness*

*She faced it with a scoff
when happiness it wore off*

*Slowly in your sleep
happiness it will creep*

*Suffering in the end
with happiness it must blend*

*They fell in love in spring
when happiness had a ring*

*Try to seize it when
happiness shows up at your den*

*When all is well
happiness will tell*

*Will it be brief
this happiness and grief*

Happy

*He has happy feet
the man in the street*

*He who can make you happy
can also make the waters choppy*

*It takes a lifespan
to become a happy man*

*Not without effort
to be happy in comfort*

*To make someone happy
when the seas are choppy*

Hard

*After a hard days toil
rub your face with oil*

*Hard to bear
the shameful affair*

*Hard to climb roofs
with cloven hoofs*

*Hard to re kindle
the fire in its dwindle*

*Very hard to pose
once you lose your nose*

Hardest

*The hardest climb isn't steep
when you have promises to keep*

Hare

*The hare it came abiding
and the tortoise came out of hiding*

Harm

*Harm is understood
better than is good*

*Many were done to harm
falling into her charm*

*The boat will come to harm
when the sailor sees a storm*

*There is hardly a harm
from an overzealous charm*

*Unspoken word has charm
without doing any harm*

Harmed

*Better to be armed
before we are harmed*

Harmful

*There is no dearth
of harmful mirth*

Harms

*He who bears no arms
cannot come to harms*

*He will come to harms
who says farewell to charms*

*Not much to say
until out of harms way*

Harried

*Full of harried men
none of whom is a gem*

Harshness

*The harshness of the light
made her eyebrows tight*

Harvest

*Good harvest is best
if you have chicks in the nest*

*The rains came too soon
in the month of the harvest moon*

Haste

*May end up as waste
things done in haste*

Hat

*When you pull it out of the hat
let it be a rabbit and not a cat*

Hatch

*After a lean patch
I had eggs to hatch*

*Batch by batch
the eggs they hatch*

*Between their legs
penguins hatch the eggs*

She had eggs to hatch
and fish to catch

Hatched
The chick is hatched
from the egg once cracked

Hatches
Somebody up there watches
as to how the egg it hatches

Hate
Always someone to hate
that is mans fate

Clean the slate
of the burden of hate

Haul
Built for the long haul
though he could hardly crawl

Hauling
Men used to hauling
loads quite appalling

Haunt
Daily it will haunt
you whatever you want

Haunting
The words though haunting
the meaning was wanting

Haven
Once there was a Raven
in a secluded haven

Having
As such
it's not about having much

Hawking
How can we be hawking
a product so shocking

Head
All day into your head
garbage is fed

Head
All the things that were fed
from childhood into my head

From whence are they fed
the voices in my head

Go fix your head
before stupid things are said

Head into her hands
to cover up her pangs

Her head it leaps
when her child she weeps

Much of it is in the head
of the reader it is said

Peril is fed
if you don't follow your head

Stuff gets into your head
and makes it feel like lead

Takes place in the head
when I am lying in bed

*The goblins in my head
I take daily to bed*

*The softness of the mound
makes the head go round*

*The web serves as a bed
where the spider can rest his head*

*They both went to bed
with a ringing in the head*

*Three times as big
as his head was the wig*

*We all go to bed
with the same thing in the head*

*What goes on in their head
in a world full of the dead*

*When the floor hit the ceiling
my head it went reeling*

*With his head in proper poise
he spoke his words with choice*

Headache

*There was a house in the hills
and headache pills*

Heads

*Heads or tails
asked the peacock to the quail*

Heal

*How to heal
what is hard to deal*

Healing

*Healing process was quick
when both of them were slick*

Healing

*The healing sound
in us is found*

Healing

*Your healing ways
with me forever stays*

Health

*Alcohol in stealth
ruined my livers health*

*Each and every breath
is a tonic for health*

*Health is best understood
by him who is starved of food*

*Hold your breath
improve your health*

*If you are happy in your health
you won't be wanting in wealth*

*New trees that sprout in health
make for the forests wealth*

Healthy

*He who early rise
becomes healthy twice*

Heap

*How big is the leap
to the top of the heap*

Hear

Can hear the music playing
but not what she was saying

Can you hear me now
while I make this vow

He couldn't hear the fax
from a earful of wax

I can hear the hum
of the taste of things to come

I wish I didn't hear
the phone in my ear

If I could hear as well as thee
where would all the mosquitoes be

Mosquitoes I hear
getting closer to my ear

Some make it clear
they prefer not to hear

That is a buzz I hear
from the flea in my ear

The only voice in my ear
is my mothers I hear

There is a ringing in my ear
which no one else can hear

Heard

Always start with a word
that is waiting to be heard

By now we would have heard
if the dinosaur was a bird

Have you heard the news
there is no orange in juice

He had the last word
until he was heard

How to find the bird
when mocking is heard

If you use the proper word
you are likely to be heard

It must first be heard
for the brain to see the word

On a hot languid summer
I heard a different drummer

Parrot is a bird
waiting to be heard

There wasn't a harsh word
from her that could be heard

Unlock the word
waiting to be heard

Until it is heard
love is just a word

Voices unheard
waiting to be heard

Hearing

Hearing is in the main
a function of the brain

Hears

Her eye lids batter
when she hears him flatter

Rhyming English Couplets

Heart

What does it take
for her heart to awake

A heart dismembered
by the pains remembered

A heart that is torn
a burden heavily borne

A tear makes sense
if a heart it will cleanse

All day he wrote jingle
to make their heart tingle

All desire is mental
for which the heart is instrumental

All things they start
from deep down in the heart

All you need is a hug
heart strings when they tug

Attack is a part
of a failing heart

Be always ready to mend
the heart of a broken friend

Before the tears they start
was a loneliness of the heart

Blame is a part
of the tear in the heart

Broken heart needs mendings
for happy endings

Heart

Child of a broken heart
that's how he got his start

Children play a part
in gladdening a mothers heart

Cry of a broken heart
why did it have to start

Darkness is a part
of the mysteries of the heart

Dear heart
from you I will never part

Deep inside my heart
the two of us will never part

Deep within the heart
love it gets a start

Do they ever part
the tongue and the heart

Don't ever part
from the delights of the heart

Don't ever part
with her stolen heart

Don't look up a chart
in matters of the heart

Don't lose your heart
to love from the start

Don't make me a part
of your careless heart

Ecstasy is a place
where the heart makes its case

Every child is a part
of the mothers heart

Every corroded heart
must eventually re-start

Every heart gets a look
at love hidden in a nook

Every heart has a leaning
that gives love its meaning

Every heart must beat
for love to repeat

Every heart must cheat
once without a repeat

Every heart must lure
love beautiful and pure

Every heart must mend
from broken dreams in the end

Every heart must think
before it puts it in ink

Every jealous heart
how does it get a start

Every wound gets a start
with a broken heart

Everytime I fell apart
the way she touched my heart

Field placing
sets the heart racing

For lies to depart
lay hand on your heart

Forever we are a part
of the intimacies of the heart

From simple little things
the heart it sings

Gnawing of the heart
from love torn apart

Hair stood on end
it's time for heart to mend

He loved her from the start
with a hand on his heart

He wanted to depart
after consulting her heart

He was all enraptured
once her heart was captured

He was made a part
of her understanding heart

He who loses his charm
must still keep his heart warm

Heart and mind reeling
from such a lovely feeling

Heart beats they hum •
like the beating of the drum

Heart beats very slow
when love is in full flow

Heart beats with a ping
when love takes to wing

Heart became warm
seeing her angelic form

Heart begins its flutter
into my ears when she mutter

Heart felt desire
needs proper attire

Heart has its reasons
to act out its treasons

Heart has the measure
of love and its treasure

Heart in repair
from music in the air

Heart is the stage
where love gets a page

Heart it bled
when love it fled

Heart it will sing
when love takes to wing

Heart must be trained
to be restrained

Heart of the matter
listen to less chatter

Heart plays a part
in thought from the start

Heart races to the skies
seeing the hair over her eyes

Heart rate picks up pace
when I watch the horses race

Heart strengthened
life lengthened

Heart strings he will pluck
while trying out his luck

Heart that is once stolen
has its moments all golden

Heart to heart
is one bridge apart

Heart you must lend
for a love without end

Heaven plays a part
in tears from the heart

Her face was built for smile
though heart breaks last awhile

Her failing part
was a broken heart

Her heart comes to me near
through the softness of her tear

Her heart is in tow
wherever I go

Her heart it spies
with dreamy eyes

Her heart made it clear
love is her only fear

Her heart she one day fixed
on a boy who was already jinxed

Her heart was quickly stolen
in a moment all golden

*Her loving heart
has played it's part*

*Her loving ways
in my heart it stays*

*Hidden in every heart
is the image of a tart*

*His amorous heart
he would instantly part*

*His heart began to plead
when love began to recede*

*His heart he bares
from the frown he wears*

*His heart it fell for candy
and his throat he filled with brandy*

*His heart was warm
though he lost his charm*

*His heart went on a chase
seeking her embrace*

*His most clamorous part
is his amorous heart*

*Holding hands together
heart felt light as a feather*

*How can I be a part
of your lovely heart*

*How can I give my heart
when we both live so apart*

*How can I part
with this love from the heart*

*How can I part
from a committed heart*

*How can I part
from the secrets of my heart*

*How can love be
what the heart cannot see*

*How can we part
from the desires of our heart*

*How did it start
this outpouring of the heart*

*How did it start
your careless heart*

*How did they get a start
these men without a heart*

*How do you play your part
oh jealous heart*

*How does it start
love in her beating heart*

*How does it start
the affairs of the heart*

*How does it tick
the heart of the romantic*

*How I long
for this heart to sing a song*

*How long must we part
from the songs in our heart*

*How to get a start
in a loving heart*

*How to make it short
love from a broken heart*

*I don't wish to part
from the rhythm in my heart*

*I fall apart
when I listen to your heart*

*I will never part
from the love in my heart*

*I wish he was told
her heart could go cold*

*If the heart were fully bared
most people would be scared*

*Images of thee
my heart got hold for free*

*Impossible gets a start
if you take it to heart*

*In her heart she felt bitter
that he missed a sitter*

*In love it plays its part
every human heart*

*In matters of the heart
get an early start*

*In matters of the heart
love plays a part*

*In matters of the heart
pizza plays a part*

*In matters of the heart
we both play a part*

*In my heart it is etched
her love that I fetched*

*In my heart there is bliss
when in absence her I miss*

*In one fleeting moment
no heart beat just lament*

*Inner workings of the heart
it can tear you apart*

*It sets me apart
when straight from the heart*

*It was left with a scar
her heart from his evil star*

*It's up to the heart
to play it's pumping part*

*Jealousy gets a start
in a loving heart*

*Jealousy is a part
of the jealous at heart*

*Joined at the heart
though far apart*

*Just don't have a heart
to tear love apart*

*Keep your heart warm
you will come to no harm*

*Like a snake charmer
he makes their heart warmer*

*Make behaviour a part
of a change of heart*

*Make me a part
of your dear heart*

*Make your heart fitter
to face love when it is bitter*

*Many a breath it takes
my heart when it breaks*

*Many a broken heart
played music from the start*

*Many a heart has found
that love is profound*

*Many a heart is broken
when love is just token*

*Many a heart will claim
love by any name*

*Many a heart must pay
when love it melts away*

*Many a heart will lure
love to it for sure*

*Many a heart will mend
from love in the end*

*Many a heart will mend
hopefully before the end*

*Many a heart will warm
at the sight of the good luck charm*

*Many a heart will weep
once love is put to sleep*

*Many a heart would sink
love if it could think*

*Message drawn from the heart
doesn't need a kick start*

*Mind is a part
of the workings of the heart*

*Mind to the heart it talks
the pretty girl as she walks*

*Moments can fill a cup
to lift your heart up*

*Mountain peaks
to the heart it speaks*

*Much of his was a part
of the country boy at heart*

*My broken heart it keeps score
while my eyes they sleep no more*

*My heart for her will sing
the eternal song of spring*

*My heart gets a lift
when I see a well wrapped gift*

*My heart gets slowly lit
from love that it finds very fit*

*My heart has eyes
for beauty where it lies*

*My heart is bound
to music and sound*

*My heart it dies
to hear your eloquent eyes*

*My heart it feels now
the slow death of love*

My heart it leaps
when my mother speaks

My heart it must nurse
her every sweet verse

My heart it shut the door
when love it came ashore

My heart it spies
her angular eyes

My heart it was sold
for a nugget of gold

My heart made an exception
for her love at it's inception

My heart made it clear
love it will endure

My heart stood still
at the phone bill

My heart stood still
in a field of daffodil

My heart stood still
when love took a spill

My heart to her I gave
before old enough to shave

My heart was stolen
when the moment was golden

My heart will keep
your smile till I sleep

My heart will speak free
once I find the key

Name dropping
heart stopping

No use looking at the chart
in matters of the heart

Nothing noble about his heart
when love so easily tears it apart

Offer them a tart
and you will win their heart

Oh bleeding heart
when will you from me part

Oh jealous heart
don't break into my heart

Oh purple heart
when will your love start

Once her heart had spoken
his love had time to awaken

Once you lose heart
difficult to re-start

Once you steal her heart
don't ever part

Once you take it to heart
it becomes of you a part

Only the heart knows well
where the hand of an angel does dwell

Open in part
window to her heart

Open wounds are a part
of many a broken heart

Our heart must one day swell
for love to turn out well

Pathos plays a part
in tears from the heart

Peace is a part
of a change of heart

Play your part
to win her heart

Reign in at the start
matters of the heart

Said the tongue to the heart
why should we ever part

Secrets get a start
in affairs of the heart

Sets the heart racing
when love does it's tracing

She broke into my heart
and tore it apart

She gave him a part
of her passionate heart

She handed me a part
of the rose that was in her heart

She is a part
of the gnawings of my heart

She is a part
of the voice in my heart

She made me a part
of her unfailing heart

She played a part
for the feeling in his heart

She plays a big part
in matters of the heart

She plays a part
in moments that lift my heart

She was all heart broken
he gave her a rose as token

Slowly it will die
the heart that is broken why

Somewhere it plays a part
love in a wounded heart

Stillness has a store
when heart has love to pour

Stomach is a part
of the way to his heart

Such was his heart
he would give everyone a part

Take heart it will soon be spring
lovers hearts will begin to sing

Tell me my heart
is this love or just a dart

The best lesson it is said
is from the heart and not the head

The bleeding part
is the wound in my heart

The days she spends in waiting
while her heart it does the debating

*The heart and mind go missing
when a mob it starts hissing*

*The heart beats softer
at the sound of laughter*

*The heart cannot be quieted
without love being requited*

*The heart feeds the liver
like a raging river*

*The heart has its desires
stoked by inner fires*

*The heart is a nest
where love is put to rest*

*The heart is a thing
to which memories will cling*

*The heart is converted
whose mind is diverted*

*The heart is towed
when love is bestowed*

*The heart it bleeds
for mercy when it pleads*

*The heart it goes fleeing
when love it comes seeing*

*The heart it goes speeding
when love it is receding*

*The heart it is said
by love it is fed*

*The heart it sings
at the lighter side of things*

*The heart it sings
when love takes to wings*

*The heart missed a beat
after prodigious feat*

*The heart must be stilled
by the eyes with tears filled*

*The heart never lies
when it sees through her eyes*

*The heart of a mother buys time
for her boy caught in crime*

*The heart of a wife
can ease my strife*

*The heart sets in motion
both love and devotion*

*The heart will buoy
from guiltless joy*

*The heart will remain
the target of pain*

*The heart you must train
to not listen to the brain*

*The language of my choice
is a heart with one voice*

*The mind it blinks
when the heart it thinks*

*The morning did start
with a throb in my heart*

*The most tormented part
was the heart from the start*

*The poetic part
it spilled from the heart*

*The road to her heart is steep
however much your love is deep*

*The sailors heart belong
to wave wind and song*

*The son he plays a part
to gladden a mothers heart*

*The voice gets a start
from a place near the heart*

*The warmth in his heart
was his best part*

*The way her heart shatters
to all and trivial matters*

*The window plays a part
to look into your heart*

*There is a fool in my heart
who loved her from the start*

*There is a secret part
in affairs of the human heart*

*They set your heart on fire
these objects of desire*

*Though we live apart
we are joined at the heart*

*Though we were ages apart
I gave to her my heart*

*Ting a ling ling
my heart is ready to sing*

*To deny a dog his bone
must have heart of stone*

*To leave with a heavy heart
they both played their part*

*Tries his best to win
our heart with a subtle grin*

*Up and down pacing
with his heart all racing*

*Virtue is not just a notion
it keeps our heart beat in motion*

*We all know the feeling
when the head and heart go reeling*

*What kind of fool am I
whose heart is broken but cannot cry*

*When did it start
this ache in my heart*

*When I hear her name
my heart never feels the same*

*When I see a good thing
it makes my heart sing*

*When my heart begins to soar
I wake up wanting more*

*When my heart fails to tell
is it death knell*

*When the heart begins to sing
love is everything*

*When will you depart
with your unfaithful heart*

Rhyming English Couplets

Where do they start
the wounds of a broken heart

Where does it start
the speakings of the heart

Where will you keep
my heart when you sleep

Wherever I go
your heart is in tow

Why did it start
this ache in the heart

Window to her heart
was open from the start

With a heavy heart I sleep
where the nights slowly creep

With his heart daylong throbbing
the robber he went on robbing

With just half a quart
she broke into my heart

Words cannot be spoken
by the heart all broken

Words from the heart
to share with you from the start

Words play a part
in feelings of the heart

Words though unseen
keeps my heart clean

Workings of the heart
love plays a part

Would you be a part
of the secret in my heart

You are a part
of moments that lift the heart

You are always a part
of the songs in my heart

You will always be a part
of my broken heart

Your heart may need pacing
if she sets your mind racing

Heartache

A heartache it took
to write a bestselling book

Heartache spared
from grief shared

Is it heartache and pain
that made us meet again

With a bite of the cake
he eased his heartache

Heartbeat

Heartbeat is the seat
of every rhythmic beat

Heartbreaks

Heartbreaks need nursing
and love needs cursing

Heartbreaks unfold
when love gets cold

Heartburn
>His heartburn betrayed
>a love that strayed

Hearted
>As soon as she departed
>he was all down hearted

>He became light hearted
>once the drinking started

>Should we have parted
>all broken hearted

>Take a big hearted look
>at every corner and nook

>They both parted
>broken hearted

>To get things started
>they became light hearted

Heartfelt
>Whatever you do for me
>was heartfelt I can see

Heartful
>Heartful things
>songs with wings

Heartless
>He was heartless and cold
>that's what made him bold

>Heartless and cold
>he was I am told

>She cast a cold eye
>at a heartless love why

>Stuck with them
>these heartless men

Hearts
>All day we pray
>for our hearts not to stray

>Bleeding hearts they chose
>just a little red rose

>Broken hearts must ache
>nothing else to take

>Broken hearts must mend
>while you still have a friend

>Broken hearts
>have many parts

>Careless hearts
>queen of tarts

>Fixing hearts
>and other body parts

>Give it a ring
>the hearts bowstring

>Hearts that never mend
>from love that came to an end

>Her hearts desire
>was to marry Mr. Esquire

>I have hearts to please
>and a home on lease

>Let me polish my grin
>I have hearts to win

*Meek surrender
my hearts only blunder*

*My favourite reading
is about hearts bleeding*

*My hearts only desire
is a fireproof attire*

*Our hearts take to wings
from the way she says things*

*People of opposite gender
have hearts soft and tender*

*Rid them of blinds
both hearts and minds*

*The hearts they screech
when love is out of reach*

*Their hearts were asleep
when love became deep*

*There is no end
for hearts that never mend*

*Though their hearts wept
promises were kept*

*Two hearts at once broken
in a place god forsaken*

*Two hearts in synch
each unable to think*

*Two hearts joined as one
until one of them is done*

*Two hearts they long
for love that is strong*

*Two hearts they must
like Iron turned to rust*

*Two hearts they speak as one
until their love is done*

*When hearts pull and tug
end it with a hug*

*When the hearts have a doubt
love gets drawn out*

*With guitars strumming
and hearts thrumming*

Hearty

*Down to his tail
he was hearty and hale*

*Every resident male
better be hearty and hale*

*Hale and hearty
and just as naughty*

*He is hearty and hale
who is supported by ale*

*He is hearty and hale
with a bend in his tail*

*He made his case
with a hearty embrace*

*He was hearty and hale
sipping his ale*

*Hearty and hale
the fish with a silvery scale*

*Hearty and hale
the last human male*

*Hearty and hale
this ageing male*

*I feel hearty and hale
when I unbottle the ale*

*To feel hearty and hale
just unbottle the ale*

*Why is the male
so hearty and hale*

Heat

*At the fireplace we meet
where there is no room for heat*

*The gravel beneath your feet
becomes hot with the mid-day heat*

*The place to meet
is the kitchen heat*

Heaven

*Be it heaven or hell
a writer should do well*

*Behind the heaven it lies
a courtyard in the skies*

*Both heaven and hell
inside us they dwell*

*Contentment was meant
to be heaven sent*

*Don't make me wait till eleven
on my last leg to heaven*

*From heaven she was sent
for me only meant*

*Getting close to eleven
send me to heaven*

*He went to heaven dejected
god had him ejected*

*Heaven and earth are mine
with love all so divine*

*Heaven has chose
her to be a wild rose*

*Heaven has opened its doors
even to the bores*

*Heaven he states
is between the gates*

*Heaven in the hills
where love had its fills*

*Heaven is a kind
of construct of the mind*

*Heaven it gives birth
to love happiness and mirth*

*How to get to heaven
before the clock strikes seven*

*I am closer to heaven
when the clock strikes eleven*

*I counted upto seven
to get pennies from heaven*

*I said how
can I go to heaven now*

Rhyming English Couplets

*I'll pick you up at seven
on my way to heaven*

*If you have a ticket to heaven
check in at seven*

*Imagine we are in heaven
before the clock strikes eleven*

*In heaven they lie
babies who die*

*In the heaven they hide
angels at high tide*

*In the kingdom of heaven
you can wake up at eleven*

*It had to be heaven
I met her at seven*

*It is already seven
and I am not prepared for heaven*

*Let's get it straight
heaven will not wait*

*Make heaven a part
of your life from the start*

*No better glimpse of heaven
than to be in love at eleven*

*Room full of heaven
when she comes home at seven*

*She and I we fled
to the heaven in our head*

*The doors of heaven he sees
when he is down on his knees*

*There is a heaven to behold
from hell I am told*

*There is a place in heaven
where all the love is given*

*There is heaven beneath the eyes
in the cradle where the baby lies*

*There is no better music in heaven
than to hear her voice at seven*

*They go straight to heaven
our thoughts morning to seven*

*Those who I met in heaven
they all died at eleven*

*Truth is well
in heaven it dwell*

*Wake up at seven
and look up to heaven*

*Why go to heaven
when I can be there by seven*

Heavenly

*A life of daily dreaming
waiting for heavenly revealing*

*From the physical state
to the heavenly gate*

*Heavenly bliss
from a simple kiss*

*It took a turn for the worse
the weather from a heavenly curse*

*Someday we will meet
on heavenly street*

*To the heavenly abode
please show me the road*

Heavens

*If the heavens fall
let it be with angels and all*

*One day we must all
heed heavens call*

*To heavens abode
through the spiral road*

*We are all living to die
to go to the heavens in the sky*

*When the heavens tore asunder
there was lightning and thunder*

*Why why
are the heavens so high*

Heaviest

*Couldn't break his bone
the heaviest of stone*

Heavily

*I spoke to a hen
who was heavily into zen*

Heaviness

*How can it be a curse
the heaviness in my purse*

Heavy

*Heavy on her mind
that his love was blind*

*The bills became heavy
with nothing to levy*

*Too many pegs
heavy in the legs*

Hefty

*He is a lefty
with a forehand that is hefty*

Heights

*They reach great heights
who burn candle lights*

*To reach heights exalted
memories must be salted*

Hell

*Just when things were well
the gates opened to hell*

*The living they dwell
mostly in hell*

*To open the gates of hell
requires a touch of the bell*

Help

*Towards us who step
may be in need of help*

Helpless

*For all the helpless hands
in far and distant lands*

Hermits
> Food is the least
> part of a hermits feast

Hesitates
> Hesitates to throw light
> on his immediate plight

Hidden
> Hidden beneath the ice
> treasures of untold price

> Hidden from your search
> words that lay in the lurch

> Hidden strife
> of the inner life

> Our worst fears are hidden
> where horses can't be ridden

> There is hidden many a gloom
> on the dark side of the moon

> We go through acts
> when hidden from the facts

Hide
> Come sit by my side
> if you have no place to hide

> No place to hide
> but the other side

> She couldn't hide her mirth
> when she saw his girth

Hiding
> Hiding in the cloud
> is a thunder very loud

> Like a bad penny
> hiding among many

High
> High up high
> where the mountain meets the sky

> When the stakes are high
> don't ask why

Himself
> He saw shades of himself
> in both giant and the elf

Historical
> Long awaited thunder
> from a historical blunder

History
> Every secret has a history
> often shrouded in mystery

> History in the making
> no mean undertaking

> History is a heap
> where thoughts old they sleep

> History takes turn
> finding people who don't learn

> Life history takes a look
> at the circumstances of the book

> The dustbin of history
> shrouded in mystery

> The shadow of history
> shrouded in mystery

*Went into history
the unresolved mystery*

*With history on the march
my collar it needs starch*

*Writing has a history
of being shrouded in mystery*

Hitch

*There is a hitch
when emotions reach a pitch*

*There is no hitch
to being young and rich*

*There isn't a hitch
to everyone becoming rich*

Hitched

*The flies they hitched
on to the ears that twitched*

Hitches

*So many hitches
rags to riches*

Hold

*For it to get hold
in the way it is told*

*Hold tight your wares
there are too many snares*

*Must hold his tongue
who is high strung*

*Put it on hold
let it gather mould*

Holding

*Holding hands they talk
on a cold winter walk*

*We climbed up the hill
holding hands till*

Hole

*Hole in one
job done*

*The hole in the cheese
lets in the breeze*

Holiday

*Once the winter is over
we will holiday in Dover*

*Man on the moon
he holidays in June*

Holy

*Men who wear beads
are good at holy deeds*

Home

*I'll soon be home
where the antelope roam*

*No place like home
when I return from Rome*

*The home lost its glue
when the crockery flew*

Homely

*I feel all homely
thinking of you only*

Homeward

*Homeward bound
with his mongrel hound*

Honest

*He sold his beans
by fair and honest means*

*The honest men
they have their hen*

Honesty

*Honesty is best
when put to the test*

*Honesty it pays
inspite of their ways*

*Like the old days
when honesty pays*

Honey

*A bee flush with honey
had a nose that was runny*

*As flying is to geese
and honey is to bees*

*She called me honey
on a day bright and sunny*

*To bees we are beholden
for the honey that is golden*

Honeydew

*The honeydew melon
is no ordinary lemon*

Honeymoon

*Hardly ever stays
your honeymoon days*

Honoured

*Others have clamoured
to be so honoured*

Hooked

*The way she looked
had him hooked*

Hope

*A beacon of hope
a bathroom with soap*

*A couple looking for hope
when there is no scope*

*Climb the rope of hope
not down the slippery slope*

*Dawn of a new hope
when snake becomes rope*

*Don't lose hope
there still is rope*

*Everything I say
hope it reaches her by May*

*First they feed you hope
that is slippery as bar of soap*

*For all the things done wrong
I hope it will make you strong*

*He was full of hope
when he found bar of soap*

He went for the rope
after losing hope

Hope is a salve
that's all we have

Hope is not trivial
it is convivial

Hope it brings
wonderful things

Hope on a rope
slippery as soap

Hope will never die
in my minds eye

Hope you make errors
that hold no future terrors

How can we cope
when there is no hope

I hope I wake up in heaven
before the clock strikes seven

I hope she can see
all I have is me

I would be lying
if hope at times seems dying

It gives you hope
when the snake turns into a rope

Messages of hope
must be large in scope

Needs a long rope
each fading hope

No need for the hang rope
once you hold on to hope

Playing pool with a rope
takes away hope

Ray of hope
slippery as slope

Slippery as soap
when it comes to hope

Some people just grope
throughout life in hope

The morning brings hope
that we both can elope

The soft and soothing breeze
hope it never will cease

The steep side of the slope
didn't give much hope

There is hope in me
pretty girl when I see

They grasp at hope
those who elope

To fulfill your hope
climb the right rope

What happens to hope
down the slippery slope

You are my only hope
with whom to elope

Rhyming English Couplets

Hopeless
> Even the homeless
> don't think it is hopeless

Hopes
> Great hopes
> need long ropes

> He climbs long ropes
> who has high hopes

> Hopes must be guarded
> for them to be rewarded

> Let our new hopes
> be based on strings and ropes

> My hopes though dashed
> in my mind they are stashed

> Towards youth I gropes
> to rekindle my hopes

Hopped
> He grabbed a paddle
> and hopped on the saddle

Hormone
> Hormone swings
> they do stupid things

Hormones
> Hormones once locked
> give reasons to be shocked

Horn
> Bull by the horn
> till the gut is torn

Horn
> Is there such a man so born
> that he later develops a horn

Horns
> A bed of thorns
> where stags lose their horns

Horoscopes
> Horoscopes on a tray
> to lead one astray

Horses
> Skinny or plump
> the horses they will jump

Host
> He played host
> to both tea and toast

> The keeper plays host
> to the goal post

Hostile
> A hostile land
> where snakes curve in the sand

Hot
> To handle he was hot
> once he was begot

Hours
> A few hours of writing
> can lead to nail biting

House
> To keep a good house
> rid it of the mouse

H

Housewife's
> Many a pot will boil
> from the housewife's toil

Huddle
> In-spite of the puddle
> they went into a huddle

Hug
> Give me a hug
> but don't pull the rug

Hugged
> Once the fire was kindled
> they hugged and bundled

> They hugged and bundled
> when fire was kindled

Human
> All of human reason
> changes with the season

> Animals have a mystery
> close to human history

> At a hot pace
> the human race

> Brinjals have feelings
> despite human leanings

> Give it a human face
> before you make a case

> How to keep pace
> with the human race

> Human flaws
> can't be fit into laws

> Human frailty
> not for the piety

> Human nature
> can slip from stature

> Human need
> how to feed

> Latent love is a part
> of every human heart

> Many a human
> is just a lemon

> Music plays a part
> in every human heart

> The human condition
> does it need rendition

> The human race
> in outer space

> They dance cheek to cheek
> because human nature is weak

> To the whole human race
> she displayed her grace

> Why is it that human
> is also part demon

Humanised
> From being demonised
> to being humanised

Humans
> Humans fight
> just for delight

Rhyming English Couplets

Humble
> He is so humble
> even the bees will mumble

Hummer
> The bees they hummer
> in my garden in the summer

Humming
> Many a flower she must
> see the humming bee first

Humor
> I would rather bear a tumor
> than an overdose of ill humor

Humour
> Humour becomes witty
> when there is incongruity

> Humour that is rich
> can have us in a stitch

> Humour will die
> from too critical an eye

> No façade this humour
> covers up many a tumour

> She could not deny
> the humour in his eye

Hump
> Before you cross the hump
> the chest you must thump

Hunches
> They all come in bunches
> all my best hunches

Hundred
> To live to be a hundred
> look after your kindred

Hung
> He was hung by a thread
> the newspapers said

> His parrot tongue
> had him hung

Hungry
> Once the tiger is hungry
> it will eat all and sundry

Hunt
> They hunt in pairs
> the great white bears

Hunted
> His growth got stunted
> from love that he hunted

Hunter
> A hunter lives and dies
> aiming at the tigers eyes

Hunting
> They went fox hunting
> holding on to bunting

> They went hunting moose
> but came back with a goose

> To go hunting moose
> carry a big noose

H

Hunts

He who hunts the whale
must return to tell the tale

Hurricanes

Stay away in May
from hurricanes they say

Hurry

He who is in a hurry
has a storehouse of worry

If you say things in a hurry
good it is not very

Hurt

He wouldn't hurt a fly
but why the elephant why

How can it hurt you
a life full of virtue

If you collect enough hurt
poetry you will blurt

In all of lifes leanings
usually hurt are feelings

Ink it hurt
his clean white shirt

It hurt so bad
it drove him mad

It might hurt your middle
the way you hold your fiddle

Many a tongue will blurt
words that can hurt

No better way to blurt
out things that hurt

Nothing can hurt you
if you have no vice or virtue

People can hurt you
if you have too much virtue

Trials and tribs
can hurt your ribs

When pinpricks begin to hurt
its time to kick dirt

Hurts

The mason works on the stone
till it hurts in his bone

Husband

The husband can tell
when all is well

Hush

They went into a hush
and talked of gold rush

Hype

She is not the type
who will fall for the hype

Hype

Too much hype
cause of gripe

Hyperbole

He ran up to bowl
and bowled a hyperbole

Hypocrisy

*He keeps himself busy
fashioning hypocrisy*

*How to see
through hypocrisy*

*Hypocrisy has a place
in many a persons face*

*Hypocrisy is a job
for the full time snob*

Hypothetical

*Is it ethical
or hypothetical*

I

Ice

> Every sheet of ice
> though slippery looks nice

Iceberg

> Like an iceberg on the fringe
> of gobbling ships in a binge

Icing

> Like icing on the cake
> snowflakes on the lake

Idea

> An idea needs a place
> to make it's own case

Ideals

> Some Ideals will work
> however deep they lurk

Ideas

> Ideas are possible
> when hatched by the responsible

> Ideas cannot at will
> be lured with a pill

> Ideas cannot fail
> unless they set sail

> Ideas he chose
> were more than grandiose

> Ideas make it plain
> that in them there is much to gain

> Ideas that are soft
> can't keep you aloft

> Ideas that glow
> with thoughts in full flow

> Ideas that take root
> must bear the best fruit

> Ideas that were hatched
> could never be matched

Idiotic

> Is it idiotic
> to be idiomatic

Idle

> Don't let him be idle
> put on him the bridle

Idle chatter
makes us feel better

Idling

Idling along
she hums her song

Idly

He stuffed himself on idly
so he wouldn't become tiddly

Ignited

A mind once ignited
cannot be quieted

Once he was knighted
he was ignited

Ignorance

If ignorance is this
I will forever stick to bliss

Ignorance and pride
seem to have nothing to hide

Ignorance has a hitch
when it reaches high pitch

Ignorance I fear
more than what is clear

Ignorance is best
put to the test

Ignorance is his
who cannot find bliss

Ignorance is his
who ignores loves' bliss

Ignorance is his
who is overcome by bliss

Ignorance makes sense
only if you confess

Ignorance of the law
mustn't be considered a flaw

Ignorance's of the past
must be rid very fast

Ignorant

Many a gem has been thrown
by the ignorant and unknown

Ignore

Just ignore the glance
when you don't seek romance

Ignoring

So many of us act
ignoring all tact

Ill

When the ill wind blows
protect your nose

Illness

His illness was here to stay
so she lamented all day

Illness and pills
as old as the hills

Illness needs a nurse
without her, death is a curse

Illnesses

> Illnesses they came
> each of a different name

Illusion

> Am I just an illusion
> of the gods in collusion

> Go beyond the illusions
> and look for solutions

> How will they fare
> these illusions everywhere

> Illusions get a chance
> in a world of romance

> Illusions shattered
> just when they mattered

> Life's illusions
> are just collusions

> So many illusions
> that were all delusions

> Some of our illusions
> are planetary collusions

Imagery

> Imagery is a kind
> of memory of the mind

Images

> Images such as this
> must be the face of bliss

Imagination

> How to ration
> imagination

> Imagination has reaches
> far into the outreaches

> Imagination is kind
> it leaves truth behind

> Imagination must be fed
> until we are dead

> Imagination runs wild
> in the eyes of a child

> Imagination takes to wings
> while the heart it softly sings

> Is there a lotion
> for imagination

> Not enough potion
> in imagination

> Of all things mystic
> imagination is cryptic

> Imaginations wild
> in the heart of a child

> Inside the head and beyonder
> where imaginations they ponder

Immature

> How to find a cure
> for the immature

> Immature for sure
> but where is the cure

> Is there a cure
> for the immature

There is no cure
for the immature

Immense
From the sound more than the sense
the joy it is immense

When sound meets sense
the effect is immense

Immortal
Heaven is the only portal
where we become immortal

Mother earth in her immortal frame
watching her children play the game

Immortality
Immortality
is mere frivolity

Impatiently
Impatiently they bear
for the timely affair

Impending
No way to impede
the impending stampede

Imperfect
Doing things that are not
we are an imperfect lot

Imperfection
Learn to ration
Imperfection

Imperfections
She never mentions
his imperfections

Imperious
His imperious touch
amounted to much

Implication
Has its implication
trace of complication

Implicit
Though implicit
the meaning is explicit

Implied
Must be untied
what is being implied

Impositions
Let them not be impositions
while we both have our positions

Impossible
Impossible it is said
a haircut without a head

Not possible to be
the impossible me

What is impossible it seems
can be conquered by teams

Imposters
Imposters have a name
though they look the same

Impression
> Create an impression
> with a good expression

> Impressions about the wig
> for a head that is too big

Improbable
> Can it be noble
> the improbable

Improper
> Nothing could stop her
> from doing things improper

Impropriety
> Impropriety
> not for the piety

Improve
> Improve your grunt
> if you have big game to hunt

> Improve your skills
> by popping pills

> Improve your smarts
> by adding up the parts

> To improve ties
> he laid his eyes

> Improves the ride
> with mirth on your side

Impulse
> They became quick of pulse
> on their very first impulse

Impulsive
> How they react
> to an impulsive act

Impulsiveness
> Impulsiveness is a part
> of the dealings of the heart

Incense
> Burning incense
> to the nostrils makes sense

Incessant
> Incessant rains
> they flooded the plains

Inches
> It's all in the inches
> when it pinches

> The shoe it pinches
> by the smallest of inches

Income
> To have good outcome
> stay within income

Incompetence
> Incompetence rules
> the country of fools

> Where incompetence rules
> we all become fools

Incomplete
> Incomplete task
> how to unmask

Incompetence
> Incompetence can
> ruin a nice man

Inconvenient
> Though inconvenient
> be subservient

Incorruptible
> Incorruptible by far
> those in power

Increase
> Why should I be younger
> it will only increase my hunger

Increased
> It increased their chance
> every embracing dance

Increases
> He increases his shame
> who plays a dirty game

Indecision
> Even indecision
> was made with precision

Indelible
> Indelible mark
> of the post mark

Indelible
> Indelible stamp
> of the lady and the lamp
>
> Indelible stamp
> of the lady with the lamp

Independent
> When will it spill
> this independent will

Indifferent
> An indifferent waltz
> caused by salts
>
> His indifferent air
> he was too willing to share

Indiscreet
> They were indiscreet
> as they walked down the street

Indiscretions
> They happen in sessions
> Indiscretions

Individual
> The common good
> is the individual food

Induct
> How to induct
> people into good conduct

Indulge
> Don't indulge in whining
> when you are dining
>
> How to indulge
> in battle of the bulge

Indulgent
> Indulgent and idle
> holding on to the bridle

Ineptitude
> Ineptitude
> from many a dude

Inevitable
> I wouldn't have been able
> if it wasn't inevitable

Infantile
> Infantile ethics
> are our only relics

Infatuation
> Infatuation has shades
> until finally it fades

Infective
> A person is infective
> who is deliberately fictive

Infested
> Shark infested shallows
> was no place for swallows

Infidelity
> Infidelity does its rounds
> where opportunity it abounds

> Infidelity
> can lead to sterility

Infinity
> Infinity is
> a state of bliss

Inflation
> Inflation rate
> is in spate

Information
> Inside information
> is it confirmation

Ingratitude
> A friends ingratitude
> increased his fortitude

> Don't lose your fortitude
> when faced with ingratitude

Inherit
> If you inherit a big purse
> consider it a curse

Inheritance
> Inheritance is a means
> of propagating genes

> Many an inheritance is free
> so go barking up a tree

> What is there to gain
> from the inheritance of pain

Inhibition
> Inhibition though strong
> can occasionally go wrong

> Lose inhibitions
> to brand new visions

> No inhibitions
> for global ambitions

Inhumanity
> Inhumanity can
> be inherited by man

Initial
>Nothing left to plunder
>after initial blunder

Injury
>Injury prone
>he was this drone

Injustice
>Injustice hurled
>at peoples of the world

>Injustice says the friend
>is death in the end

>Injustices of our time
>to tolerate is not fine

Ink
>Ink and quill
>to make me tranquill

Innocence
>Innocence once torn
>never again born

Innocent
>Bees that devour
>every innocent flower

>Innocent pastime
>that doesn't cost a dime

>Innocent until proven
>so said the raven

>The innocents will trust
>like the grown ups must

Insane
>For man to have a mane
>is in no way insane

Insanity
>Insanity plea
>of the biting flea

Insecure
>How to find a cure
>for love so insecure

>Nuggets that cure
>the insecure

>There is no cure
>for the insecure

Insensitive
>The insensitive word
>is forever heard

Insight
>He gets his insight
>on lonely dark nights

Inspired
>Whatever transpired
>must have been inspired

Instant
>Instant paradise
>where all things are nice

Instead
>Instead of bonding
>he is absconding

Instinct
*Make it extinct
your worst instinct*

*When the message isn't succinct
use your instinct*

Instinctual
*How to purge
this instinctual urge*

Insults
*Insults will live
long after we forgive*

Intact
*Come out intact
if you are caught in the act*

*Head intact
after eye contact*

Integrity
*Oh the nitty gritty
of integrity*

Intellectual
*Is he really clever
the intellectual forever*

Intemperance
*Intemperance makes sense
as a death sentence*

Intemperate
*Intemperate action
does it need traction*

*Intemperate remarks
about people in the parks*

Intense
*When the sound makes sense
the joy is intense*

Intensity
*No intensity
will not provoke pity*

Intentions
*Good intentions
cloaked in pretensions*

*Good intentions
end up as contentions*

*Intentions feed
relentless greed*

*Intentions good
like spicy food*

*Once ensnared
intentions bared*

*Showers that fade fast
had no intentions to last*

*When intentions
become contentions*

Interact
*Use tact
to interact*

Interest
*Didn't interest the lasses
boy with the pebble glasses*

*Once your interest is vested
you don't like it to be tested*

*Put it to rest
your short term interest*

Interesting
*Interesting times
when dimes are called dimes*

Interference
*Interference is swell
if it helps you do well*

Interpret
*Incomprehensible and vast
how to interpret the past*

Interpreter
*I need to learn better
how to be interpreter*

Interrupts
*The bottle when I see
she interrupts always me*

Intervention
*Divine intervention
never gets a mention*

Intimacy
*Intimacy is heard
best through the word*

*The intimacy with words
not given to the birds*

Intimate
*Intimate things aren't spoken
not even in jest or token*

Intoxicated
*He is intoxicated
and oxygenated*

Introduction
*After a brief introduction
they had the induction*

Introspection
*Introspection means
sticking to beans*

Invade
*Don't invade
my privacy in the shade*

Invented
*Lies are invented
they then get cemented*

Invention
*Against all contention
this game called invention*

*Social conventions
are whose inventions*

Investments
*His voice would choke
when investments went broke*

Invincibility

> Invincibility
> is about ability

Invisible

> The invisible quest
> must be cleverly dressed

Invitation

> Formal invitation
> came with trepidation

> Invitation needs no battery
> but it ends up as flattery

> Invitation to gripe
> eating fruit that isn't ripe

> No invitation
> start of palpitation

Invite

> If you go forth and back
> you will invite flak

> You will invite mockery
> if you don't have crockery

> My eyes they were invited
> to her smile that was requited

Inviting

> All this infighting
> much too inviting

> Good writing
> very inviting

> He makes his fine writing
> to read very inviting

> Reading, writing
> oh so inviting

Invoke

> Don't invoke their ire
> by simply shouting fire

> To stray from the path
> is to invoke wrath

Invulnerable

> Season after season
> he is invulnerable to reason

Irate

> Don't be irate
> if they seal your fate

Ire

> He can walk through fire
> and anyones ire

Ironical

> If it isn't comical
> it isn't ironical

Ironist

> He says things with a twist
> the ironist

Irony

> Can't you see
> the irony

> Irony must suffer
> at the hands of metaphor

> Irony will be dead
> if poetry isn't fed

Irrational
> *Irrational fears*
> *make us drink beers*

Irregularity
> *Irregularity*
> *cannot bring parity*

Irresistible
> *Her irresistible charm*
> *keeps me all day warm*

Irreverent
> *How to train*
> *this irreverent brain*

Island
> *On an island marooned*
> *we both sat and crooned*

> *The islands must be seen*
> *in their best coat of green*

Itch
> *Went to a high pitch*
> *the unremitting itch*

J

Jealous

> Don't make me a part
> of your jealous heart

> How to tear you apart
> from my jealous heart

> Oh jealous eyes
> why so many spies

> Oh jealous heart
> can I appease you with a tart

> Oh jealous heart
> don't tear me apart

> Oh jealous heart
> how did you get the part

> She made it clear
> he has a jealous ear

Jealousy

> Jealousy and rage
> how to assuage

> Try and stay apart
> from jealousy of the heart

> With jealousy in his kit
> he didn't know where to sit

> Deep down in hell
> jealousy is alive and well

> How does it get a start
> the jealousy in the heart

> I am no sage
> I have jealousy and rage

> Jealousy by the quart
> to fill a jealous heart

> Jealousy gets a start
> in corners of the heart

> Jealousy must sit
> where the heart thinks it fit

> Love can be killed
> by jealousy that is spilled

> Must be snuffed out at birth
> before jealousy it gains girth

> Once set in motion
> jealousy becomes emotion

Rhyming English Couplets

Why did it start
jealousy in the heart

Jellyfish

If you have the means
live on jellyfish and beans

Jerks

Men with too many perks
end up becoming jerks

Jingles

Where do they hang their shingles
those who like jingles

Job

A job well done
can only be fun

Until the job is done
go get the next one

When she was being watched
the job at hand she botched

Joke

It is no joke
the dagger beneath the cloak

It is no joke
to be stripped of your cloak

It is no joke
when the toad begins to croak

It wasn't just a joke
that we all go up in smoke

Many a bloke
fell for the joke

The joke is on you
on that you can chew

They are not the kind of folk
who will laugh at your joke

An old frog he croaks
while feeding on his jokes

Jolly

Allow them their folly
if it makes them jolly

Allow them their folly
just to keep them jolly

How can I be jolly
without any lolly

Journey

A journey of pondering
without much wandering

A journey that takes awhile
can be shortened by a smile

Don't lose sleep
though the journey is steep

Journey without strife
gives meaning to life

Journey

My life's journey over
I sit and chew upon clover

*She came with me on a journey
and we both ended up in gurney*

*The journey was full of surprises
and occasional prizes*

*At journeys end
there still was a bend*

Joy

*Don't go and purge
joy from the scourge*

*Grew up to be a joy
the sweet little boy*

*He works with such joy
the shoe shine boy*

*How to spread joy
without single toy*

*If it brings you no joy
get rid of the toy*

*Joy beneath the gloom
must someday bloom*

*Joy to you while reading
as much as I had while writing*

*The joy is immense
if the sound makes sense*

*The joy of setting sail
ends up as a sting of the tail*

*There is so much joy
in trying to annoy*

*You don't have to be clever
to find joy forever*

Joys

*A sample of her joys
she dished out to the boys*

*For all those lost joys
that were broken like toys*

*Forever some will miss
the joys of eternal bliss*

*Said to me the sparrow
share your joys and sorrow*

*With shared joys
men become boys*

Judge

*If you judge them by their looks
what would happen to books*

*It took hours of schooling
for the judge to make a ruling*

*Judge yourself harshly
before you eat parsley*

Judged

*We are always being nudged
to where we are judged*

Judgement

*Good judgement is a cure
for past mistakes for sure*

*Judgement becomes strong
when perspectives are long*

*Judgement when it is good
is easily understood*

*The law changes its hue
when the judgement is due*

Judicial

*Judicial solution
without resolution*

Juice

*Put it to use
when you pump up the juice*

*You are no use
like an orange without juice*

Juices

*He has uses
for formenting juices*

July

*July will be soon
after May and June*

Jumper

*They all look plumper
in a wooleen jumper*

Jumping

*Words jumping the queue
to make sentences new*

Jumpstart

*Coffee it may
jumpstart your day*

Juncture

*At this precise juncture
I need a bowl full of tincture*

Jungles

*No room for bungles
in the teeming jungles*

Justice

*Justice awaits
him who waits*

*Justice grinds slowly
for the high and the lowly*

*Whether high or lowly
justice grinds slowly*

K

Kangaroo

>Pouch gives a clue
>to the baby Kangaroo

>With each forward leap
>Kangaroo takes time to sleep

Keen

>With her keen eye
>she caught him when he lie

Kept

>Suitors kept at bay
>waiting for their turn to say

Key

>Many things we cannot see
>because we cannot find the key

Kick

>The mule gets its kick
>with a hoof that it can flick

Kill

>Dressed to kill
>with money to spill

>Generosity can kill
>if you have money to spill

>He won't kill the viper
>if you pay the piper

>If you fix what ain't broke
>you will kill it in one stroke

>More than meets the eye
>things that kill you why

>Pop a pill
>before you go for the kill

>Summer without the showers
>would kill all the flowers

>They went nuclear at will
>they had roaches to kill

Killer

>Let it not turn mean
>the killer gene

Kills

>With well honed skills
>the lioness she kills

Kind

*Do I need to remind
you are one of the kind*

*He has the kind of middle
that can be described in a riddle*

*He is being kind
who says love is blind*

*He is one of a kind
to his flaws very blind*

*He was the animated kind
with an electric mind*

*He who can
be kind to beast and man*

*In every land
we need a kind hand*

*It suited her to be kind
to the dog that was blind*

*Minefields of a kind
in the corners of the mind*

*Please be kind
to the wanderings of the mind*

*There is a kind of knowing
that makes love mind blowing*

*Towards her he felt kind
after an all too rested mind*

*Unwavering kind
the wayward mind*

*What kind of blinds
are these closed minds*

*What kind of bliss is this
that needs to be sealed with a kiss*

*What kind of this shop
that doesn't sell lollipop*

*Who has a silly mind
is a weak kind*

*You must be blind
if you think the ocean is kind*

Kinder

*He couldn't have been kinder
as he walked behind her*

Kindness

*He has the kindness of a clam
and the wildness of a ram*

*Kill them with kindness
till they complain of blindness*

*Kindness has a way
of keeping blindness at bay*

*Kindness stays
once you mend your ways*

*The world is full of blindness
especially towards kindness*

*When you consider his kindness
make sure it isn't blindness*

Kinds

*All kinds of doom
from the womb to the tomb*

*How to wear leather
in all kinds of weather*

King

*Can the pauper ever sing
better than his king*

*Head to toe he is king
except for a broken wing*

*The fish they don't sing
where the kingfisher is king*

*The penguin is king
where the albatrosses sing*

Kingdom

*Let us sit in the kingdom
where whiskey is the wisdom*

*There is a kingdom where rubies
are given away as freebies*

*There once was a sleepy kingdom
where everyone had their freedom*

Kingfisher

*If you need a well wisher
hire a kingfisher*

Kings

*Cabbages are things
fit only for the kings*

*Kings in palaces
willing to trade places*

Kiss

*A bolder statement than this
can be made with just a kiss*

*Don't involve kiss
in the pursuit of bliss*

*Gallantly he would kiss
all except cobras that hiss*

*No greater joy than this
than to forgive her with a kiss*

*The absence of bliss
can be remedied with a kiss*

*The cobra will hiss
waiting to kiss*

*To improve upon her kiss
she whispered the word bliss*

*Under the starlight they kiss
on a night such as this*

Knees

*Fleas have knees
and so do bees*

Knight

*Where was the knight
when the dark horse came to light*

Knighted

*For him to have been knighted
the queen was probably short sighted*

Knock

*The knock inside the shell
told us the chick is well*

Adam and Eve had a plot
to tie us up in a knot

It takes a lot
to cut through the knot

We are all in this knot
from Adam and eve's plot

Knots

Tied up in knots
from love that is lots

Know

Do the polar bears know
when it will snow

Doesn't know where to go
he who isn't in the know

Everywhere I go
I meet someone I know

If you tell all you know
where will you go for more

Once you are in the know
just don't let it go

Knowing

Let's keep going
but not without knowing

They just keep going
who are all knowing

Though he is all knowing
he doesn't know where he is going

Knowledge

Action will bear fruit
with knowledge at its root

Dams were built by the beaver
who has knowledge of the river

If knowledge is this
why is ignorance bliss

Knowledge fills these pages
collected over the ages

Knowledge has no limit
once the lamp has been lit

Knowledge is a fire
fuelled by desire

Knowledge knows no bounds
if you know where it abounds

Knowledge needs learning
to improve your earning

Knowledge once stored
cannot be ignored

Knowledge put to use
will slowly diffuse

There is no college
that teaches self knowledge

When knowledge flows like a river
the spine it feels the shiver

K

L

Labour
>Fruits of your labour
>for others to savour

>Too much labour
>to rattle your saber

Lace
>Don't wear your lace
>when you go to that place

>She sat there making lace
>at the fire place

Lacking
>Not lacking in bite
>when being impolite

Laid
>Once we are laid to rest
>can never be somebodys guest

Lake
>A fish with no lake
>is like an Eden without a snake

>In every lake I wish
>there is a single fish

Lame
>Even the lame duck
>shows a little pluck

>He is stuck
>being called lame duck

Lament
>Soon he will lament
>who created a ferment

Land
>Land without trees
>attracts no bees

Landscape
>Landscape in the main
>was beautiful terrain

Language
>He doesn't need toddy
>whose language is shoddy

>His language is crisp
>mustache just a wisp

>How to decipher
>the language of the viper

If Language becomes your master
you will lose your friends faster

Language cannot be glorified
unless by experience fortified

Language has links
to how we thinks

Language has meaning
that can be demeaning

Language is nice
as a reporting device

Language it slips
through mothers lips

Language must have its verve
to negotiate the curve

Language of the apes
takes many shapes

Language of the heart
where does it start

Language of the mind
can be cruel or kind

Language of the soul
is what makes music whole

Some they handle language
as if it were baggage

Their language is simple
but the message is ample

There is language in this page
befitting a sage

Last

Aspersions when you cast
have a tendency to last

He who is the last man
cannot do what adam can

He will not last
who tries to change the past

How can it last
if you fall into it fast

One last time
if it isn't a crime

The shoemaker went on a fast
because his shoes they didn't last

Things have been said better
down to the last letter

Lasting

To write things that are lasting
do it while fasting

Late

Can't be late
have to fill the slate

Don't be late
for your appointment with fate

Don't be late
in finding a suitable mate

How to fix your state
if you get up late

I came upon it late
this exalted state

L

*If you come late
I will decapitate*

*It was too late to call
when the sword was ready to fall*

*Never be late
for a dinner date*

*Never too late
to redeem your fate*

*Somethings of late
were written into fate*

*There is a road sign to the gate
so don't be too late*

*There was a locked gate
and the hour was late*

*Too late to be jolly
once he found his folly*

*Was an exalted state
though it came late*

*We were stopped at the gate
by a minute we were late*

Lately

*What have you done lately
that makes you look stately*

Latent

*Ceases to be latent
once it is blatant*

*Latent in some fellows
bile that is all yellow*

*Do anything but scoff
to get a laugh*

*Don't scoff
just laugh it off*

*Enough laugh lines
that shored up good times*

Laughter

*Laughter as such
doesn't say too much*

*Laughter followed the gloom
and love began to bloom*

*Laughter on the whole
good for the soul*

*Laughter will sit
on the men of wit*

*Who generates much laughter
is most sought after*

Lavish

*Lavish feasts
not without beasts*

Lavishness

*Lavishness was due
to the fortunate few*

Law

*A law once broken
has loudly spoken*

*Change the law
that is laden with flaw*

*Doesn't much it take
for a law just to break*

*In each and every land
the law lends a helping hand*

*Many have faltered
trying to get a law altered*

*No such thing called bungle
in the law of the jungle*

*The helping hand of the law
must act without a flaw*

*The law must not choose
what is beyond its ordinary use*

*Bad laws must be broken
not just as token*

*How improperly they sit
laws that don't fit*

*Laws that are nice
are never used twice*

*Many laws in use
potential for abuse*

*Tiger with sharp claws
need not obey laws*

*We appear like flaws
to a life governed by laws*

Lawsuits

*Lawsuits bear fruits
in the form of loots*

Lay

*Rather bland
the lay of the land*

Laying

*It's like laying an egg
standing on one leg*

Lays

*A hen lays her egg
without us having to beg*

*The chicken lays her egg
without us having to beg*

Lazier

*Man finds it easier
to become a little lazier*

Lazy

*Can they be called lazy
people who take it easy*

Lead

*What we say goes
we lead them by the nose*

Leader

*Each man has a plan
to be leader of the clan*

*Leader of the pack
leads the attack*

*Why are they baiting
the leader in waiting*

Leaf

>Can't be fig
>if the leaf is big

League

>I have a colleague
>in each and every league

>When it came to intrigue
>he was in a different league

Leaguer

>Can't be a meagre
>and a big leaguer

Leak

>When the bottle began to leak
>messages they began to speak

Leaks

>Can make you think
>a pen that leaks ink

Lean

>He was lean
>mean and scalene

Leaning

>He has a leaning
>for words without meaning

>Must have a leaning
>to coax out the meaning

>The way she was leaning
>he got the meaning

>I have leanings
>for cheese and wine evenings

Leap

>After a quantum leap
>he fell in a heap

>All in one leap
>the leopard grabbed the sheep

Learn

>Each of us in turn
>have lessons to learn

>I have yet to learn
>about ending up in the urn

>Learn how to stop
>once you reach the top

>Learn how to treasure
>love in good measure

>Learn to be tranquil
>without use of the pill

>Learn to deal with chaffe
>once you make a gaffe

>Learn to face the storm
>wherever you are from

Learn

>Learn to grapple
>with the bad apple

>Learn to inspect
>what you expect

>Learn to open doors
>on all fours

*Learn to ration
an interrogation*

*Learn to react
to both fancy and fact*

*Learn to repair
a life of despair*

*Learn to ride
both time and tide*

*Learn to sample
many an example*

*Learn to say enough
whatever is the stuff*

*Learn to take stock
when you are in shock*

*Learn to trust
first you must*

*Learn to understand
each and every brand*

*Once you learn to spell
you will never be a frog in the well*

*To learn about a cat
must listen to the rat*

*To learn is to grow
the mind from being slow*

Learned

*A lesson never learned
had him all burned*

*He learned to bowl a googly
on the banks of the hoogly*

*It's not hard to tell
he learned his lesson well*

Learning

*A little bit of yearning
needed for all learning*

*Is it a sign of learning
the feet when they are burning*

*There is no turning
away from learning*

*Things that foster learning
must be based on yearning*

*We must often go returning
to the basics and learning*

Learns

*He learns to despise
who thinks he is wise*

Leave

*Adam and eve
they had apples to leave*

*If you leave out the chaff
you have nothing but gaffe*

*Just leave it to them
to write with their pen*

*Leave me alone
I am muscle and bone*

*Leave me alone
I want to be a clone*

Leave me alone
said the bee to the drone

The leaves they wither and fall
from trees both short and tall

The leaves were green
where the parrots have been

Left

If what you say is true
there is nothing left to rue

Nothing left to rave
once beyond the grave

Legal

Everything is legal
as long as it is frugal

Legally

People need reminding
that it is legally binding

Legend

Don't offend
the living legend

Legend

The seeds were sown
where his legend had grown

The sea will keep
its legends of the deep

Leisure

Palaces of leisure
caters to their pleasure

To wipe out your leisure
drink many a measure

Travel and leisure
without a single seizure

With eyes that leisure will see
sipping and tasting green tea

Lend

Don't ever lend
money to a friend

Ears we must lend
to the words of a friend

Less

More or less
for you to guess

The things she does and says
doesn't make it less

Lessen

Lessen your load by sharing
it with someone who is caring

Lesson

Fingers burned
lessons learned

Lessons that are taught
are forget me not

Letter

A letter I found on the street
about two hearts tangled all neat

As a man of the letter
he seems to be getting better

He came upon good fetter
when he read her letter

Letter writing is an art
to penetrate the heart

She dabbed a bit of scent
on the letter before it was sent

She wrote him a letter
she found someone better

Liable

Liable to get hung
who speak with a different tongue

Liar

Got to be a liar
to write good satire

Liberty

Liberty of thought
can be a ruinous plot

License

License to thrill
with paper and quill

Lie

A lie for a lie
can kill someone why

A lie has it's abode
on the back of the toad

A lie has ties
to more than the flies

Cheating eyes why
they say they never lie

Easy to lie
but they don't know why

He cannot lie still
who is worthy of his skill

He dispenses a lie
and slowly lets it die

He spilled each lie
with a one shut eye

How to see a lie
without blinking an eye

Knowing it is a lie
is to watch them deny

Nothing but a lie
can infect a fly

Oh to lie still
in fields of daffodil

Someday I will
finally lie still

They don't lie still
who live in notting hill

Lied

He was never tongue tied
whenever he lied

I could have lied
that I wasn't mortified

Lies

A series of lies
have family ties

He was caught with lies
like a fish with flies

His family he ties
with a rope full of lies

How much we matter
lies all in the chatter

Lies and bluff
are his usual stuff

Lies will bear fruit
be economical with the truth

Lies will slip
into every gossip

Not for others to see
what lies within me

On lies it will feed
many a misdeed

Reluctance lies
in her half closed eyes

The answer lies
between the lines

They caught on to his lies
not once but twice

Uneasy lies the head
whose mouth hasn't been fed

Life

A life driven by need
gains momentum and speed

A life full of joy
without a single toy

A life long learning
the ecstasy of yearning

A life that is wasted
was hardly ever tasted

A life without risk
can protect your disc

A life without words
we would be like the birds

A sense of belonging
all life longing

A well settled life
free of strife

Across the span of my life
commas and stops made it nice

All guts and glory
his whole life story

All I wish to do
is spend my life with you

All in this life
the man said to his wife

All life is sacred
both feathered and naked

All life long
their love was strong

All life we keep guessing
what in our life is missing

All my life I lay brick
in the meantime I miss a trick

All shapes and sizes
they come life's prizes

Barks many a toad
at life along the road

Bread butter and knife
is all we need in life

Decadent life
breeds no strife

Denied by the storm
was a life of calm

Do all the things you can
while there is life in your man

Don't covet your neighbours life
it may be filled with strife

Each generation has strife
based on the new facets of life

Ease your strife
celebrate life

Episodes from our life
stick out like knife

Every grain of rice
adds spice to your life

Every moment of life
Filled with love and strife

Every square foot less
made my life a mess

Full of poor taste
his life it was a waste

Half my life is over
and I haven't even reached Dover

Have I wasted my life
or is it just the strife

He could ease away his strife
by the lifestyle in his life

He lived a genteel life
used a fork without a knife

He that takes a life
need not be with knife

He who is pensive
can make life expensive

He who stops trying
will spend his life crying

His life he laid
after he got paid

How can pox be small
that takes your life and all

How to handle strife
in the orchestra of life

L

*If life comes a bit late
meet it halfway at the gate*

*If life were only this
what is it we miss*

*In life he choosed
to stay always amused*

*In life it pays
to mend your ways*

*In life we make choices
based on inner voices*

*In life you will be meeting
many things that are fleeting*

*In order to better your life
be good to your wife*

*In spite of being a yawn
life goes on*

*In the affairs of life
be as sharp as a knife*

*In this little spring called life
so much dullness without a wife*

*Inner life
under the knife*

*Is it worth living
a life without loving*

*It's how you look at strife
that defines the quality of life*

*Life becomes a bore
when modesty is no more*

*Life becomes easy it seems
once you refine your dreams*

*Life beyond the grave
is there need to shave*

*Life can be boring
if you don't sleep snoring*

*Life ends with a groan
for both man and the drone*

*Life from the source
is on a collision course*

*Life gets a sheen
once love is seen*

*Life goes on
for man and swan*

*Life has not been shortened
by whatever that has happened*

*Life however brief
experiences a touch of grief*

*Life in the navy
not all gravy*

*Life is a bed of feathers
for all the loving mothers*

*Life is a bit bland
with no one to hold my hand*

*Life is a bubble
that portends trouble*

*Life is a bumpy ride
if you have things to hide*

Life is a daily grind
from which we must unwind

Life is a gift
give it a lift

Life is a part
of love and the heart

Life is a riddle
with men in the middle

Life is a waste
with no fragrances to taste

Life is about bobs
sniffles and sobs

Life is about risk
ignoring your disc

Life is about traffic
and a love that defies logic

Life is completely wasted
that isn't fully tasted

Life is for living
and for forgiving

Life is full of snares
in addition to all the cares

Life is full of swindles
as the money dwindles

Life is in the main
about controlling the brain

Life is in the main
about getting on the train

Life is just a glance
without a second chance

Life is just a ride
by airplanes on the side

Life is lived in fear
that death may anytime be near

Life is lived in the head
so it is usually said

Life is meant
for contentment

Life is meant
with love to be spent

Life is never bland
full of a friendly hand

Life is never whole
for the tormented soul

Life is on a lease
death will bring release

Life is short it seems
for those who live off their dreams

Life it seems
dull without dreams

Life it teems
with inherited genes

Life lived in grace
at a slow steady pace

Life lived just for fasting
can be self defeating

Life long penance
is a repentance

Life needs lengthening
love needs strengthening

Life not tasted
is time wasted

Life of action
is the main attraction

Life of stagnation
no explanation

Life was so absurd
he changed into a bird

Life we must face
with a new state of grace

Life will be never
as good as ever

Life will become fonder
for death it will last longer

Life will lose its wonder
if god holds back the thunder

Life will taste like honey
make friendship with money

Life without spice
for men with no vice

Life would be bland
no one to hold your hand

Like a runaway train
life is in the main

Live a life of brave
don't wait for the grave

Long life span
for the diehard fan

Long life span
for the honest man

Luxury is a master
of making life softer

Make your amends
before your life it ends

Many a life is led
by feeding off what was said

Many a life it has stole
the malignant mole

Many things in life
put to the less than sterile knife

Movies are rarely made
of a life in the shade

My back is bent
from a life well spent

My life I must bend
towards a new end

My life took a turn
for her when I yearn

My life without you
is a feeling quite new

No need for enunciation
about a life of renunciation

No walk of life
without grief or strife

Not without strife
many a persons life

Not without strife
the lotus eaters life

Oh gentle life
why this mantle of strife

Once he caught her fancy
his life became chancy

Once you are attached to life
face up to joy and strife

One life to the next
we must change the text

Parts of life are rough
without too much stuff

Relishing life
smoking pipe

She came into my life
without becoming wife

She changed my life
who was not my wife

She eased all my strife
and brought meaning to life

So many years are wasted
without life it being tasted

So much of life
devoted to strife

Some will make it their sport
to spend their life in court

Somewhere he lost his way
life it made him pay

Spend your life giving
to make it a good living

Sun and sand
where life is grand

The life of a spider
is to spread his web–wider

The life saved is a fact
by a single act

The life that we know
is all shimmer and glow

The meaning of my life
without her would be strife

The ocean and its swell
many a life it can quell

The purpose of life
is to chase away strife

The thing that changed my life
was the constant strife

The things we miss in life
mostly the cause of strife

Their life was a portrayal
of loves betrayal

There are people in our life
who see us through strife

They fill you with strife
the people in my life

———

Those who go on forgiving
find life worth living

———

To survive you must be strong
for life can be very long

———

To the relief of all my strife
she came into my life

———

Try and live life
like a neighbours wife

———

Try to part with strife
in all facets of life

———

We both bumped into life
and forgot our strife

———

We spend our life seeking
love that is worth repeating

———

What do they know of life
if they haven't faced any strife

———

What you get out of life
it takes back as strife

———

When I am in her company
life is one big symphony

———

When life becomes bland
go play in the sand

———

When my life is all done
I leave behind a loved one

———

Where is it leaning
this life without meaning

———

Why look for another you
when daily our life is new

———

Without a true calling
life would be appalling

———

Without the sweet life
it is all about strife

———

Without you in my life
sharpening a knife

———

Years of active life
without a hint of strife

———

You give them a knife
they will take your life

———

Your life could become maybe
if you touch tar baby

———

Your personal life
can't go under the knife

———

Every day I try to reach her
my life's greatest teacher

———

Life's joys are felt
when properly dealt

———

Life's little blunder
pirates and plunder

———

Life's little jolts
from loose nuts and bolts

———

Life's little things
have the biggest wings

———

Life's ups and downs
add to the frowns

———

Make it a duty
to unearth life's beauty

Many of life's sproutings
tinged with some doubtings

Newspapers they rattle
with life's every battle

Lifelong

A lifelong of help
from a single false step

Lifelong he will brood
for having said something rude

Lifelong I savour
her every favour

Lifelong it stays
your careless ways

Lifelong we dread
of the things that were not said

Lifelong we keep waiting
while death it keeps baiting

Too long in the end
the lifelong friend

Lifespan

Gold he must pan
in one lifespan

Lifestyle

To keep up your lifestyle
you need both cunning and guile

Lifetime

A lifetime it took
to learn to look

Lifting

Through the lifting fog to the winds
birds they flutter their wings

Light

By the light of the mid-night moon
they said lets get married soon

Don't let it thin
the light within

From day to the night
where there is little light

From the luminous light
into the depth of the night

How to know what's right
through the blinding light

In the clear light of day
she said you may

In the evening village light
two cocks made to fight

Light it will fill
the lighthouse on the hill

Like a beacon in the night
the lighthouse and its light

Like switching off the light
when it isn't yet night

She is my light
all through the night

She travels very light
as a flower it might

The evening light must probe
her resplendent robe

The radiant light
of fireflies in flight

To light is my desire
of my own funeral pyre

When the air is light
thoughts of love in flight

Who should provide the light
said the sun to the night

You are the light on my coast
who feeds me with toast

Your chance to get him
where the light is dim

Lighthouse

The lighthouse on the hill
makes the ship stand still

The lighthouses crumble
to the ocean and its rumble

Lightning

He was lightning quick
when he caught the nick

Lightning and thunder
a child's first wonder

Like

Like the cold in the fridge
the winds over the bridge

She is a wife and mother
like no other

Limit

Is there a limit
for the abandoned spirit

We are both in it
without so much as limit

Every five minutes
he would reach his limits

If you drink beyond your limits
it won't lift your spirits

Linguistic

Say things upside down
with a linguistic frown

Link

There is a vital link in the chain
of the paddy to the grain

Lions

Lions have claws
which make the jungles laws

What is the hen
doing in the lions den

Lipped

The wings once clipped
made them tight lipped

Liquor
>He seems to get slicker
>when he sees a bottle of liquor

>Let me drown in liquor
>till the last flame it flicker

List
>Make a list
>before the tryst

Listen
>Better to listen to symphony
>in mixed company

>Tea leaves in the summer
>as I listen to the drummer

>To listen be ready
>her sweet melody

Listened
>Inside the barn
>she listened to his yarn

Literature
>Literature will die
>from too critical an eye

Little
>As such
>little is much

>Her every little ailment
>fills me over with torment

>Little girl fills
>her vase with daffodils

>Very little lull
>from the seagull

Live
>Can't judge the outcome
>if you live beyond your income

>Don't be afraid to live
>we all have something to give

>He is slippery as moss
>and can live through the loss

>He who is afraid to live
>has only one life to give

>Her will it was strong
>to live very long

>How can we live long
>while the body withers along

>How easy it seems
>to live above your means

>How to live apart
>with such a heavy heart

>How to live with rabbits
>and still keep your habits

>I wish I could live on a star
>where there is no war

>Just ask the knave
>how to live in a cave

>Live music is living
>and totally unforgiving

Make it clear
I will not live in fear

Not hard to believe
we all want to live

Once you live on the cheap
pennies will become a heap

Somethings got to give
if you have long enough to live

The longer you live
the less you have to give

The longer you live
you have less to give

There is nothing left for me
but to live up in the tree

They live and die as men
who once lived in a den

They live in grace
at their own pace

To live a daily lie
is to question daily why

To live well for a day
kneel down and pray

To live well for a week
be silent and don't speak

To live well for a year
have good cheer

We live in groups
and sip on soups

What use is it to live
for I have nothing else to give

Words to live by
till the day we die

Lived

He lived in a hut
the total coconut

His life he lived hotch –potch
with his daily dose of scotch

Once there lived a toad
in the middle of the road

There lived a little skunk
on an old tree trunk

Liver

The fingers they quiver
from a failing liver

Was it my liver
that caused all the quiver

Lives

He that lives on toast
has not much to boast

Husbands and wives
leading separate lives

In both town and county
he lives off his bounty

Like bees in their hives
moments in our lives

Of fish he is fond
who lives in a pond

Parallel lives
of husbands and wives

Poetry lives on
long after I am gone

She lives in every page
with a sparkling image

So many lives wasted
without victory being tasted

Sunset of our lives
we must dedicate to our wives

When their lives needed some wattage
they went to the cottage

Living

Even when you make a living
lace it with a bit of loving

He made a living
by being unforgiving

I've had my share of living
and mistakes that needed forgiving

If you blink before giving
how to make a living

Living

No end to giving
if life is worth living

There is no living
without a bit of giving

Small things and nothings
also make livings

Lizard

Yet to see a lizard
born without a gizzard

Loan

Loan shark barks
at dogs in parks

Lock

Lock it up in a vault
every single fault

Logic

All sense to logic
is lost when I see magic

If it has any logic
it can't be magic

There is no logic
to re-capture the magic

Trying to create magic
beyond all logic

Why is there no logic
for things that have magic

Loneliness

Nothing like onlyness
to breed loneliness

Lonely

All alone hurled
into a lonely world

L

*For you and you only
I write when I am lonely*

*How lonely one can be
without being carefree*

*On his back was the lonely hunter
when the horse he began his canter*

*Standing room only
will make you very lonely*

Lonesome

*Lonesome in the night
how did I reach this plight*

*Take red eye flight
if you are lonesome tonight*

*The lonesome they strum
to the music as they hum*

Longing

*Why does this longing
keep us both hanging*

Look

*All it took
was one last look*

Look

*Don't look at the mirror
hoping to find your liver*

*Don't look in the mirror
if you are looking for your liver*

*Faraway in the arctic
don't look for the attic*

*His lean and hungry look
makes her want to cook*

*Many it seem
look for esteem*

*See things in a new way
look at grass and call it hay*

*The fish they don't look
at the bare hook*

*When I look thee in the eye
I see another guy*

*Hey good looking
what are you cooking*

*I made a trip to Goa
looking for a boa*

Looks

*A fox that is slick
looks for a lamb to lick*

*All looks yummy
for the empty tummy*

*Carpet beneath the feet
looks quite neat*

*Go by looks
when you choose your books*

*He was driven to her looks
but wouldn't give up his books*

*In the company of books
and her good looks*

*In the company of books
to improve my looks*

Loon

*Cannot catch a loon
with a harpoon*

Loopholes

*Loopholes have a hitch
when they miss a stitch*

Looseness

*Looseness of the tongue
can get you hung*

Loot

*How to loot
from the tree the fruit*

*How to loot
the high hanging fruit*

Loots

*Of all the brutes who wore suits
he was the one who loots*

Lord

*Said a lord to the lord
we were favoured by our god*

*Said the fish to the Lord
your behaviour is odd*

*Wasn't so at birth
became lord of the girth*

*A place to be at odds
is not the house of Lords*

Lose

*Not much more to lose
without you I am no use*

*The more you use it
the less you will lose it*

Loss

*Bring out the floss
to stop tooth loss*

*He is never at a loss
like a snake through the grass*

*He was at a loss
why he was cross*

Losses

*Pandering to the bosses
caused all the losses*

Lost

*He became a goner
when he lost his soft corner*

*He lost all his jolly
when he found his folly*

*He lost his treasures to the sea
in the hours of the morning wee*

*How much did it cost
what you have lost*

*Husband lost his voice
and had to give up his choice*

*The blue of the sky
is lost to the closed eye*

*The flying pig
lost his wig*

*The loan was lost in the end
so was my good friend*

*The shepherd bears the cost
of the sheep that was lost*

*What is the cost
of mornings that are lost*

*Where have your been
have you lost your sheen*

Lotion

*Give me that lotion
to ease this commotion*

*The soothing power of lotion
to ease all commotion*

Lotus

*The lotus has a stem
but more than that a gem*

Lotuses

*Lotuses are they fond
of the lillies in the pond*

Loud

*He rode away in a cloud
to hoofbeats very loud*

*He rode the dark cloud
to where the thunder was loud*

*The moon makes it loud
the silver lining of the cloud*

*Why does it have to be loud
when it speaks the cloud*

Love

*Interest sustained
love retained*

*A dislike of sorts
for love and its warts*

*A failing love must part
from desires of the heart*

*A heart that is haunted
by a love that is wanted*

*A life of love
is love of life*

*A love at once fractured
for want of being nurtured*

*A love once divided
cannot be avoided*

*A love once parted
consider it departed*

*A love short on kisses
falls short of blisses*

*A love story re-told
puts your heart on hold*

*A love without a name
is the way they played the game*

*A message was sent through the mynah
to my love in the border with china*

A new way of thinking
about love without blinking

A remembered love will last
though a shadow of the past

A tear so easily dries
when love gets in your eyes

Afraid of losing
the love of my choosing

Again an again
love is pain

All feelings drained
but love it remained

All happiness was riding
on love that came inviting

All I need is you
for love to renew

All is fair
in love affair

All love is moral
if you gift her a coral

All miracles lie still
unless love has the will

All my love I shower
to the beauty of this flower

All my love slowly drained
washed away when it rained

All said and done
love is a lot of fun

All shapes and sizes
love has its devices

All the way she sobbed
from love once robbed

All true to form
love ran into storm

All we need now
is work and love

All wrapped up in a tune
love in the month of June

Almost there
their love affair

Along the way
love will find a way

An early winter tryst
that love almost missed

An ill wind it blows
at love when it glows

Another time another place
love made its case

Answers do not question
why love is in detention

As long as you do
I love you too

As she stretched her way up
love it filled his cup

As such
I love you very much

L

As the evenings got longer
their love became stronger

As the waves hit the rocks
they made love talks

At a fast clip
love reached her lip

At their past love they scoff
once they call it off

Be a little wary
for love can be scary

Be the solute
in love absolute

Beat it away with a stick
love that is sick

Bee tries to devour
the love in the flower

Before her love it died
she was all starry eyed

Beginnings are a part
of love falling apart

Better be game
when love calls your name

Between two egrets
love and regrets

Blinking makes it go
when love is in full flow

By any other name
love it wouldn't be the same

By then it's too late
after love turns to hate

Can easily be spilled
love unfulfilled

Can love be found
on the rebound

Can make love tick
the candlestick

Can put them to sleep
love that is deep

Can't happen too soon
love in the afternoon

Can't see things clearly
when you love her dearly

Cannot last long
without love and a song

Coffee will blend
with love in the end

Comfort and love
like hand and glove

Coo said the dove
and be my love

Couples in love
like the cooing dove

Deep down to my bone
I love you and you alone

Deep inside
loves' big surprise

*Deep love is unspoken
not even as token*

*Depending on the weight
love it goes by freight*

*Difference in the end
by the love that you send*

*Dined and wined
love gets defined*

*Dinosaurs love to munch
other animals for lunch*

*Distance made it clear
that love for them was dear*

*Does it mean much
love as such*

*Does love play a part
in matters of the heart*

*Don't be a bore
when love comes ashore*

*Don't be aghast
love can dissipate fast*

*Don't be unkind
to whom love is blind*

*Don't belittle
love that is little*

*Don't fall asleep
when love it is deep*

*Don't fall behind
just make love blind*

*Don't get irate
if love turns to hate*

*Don't go lamenting
that you're love is not cementing*

*Don't go stalling
when love comes calling*

*Don't hold back
the love attack*

*Don't leave me all hanging
to love we both belonging*

*Don't let it slip
your love relationship*

*Don't let love rust
before you hit the dust*

*Don't look for cure
when there is love to endure*

*Don't lose sleep
over love that you can't keep*

*Don't make it the ending
if your love it needs bending*

*Don't push and shove
just to welcome love*

*Don't push and shove
without depth in your love*

*Don't tear it apart
love when it makes a start*

*Each and every dove
has the company of love*

L

Each and every pair
must have love in repair

Each in its spate
both love and hate

Easy to remember
love in September

Easy to tell
when love life is well

Eden is in the East
where love is a feast

Element of surprise
when love was the prize

Encumbrances of love
are remembrances now

Endearing plight
love at first sight

Ended with a sob
love and its throb

Enriched beyond measure
love is a treasure

Eternal delight
of love in its flight

Even for the sage
love came of age

Even the fish they weep
when love is deep

Every flower must sit
where love finds it fit

Every sacrifice
for love is very nice

Every shepherd has his love
while the sheep they push and shove

Everywhere I go
love keeps its glow

Eye plays a part
in love from the start

Far away it stood
love promised as good

Fear is strong
that love can go wrong

Fender bender
love me tender

Find a new angle
for the love triangle

For each other when we pine
love it feels divine

For love he dies
and her Spanish eyes

For love I aspire
to fulfill a desire

For love to be blind
it takes a certain kind

For love to be generous
it must not be onerous

For love to cement
fulfillment is meant

Rhyming English Couplets

*For love to keep
bury it very deep*

*For love to take hold
writ in letters of gold*

*For things to get better
write a love letter*

*Forever and ever
our love needs a lever*

*Forever I will keep
love that comes in my sleep*

*Forever it was meant to be
love between you and me*

*Forever love will stay
even if you go away*

*Forever we must keep
love that is deep*

*Friends can tell
whose love is well*

*From season to season
love is the reason*

*From tears I refrain
though love is a pain*

*Furthest from my mind
that love for you is blind*

*Garlands are woven
to the love once proven*

*Get on with it now
how deep is your love*

*Give love a rest
to put it to the test*

*Give up all things gladly
for whom I love madly*

*God is a friend
of love in the end*

*Goes to the head quicker
both love and liquor*

*Good bye is a part
of love from the start*

*Grow up quick
there is love to pick*

*Half forgotten love
remembered quickly now*

*Handle all your love
with a sensuous glove*

*Hard to maintain
love like a fountain*

*Hardwired into the brain
our love will remain*

*Has it occurred to you then
that love letters need a pen*

*Has its own splendour
love for each gender*

*Hatred as such
is not about love as much*

*Have to keep them fanning
love thought and planning*

He bid farewell to charm
when his love it came to harm

He clings to the delusion
that love is an illusion

He fell in love with sleep
but how long would it keep

He felt a strong jitter
when love became bitter

He found it hard to face
love when it made its case

He lusteth not
in love to be caught

He must have been blind
when he left his love behind

He needs to be reminded
that to love he is blinded

He overheard her whisper
that their love was getting crisper

He ran away to gloom
when love failed to bloom

He sang her a love song
though he was mister wrong

He spoke with a certain halting
when love it came pole vaulting

He told her his mind
until her love it went blind

He turned every stone
for love alone

He was ever so gentle
when love was all mental

He was undismayed
by the love that strayed

He who dares to love
she drops instantly her glove

He who is a knave
makes love his slave

He who speaks in riddles
for him love it sizzles

Heartache it ends
if love pays dividends

Her beauty when faded
their love became jaded

Her love isn't beyond reach
if you gift her a peach

Her love it came unrelenting
and she said it needs cementing

Her love it made me wise
with love requited eyes

Her love she revealed
until then concealed

Her love was caught
in an undercurrent of thought

Her love was delayed
my heart it strayed

Her love was not slated
to be expiated

Rhyming English Couplets

Her message was very clear
that love would cost him dear

High above the skies
love in repose lies

High and the mighty
whose love is all flighty

His back he turned
to love once burned

His life he lived comically
and love life economically

His love and admiration
with her approbation

His love she became blonder
and he began to ponder

His love sounded coarse
when his voice turned hoarse

His love to her was dear
she gave him her full ear

His step had a spring
of the love it would bring

Home is a place to take
love that takes the cake

How best to keep
love that is skin deep

How can I bless
love that is less

How can I ever part
from her love in my heart

How can I go to bed
without love in my head

How can I hide it now
a mind so giddy with love

How can I love you tender
after the fender bender

How can I make a bid
for her love where it is hid

How can I mend
the love of a dear friend

How can I part
from the love in my heart

How can I sample
her love that is ample

How can it be blatant
love that is all latent

How can it be deep
if love happens in your sleep

How can it be deep
love that is asleep

How can it give you a lift
love packaged in thrift

How can love be true
if there is no glue

How can our love end
when your words are my best friend

How can you now
live without her love

L

How could she deny
love in the corner of her eye

How did I live
without love to give

How did you guess
that love is stress

How easily it dries
when love gets in your eyes

How much have I gained
from love that was drained

How must I touch
love that is too much

How to comment
about love as torment

How to elope
with love slippery as soap

How to forsake
my love for the cake

How to frisk
love that is brisk

How to get love
without push and shove

How to give it a name
love that flickers like a flame

How to go defining
love with rhyming

How to make it glow
when love life becomes slow

How to nurture
love that is torture

How to please
this love for cheese

How to put it to bed
love without being fed

How to quell
the love unwell

How to repeat
love in the summer heat

How to replace
love from its place

How to savour
love and its flavour

How to say things
so love takes to wings

How to sleep
with so much love to keep

How to tell
what love for us befell

How well they fare
with their love in repair

I close my eyes and think
how our love gets to link

I close my eyes and think
how to put my love into ink

I daily hope and pray
love for her will stay

I didn't know what to say
when love came back to stay

I have enough to spare
love for us to share

I have her love to keep
when I wake up from my sleep

I have lived through now
all aspects of love

I long for your love in may
when we can romp in the hay

I love her more
than I can keep score

I love his stumblings
after overdose of dumplings

I love my porridge
better than my marriage

I love you like a friend
right till the very end

I will one day return
when our love gets its turn

I will write you a letter
when our love it feels better

I would love to live in the stars
where there are no cars

If you fall in love with pity
don't live in the city

If I am not mistaken
our love is more than token

If it needs repair
love isn't fair

If it stays in your mind
love can be blind

If love has its way
two hearts will sway

If love is a vice
it is graceful and nice

If love is this
what happened to bliss

If love was just a notion
why is my head in commotion

If our love was never meant to be
why did we bark up the tree

If this ain't love
I'll become a cow

If you do not love with passion
you will go out of fashion

Imperfection is a part
of love from the start

In a cottage by the sea
where love it came to be

In a world without care
love will very well fare

In an endless play
love will stay

In every heart will blossom
love that is quite awesome

L

In her memory it dwells
love like the ocean swells

In life's every scheme
love is a common theme

In love he gambles
with life in shambles

In love it is the norm
to wait for the cosmic form

In love it pays
to mend your ways

In love it will matter
to have a heartfelt chatter

In love they stand tall
not knowing they might fall

In love with her most
the light on my coast

In order to make love flicker
an ounce of romance liquor

In sleep I count sheep
though love is deep

In so many different ways
love it spends its days

In the fancy flight of love
I have a gift for you now

In the ship he sailed
after love got derailed

In their longing eyes
their love it lies

In times good or bad
love it can be had

In times so tainted
love can be painted

Into her heart she lured
his love until it was cured

Is it ever enough
love and that kind of stuff

Is love just a notion
or a true lotion

Is love put to bed
once we are dead

Is there a lotion
for love in slow motion

Is there such a state
as no love or hate

It came to me in a dream
love and her as a team

It came upon by chance
love at the annual dance

It has its ups and ends
the love of distant friends

It has to be towed
once love is bestowed

It is a cause for worry
that love is transitory

It is worth your knowing
her love for you is glowing

*It isn't just a manner of speaking
when we say love is what we are seeking*

*It isn't very clear
why love is also about fear*

*It led them to the altar
though their love began to falter*

*It put out the fire
of love and desire*

*It shatters me to think
love can happen in a blink*

*It takes on a new angle
when love begins to strangle*

*It took one long year
to bring love its cheer*

*It was a season to savour
love and its flavour*

*It was all over in a blink
love before we could think*

*It was never made clear
why love should end right here*

*It wasn't all that bad
the love we nearly had*

*It's hard to break the spell
when there is love still to quell*

*It's such a shame
love is never the same*

*Kept him forever haunted
by the love for her he wanted*

*Know not why
love it must die*

*Let it be let it be
love between you and me*

*Let it not be in haste
one last love to taste*

*Let love for her be mine
each and every time*

*Let love have say
on a cold wintry day*

*Let love make its case
straight to her face*

*Let my love be a part
of your wandering heart*

*Let not love sleep
when my feelings are deep*

*Let the light be shone
to where the love has gone*

*Let your eyes speak
when love becomes bleak*

*Let's have tea and buns
and love by the tons*

*Let's take a peep
at love that is deep*

*Letters written on the sand
love is at hand*

*Life of love is trouble
like a soap bubble*

*Life's biggest treasure
love when it is pleasure*

*Lifes miracles shared
love can be repaired*

*Like a flat tyre
love is a desire*

*Like a flower unfold
love we are told*

*Like a fragile bubble
love is a struggle*

*Like a mother to her fawn
to love she was drawn*

*Like a well rehearsed love
the cooing of the dove*

*Like love it slowly fades
the rainbow and it's shades*

*Like the scent of a rose
love told as prose*

*Locate it fast
love that is lost*

*Looking for a heart to love
a heart beat here and now*

*Loosen the fetters
with love letters*

*Love affair by far
destructive as war*

*Love affair
in disrepair*

*Love aims to please
under the fresh summer breeze*

*Love and affection
your daily reflection*

*Love and amity
is the cure for calamity*

*Love and belonging
of a heart that is longing*

*Love and betrayal
a common portrayal*

*Love and bonding
why are they absconding*

*Love and charm
her daily balm*

*Love and despair
a likely pair*

*Love and emotion
cause of commotion*

*Love and fear
to each other very near*

*Love and hate are passions
that live off daily rations*

*Love and hate
are passengers on a plate*

*Love and hate
through a common gate*

*Love and hate
two sides of fate*

Love and hate
two sides of the slate

Love and infatuation
a potent combination

Love and it's pain
runs through her vein

Love and it's texture
was felt without a lecture

Love and it's themes
has it's own schemes

Love and its plight
is an endless delight

Love and its pulse
can never be repulsed

Love and its woes
head to toes

Love and respect
is the least I expect

Love and survival
both need revival

Love and vanity
to lose is calamity

Love as it was known
was fully home grown

Love as it was then
was known to men and women

Love at first is sweet
from the maiden when she greet

Love at first sight
is a welcome plight

Love at first sight
worsened my plight

Love at him she hurls
the pretty girl with curls

Love at its best
is only a quest

Love at its best
must withstand the test

Love awakens to thoughts
of her and what nots

Love became bigger
from her mythical figure

Love became divided
when each other they chided

Love became heady
when both were ready

Love became rubble
from emotional trouble

Love became whole
with her in my soul

Love becomes a pattern
the closer we get to Saturn

Love becomes a word
waiting to be heard

Love becomes awesome
if the person is a possum

Love becomes fluent
for the very affluent

Love becomes limited
if you are not committed

Love becomes ripe
once you put it in your pipe

Love becomes simple
when I see a dimple

Love beginneth
when her heart you winneth

Love betrayed
all over sprayed

Love bites at night
total delight

Love blossoms in seclusion
released from it's occlusion

Love boat it seems
a place for aspiring dreams

Love both precious and little
turned out to be brittle

Love brings fortitude
and a new attitude

Love brings good cheer
and wafteth away all fear

Love by another name
wouldn't be the same

Love by itself
can't improve yourself

Love came alive
before the nose dive

Love came back twice
by way of surprise

Love came by passing
made for a chance romancing

Love came in an instance
and went the whole distance

Love came so quick
he couldn't light the wick

Love can be a trigger
for accomplishments bigger

Love can be blind
from distortions of the mind

Love can be bridged
by time abridged

Love can be brimming
for those of us living

Love can be deep
but getting there very steep

Love can be delightful
and equally frightful

Love can be demeaning
with the loss of all its meaning

Love can be fleeting
after a single meeting

Love can be found far and deep
whether she is awake or asleep

Love can be frightening
belt needs tightening

Love can be had
when two people are glad

Love can be healing
to a heart without feeling

Love can be jinxed
by messages that are mixed

Love can be mean
like a bad dream

Love can be nifty
well past fifty

Love can be potent
though it is latent

Love can be potent
though it is nascent

Love can be revealing
with frankness and feeling

Love can be slit
by his caustic wit

Love can be teasing
and stop your wheezing

Love can be trapped
and gift wrapped

Love can become a heap
even in your sleep

Love can become blurred
by a single unkind word

Love can correct a wrong
with a single love song

Love can drain you faster
if you don't know how to master

Love can easily part
from a feebleness of the heart

Love can go wrong
for the weak and the strong

Love can inspire
colourful attire

Love can kill you why
find out before you die

Love can kill
against your will

Love can make you happy
even when it is choppy

Love can make you cry
until the tears run dry

Love can never be dead
once the angel enters into your head

Love can never be found
without her voice sweet and sound

Love can reform
a human in any form

Love can spell trouble
fragile as a bubble

Love can trigger
thoughts to figure

Love can turn cold
even for the very bold

Love can turn you grey
unless you daily pray

Love can't be far
if you be the way you are

Love can't be split
just because of guilt

Love cannot be dead
if it happens in your head

Love cannot be delegated
nor possibly relegated

Love cannot be in the air
if both have nothing to share

Love cannot be spoken
when you are heart broken

Love cannot be started
without being whole hearted

Love cannot win
when poverty is in

Love comes back aching
just for the taking

Love comes dancing
to a heart that is romancing

Love comes face to face
for those who do not chase

Love comes into play
before death takes it away

Love comes so slowly
for the rich and the lowly

Love comes to an end
to those who pretend

Love comes to you greeting
just as the wound is fleeting

Love conquered all
when they met in the mall

Love conquers all
fears great and small

Love constantly fed
upon something that she said

Love contrived
hasn't arrived

Love could be forever
if we both are clever

Love could face a damper
if you forgot your camper

Love does it's duty
by giving her all it's beauty

Love doesn't come easy
for her who is choosy

Love doesn't say good – bye
to people when they die

Love doesn't say marry
but readily says sorry

Love don't pay the bills
nor cure the ills

Rhyming English Couplets

Love drops its woes
from head to toes

Love engenders fear
why it is not clear

Love enters in part
to fill her open heart

Love for her he invented
until she relented

Love for Lovella
resulted in novella

Love for you and me
let there daily be

Love for you will last
through memories from the past

Love forgettable
but not regrettable

Love from far away
can begin to stray

Love from its source
can it go off course

Love gains a friend
always in the end

Love gets a dent
though she never meant

Love gets a new start
when you leave with a heavy heart

Love gets a spark
when sunlight becomes dark

Love gets a start
from music in the heart

Love gets a start
from two willing hearts

Love gets a start
in every willing heart

Love gets a start
straight from the heart

Love gets a start
when feelings play a part

Love gets a treat
with each heartbeat

Love gets its meaning
when one of them is scheming

Love gets its sheen
from what might have been

Love gets its showers
from the petals and the flowers

Love gets its sleep
and angels wake up to peep

Love gets its turn
like heartburn

Love gets to its peak
to hear a baby speak

Love gets to peep
at her while asleep

Love gets unbound
where lovers are to be found

L

*Love goes running
to where couples are sunning*

---

*Love got a demotion
overcome with emotion*

---

*Love got meaning in the shade
after the escapade*

---

*Love got promotion
by feeding on emotion*

---

*Love had destroyed
feelings once buoyed*

---

*Love had lost its grip
after the heavenly trip*

---

*Love had passed him by
after the first good-bye*

---

*Love half blessed
needs to be caressed*

---

*Love has a feature
the hearts best teacher*

---

*Love has a fondness
for men with baldness*

---

*Love has a future
if you have teacher*

---

*Love has a heart
that's the scary part*

---

*Love has a history
shrouded in mystery*

---

*Love has a history
steeped in mystery*

---

*Love has a leaning
to give life meaning*

---

*Love has a longing
to be a lovers belonging*

---

*Love has a moment
that needs a lot of cement*

---

*Love has a new attire
putting pressure on desire*

---

*Love has a razzle
and picks it's time to dazzle*

---

*Love has a scheme
to make us dream*

---

*Love has a short fuse
so quickly drink your juice*

---

*Love has a stake
in the fatal mistake*

---

*Love has a way
of making hips sway*

---

*Love has a way
of stealing hearts away*

---

*Love has appeal
and the power to heal*

---

*Love has appeal
because it is a feel*

---

*Love has cures
for the eternally yours*

---

*Love has died for some
under the influence of rum*

Love has eyes
blue as the skies

Love has found
it always comes around

Love has gone wrong
for both weak and the strong

Love has gone
to where the light is shone

Love has happy endings
also heart felt blendings

Love has it's sorrows
both to day and to-morrows

Love has its abode
in a single episode

Love has its riches
and also its hitches

Love has its snags
and also its pangs

Love has lost its sheen
once she became my queen

Love has lost its sheen
where have you been

Love has many paths
and also its wraths

Love has me dreaming
with whom I should be teaming

Love has much to gain
from deep sorrow and the pain

Love has much to gain
when both get wet in the rain

Love has never known
such moan and groan

Love has no use
if it only confuse

Love has often fought
for unlimited thought

Love has seen
that life can be mean

Love has shown
it's better to be alone

Love has the feel
of eternal appeal

Love has the power
to blossom in the shower

Love has ties
to untold lies

Love has wings
in my rememberings

Love has wings
swift as the winds

Love hate or wealth
there will always be a death

Love he had known
deep down to the bone

Love his only goal
the pathetic soul

Love holds me tight
through the dreary night

Love hormones
can rid you of moans

Love ignored
when he was bored

Love illusions
are they delusions

Love in all its glory
enough for one life story

Love in all its layers
peels with daily prayers

Love in full bloom
is the fruit of the loom

Love in full flight
is a source of delight

Love in full flow
her cheeks tend to glow

Love in part
is key to her heart

Love in the end
drives you round the bend

Love in the end
is a dubious friend

Love in the end
is someone to offend

Love in the heart it stays
once the mind it mends it's ways

Love in theory
made them weary

Love is a big part
of functions of the heart

Love is a blessing
improved by caressing

Love is a calling
mostly about falling

Love is a choice
of the inner voice

Love is a choice
we must make with poise

Love is a contract
with everything abstract

Love is a cure
if you can endure

Love is a decision
the heart does with precision

Love is a delicate wisp
makes her thoughts crisp

Love is a desire
down to the wire

Love is a desire
that will never tire

Love is a distraction
from the main attraction

Love is a drunken state
caused solely by your mate

Love is a fatal attraction
filled with love no retraction

Love is a fear
in camouflage my dear

Love is a feel
with a special appeal

Love is a feeling
for two hearts appealing

Love is a feeling
that is most appealing

Love is a feeling
that is very appealing

Love is a feeling
with the promise of meaning

Love is a fever
for both man and the beaver

Love is a fire
that can crimple your attire

Love is a flame
that doesn't stay the same

Love is a flavour
that only you can savour

Love is a flimsy thread
where spiders fear to tread

Love is a freedom
we all really needum

Love is a friend
of greatness in the end

Love is a game of chess
where the king asks the queens to bless

Love is a game
like the flicker of a flame

Love is a game
played around the candle flame

Love is a gift
given without thrift

Love is a gift
that gives you a lift

Love is a gift
through which we must sift

Love is a gift
without any thrift

Love is a growth
also known to the sloth

Love is a kind
of an absent mind

Love is a kind
of leap of the mind

Love is a kind
of phantom of the mind

Love is a kind
of sparkle in the mind

Love is a kind
of treasure of the mind

Love is a longing
and a need for belonging

Love is a longing
that can leave you hanging

Love is a longing
that leaves you hanging

Love is a memory
like crème and cherry

Love is a notion
full of emotion

Love is a notion
needs no translation

Love is a one way street
to travel with stamping feet

Love is a pain
from which neither will gain

Love is a pantomime
that defies tide and time

Love is a part
of a heavenly heart

Love is a part
of both head and the heart

Love is a part
of every human heart

Love is a part
of every pining heart

Love is a part
of experience from the start

Love is a part
of feelings from the start

Love is a part
of feelings of the heart

Love is a part
of the emboldened heart

Love is a part
of the failings of my heart

Love is a pearl
in the heart of a girl

Love is a phantom
measured by the quantum

Love is a piece of heaven
but where does it go at seven

Love is a plight
resolves itself by night

Love is a predicament
that has no medicament

Love is a prize
more than surprise

Love is a reminder
that the heart will surely find her

Love is a scheme
that has no theme

Love is a search
ends up in church

Love is a secret longing
and a sense of belonging

Love is a secret thing
makes two hearts sing

Rhyming English Couplets

Love is a serious matter
from the former to the latter

Love is a serving
for whose heart is deserving

Love is a slippery slope
that relies only on hope

Love is a song
that can take very long

Love is a song
with feelings very strong

Love is a spark
that happens in the park

Love is a spark
that shows up in the park

Love is a state of mind
for the deaf or the blind

Love is a token
of a heart all broken

Love is a treasure
excitement beyond measure

Love is a treasure
for which there is no measure

Love is a treasure
that is lifes greatest pleasure

Love is a vision
like light through a prism

Love is a wishing
cannot be got by fishing

Love is a wonderful thing
until it begins to sting

Love is a yearning
doesn't need learning

Love is a yearning
when the tide is turning

Love is about craving
love and its raving

Love is about dreams
more than it seems

Love is about longing
for all your belonging

Love is about shedding
all thoughts of a wedding

Love is about the self
being beside ones self

Love is about trusting
feeling that need dusting

Love is affection
that needs no deflection

Love is all mental
can become monumental

Love is all you need
when you wish to feed your greed

Love is also deep
between two sheep

Love is an emotion
of selfless devotion

L

Love is an endless chain
while two hearts they bear the pain

Love is an endless rhyme
painful yet divine

Love is an illusion
doesn't need another delusion

Love is an illusion
of minds in collusion

Love is an illusion
of the two in collusion

Love is an itch
reaches fever pitch

Love is appealing
if he says it while kneeling

Love is appealing
to those who have feeling

Love is at it's best
when it stands the test

Love is best
at her behest

Love is best
when put to the test

Love is better had
when both of us are glad

Love is bliss
but what is this

Love is collusion
of many an illusion

Love is delight
when the moon is bright

Love is distilled
by the very skilled

Love is divine
like sweet tasting wine

Love is divine
not intoxicating wine

Love is easily spilled
by being strong willed

Love is elastic
unless you are plastic

Love is enough reason
during holiday season

Love is fed
by what's in the head

Love is for the birds
and for buffalo in their herds

Love is forever
not something to sever

Love is full of trifles
they both go for rifles

Love is giving
to all that is living

Love is gold
for both young and old

*Love is hard to explain
though it seems so plain*

*Love is heard
in the songs of a bird*

*Love is here to stay
as life it wears away*

*Love is here to stay
like milk and honey in May*

*Love is here to stay
we are on tranquility bay*

*Love is in need of crying
to stop it from dying*

*Love is in part
appealing to the heart*

*Love is in the main
of singing in the rain*

*Love is in the air
at Scarborough fair*

*Love is in the air
but where is the affair*

*Love is in the main
about not having to explain*

*Love is in the main
about pain and a bit of gain*

*Love is in the main
about pangs and the pain*

*Love is in the main
about psychic pain*

*Love is in the main
poetry for the brain*

*Love is inclined
to be wined and dined*

*Love is infatuation
without punctuation*

*Love is just a flame
needs fanning all the same*

*Love is just a swish
between two passing fish*

*Love is just a thought
so why are we in it caught*

*Love is just play
unless we are of clay*

*Love is large
not a mirage*

*Love is learning
that it's better when returning*

*Love is like a feather
that floats in all weather*

*Love is lost
between fire and frost*

*Love is made whole
by happiness in the soul*

*Love is more than fun
after the day is done*

*Love is more than gold
within the family fold*

Love is nascent
unless it is recent

Love is never the same
for those who play the game

Love is not a myth
it is the essential pith

Love is not platonic
when both are satanic

Love is overdue
from all the changing hue

Love is protection
that defies detection

Love is recovery
after self discovery

Love is seems
has inveterate schemes

Love is severed
when fault is discovered

Love is shallow
where the earth is fallow

Love is stilled
by grief distilled

Love is sublime
a twinkle in the face of time

Love is sweet
on the repeat

Love is swell
in the darkness as well

Love is the dart
like arrow in the heart

Love is the duty
you do to all beauty

Love is the essence
about fluorescence

Love is the fire
of the hearts desire

Love is the food
of your changing mood

Love is the freedom
in gods little kingdom

Love is the glue
between the two

Love is the glue
that can turn your face blue

Love is the glue
that holds us two

Love is the glue
to make the meaning come true

Love is the lotion
for selfless devotion

Love is the remedy
for a life without melody

Love is there to relish
if you don't make it a fetish

Love is twofold
so we are told

Rhyming English Couplets

Love is uncovered
as soon as discovered

Love is unique
like a parrots red beak

Love is very clever
makes you think it's forever

Love is very inviting
when there is no in-fighting

Love is voided
once the heart is divided

Love is well
like a pearl within a shell

Love is wide
like the ocean tide

Love is withdrawn
once you become a yawn

Love isn't bad
if it doesn't make you sad

Love isn't the same
until I hear your name

Love it appears
had left them in tears

Love it became ready
to listen to the melody

Love it becomes chancy
when the hearts they become ancy

Love it becomes crisper
when spoken in a whisper

Love it becomes heady
for people who are ready

Love it belong
to desires that are strong

Love it belong
to sentiment and song

Love it binds
to cultivated minds

Love it brings health
far more than wealth

Love it brings
life's meaningful things

Love it came late
so it was his fate

Love it can die
without glint in her eye

Love it can fan
the many instincts of man

Love it can hamper
your ever ready temper

Love it can muster
feelings filled with lustre

Love it can reach
beyond the breach

Love it cannot be fed
by so slender a thread

Love it cannot bear
an extra love affair

L

Love it cannot hide
with you by my side

Love it chooses
its own excuses

Love it chose
rational repose

Love it commences
within the six senses

Love it commenses
what I feel through the senses

Love it confuses
as and when it chooses

Love it cries
when the flame it dies

Love it died
once easily denied

Love it dies
from prying eyes

Love it doesn't need a name
that's the name of the game

Love it drives
their parallel lives

Love it dwells
in brain cells

Love it embraces all
her problem both trivial and tall

Love it ended up sour
like the withering of a flower

Love it faded
after they were jaded

Love it feels light
from a great height

Love it flickers why
like a glow in the sky

Love it has a span
differs from man to man

Love it has proved
that fortunes can be improved

Love it has taught her
not to write on water

Love it has taught
it can never be a whole lot

Love it improved its ties
because of the jasmine in her eyes

Love it increases doubt
once humour is out

Love it is said
is mans daily bread

Love it leaks
when the heart speaks

Love it lies
in the tears from her eyes

Love it may be mentioned
must never be questioned

Love it minces
with the soul and its glimpses

Love it must be near
every hesitant tear

Love we must trace
to its hiding place

Love it needs fetching
more than just your etching

Love it needs mending
without each other bending

Love it needs
flowering seeds

Love it pays
once you mend your ways

Love it plays a song
all life long

Love it plays
in unintended ways

Love it protested
that it was not attested

Love it rents asunder
the lovers only blunder

Love it seeks
ever greater peaks

Love it seems swims
in forbidden streams

Love it seems
can be more than in dreams

Love it seems
is about selling dreams

Love it slips
when friendship dips

Love it stayed
even though it weighed

Love it stays
despite their separate ways

Love it stays
like the good old days

Love it stays
more than two days

Love it stays
with just enough praise

Love it strayed
from trust betrayed

Love it strays
from haphazard ways

Love it strays
in so many ways

Love it suits
all pursuits

Love it takes a peep
while both of them are asleep

Love it takes turn
in being taciturn

Love it teaches
as we stroll the beaches

Love it took
to write this book

Love it turned rancid
after becoming placid

Love it was deeply woven
by two hearts that were stolen

Love it was hatched
under the roof that was thatched

Love it was kept
like an eternal debt

Love it was meant
to be an event

Love it will breach
once out of reach

Love it will languish
in delight and anguish

Love it will renew
when I am without you

Love it works
because of the perks

Love it wouldn't part
form his humble heart

Love it yields to appealing
from the ground to the ceiling

Love keeps yearning
for feelings to be churning

Love kept its hold
on lover's who were bold

Love knit tight
can set things right

Love knows how to hide
in the labyrinths of the mind

Love lets you peep
at the thought that is deep

Love letters abound
once love is found

Love letters by the hand
near the ocean and the sand

Love life has a tune
best heard on the moon

Love life is healing
and so appealing

Love life it quickly ends
whose knees refuse to bends

Love life loses its glow
when each other they come to blow

Love life under the knife
produces all the strife

Love looks for clues
why the heart it rues

Love loses its gleam
as a part of natures scheme

Love loses its glitter
when you miss a sitter

Love lost its need
after a slow bleed

Love lost its power
like the fallen flower

Rhyming English Couplets

Love lost without deserving
from doing things self serving

Love made him wise
while it slowly dies

Love made it fun
for two hearts to speak as one

Love made its case
and stared him in the face

Love made them dizzy
also kept them busy

Love makes a call
when the rains fall

Love makes connections
based on your selections

Love makes it clear
it is filled with tear

Love makes it clear
it is not based on fear

Love makes it clear
it is the opposite of fear

Love makes it clear
many things to fear

Love makes it clear
no love without tear

Love makes it clear
that in it there is fear

Love makes it clear
that memories are dear

Love makes it clear
that our future is right here

Love makes it clear
that the opposite is fear

Love makes it clear
that the present is right here

Love makes it clear
will not tolerate fear

Love makes it whole
the fragments of the soul

Love makes it whole
the meetings of the soul

Love makes it whole
the music in my soul

Love makes its case
in a subconscious place

Love makes its case
in a very private place

Love makes its presence
felt in her absence

Love makes me ill
please give me a pill

Love makes me peep
at her gentle sleep

Love makes no deal
if it has an ominous feel

Love makes selections
among close connections

Love makes them say
things out of the way

Love makes us whole
both body and soul

Love may be strong
but things can go wrong

Love may have cures
but will it be yours

Love may seem
impossible dream

Love me tender
but don't offend her

Love me tender
she said to the other gender

Love me till the end
I have my heart to mend

Love misplaced
cannot be replaced

Love must be avoided
once it is divided

Love must be fed
before it is dead

Love must be fed
by thoughts in the head

Love must be fed
with music in the head

Love must be groomed
to stop from being doomed

Love must be made
in the moonlight or the shade

Love must be near
if it drops a single tear

Love must be protected
after the lovers have defected

Love must be stored
for times when you are bored

Love must be weighed
before it is conveyed

Love must combine
a visit to the shrine

Love must demise
so say the wise

Love must enjoy
liberation and joy

Love must not ration
fidelity and passion

Love must not ration
the heart and its passion

Love must restrain
this runaway train

Love must take its chances
between two romances

Love must take the blame
I'll never be the same

Love needed reminding
that moonlight is not blinding

Love needs a ferry
to make them both merry

Love needs a partner
and a good Gardner

Love needs a stronger beat
this I will repeat

Love needs repair
in times of despair

Love needs to be ready
with the right melody

Love never dies
from family ties

Love never dies
with friendly eyes

Love never refuses
joy and its juices

Love of a different fate
left behind at the gate

Love of a different kind
to make you unwind

Love of extremes
and adventure themes

Love of my life
she gives me no strife

Love on demand
becomes a command

Love once declared
had the couple very scared

Love once it is parted
in directions different they departed

Love once it turned
it never returned

Love once set in motion
causes all the commotion

Love opens the blinds
for two patient minds

Love owes a gratitude
to the sweet sounds of solitude

Love played a part
in her retreating heart

Love played a part
in the readings of her heart

Love plays a part
for the song in my heart

Love plays a part
in couplets from the heart

Love plays a part
in every broken heart

Love plays a part
in his wandering heart

Love plays a part
in matters of the heart

Love plays a part
in mending a restless heart

Love plays a part
in music and art

Love plays a part
in purifying the heart

Love plays a part
in the corners of your heart

Love plays a role
in making your life whole

Love plays its game
like a moth to the flame

Love plays its game
like the flicker in the flame

Love plays its part
in matters of the heart

Love please be kind
I am going out of my mind

Love potion
is not just a notion

Love pours in a flood
when the rose is red as blood

Love recaptured
had them all enraptured

Love remains a part
of the intimacy of the heart

Love repaired
by disquiet shared

Love requires clarity
and a bit a of charity

Love restrained
was slowly drained

Love retains
its aches and pains

Love returned
must be earned

Love say the wise
comes as no surprise

Love scales the peaks
when to me she speaks

Love she could not efface
that was written all over her face

Love she defies
with intrusive eyes

Love she had ample
for the whole family to sample

Love she hears
with burning ears

Love she will find
in the waters of the mind

Love so long standing
defied understanding

Love so profound
can never be found

Love songs he sing
for a pretty thing

Love stayed in the heart
though they were heavens apart

Love stays hot
says forget me not

Love sticks the parts
of two open hearts

Love stops at the gate
if that is your fate

Love story must be told
before the ink it turns cold

Love taken through its paces
makes the heart jump as it races

Love takes a peek
at teardrops down her cheek

Love takes a peep
at the heart that is asleep

Love takes it's toll
on both the heart and the soul

Love takes its course
with a new life force

Love takes its time
to become all divine

Love takes its time
until it has reason to rhyme

Love takes me home
where the heart can freely roam

Love takes to wing
when the churchbells sing

Love talk became crisper
as she spoke in a whisper

Love tears you apart
from the happenings of the heart

Love tears you apart
why so does it start

Love that appeared
had my sorrow all cured

Love that came first
not enough for thirst

Love that comes with ease
is more likely to cease

Love that fades fast
was not meant to last

Love that is blind
is one of a kind

Love that is deep
forever we must keep

Love that is deep
so easy to keep

Love that is enduring
also very alluring

Love that is filled
is fulfilled

Love that is fleeting
is a form of cheating

Love that is hidden
must have been forbidden

Love that is obvious
could also be dubious

Love that is pure
is the best cure

Love that is pure
must be bottled for sure

Love that is slow
has eternal glow

Love that is vicarious
can turn precarious

Love that needs so much care
is sometimes hard to bear

Love that will last
is a thing of the past

Love they chases
in godforsaken places

Love they said was blind
lovers of a tender mind

Love they say is found
by goldfish in the pond

Love though deep
disappeared in my sleep

Love though divine
can be sweetened by wine

Love takes it's birth
when sunlight hits the earth

Love together we can craft
floating on a slow raft

Love took a peep
with a promise to keep

Love took off in a bus
with just the two of us

Love took shape
in a dreamy escape

Love torn apart
it tells on the human heart

Love turned cold
before it took hold

Love turned into half
on my behalf

Love turned to doubt
like a candle burnt out

Love understood
is the best food

Love unscripted
gets interrupted

Love unspoken
couldn't be just token

Love unspoken
not just token

Love untold
have secrets to unfold

Love up on the hill
where love it stood still

Love was begun
at a season in the sun

Love was blind
for his troubled mind

Rhyming English Couplets

Love was kept simple
with a smile and a dimple

Love was meant to be
like honey is for the bee

Love was meant
for the inside of the tent

Love was never meant
to be cause of discontent

Love was planted on his cheek
with a peck from her beak

Love was preserved
like pickle that was served

Love was restored
when they both got bored

Love was rewarded
once the heart was scalded

Love was so deep
it put me to sleep

Love was so strong
I burst into song

Love wasn't the same
when the roses never came

Love wasted in sorrow
deep down to the marrow

Love we must savour
without fear or favour

Love we need to live it
without an outer limit

Love when it comes
the guitar string strums

Love when it smiles
shortens the miles

Love when you are bored
can be bottled and stored

Love will alight
on those who delight

Love will always be
about the drone and the bee

Love will be brief in the end
who has many desires to fend

Love will be dead
if improperly fed

Love will be ensuing
once the coffee is brewing

Love will forever be
about metaphor and irony

Love will forever be
heaven for you and me

Love will forever stay
if they both mend their way

Love will get you there
where all is well and fair

Love will go away
if you share the ash tray

Love will have its say
whether it is April Or May

L

Love will last
of all things past

Love will never be bland
where the ocean meets the land

Love will never fail
to wait for her mail

Love will play it's part
if you follow your heart

Love will remain
as rapture and pain

Love will remain
our most prominent pain

Love will remain
unfamiliar terrain

Love will remember
the moonlight timbre

Love will retreat
in the mid-day heat

Love will run dry
too hard if you try

Love will see us again
through the pouring rain

Love will soothe
when the ride is smooth

Love will take us far
where the blue skies are

Love will unfold
treasures of gold

Love will whittle
whose heart is brittle

Love will yield
to lilies in the field

Love without a moan
is like a dog without a bone

Love without veneration
cannot last a whole generation

Love without you
like a morning without dew

Love written in bold
threads of gold

Love written with faded ink
wasn't enough to draw a blink

Love you must send her
while she work at the blender

Love you will find
in the attic of the mind

Love's little trifles
can't be cured by rifles

Love's only offering
untenable suffering

Lovers they rave
until love hits the grave

Make it last awhile
the love in your smile

Make love a part
of the meetings of the heart

Rhyming English Couplets

*Makes my heart soar
love all the more*

*Many a love is on hold
because the two of them are not bold*

*Many a Love it fell
from secrets not held well*

*Many a love must fade
to a quiet place in the shade*

*Many a love was broken
by words carelessly spoken*

*Many a love was found
the second time around*

*Many a love was torn
after it became worn*

*Many a song he sang
to ease love of it's pang*

*Many a south sea isle
can make you love her smile*

*Many a wish can sway
love that makes its way*

*Many are deceived
by love once conceived*

*Many have vied for love
without the push and shove*

*Many levels of giving
love to the living*

*Many times they wished
their love was replenished*

*Many ways to measure
when love is a treasure*

*Memories I have that sing
that love is the only thing*

*Men they easily break
when love is at stake*

*Men they push and shove
for their daily dose of love*

*Message of love becomes clear
when she comes to me very near*

*Messages sent through a dove
some of the things we do for love*

*Meteoric and fast
love was made to last*

*Moments that are soft
can keep our love aloft*

*Mostly essential
love and its potential*

*Much of love is meant
to make them both content*

*Much of our longing
is about love and belonging*

*Much too much to lose
when love has too many hues*

*Must it be spurned
love quietly returned*

*My eyes go and rest
where love is caressed*

L

My eyes have seen
where her love has been

My eyes must daily be fed
with sweet love it is said

My failing is in my heart
love in it is a part

My hair needs care
and love needs repair

My love for her has seen
both love and nicotine

My love it cries
for her Spanish eyes

My love needed a plumber
when it went into slumber

My love she happily carried
though about to be married

My love to her crying eyes
said I love her till I dies

My love with all her charms
how far away from my arms

Need a love to hug
after beer from the mug

New and forever
love if you are clever

Nice descriptions
of love prescriptions

Night stars as they blink
love begins to think

Nightmares in pairs
after love affairs

No better god than this
the love of a mothers kiss

No greater love than this
though there wasn't a single kiss

No greater tonic
than love that is platonic

No love without a tear
that's what makes it clear

No more love to spare
after this affair

No more tears to shed
love is good as dead

No need to dwell
on love that isn't well

No need to sift
true love is a gift

No one but you have seen
where my love has been

No one can succeed
without love to feed

Nobody has a clue
why love can turn blue

Nobody has a clue
why love is the greatest glue

Not easy to forget
when love is put to the test

Not easy to harbour
love thy neighbour

Not enough love to hoard
for the days when we are bored

Not enough love
to please the dove

Not just a manner of speaking
that love is too intriguing

Not so easy to walk
when love begins to talk

Nothing else matters
when love it shatters

Nothing is above
motherly love

Nothing more tonic
than love all platonic

Nothing to fear
once love makes it clear

Of the love in my heart
she played a part

Oh what a place to be
where love and moonlight are free

On a perfect morning day
love has something to say

On a starlit night
love is a delight

On days when the moon is fuller
I will lean on her love like a pillar

On each festival night
love came to light

On his last leg
for love he beg

Once all is said and done
love in the end was fun

Once estranged
love re-arranged

Once he was lured
of love never cured

Once her heart is won
love says it is done

Once his mind cleared
it was love that he feared

Once it ceases to be a dream
love is not what it may seem

Once it comes upon frost
love consider it lost

Once it goes sour
love brings you no flower

Once it loses its glow
love ceases to flow

Once it loses magic
love it becomes tragic

Once it takes to flight
love can be a delight

Once love is done
there is setting of the sun

L

Once love is put to sleep
where is the need to weep

Once love is time tested
time musn't be wasted

once love it is blown
makes you all alone

Once love loses its sheen
ask where have you been

Once set in motion
love can be commotion

Once that he had
the love it went bad

Once the mascara faded
their love became jaded

Once there lived a moose
who fell in love with a goose

Once turned away
will love ever stay

Once you are over the hill
love it stays still

Once you prove your worth
a new love takes birth

Once you show me the meaning
love will get back its feeling

One day she just ravished
with our love fully tarnished

One love bloomed
while the other doomed

One man show
with love in full flow

One thing is clear
love engenders fear

Only in gods kingdom
love gets its freedom

Only love it can mend
broken heart in the end

Only the brave
they send love to the grave

Ordinary folks
love red yolks

Ornamented by love
messages through the dove

Others they appear
and make their love clear

Our hearts must mend
once love comes to an end

Our love became a speck
we both said what the heck

Our love became bright
when she showed me the light

Our love came upon doubt
which it couldn't do without

Our love is a treasure
far beyond measure

Our love is beyond reason
hope it lasts the season

Our love is here to stay
let's build a cottage by the bay

Our love is here to stay
till the end of May

Our love it needs peeling
so it is more revealing

Our love it needs peeling
to make it more appealing

Our love was so deep
I couldn't get to sleep

Our love will get bolder
is what I told her

Ours alone my dear
when love it appear

Out of control
when love takes a stroll

Out the window went reason
faced with love during season

Over morning coffee they presided
on their love totally divided

Over the years she gemmed
into a love all well hemmed

Overcome with grief
at the thought of love being brief

People seldom keep
love that is deep

Petals were once showered
on love that just soured

Please find a cure
where love can endure

Poetry from within
love finds a way to win

Posing in different hues
love asks for its dues

Prudence makes sense
when love is intense

Put love to use
once you turn it loose

Quickly and now
invest in love

Renew your love every morning
by being to her very charming

Season for love
let it be now

Seeds of love once planted
can grow up straight or slanted

Seeds of love once planted
never will they grow all slanted

Self love must be purged
lest other loves get submerged

Shades of subtle meaning
in love expressed as feeling

She came home and she prompted
me to love her as she wanted

She couldn't find words to speak
when love reached its peak

She eased into the song
and made our love strong

She gave me the mould
upon which love took hold

She has a quick ear
to love when it is near

She is too much a part
of the love in my heart

She made it very plain
her love was without pain

She made them into beads
her love seeds

She plays a part
for the love in my heart

She put love to repair
with pin flowers in her hair

She rode away her colt
with her love in revolt

She said good –bye
with love in her eye

She untangled her hair
when love was in the air

She was all frivolity
when her love became quality

She was light of heart
love when it fell apart

She was loyal to his love
like dove to dove

She was seriously attached
to their love that was hatched

She went aghast
that for love he would fast

She worked on him her magic
and his love defied all logic

Should we ask why
love should ever die

Silence is a part
of love from the start

Sit beside me my love
let me take off your glove

Slippery as moss
love and its loss

Smoke without fire
like love without desire

So little trust
when love begins its rust

So many kinds of love
some push, some shove

So much better heard
love through its whispered word

So much love received
though at times deceived

So much wrath
in love and its path

So why bargain
when love has nothing to gain

Rhyming English Couplets

Someday our love will come
to where once more it was fun

Something in me cries
when her love for me it dies

Something to hold on
though love it has gone

Sooner or later
for love we must cater

Sorrow is a distraction
while love is in construction

Sow the right seeds
of love and its needs

Speed up your ticker
to make your love flicker

Stay with me till
I pop this love pill

Story is making the rounds
that their love life's out of bounds

Such a fragile bubble
love is so much trouble

Tear love apart
once broken from the heart

Teary eyed
from love that has died

Ten winters old
our love still has a hold

That love is the best food
is least understood

The banyan tree was made
to make love in its shade

The broken nest
put love to the test

The candle flames flicker
making the love come quicker

The days are yet to come
when the songs of love she will hum

The door was bolted too long
for their love to become strong

The evening shadow can tell
if our love will be well

The falling star needs catching
while love it goes on hatching

The flame of love will flicker
if you don't go home quicker

The flames of love need a fan
once she gets her man

The glide of the landing swan
like love that is newly born

The head it goes reeling
when love shows up as feeling

The heart it can see
love wherever it be

The heart it leaps a mile
when love breaks into a smile

The heart it learns to sing
when love it takes to wing

L

The heart needs to be instructed
that love must be constructed

The lady's love is a favour
life long you must savour

The letters I love most
when I wait for the post

The light within
where love is in

The limerick made it clear
that love came very near

The love he projected
summarily rejected

The love I have for you
is not of common hue

The love in me
trying to break free

The message gets crisper
from the love of a whisper

The mind gets all bent
when love sits in a tent

The mind it must be fed
with love until we are dead

The night of the full moon
for love it was a boon

The nitty gritty
of love in the city

The only thing in season
is love without a reason

The other side of love
is no white dove

The paint went peeling
when love hit the ceiling

The pangs of love they smart
when two loves decide to part

The price can be steep
if your love is deep

The purest of human treasures
is love that has no measures

The queen bee will moan
for the love of the drone

The river and its murmer
made their love much firmer

The road to love is steep
this is no time to sleep

The road to love though steep
they both end up in a heap

The snow each Christmas must fall
when love gets a wake up call

The sound and the sense
of love intense

The time has come
for our love to become numb

The time has come
for our love to become one

The way love took hold
made her very bold

*Their daily love talk
was on the skywalk*

*Their dialogues bore fruit
and love it took root*

*Their love at first sight
didn't last through the night*

*Their love became firmer
listening to the river and its murmur*

*Their love became stronger
as the shadows they became longer*

*Their love developed a frost
but it was never lost*

*Their love was quite awesome
more than any blossom*

*Their love it was fated
to be re-decorated*

*Their love life was squandered
when their minds wandered*

*Their love needed defining
and a little bit of refining*

*Their love was deep
though both they were asleep*

*Their love was properly matched
by the number of chicks they hatched*

*Their love was slated
to be detonated*

*There are places in the mind
where love is easy to find*

*There are things to do must
when love begins to rust*

*There is a man in the moon
for love to swoon*

*There is no cure
for love and its allure*

*There is no eye or ear
that love cannot see or hear*

*There is no greater wine
than love most divine*

*There is no measure to tell you
how much I really love you*

*There is no solution
for love is just an illusion*

*There is so much love to pick
better to grow up quick*

*There was a secret history
of love life and its mystery*

*There will forever be
fragrance of her love for thee*

*They all want a slice
of love when it is nice*

*They are a loving couple
whose love they say is supple*

*They both blundered
and their love floundered*

*They both can tell
when love needs to quell*

L

*They both sat in the shade
that's where love is made*

*They both were afflicted
by the love that was inflicted*

*They both were rankled
by their love all entangled*

*They climbed up the hill
and let their love spill*

*They did not need any tuition
to bring their love to fruition*

*They fell in love in may
in an innovative way*

*They found that their fetchings
were love in all its etchings*

*They found their forgotten space
where love made its case*

*They resort to love chatter
when the rains go pitter patter*

*They say love is fed
by the people in bed*

*They turned out to be bland
love letters in the sand*

*This love was fun
like a practice run*

*Those who don't feel your love
forget them quick and now*

*Though booted and spurned
his love always returned*

*Though it is plain
love hard to explain*

*Though love it was near
he was deaf in the ear*

*Though slippery as eel
love has appeal*

*Though the cost can't be measured
lost love is much treasured*

*Through weakness and frail
she left love in her trail*

*To cast its spell
love must be well*

*To each other they have a duty
both love and beauty*

*To go back in time
when love was divine*

*To go where love will
you need a skill*

*To her love belongs his ear
that he made it clear*

*To him whom we love most
this drink will play host*

*To love and be loved
is a message very loud*

*To love he is blind
is he losing his mind*

*To love in vain
is the biggest pain*

To love it belongs
the immortal song

To love live and die
how hard they try

To love once converted
his mind got inverted

To make the heart sing
song of love you must bring

To mix them how
both marriage and love

To my love she was blind
from the meanderings of her mind

To put love into song
I had to think very long

To see me she was glad
for the love that I had

To the one I love most
this book will play host

To-day to-morrow and forever
our Love will die never

Told in many ways
love it stays

Too great for mending
after love sees the ending

Too many whys
why love dies

Too soon assumed
that love it was doomed

Total trust
in love is a must

Treasured love will last
from memories of the past

True love will find
a gate open to the mind

Tulips in the spring
and love songs to sing

Twins at the gate
both love and hate

Two eyes when they share
the love that is in the air

Two hearts that meet as one
until love is done

Uncontained
love it pained

Under the starlit sky
how can love we deny

Uninterrupted
love it erupted

Unstoppable at its source
love as a force

Until it is felt
love is just pelt

Until it is immense
love doesn't make sense

Until love is renewed
life is skewed

L

Until we meet again
our love must not be slain

Waiting for love to shower
on my final hour

Waiting for you
for love to renew

Waiting waiting
for love to come baiting

Was it unkind
for love to be left behind

Way deep in the past
when I thought love would last

We came to the conclusion
that love is an illusion

We must all turn the page
for love is just a stage

We must expiate
love for the opiate

We must go our separate ways
so love no longer it stays

We must re-do things
for love to take to wings

We were both appalled
at love that was stalled

We were fulfilled
by love distilled

Wear your best vest
and put love to the test

Weaving love into fiction
can be an addiction

Were they in love
or boxing without glove

What does it take to keep
love that is very deep

What good is love
if it can't be now

What happens now
in a climate of love

What has it to gain
love by causing pain

What has love to gain
by causing all this pain

What is gained
by love restrained

What is it you have lost
when love turns frost

What is the cost
of love that was lost

What is the mystery
of love and it's chemistry

What is the mystery
of love and it's history

What kind of love is this
that tears me away from bliss

What kind of love is this
when you don't top it with a kiss

What makes them tick
both love and music

What wouldn't I give
for a love to re-live

Whatever love is remaining
has lost its sense of meaning

Whatever the season
love will find a reason

When I think of it I float
of the love that is remote

When love becomes grief
where to find relief

When love begins to mutter
it sounds like a stutter

When love came expecting
she was unsuspecting

When love comes around
it improves mind body and sound

When love gives you permission
just go on a mission

When love is compact
it has impact

When love is food
you feel good

When love is here to stay
it is best to sit and pray

When love is put to the test
go to your love nest

When love is secure
ills have a cure

When love is strong
weave it into song

When love is to and fro
I also miss you so

When love isn't bonding
where is it absconding

When love it comes kneeling
the heart it goes fleeing

When love loses its glitter
the memories turn bitter

When love made a choice
it made me its voice

When love makes a call
be a fly on the wall

When love makes a call
be prepared to lose it all

When love makes its case
don't give up the chase

When love needs a chase
it's just a passing phase

When love needs help
I get a spring in my step

When love ran aground
a new love was found

When love re-groups
it sends them into loops

When love says no
can't get up and go

When love takes hold
heart turns to gold

When love takes to wings
it bares all things

When love takes to wings
loosen your purse strings

When love turns to fear
the mind is unclear

When love was in the air
my heart was in repair

When men start to feel
love is slippery as eel

When my heart needs a mender
I seek love and its splendour

When our love was burning bright
the stars they sparkled at night

When she took the pill
love stood still

When spring meets love
they release white dove

When the angels sing me a song
in love there is nothing wrong

When the heart has a need
love plants a seed

When the moonlight it does you a favour
it's time for love for us to savour

When the pace is slow
let love flow

When will it derail
a love so frail

When will it dissolve
this memory of her love

Where does it stem
what love does to them

Where have you been
love not to be seen

Where have you been
my love not to be seen

Where is she now
my one great love

Where shall we go now
for a different kind of love

Where the cottages are small
and love gets a call

Wherever love you roam
come back to our home

Whether 20/20 or blind
love it vexes the mind

Who said it was easy
when love gets to be queezy

Who will it pick
love when it is quick

Whoever says love is well
doesn't know what is hell

Why are you complaining
when love doesn't need explaining

Why didn't it stay
the love that got away

Why do we wilt
when love comes with guilt

Why do you bicker
choose between love and liquor

Why does it seem
love is just a dream

Why does it seem
love is just a scheme

Why don't you come back soon
love in the afternoon

Why is it that falling
in love is so appalling

Why it makes sense
love so intense

Why make a fuss
this love is about us

Why must we part
said love to the heart

Why not sit and pray
love is here to stay

Why we love and lose
where can I seek the clues

Why would love fade
while sitting in the shade

Will love still be deep
once I fall asleep

Will make you feel better
love to the last letter

With a single glance she fed
him with much love it is said

With each passing year I long
for our love to become strong

With each sip at the straw
nectar of love he draw

With his tail swinging gladly
In love he fell madly

With love losing sheen
she asked where have you been

With love once smitten
he gifted her a mitten

Within me it lies to choose
how to put love to use

Without her now
what will happen to love

Without love as subsistence
there is no existence

Words of love he uttered
though he always stuttered

Words of love to mutter
how can I without stutter

Words they fall
when love makes a call

L

Words we whisper
for love to be crisper

Would it be the same
love without a name

Wounds that surface now
mostly due to love

Wounds will leave a scar
from love that goes too far

You and I belong
to where our love is strong

You and I forever my love
together both, like hand and glove

You can end up in a pickle
from the love tickle

Your twinkle though it is far
I love you as you are

How to forget
love's little fret

How to repair
love's despair

Love's collusions
are beyond illusions

Slowly it became firmer
Love's distant murmer

To be content
is love's intent

To learn of love's meaning
he comes home beaming

Lovebirds

Unspoken words
between lovebirds

Loved

Hard to undo the tether
once you have loved another

He bid farewell to the host
whom he loved dearly most

He told her oh so clearly
that he loved her almost nearly

He told her very clearly
that he loved her very dearly

How to push out the other
once you have loved another

No man ever loved
who was pushed and shoved

Nothing less will do
than to be loved by you

She loved his leanings
for cleaning her ceilings

They both loved cherry wine
when they went out to dine

To be loved by a man
is her only plan

What have you to gain
causing loved ones pain

Loveless

They were both clueless
why they were loveless

Loveliness
How can you mend
loveliness in the end

Lovely
He played a lovely tune
while she looked at the moon

Her hair made up in a braid
she made for a lovely maid

Lover
Doesn't care about the cover
the book lover

How to make it brief
the lover and his grief

I put her lover to the test
like I know how best

Imaginary lover
how can I forgive her

The lover comes kneeling
with words that are appealing

Engaged in deep thought
lovers in mid night caught

How to atone
a lovers moan

It is the lovers wish
to be with a school of fish

Lovers are a breed
who make each other bleed

Lovers have nothing to gain
when loneliness is a pain

Lovers show they care
when music is in the air

Lovers they greet
on thread needle street

Lovers they grumble
if the hearts don't tremble

Lovers they met at will
on top of the windy hill

Lovers to their homes they run
on the back of the evening sun

Moonbeams of light
lovers first delight

Parrots beak to beak
and lovers cheek to cheek

The winter air is crisper
two lovers when they whisper

They travel many lands
lovers holding hands

When lovers they say sorry
one of them doesn't want to marry

Loves
Best to be glad
about the loves you have had

Book is a friend
who loves you no end

*Don't play host
to the old loves ghost*

*From past loves slain
lie many a hidden pain*

*Her arrival
loves' revival*

*Her flowers she loves them yellow
whoever is the fellow*

*If the sheep loves the fox
he could get small pox*

*Let me be the vector
for loves best nectar*

*Like two cooing doves
discussing their loves*

*Loves best offering
ends up as suffering*

*Loves best prize
is the big surprise*

*Loves darkest fears
can bring out the tears*

*Loves embrace
dispels all grace*

*Loves every passion
doesn't need a mansion*

*Loves grief
no relief*

*Loves highest pleasure
must be sought in leisure*

*Loves true desire
is a new attire*

*Loves' biggest prize
thoughts that surprise*

*Many a vexation
from loves fixation*

*Moves sideways faster
him who loves a lobster*

*No two loves are the same
so don't dish out blame*

*Once it is lost
loves labour has cost*

*One of loves essences
is to heighten your senses*

*One of loves wrinkles
face full of pimples*

*She loves it best
her own nest*

*The hostess loves most
who is a walking ghost*

*They have a propensity
to experience loves intensity*

*Two loves that feel like one
while they romp in the sun*

*We are all on a mission
to capture loves passion*

*What have we to gain
from loves every little pain*

Loves' best friend
is a diamond in the end

Loves' embrace
is gods grace

Loving

Half way up the stair
she gave him a loving air

Improve ties
with loving eyes

It pays
to have loving ways

Something in the air
made them a loving pair

Tender loving care
doesn't tame the bear

They were a loving pair
whose love needed repair

Lovingly

Every colour of feather
lovingly brought together

Would lovingly sit beside her
even the arachnid spider

Loyal

Easy to be loyal
to the lovely royal

Loyal and devoted
once they are voted

Subjects remain loyal
to kings queens and the royal

Loyalties

Loyalties divided
end up as voided

Loyalty

Loyalty and devotion
is it just a notion

Loyalty on the whole
is about a flag and a pole

Luck

Bad luck can devour
men in their ivory tower

Create your luck
with a bit of pluck

Every flower that I pluck
I give to her for good luck

Good luck and pluck
can get you unstuck

He had a penny for luck
and a quack for the duck

He ran out of pluck
but never out of luck

He who is pluck
gets stations of luck

I came upon luck
and was totally stuck

L

*If you pick upon your luck
you will get back your buck*

*It will bring you luck
if you pass the buck*

*Let's have a beer
before luck stops here*

*Nothing seems to work
where bad luck it lurk*

*Out of luck
disaster struck*

*She said best of luck
you need more pluck*

*To survive you need luck
and a little bit of pluck*

*When you are stuck
invoke your luck*

*With a sudden pluck
he ate an apple for luck*

Luckiest

*Friday in May
is the luckiest day*

Lucky

*How it took shape
the lucky escape*

*Lucky it was a pellet
and not a speeding bullet*

Lumbers

*He who lumbers
can't be good with numbers*

Luminous

*How to forsake
this luminous ache*

*Luminous sights
of the starry delight*

*When things look ominous
the background gets luminous*

Lunatic

*The less said
about the lunatic in the head*

Lunch

*I have a hunch
we will meet at lunch*

*Let's have lunch
there is food to munch*

Lure

*Old age is a lure
for many a cure*

*The spider will always try
to lure the unsuspecting fly*

Lures

*So many lures
to supposed cures*

Lurks

*Don't look for perks
danger where it lurks*

Luster

*To recover some of the luster
better to lance the blister*

Lustre

> To restore the lustre
> just use a duster

Lustrous

> Let it remain
> her lustrous mane

Luxurious

> Jumping rabbits
> have luxurious habits

Luxury

> Luxury it is said
> is in the softness of your bed

Lying

> Here was a peach
> lying on a sandy beach

> Lying on the green grass lawn
> they sang ghazals into the dawn

> There is no denying
> he has no fear of lying

Lyre

> Sitting by the winter fire
> she plucks away at the lyre

> The girl who played the lyre
> wore a pink attire

> The lyre has strings
> that pluck when it sings

M

Machine
> Everyday he toiled
> like a machine well oiled

Macon
> Let us go to macon
> to buy butter eggs and bacon

Made
> Made him forlorn
> being an object of scorn

Madness
> In a world full of madness
> there is sadness and gladness

Magic
> A magic wand is such
> that it can give you much

> Couplets without logic
> retain all the magic

> Fast fingers and magic
> for the rabbit has no logic

> I could make her very fond
> if I had a magic wand

> If it doesn't have logic
> it loses its magic

> In the magic world of mirrors
> that give you cold shivers

> Magic is found
> in the magical sound

> Magic was no news
> to her new pair of shoes

> More than just a notion
> this magic potion

> The bottle with the magic
> was hidden in the attic

> The magic in his prose
> pinker than the rose

> The magic of her smile
> hasn't shown up in a while

> There is magic in the air
> from the love they share

> Unstable logic
> will lose its magic

Magical
> Words with magical sounds
> and children making rounds

Magnificent
> Magnificent obsession
> is a whole life session

Magnify
> If you magnify your toe
> it could become your foe

Maid
> He who is staid
> cannot win the maid

> He who is staid
> will not find a maid

Majestic
> Every majestic peak
> clouds their company keep

> Every mountain has a story
> that speaks its majestic glory

Majesty
> I have yet to see our tapestry
> so she said her majesty

Make
> How to make it go
> that ain't at all so

Makeover
> No take over
> without makeover

Maker
> Not only is he a maker
> man is a risk taker

Male
> If the peacock is pale
> it is not a male

> The male puts to the test
> the female in the nest

Malice
> Much of it was malice
> when he emptied the silver chalice

> There is malice in this fox
> he is combing his locks

Malicious
> A malicious chap
> with a tilted cap

Mammal
> Whale is a mammal
> so is the camel

Man
> I'll do what I can
> they said man to man

> Man blinketh
> as he thinketh

> Man in the moon in seems
> sends all the moonbeams

> Man is in the main
> about causing god much pain

Man must toil
to make the pot boil

The man is still within
the moon when it is thin

Manipulate
To make things look bigger
manipulate the figure

Manipulated
until they capitulated

Mankind's
Mankind's curse
how to fill the purse

Manner
All manner of characters
ply the ocean waters

Her manner was slow
without losing her glow

Was his own doing
his manner of going

Wearing trousers and shirt
his manner was curt

Good manners and what not
I do not wish to be taught

Mantelpiece
Her photo my best piece
upon the mantelpiece

March
Mid-day in march
the weather it will scorch

Mares
He who rides two mares
need not keep any spares

Many mares and their colt
live in the town of Odebolt

Marginal
Adam was original
all the rest were marginal

Marigold
The marigold and the mould
live in each others fold

Marital
Marital bliss
not just his

Marital woes
down to his toes

Our marital choices
based on inner voices

Market
The market it crashed
and the potato got mashed

Marriage
A marriage that is filling
for every gut feeling

Cricket twenty twenty
marriage fifty fifty

Don't look for porridge
outside your marriage

Happy eating porridge
though unhappy in marriage

How to re-arrange
a marriage so strange

Marriage as an institution
headed for destitution

Marriage gives you a start
so both can play a part

Marriage has its nights
and fights under the lights

Marriage has its nights
and its delights

Marriage has logic
if it is biologic

Marriage is a matter
where it rains pitter patter

Marriage is a venture
a mindless adventure

Marriage is desired
for parents who have sired

Marriage is no scourge
if you have the urge

Marriage it stares
at our daily cares

Marriage it was hatched
before they were matched

Marriage repairs
your daily cares

Who has ever heard
that marriage is absurd

Why is marriage the rage
if both end up in a cage

You're marriage will be fitter
if both of you are not bitter

Hell gave birth
to some marriages on earth

Marriages are made in heaven
at half past seven

Married

Married in haste
can't find toothpaste

Married in secret
after consulting the egret

She is married to someone other
cannot undo the tether

She married a miller
who was strong as a pillar

She was married to a wild
man who still was a child

The landed married the gentry
for the good of the country

Though he was married
he was happily harried

When married life upended
no one was offended

Marrow

Down to his marrow
he was straight and narrow

Marry

Marry a householder
is what I told her

Much weight it will carry
if you ask her to just marry

The burdens we carry
after we marry

The days will be more sunny
if you go and marry a bunny

Mask

Was it too much to ask
what lay behind his mask

Master

A husband must be a master
at doing all things faster

Better learn faster
you're dealing with a master

How can he master
who reads poetry faster

How can we master the night
without a flash of light

It gets done much faster
if you learn from the master

Man is a master
at forgetting the past faster

Master has his say
but the dog has his way

Run away from him faster
who is a bad task master

Run from him faster
he who is your master

The dog runs faster
when he sees his master

The hand of the master
gets to it faster

They catch up with you faster
the things that you don't master

Why burn the toast faster
when you think you are the master

Mastered

All the eggs have mastered
how to hatch while plastered

Mastery

Mastery of words
by nightingales and birds

Mastery over time
makes it easy the climb

Matador

The matador is well
though the bull it was that fell

Match
How to keep score
if the match is a bore

Match
The match then will clinch
if you give them an inch

There must be a catch
when deeds don't match

There was nothing to match
the jeans full of patch

Two points from the match
ran into a bad patch

When you strike a match
a fire it did hatch

When you strike a match
a flame it will hatch

With pajamas that match
she found him to be a good catch

Material
Material wealth
doesn't improve health

Maternal
She kept it open and wide
her maternal side

Maternity
A small slice of eternity
time taken for maternity

Mathematical
Mathematical blunders
from dancing numbers

Matrimony
The key word in matrimony
is not matri but money

Matter
Does it matter
the silly things they chatter

These things matter
when you sit down to chatter

Me
Me and her
have each other to purr

Me and my pup
go for the milk in the cup

Meal
No fish no meal
for the monk seal

They hit the wheel
after the meal

Like two seals
sharing meals

Three meals a day
and a place to stay

Mean
All painted in green
doesn't mean he is mean

*Forces unseen
that can make you mean*

*Have to come clean
both lean and the mean*

*He became mean
from too much jelly bean*

*He could be called mean
who keeps your wounds green*

*His halo may be clean
but he still can be mean*

*It would be mean
to feed him just a bean*

*It's that puff of nicotine
that makes him so mean*

*Lean and mean
where have you been*

*Men with mean feet
make bullets hit the street*

*Sometimes serene
other times mean*

*Though feeble and lean
his temper is mean*

Meander

*Don't meander
get down to candor*

Meaner

*He became leaner
also very much meaner*

Meaning

*I couldn't find any meaning
the way they were leaning*

*I heard the meaning
from the way she was leaning*

*Like a kaleidoscope beaming
each read a change of meaning*

*Meaning must be fed
to that which is unsaid*

*So many levels of meaning
not at all demeaning*

*Some have a leaning
to discover the hidden meaning*

*The meaning may not be clear
but it has no peer*

*The well meaning leech
made his skin bleach*

Meaningful

*Meaningful rhymes
for difficult times*

Meaningless

*Elephants they hang around
making meaningless sound*

Means

*Behind the scenes
are the men of means*

*Go find your Samson
even if it means ransom*

Rhyming English Couplets

He who spills the beans
better be a man of means

How to clone the genes
of the men of means

Once you have the means
go buy the beans

What all this means
is a hill full of beans

Whatever your means
live within your beans

Why they wear jeans
these men of means

With holes in his jeans
he lived beyond his means

Meant

A scent that is meant
only for the rose to vent

For her this rose was meant
with every bit of its scent

How can we see
what we were meant to be

Me and he meant to be
so said she

Snowman was meant
to eventually melt

Some things are meant to be
said the drone to the bee

Somethings are meant to be
whether you be he or she

The camel isn't meant
to be in a tent

The closed door was meant
to show where she went

Whiff of a scent
for her only meant

Measure

A virtue once lost
can't measure the cost

How to measure the speed
of his incessant greed

Measure by measure
he secures his treasure

Medal

It was not for the medal
they put foot on the pedal

Medicine

Medicine is an art
that sets it apart

Mediocrity

Easy to tell
that mediocrity will sell

Mediocrity cannot be cured
by simply being endured

Mediocrity dwells
on the stories it tells

Medium

Butter is the medium
to ease the tedium

Meek

How can she be meek
who has pink in her cheek

Which one is meek
when two people speak

Meet

How shall we meet
the dangers in the street

Meeting

Better to be late
in your meeting with fate

I have set up a meeting
with death to come greeting

Why should every meeting
of ours be so fleeting

Meets

Every now and then
paper it meets my pen

Man meets woman in a garden
without being seen by the warden

When bad meets good
they offer each other food

Mellow

He is a mellow cat
who wears a tilted hat

Melodies

Soft melodies to behold
from the flowing river all cold

To melodies belong
the universe and its song

How to fix it soon
this melody out of tune

Melody and rhyme
with the passage of time

When the melody is plain
it will soothingly remain

Memories

A man without a past
whose memories couldn't last

At me they scream
memories from my dream

Both hers and his
sweet memories made of this

Days when I was young and strong
to far off memories belong

Fond memories are here
wherever they appear

Fond memories they hold
feelings both hot and cold

For memories to thrive
they must come alive

From memories they bubble
without any trouble

Her memories could be other
than discussing just the weather

How can they be wrong
memories so strong

I have memories to forget
before I get set

I have memories to thank
but no money in the bank

In memories long
a beautiful song

In the cobwebs of the mind
memories of a kind

Into memories seared
things most feared

It's all in the sound
where memories abound

Leave the past behind
as if our memories are blind

Lingered into the twilight
memories of the night

Memories abound
in every little sound

Memories and the pain
engraved in the brain

Memories are in the main
about love and its pain

Memories as such
need a featherlite touch

Memories bring tears
until the mind clears

Memories can be had
of both sad and glad

Memories from the past
beyond death they will last

Memories from the past
reclaimed to make them last

Memories from the past
some they do last

Memories have a duty
seek loves beauty

Memories have eyes
all the way to the skies

Memories I must prize
of words and wisdom both twice

Memories I was fond
in the town of fishpond

Memories I wish
were always made of this

Memories made of bliss
how can they be better than this

Memories made to last
sweet things from the past

Memories must be stored
so you won't be bored

Memories my dear
become crystal clear

Memories of bliss
hers or his

Memories of bliss
were made of this

Memories of delight
soon out of sight

Memories of our bliss
much more than this

Memories old and new
filled with love anew

Memories remain
of the sounds in the rain

Memories sublime
through the windows of time

Memories such as this
how could ever we miss

Memories such as this
the cobra and his hiss

Memories suppressed
suddenly expressed

Memories that are frozen
were carefully chosen

Memories that are lasting
never lose their frosting

Memories that I let
easily forget

Memories that last
are things from the past

Memories that last
from the unforgettable past

Memories that linger
can be counted on a finger

Memories they keep
well in my sleep

Memories they lie in a heap
unattended while I am asleep

Memories to cling to
and to sing too

Memories to cling
and songs to sing

Memories unwanted
had me all haunted

Memories we are told
have the value of gold

Memories were made of this
says the cobra with a hiss

Memories will hatch
when you have love to catch

Memories will stay why
from the corner of her eye

Memories worth saving
about love and its craving

Much better clutched
the memories untouched

My memories will stay
how graceful she was in grey

New synapses are built
so memories they don't wilt

M

Rhyming English Couplets

*Nothing closer than this
to memories made of bliss*

*Old memories raked
need to be freshly baked*

*Printed words have memories
enhanced by eating celeries*

*Somewhere in the past very deep
I have memories that keep*

*Tenderly dealing
of memories with feeling*

*The eye only sees
the water colour memories*

*The past we must greet
of memories that were sweet*

*To re-live the past
memories must last*

*Touch not and they will last
memories from the past*

*Turn the face of sad
through memories that are glad*

*When I think of you and sing
fond memories they bring*

*Why don't they last
memories from the past*

*With fond memories only left
that were kept hidden in her breast*

*With her memories rife
best moments of my life*

*With memories all distorted
we politely gracefully parted*

*With memories to cling to
and a heart to sing to*

Memory

*A memory once stored
can be restored*

*Always in my memory
us both eating celery*

*Before the memory erases
I love to sing your praises*

*clings to the memory
better than celery*

*Distant reaches of the memory
where love is stored cleverly*

*Dormant synapses
memory lapses*

*Down memory lane
where the windows have no pane*

*Every distant memory
recounted all for free*

*Failing synapses
cause memory lapses*

*He had an unfailing memory
from all the celery*

*Her smile in my memory green
waiting anxiously to be seen*

M

His memory went pale
once filled with ale

I recorded her love in memory
when I chewed upon celery

In my memory they last
some glimpses of the past

In the recesses of my memory
I can smell the taste of celery

It must have been the celery
building blocks of memory

Like cherries on the tree
sweet memory

Memory and action
have their own traction

Memory can be taught
when you put sound into thought

Memory failing
mind derailing

Memory gets caught
in useless thought

Memory has been found
to be based entirely on sound

Memory has much to gain
if we sleep again and again

Memory I hear
is to make the past clear

Memory is a kind
of molecule of the mind

Memory is a pot
that needs stirring a lot

Memory is a thing
to which we all cling

Memory is bound
to music and sound

Memory is deep
for fragrance that is sweet

Memory is strong
for opinions that are wrong

Memory is strong
when there is love in a song

Memory it treasures
loves best pleasures

Memory lapses
from aging synapses

Memory loss
is paradise lost

Memory molecules spewing
without any reviewing

Memory of stays
in new and original ways

Memory takes to wings
from dissimilar things

Mind collapses
from memory lapses

Tastes worse than celery
the details in my memory

The daily tussles
of our memory muscles

The memory pot
gets stirred a lot

Their memory is long
whose acumen is strong

Their memory is short
who have temptations to thwart

To memory you must commit
without any limit

Where have you been
while my memory wears thin

Men

Men were not at hand
when dinosaurs roamed the land

Men will never tire
of wearing new attire

Mend

Bent it stays
if you don't mend your ways

Every old friend
has fences to mend

Find ways to mend
the beginning and the end

Forever it stays
once you mend your ways

How to mend the breach
that is totally out of reach

How to mend your ways
in ten busy days

I have fences to mend
with god in the end

I hope his heart will mend
forever in the end

I only stays
if you mend your ways

In life it pays
to mend your ways

Make them pay
who don't mend their way

Mend fences
with broken sentences

Mend your way
for love to stay

Mend your way
or love won't stay

Mend your ways
or I don't stays

Mend your ways
or number your days

Mend yourself fast
in ways that will last

Miles apart they stays
who don't mend their ways

So many things to mend
and hearts in the end

*So much to mend
and people to offend*

*They will part ways
who don't mend their ways*

*Too late to mend
your character in the end*

*When will it all end
so many things to mend*

*When your career needs a mend
go to the temple and bend*

*Works out in the end
when you have fences to mend*

Mendacity

*He is all audacity
with a little mendacity*

Mended

*Don't be offended
if my mind isn't mended*

*His mended ways
were bygone days*

Mending

*Broken hearts need mending
and a bit of welding*

Mends

*Husband stays
who mends his ways*

Mental

*Mental floss
doesn't stop tooth loss*

Mental

*Mental illness
has a kind of stillness*

Mention

*Don't ever mention
your distension*

Mentor

*I want to meet your mentor
he said to the tormentor*

Merciful

*Better to be at least
merciful to the beast*

*Merciful release
if you please*

*Oh merciful god
give their love the nod*

Mercifully

*Mercifully it ended
with our hearts all mended*

Merciless

*The merciless have shown
the way to the throne*

Mercy

*Angel of mercy
was not a heresy*

*Don't offend
for mercy is a friend*

*Have mercy now and then
in the use of your pen*

Rhyming English Couplets

Mercy is the least
you can be to the beast
———
Mercy lies in heaven
if you get there by seven

Mermaid

Mermaid in the river
gave him a shiver
———
Every mariner has eyes
for mermaids on ice
———
He goes to sea
hoping mermaids he will see
———
Sailing sea to sea
wherever mermaids may be
———
The wonder that is the sea
where mermaids are meant to be

Merry

First have your say
then go your merry way
———
Many a merry dart
he collects in his cart
———
Said the cat to the canary
why are you so merry

Mesmerizing

Mesmerizing tale
about the blue whale

Mess

Why this mess
it's only chess

Message

A message it hums
the jungle drums
———
Get to it faster
message from the master
———
He became very livid
when the message he got was vivid
———
If you talk too fast
the message won't last
———
It starts with a simple word
whose message is easily heard
———
Message in a bottle
was meant to startle
———
Message it sends
to different friends
———
Message they strums
through jungle drums
———
Message though clear
we prefer not to hear
———
The message couldn't have been crisper
though a thin whisper
———
The message gets lost
when news travels fast
———
The message in a bottle
was all filled with prattle
———
The message went out
the problem was too stout
———

M

The pig got the message
he could end up as sausage

There was something in her whisper
the message couldn't be crisper

Whose is it loss
when message doesn't get across

It has messages to send
when your hair stands on end

Messages divine
between the lines

Messages of love
in the flight of the Dove

Messages that are mixed
must have been jinxed

Messages we are fond
from the heavens and beyond

Messages you will find
in the recesses of the mind

The mirror it will send
messages that offend

Metal

They went in search of metal
to turn it into gold petal

Metaphor

What are you waiting for
come up with a metaphor

What is it for
this metaphor

Methods

All methods must rest
after they fail the test

Methods you must borrow
how to conquer sorrow

Metric

Metric might
is always right

Midnight

It is past the midnight hour
I look for food to devour

The midnight has jaws
and teeth in its claws

Might

Don't bring it up
it might fill the cup

How can it be seen
what might have been

Might as well be rope
when they dish out hope

What might have been
has now lost its sheen

What they might say
can make you pay

Mighty

High and the mighty
can be a bit flighty

Mild

Many a parent mild
begets a thankless child

Miles

I have many miles to log
before I reach Prague

Many miles they logs
who go from clogs to clogs

Many miles to log
footsteps in the fog

Many miles to log
in a curtain of fog

Many miles yet to be logged
before my arteries become clogged

Many miles to log
before I meet Mr. Hogg

Miles and miles she logs
on her clipity, clipity clogs

Miles he logs
clapping his clogs

Milkman

In the early morning mist
the milkman to his tryst

Million

Million miles to go
to find love in all its glow

Red faced camelion
one in a million

Mind

A mind made up
can fill your cup

A mind made up
can it fill the cup

A mind re-arranged
has it really changed

A mind subdued
cannot ever feud

A mind without a master
gets into trouble faster

A new way of looking
at what the mind is cooking

A question with two sides
is in the mind of all brides

A receptive mind
will not be blind

A state of mind
happiness is a kind

Be ready for the grind
with an open mind

Better than my own
the mind of a drone

Brain begins to talk
when the mind takes a walk

Can it be curbed
the mind disturbed

Don't be blind
to the workings of the mind

Don't fall behind
you are always on my mind

Don't let your mind falter
when you step up to the altar

Don't think I am blind
you're always on my mind

Each other they find
the brain and the mind

Each other they find
the music and the mind

Enclosed you will find
things that tickle your mind

Forever wandering mind
to obvious things very blind

He asked his mind to spare
what was already in there

He woke up to find
he had lost his mind

Her mind becomes a haze
with every wandering gaze

His mind it became blurred
from her every teasing word

His mind moved to the braids
when he was with the maids

His mind was all glitter
when he missed a sitter

How can I mend
this mind no end

How can it be blind
the well prepared mind

How can we be blind
to images in the mind

How can we be blind
to the myriad facets of the mind

How to find
the recesses in the mind

How to go forward
with a mind that is wayward

How to set ablaze
your mind through the haze

How to train
a mind with no brain

If you have axe to grind
do it with a clear mind

If you listen to a good tape
your mind it will take shape

Just for starters
take your mind off matters

Let us meet behind
the further reaches of the mind

Man must have his tent
so his mind doesn't get bent

Many a day he toiled
to get his mind all oiled

Many a mind set
may not be an asset

Mind and body
both need toddy

Mind can take you where
no one else is there

Mind filled with terror
prone to make error

Mind is a palace
where we get solace

Mind laid bare
from here to there

Mind your cap
you're on the last lap

Mind your longings
they end up as belongings

My mind is in a grip
when my heart takes a trip

My mind it has taught
me how to say forgot

Newness you will find
in the newly wired mind

No more beers
until the mind clears

No point in dithering
when the mind is withering

Nothing escapes her mind
though partially blind

Once they read your mind
they can rob you blind

Our mind is the foe
said the average joe

Penguins they don't mind
when snow storms make them blind

Please be kind
to the mutterings of my mind

Please be kind
to the stammerings of my mind

She put ease into his mind
when love for him was blind

So much of their mind
to each other blind

Some parts of the mind
why are they blind

Stories they will find
to unsettle the mind

Stuff happens
mind sharpens

That's how my mind was made
up in the sunshine and shade

The corners of my mind
I once thought were blind

The ear and the mind
is enough for the blind

M

*The eye is blind
to corners in the mind*

*The galloping mind
to many things blind*

*The mind can take you places
where the shoes have no laces*

*The mind has lost all reason
depending on the season*

*The mind I have found
is wired only for sound*

*The mind in a clutter
speech is a stutter*

*The mind is a bottomless pit
don't know where these thoughts sit*

*The mind is a kingdom
where memories store wisdom*

*The mind it is caught
in a tapestry of thought*

*The mind it races
to uncharted places*

*The mind it sings
enchanting things*

*The mind thinks of the senses
as just pretenses*

*The mind will settle
for coffee in the kettle*

*The mind would heal
if the brain could feel*

*The unprepared mind
is one of a kind*

*To a man without his mind
the world would be blind*

*To the higher reaches of the mind
I reach out in a bind*

*Uncluttered mind
can afford to be blind*

*Vagaries you will find
in the deep thinking mind*

*What will we find
in the recesses of the mind*

*When I am in a bind
I say never mind*

*When I spoke to her my mind
her love it became kind*

*When it crosses your mind
pretend you are blind*

*When the mind spins its magic
where is the need for logic*

*When your mind is narrow
you look like a sparrow*

*Who are not of one mind
need not be called blind*

*Whose mind it needs fixing
with him don't go mixing*

With every ticking of the clock
the mind ends up in a lock

With you on my mind
how can I fall behind

Mindedly

Single mindedly
he made to her a plea

Mindful

Mindful of his passions
she adjusted her fashions

Mindless

A mindless impulse
has its own pulse

Minds

Find a better way
to make their minds sway

In my minds eye
I hope I never die

Minds profound
on spaceships bound

More than just a read
we have minds to feed

Our minds we need to reign
In London or in spain

Two minds they treasure
love in equal measure

Will it always remain
the minds' dark terrain

Wisps of thought
form the minds parking lot

Mine

She said she will be mine
if we both go out to dine

Miner

The miner he gets hold
of a mine full of gold

Mingle

Don't hang your shingle
where sand and water mingle

Finger tips when they mingle
beginning of a tingle

I walked upon the shingle
where the ocean waters mingle

If you mingle with new races
you will get to know their faces

It is better to mingle
if your name is Dingle

With jug of beer they mingle
and with pockets that jingle

Mint

She passed him the mint sauce
as he slipped and fell on the moss

The repeated mint
of a genetic misprint

Minute

Minute by minute it spews
the good and the bad news

Miracle

*Miracle happens now
and then where there is love*

*Miracles don't happen
as nearly as often*

*Miracles make a noise
and give us a new voice*

*Miracles they come and nod
if you put your trust in god*

Mirror

*Look yourself in the mirror
and get a cold shiver*

*Mirror has its say
wherever you be may*

*Mirror mirror on the wall
why wait for my teeth to fall*

*Short or tall
the mirror says it all*

*Hall of mirrors
spine full of shivers*

Mirthful

*Every mirthful boy
brings his mother joy*

Misadventure

*He lost his denture
from a misadventure*

Misbehaves

*He has close shaves
who misbehaves*

Mischief

*Stay a bit longer
you mischief monger*

*When mischief it tempts
no one pre-empts*

Miseries

*He collected miseries
as if they were treasuries*

Misery

*Man is at his best
putting misery to the test*

*Misery is no symphony
in any kind of company*

*Misery will ride
on the spoils of pride*

Misfortune

*Don't play the tune
that spells misfortune*

*Misfortune say the cats
is when they run out of rats*

Misguided

*The mind misguided
must be avoided*

*They need to be chided
those who are misguided*

Mislead

*To mislead is in the main
the job of the brain*

Misleading
Misleading stories
of past glories

Misplaced
Effort misplaced
when a mirage is chased

Miss
All we have is us
let's not miss the bus

Do not miss
this sonic bliss

Everyday I miss you
with teardrop on tissue

How did I miss
a blessing such as this

Not a thing you will miss
in-spite of ellipsis

On days such as this
how can I not you miss

Missed
For every step that he missed
there was a sound that hissed

Missing
When a feather goes missing
my cap does the hissing

Mission
He is on a mission
to acquire erudition

Make it an obsession
your fact finding mission

My peripheral vision
is on a fact finding mission

Our life's only mission
to stop nuclear fission

What is its mission
this thing called inhibition

Missionary
Missionary zeal
has widespread appeal

Misspoken
Of all the misspoken words
this one must be heard

Mist
Gradually became thin
the mist as it came in

Mistake
All it takes
is one mistake

Mistake made twice
happened in a trice

Mistake of my life
to be into strife

What can I make
of this mistake

M

Mistaken

A hat full of thorns
can't be mistaken for horns

A mistaken belief
brings no relief

A step once taken
turned out to be mistaken

He was mistaken
when his private knowing was broken

I was mistaken
about the bribes that were taken

Mistakes

How to stick a knife
into the mistakes of my life

Mistakes are a part
of a vision that is short

Mistakes belong
mostly to the strong

Mistakes can be made
in the sunlight and in the shade

Mistakes from the past
cumulative and vast

Mistakes from the past
get rid of them fast

Mistakes from the past
how long will they last

Mistakes from the past
long shadows they cast

Mistakes have the power
to send you to the shower

Mistakes that are small
are better than that are tall

Mistakes that were made once
I ended up looking the dunce

Mistakes though vast
can be made not to last

Mistakes though vast
we must bury the past

Mistakes when they pile
wipes away the smile

Mistakes will be made
in the sunshine and in the shade

The printer had a hand
in mistakes where they stand

Why are they made
mistakes in the shade

Mistook

Mistook for swagger
his precarious stagger

Misunderstanding

Every misunderstanding
gets an ovation standing

Misuse

Don't misuse
your tongue when in use

Moan

Better to moan
in the presence of your drone

Better to moan
in the privacy of your home

He sat alone
with a scornful moan

Moan and groan
through every stepping stone

Said the bee to the drone
why do you so moan

Said the queen bee to the drone
why do you so much moan

Mob

They will make you sob
if you hob-hob with the mob

Moderation

Moderation is fatal
unless it is total

Modest

He who is modest
doesn't speak the loudest

Moment

Every moment matters
well dressed or in tatters

For every moment he sought her
he became an inch shorter

The moment maketh the man
the only way he can

Momentary

The momentary surges
of dissipating urges

Moments

Moments from the past
how to make them last

Moments maketh the man
that must be gods plan

Moments of trauma
not without drama

Moments re-captured
had me enraptured

Moments such as this
feel like eternal bliss

Moments that are fearful
can also be tearful

Moments that were golden
from our youth were stolen

Moments unfold
that are shiny as gold

Sacramental moments
need no comments

To re-live there is a cost
of moments from the past

Money

Bees make honey
man makes money

Bees will give you honey
for a little bit of money

Can't be got by stealth
money or good health

Eggs for money
and hen for a penny

Enough money for the cab
in my string net bag

Follow the money
till the nose gets runny

Go to the market
with money in the pocket

He called her honey
and ran through her money

He collected bags of gunny
to put all his money

He has money to spare
who spends it with care

How to earn money
in life to buy honey

It's not about money
this thing called alimony

Like bees to honey
people to money

Money and learning
both come from yearning

Money can change
even the very strange

Money earned from pottery
he spent it all on lottery

Money has influences
on their affluences

Money has them beaming
at a life without meaning

Money in the pocket
eye in the socket

Money is a buffer
to borrow is to suffer

Money is a plague
whose cause is vague

Money is about blending
both earning and spending

Money is just a means
of filling pockets with beans

Money is mine to lose
not for them to use

Money is the cure
for the sound and secure

Money is the test
of which friend is best

Money it seems
goes to men of means

Money rarely lingers
it slips through the fingers

Money they say
goes a long way

M

*Money we must nurse
for purse is a curse*

*Money we must pay
for what we need in a day*

*Money will end
friendships on the mend*

*My joy will be unending
if you send me money for spending*

*No money to burn
if you don't earn*

*Not enough money
until it fills the gunny*

*Put your trust
in money you must*

*Save every penny
when time is money*

*Sign of decay
is money they say*

*Spend money for sure
to live rich and die poor*

*The mind remembers
money is numbers*

*There is no knowing
when the money stops flowing*

*They call you honey
just to get your money*

*They eat into your penny
money who need many*

*Though money is expendable
he was very dependable*

*We each will get our turn
but not without money to burn*

*When money is tight
so is your plight*

*When my angel calls
I take money to the stalls*

*With money he won't part
he who is smart*

*Your days will be good
if you spend money on food*

Monk

*The monk who came to tea
was bitten by a flea*

Monogamy

*Don't tell
but monogamy is well*

*Gin rummy
and monogamy*

*If monogamy could be stored
someone would be bored*

*Monogamy has pleasures
also many treasures*

*Monogamy is for the birds
and for the bison herds*

*Oh so yummy
Monogamy*

Monster

Close shave
from the monster wave

He should rid himself faster
of the part of him that is a monster

Mood

Altered mood
from tinned food

Change is food
also for the mood

Don't brood
recapture your mood

For some it is food
changes in the mood

He considers it his food
who chooses his own mood

He eats cakes
whenever his mood takes

Items of food
for the right mood

Mood is never blue
when friends they are true

No chance of mood
when cat sees food

Moon

Dark clouds they swoon
when they see the full moon

Dark side of the moon
harbours a baboon

It is never too far
the moon from the little star

On a dark mid-night in June
the only light was in the moon

On the night of the full moon
they danced at the saloon

The moon must make room
for the sun in the morning soon

The moon was in its arc
without losing its spark

The new full moon
to make you hum a tune

There is a lagoon
on the dark side of the moon

Through the cold I swoon
at the full winter moon

Why is the moon
so dull at noon

Moonlight

Holding hands in June
in the moonlight and perfume

Moral

Go look for a moral
deep down in the coral

He was perfectly moral
and shiny as coral

It better be sound
the moral ground

Moral collapse
has many a relapse

There must be a moral
if you win her heart with a coral

There must be a moral
why the reef is all coral

Morals take to flight
on many a drunken night

When you dive for corals
abandon your morals

Moribund

Not enough fund
for the cause moribund

Morn

On his deathbed in the morn
he ate pop corn

Where have the sparrows gone
so early in the morn

Morning

As a morning starter
tighten your garter

Drops of the morning dew
on petals of every hue

In the early morning chill
when sleep has had it's fill

In the morning as it wings
the nightingale it sings

Morning it rings
when the nightingale sings

Out of the house storming
on a cold Monday morning

Rose petals in the morn
the morning dew they adorn

The early morning scene
in England must be seen

The early morning sun
scales mountain peaks for fun

The morning fog must call
on mountains short or tall

The morning must be well
there is a tolling of the bell

The morning once broken
moon and the stars just token

The morning sky was flush
and the grass all green and lush

The morning sun had a flare
and I had a breakfast to share

The spotted deer they run
to the colours of the morning sun

To-morrow it comes yawning
long before the morning

Mornings of egg and bacon
with a pinch of salt must be taken

M

Morrow

Wakes up to a bright morrow
he who relinquishes sorrow

What morrow might bring
might give me cause to sing

Mosquitoes

Mosquitoes singing loud
under rain cloud

Mosquitoes take to flight
on a warm tedious night

Why do mosquitoes sing
just before they sting

Mother

All the things I didn't do
for a mother who once I knew

Mother will often spy
her child with a watchful eye

She asked her mother why
with a babies trusting eye

She turned the baby loose
the mother goose

Motion

Indifferent to motion
he sat and rubbed lotion

Set it in motion
eternal devotion

The river stops its motion
once it reaches the ocean

The waters of the ocean
constantly in motion

Waters of the ocean
constantly in motion

Motives

Motives are best
put to the test

Mould

How to spin gold
from a simple little mould

Mould it stays
from the good old days

Mountain

Mountain top
is the final stop

Snow melts and leaks
when the mountain top speaks

The fog it stops
at the mountain tops

The mountain aims to win
where the air is soft and thin

Mountainous

No place on earth
with this mountainous girth

Mountains

Mountains of sand
make for a big land

*Mountains steep and tall
comes the flowing waterfall*

*The mountains they play their song
with a plume that floats very long*

Mouth

*His mouth was drawn
to envious scorn*

*Keep your eyes peeled
and the mouth sealed*

Move

*They make their move
when they have things to prove*

*He moved from town to town
adding lines to his frown*

*The monkey on its haunches
moves along the branches*

Much

*As such
didn't add up to much*

*No such thing as such
called much too much*

*They make of it much
his midas touch*

Multiple

*He is no elf
he has a multiple self*

*One of them is an elf
of his multiple self*

Multitude

*They can be wrong
the multitude though strong*

Mum

*How to keep him mum
without opium*

Murmer

*The stethoscope was pressed firmer
to elicit the soft murmer*

Muscle

*As the words tussle
with the writing muscle*

*Build your muscles
for everyday tussles*

*Muscles went into a quiver
as he jumped into the river*

Muscular

*These are just pegs
not muscular legs*

*They start their sparring
with a muscular warning*

Music

*Defies all logic
for she is my music*

*In a manner of speaking
music is living*

*In parts of my head
music is dead*

M

*Is it the music or the motion
the cause of all commotion*

*More than a passing interest found
in the music that filled the sound*

*Music and song
to love they belong*

*Music and song
to the artist belong*

*Music and sound
makes the world go round*

*Music does it best
but poetry is next*

*Music has a gear
in the right hemisphere*

*Music has a sound
that makes thoughts nice and round*

*Music has touch
appreciated much*

*Music is a choice
of your inner voice*

*Music is a feeling
to the ear very appealing*

*Music is a force
with a permanent source*

*Music is a juice
we just can't refuse*

*Music is a kind
of oxygen for the mind*

*Music is a part
of memories of the heart*

*Music is a part
of us from the start*

*Music is fed
by the orchestra in my head*

*Music is fed
to the hotline in the head*

*Music is in part
food for the heart*

*Music is in the main
about the human brain*

*Music is kind
to the person who is blind*

*Music is neat
like the heart beat*

*Music is well
that has taste and smell*

*Music it can train
our emotion and the brain*

*Music makes it clear
meant to bring out a tear*

*Music makes sense
while smelling incense*

*Music on the whole
is good for the soul*

*Music on the whole
makes up the soul*

Rhyming English Couplets

Music will pick
up even the sick

No music can match
what the nigthtingale can hatch

Song of the road
is music for the toad

The mind tends to pick
word set to music

The music of the mountains
lie in the dripping of their fountains

The words make it round
the music and its sound

There is music in the air
of the dancing pair

There is music in the rain
also in the train

There was music in my head
the day we were to be wed

To keep moving along
play music and song

Words set to music
that sound very slick

Musical chairs
no room for pairs

Musical

Musical memory
improved by celery

Must

If you cannot decipher
you must be a heifer

Other than a wasp
all else we must grasp

Myopic

Myopic and blinkered
they don't wish to be tinkered

Mysteries

All manner of mysteries
that hold on to their histories

All of life's mysteries
are in men's histories

How can she be blind
to the mysteries of the mind

Mysteries they shroud
within the wandering cloud

Mysterious

Children are so curious
for all things are mysterious

The mysterious spark
that makes a dog bark

Mystery

Born into this mystery
of love and its history

I leave it to history
and an element of mystery

I'll leave it to history
to unravel the mystery

M

*In mystery it was shrouded
together when they crowded*

*My life is so crowded
and in mystery shrouded*

*Mystery revealed
signed and sealed*

*Mystery shrouds
the man who made clouds*

*No more mystery
about the brain and its chemistry*

*Shrouded in mystery
unsavoury history*

*The mystery of dawn
to admire we were born*

*Way back into history
to unravel earths mystery*

Mystic

*Make it your theme
this mystic scheme*

Mystical

*Every mystical meeting
turned out to be so fleeting*

*Mystical source
takes a devious course*

*Seen through her face
was a deep mystical place*

*The mystical source
is on course*

Myth

*Described with pith
though shrouded in myth*

*Myth has power
hard to devour*

*Where is thy pith
or is it just myth*

Mythical

*How can it be ethical
just because it is mythical*

*Of all the mythical tales
it's the one about the whales*

Myths

*Images that shatter
myths that matter*

*Puranic myths
are made of piths*

N

Name

*By any other name
she wouldn't be the same*

*His name was charley
he lived on wheat and barley*

*Street without a name
where children play the game*

Naps

*Don't let your synapse
take silent naps*

Narrow

*From the straight and the narrow
strayed the sparrow*

*In narrow streets of cobbled stone
they wished upon a wishbone*

*Narrow strip of the moon
clearly seen in June*

*Options become narrow
with just bow and arrow*

*Options become narrow
if you use bow and arrow*

*With a mind so narrow
he could be mistaken for a sparrow*

*Your vision will be narrow
if you are a sparrow*

Nation

*He made his nation proud
with eloquence that was loud*

Nature

*All of nature is a part
of a beating universal heart*

*Good nature is a feature
of a well brought up creature*

*Human nature
is a solemn creature*

*Human nature
is a true poacher*

*Human nature
not a good teacher*

*It's the nature of the lie
don't ask why*

Nature does her rounds
to the howl of the wolf and hounds

Nature does not brood
when butterflies search for food

Nature has done it's best
but man hasn't stood the test

Nature keeps her feature
and protects every creature

Nature takes pains
to bury our remains

Nature will be abiding
if you come out of hiding

The nature of her craft
was how to make love soft

With nature as my teacher
I practiced being a preacher

Men must make it a duty
to preserve natures beauty

Natures best call
snowflakes when they fall

Naughty

Man who is haughty
tends to be naughty

Navigate

I can navigate any land
with the help of her steering hand

Near

Make it clear
D-day is near

Neat

To think on your feet
is so very neat

Necklace

So much solace
from the beaded necklace

He is all pockets
necklaces and lockets

Nectar

The bee has a nose so long
it finds nectar where it belong

Need

A man needs nine lives
to have as many wives

A rough and ready stand
in need of a steady hand

All I need is wine
and all things divine

All you need is speed
to fulfill your need

Breakneck speed
where is the need

Do they need a reason
to celebrate the holy season

Do they need wings
these lofty things

*Do we need rifles
when the world is full of trifles*

*Every day we feed
our greed and our need*

*Every ingot will buoy
our need for a bit of joy*

*Every mammal big
need not wear a wig*

*Every pipe needs a lug
of tobacco plug*

*Go for the toast
when you need it most*

*Greed beyond need
doesn't need a seed*

*He knelt down wearing tweed
fulfilling her every need*

*I am on my last leg
all I need is a peg*

*I don't need reminding
that the grain needs grinding*

*I need to be belonging
to a deep sense of longing*

*Let's start anew
now that I need you*

*Need I be smitten
by every script written*

*Need I say more
than ever before*

*Need more than dimes
for modern times*

*No need to be wary
about the house on the prairie*

*No need to brood
poetry is a mood*

*No need to freeze
it's the soft summer breeze*

*No need to gloat
you're in my boat*

*No need to goad
a croak from the toad*

*No need to quell
fragrance that is well*

*No need to ration
anything filled with passion*

*No need to shave
for I am going to my grave*

*No need to take stock
when key fits the lock*

*No need to wait
your fires will burn straight*

*Rest was the need
for man and his steed*

*Self destruction is the need
for man and his creed*

*She who is nimble
doesn't need a thimble*

*The cutting edge
does it need a wedge*

*There once was a giant
who didn't need to make a point*

*They need many a hand
who work on the land*

*They need their daily fodder
the established order*

*They need their solace
who live in a palace*

*To eat without a halt
you need to add salt*

*To fulfill your need
plant the right seed*

*Upon the prey he feed
whenever the cheetah has a need*

*What I really need
is a leech to bleed*

*Whatever the season
men need a reason*

*When the goldmine is big
do we need to dig*

*Why do we need words
when we can speak like the birds*

*Words with good upbringing
we need to be stringing*

*You need to alter
thoughts that easily falter*

*You need to be a stalwart
for the great leap backward*

*You don't need gall
to make the phone call*

Needed

*He got all he needed
whenever he pleaded*

*He quickly heeded
to things that she needed*

*There was this man in Dorset
whose hernia needed a corset*

*When our feet needed washing
the sea it came lashing*

Needle

*Some they go why
through the needle with the eye*

Needs

*A plan that fits your needs
must have all the beads*

*All it needs is a peck
the cure for a stiff neck*

*Bad deeds
have bad needs*

*Fuel needs no fire
nor someone else's ire*

*He needs to mellow
the strange bed fellow*

*He needs two things now
both cow and the plough*

He wears many beads
who has unfulfilled needs

His needs were met
once the beads were set

Men have needs
so they count beads

Men who wear beads
have very few needs

Needs her daily pat
the Cheshire cat

Needs no helping hand
he is a one man band

Needs no reminding
we all need unwinding

Needs of the body
a little more than toddy

People of lesser needs
they plant less seeds

Plant more seeds
for our doubling needs

Somehow or other
every nest needs a feather

Tailor your deeds
to fit your needs

The bottle needs unscrewing
to find out what is brewing

The crocodile in the moat
has his daily feed of goat

The horse that waddles
needs no saddles

When he needs a fix
he sticks to aesthetics

Wherever it leads
it must suite your needs

Who needs a rose
when I have your prose

Writer in his den
needs paper and pen

Negotiate

Don't negotiate
when you are irate

It's better to officiate
than to negotiate

Negotiating

Negotiating kills
all manner of skills

Negotiating skills
don't come in pills

Negotiating skills
is a battle of wills

Neighbour

Find a good neighbour
who doesn't rattle his saber

Ill will towards your neighbour
both will pull out the saber

Neither

>Neither can gain
>causing each other pain

Nerd

>In each of us is a nerd
>waiting to be heard

>If birds could speak our words
>we would sound like nerds

>They are not nerds
>men of few words

Nerve

>Every nerve cell
>in the brain decides to tell

>He lost his nerve
>when the ball began to curve

>Once you lose your nerve
>the serve will lose its curve

Nerves

>Hold your nerves
>through the curves

>When you have nerves to settle
>go boil the kettle

Nervous

>He was a nervous wreck
>until she gave him a peck

Nesting

>Nesting boxes
>can test the foxes

Never

>I have yet to meet a yak
>that has never heard a quack

>I will never give you up
>he told her over tea cup

>In never never land
>with no cash in hand

>Never alone the dog
>when he has a bone to hog

>She can never be a brother
>the fairy godmother

>Yellow fever never
>hits the beaver

New

>Do you have it in you
>to say something new

>It may not be new
>if it happened to you

Newborn

>At the newborn is hurled
>a merciless world

>To run is the goal
>of the newborn foal

>To the newborn is hurled
>the state of the world

Newfound

>Serve him toast
>your newfound host

News

> For news to be good
> bad news is food

> He made news
> wearing just hat and shoes

> News it will dwell
> on things that sell well

Newspapers

> Newspapers are bound
> to lose their ground

Nexus

> He had a nexus
> with her plexus

> He made a nexus
> with his solar plexus

Nibble

> Don't quibble
> just nibble

Nice

> Avarice is nice
> when you throw the dice

> Cut price is nice
> if that's your vice

> Everything is nice
> until it happens twice

> Folks who say things twice
> are usually very nice

> Folks without a vice
> may not be all that nice

> He didn't think it was nice
> that his folly became a vice

> How to be nice
> about something bad twice

> It was a nice token
> the ice once broken

> It was so nice
> they did it twice

> It would be nice
> if it caught mice

> Pieces of Ice
> in champagne is nice

> Silk and spice
> to trade would be nice

> War cannot be nice
> it is all about vice

> What was meant to be nice
> must be read twice

Nifty

> Be nifty
> you've hit fifty

> Fifty – fifty
> sounds very nifty

Night

> Hands held at night
> under the moonlight

> If you wake up at night
> could you be half right

*Like a pinprick might
cause pain very slight*

*Night time is the best
time to rest*

*On a bitter cold night
sleep cosy and tight*

*Rays of light
from the starlit night*

*The birds in flight
through the clouds at night*

Nightingale

*Nightingale sings
fluttering her wings*

*She sings up to scale
the morning nightingale*

*The nightingale she chirp
while her chicks they burp*

*Waiting in the wings
the nightingale sings*

*We both sing along
with the nightingale and her song*

*The nightingales as they sing
to the tulips in the spring*

Nightmare

*He woke up to stare
at the passing nightmare*

*Nightmare days
from a mind that strays*

*Until the nightmare
they were a lovely pair*

*Don't convert your cares
into nightmares*

Nights

*Insights need no lights
on days or nights*

Noble

*Every noble cause
has a because*

Nod

*At each other they nod
two peas in a pod*

*They gave each other the nod
the two peas in the pod*

Noise

*Less noise
more poise*

*Noise and clutter
makes me stutter*

Nonetheless

*I will nonetheless
go where the angels bless*

Nonsense

*Nonsense unexpected
must be respected*

*To always make sense
is such nonsense*

Nose
*There goes the nose
ruining my pose*

Nothing
*Nothing can be had
if you go from good to bad*

Nourished
*Better nourished
health flourished*

Novice
*The novice in me
buzzes like the bee*

Nuclear
*Nuclear waste
is no ordinary paste*

*When you are near
I become pro-nuclear*

Number
*A number and a letter
makes the reading much better*

*They pinned on him a number
to wake him up from his slumber*

O

Obedient
*My obedient brain
has become a runaway train*

Obese
*He became obese
from too much cheese*

Obsessed
*He is obsessed
to being the best dressed*

Obsolete
*When the tiger gets his meat
one life becomes obsolete*

Obviously
*Obviously true
when it is flu*

Occasionally
*The pair they bond to feed
and to occasionally breed*

Ocean
*All thinking ceases
as I face the ocean breezes*

*Arctic ocean has the clue
why the blue whale is blue*

*By the ocean waves lulled
their wedding they annulled*

*Down in the ocean deep
the tortoises where they sleep*

*Every single ride
on the ocean waves and tide*

*From waves that abound
come the ocean sound*

*He went out to swim
in the ocean on a whim*

*Into the ocean depth
where the sun at night is kept*

*Little birds they nabs
tiny ocean crabs*

*Many a gull
flies when the ocean is lull*

*My boat began to stall
as the ocean turned into a wall*

*On the ocean waters they float
seagulls like a little boat*

*On the ocean waters they mull
both he and the she gull*

*Polar bear is found
where the ocean is Ice bound*

*Said the gull to the gull
why is the ocean so lull*

*Scenic and serene
the ocean waters green*

*Scour the ocean bed
looking for things that are dead*

*Seagulls they fly
to where the ocean meets the sky*

*She stood by the ocean why
staring at the sunset sky*

*Sitting by the ocean
I have her devotion*

*Sitting by the ocean
watching the waves in motion*

*The cliff by the ocean
stops the wind in its motion*

*The ocean and the swell
can they the weather tell*

*The ocean is very deep
where colourful corals they sleep*

*The ocean makes a plea
to the sand dunes by the sea*

*The ocean waves they slap
like two hands when they clap*

*The snow on the ground
is ocean bound*

*The surfer raves
about the ocean waves*

*There are things beyond the ocean
it is not just a notion*

*To swim is an undertaking
as the ocean waves are breaking*

*Under the ocean dark
swims the great white shark*

*Under the ocean deep
pearls in their shells asleep*

*We all have our sides
like the ocean has its tides*

*What makes an ocean
is little drops in motion*

*Where the ocean meets the land
and the orchestra is at hand*

*With great skill he plied
the ocean long and wide*

*You know the ocean is well
when it breeds a big swell*

Oceans

*Across the oceans green
mermaids waiting to be seen*

*Beyond the oceans far
that's where they jump and spar*

*Many a fish would cry
if the oceans all went dry*

*Oceans have a plan
for each and every clam*

*Once the oceans run dry
do we need ships why*

*Sunset is a treat
oceans where they meet*

*The blueness will remain
with the oceans in the main*

*The sun leaks its gold
into the oceans fold*

*To sail the oceans choppy
really makes me happy*

Offend

*Don't give him a pear
you might offend the bear*

*Don't offend
neither family nor friend*

*Everyone in the end
they try to offend*

Offending

*Don't go offending
with a squeal at the ending*

Offer

*He looked up his coffer
before he made the offer*

*What have you to offer
let me see your coffer*

Often

*All too often
they forget to soften*

Old

*Can he do the can can
the very old man*

*He was an old hand
at tilling the land*

*Old men need nurses
and big fat purses*

*Old world charm
will cause no harm*

*Rejuvenated I stay
from a whiff of the old bay*

*The old man though hard nosed
with his bowler hat he posed*

*Though old and gaudy
he still has a strong body*

*Though old as the hills
he hadn't done his wills*

Omission

*Omission and commission
both need permission*

Onions
> Onions have a feel
> better with each peel

Opaque
> Even the opaque mind
> is not totally blind

Open
> Don't open the door
> if you can't keep score

> He who is well spoken
> to him the way is open

Opinion
> Don't let it smother
> the opinion of the other

> Good opinion cannot be had
> of the scorpion who is bad

> My opinion of the guest
> is not the very best

> The opinion of the other
> creativity it smother

> What is wrong
> if your opinion is strong

> Opinions keep shifting
> whether love can be uplifting

> Our opinions must be subtle
> of the things they wish to scuttle

Opponents
> Opponents must be fed
> by clever lines that are said

> To make opponents stall
> is the point of it all

Opportunity
> Don't tend to your locks
> when opportunity it knocks

> When opportunity and desires meet
> each other they greet

Opposition
> Don't get bored
> when the opposition scored

> His majestys position
> is have no opposition

Optimism
> Optimism is a bubble
> waiting for trouble

> Sun through a prism
> reckless optimism

Optimist
> He can see through the mist
> the optimist with a twist

Option
> Read this caption
> I have an option

Orchids
> Orchids in full bloom
> to lift the gloom

Ordinary
> When there is cinder in the eye
> it is now ordinary stye

Original

> Can't be more original
> than the aboriginal

> Make it original and bold
> that which is re-told

Ouch

> Ouch!
> I don't like this couch

Ounce

> Ounce for ounce
> it will make you bounce

> Ounce for ounce
> why does it bounce

Outsider

> Don't go and chide her
> if she is an outsider

Over

> Before it's all over
> I'd like to move to Dover

Oversell

> He who speaks well
> does not oversell

Overstepped

> Overstepped in haste
> the bounds of good taste

Overtake

> Never overtake
> the undertaker

Owes

> Many a cap has a feather
> that he owes to his mother

Owned

> Owned by few
> the well leathered shoe

Owner

> Every new owner
> turned out to be a moaner

> Many a loose tongue
> has had the owner hung

P

Pace

At her own pace
she knitted lace

It picked up pace
after the embrace

It picked up pace
the horse in the race

Make your case
at your own pace

Not enough pace
to jump into the race

Slow meandering pace
has its own grace

The two horse race
is gaining pace

To win the race
you must pick up pace

When the pace gets hot
drink from the pot

Paces

Putting her through her paces
brings contortion to their faces

Pack

They each pick up the slack
when they hunt as a pack

Pact

They made a pact
to do things with tact

With one small act
we made a pact

Paddle

To paddle your canoe
is nothing new

Page

He expressed his rage
from the pen to the page

How can it turn to rage
the writings on a page

Page after page
his writing filled with rage

*The voice of a sage
can't be written in a page*

*Two birds in a cage
are on the same page*

Paged

*I get always paged
when fully engaged*

Paid

*He has paid his dues
who wears blue suede shoes*

*He was waylaid
for having not paid*

Pain

*Added to his woe
he has pain in the toe*

*Both pain and bliss
why so is this*

*Eager to suffer pain
with not much to gain*

*Every ounce of her pain
affected me in the main*

*Every pain must drown
with a single frown*

*He who causes pain
will always so remain*

*How to forget the pain
that they do to you for gain*

*I feel the pain
of money down the drain*

*In the beginning there was pain
but birthdays they remain*

*Monogamy is a pain
with few things to gain*

*Much less pain
once the foe is slain*

*No greater pain than this
when there is love without a kiss*

*Nothing to gain
by feeding their pain*

*One disastrous reign
that caused all the pain*

*Pain and it's pangs
by people with fangs*

*Pain came home in a heap
once love was put to sleep*

*Pain in the head
from my daily dread*

*Pain in your toes
will ripen your woes*

*Pain is a part
of every aching heart*

*Pain say the weak
we don't wish to seek*

*Pain takes to flight
when love walks in at night*

Pain will speak
when two shoulders meet

Pain will teach
that things aren't out of reach

Pour water to the pain
but from salt refrain

She said she would remain
just to soften the pain

Sipping is a pain
of bubbly champagne

The bull frog hides from the rain
away from the droplets of pain

The pain in your snout
is not from the gout

The pain of love searing
needed much repairing

The pain when you lose
is more than you choose

The phantom pain
will forever remain

The source of all my pain
was mostly love in the main

The terminally ill
need pain pill

They are able to cause you pain
with so little to gain

Though I have nothing to gain
I will always feel your pain

Though it pain
it is best to abstain

To rid it was in vain
the nagging of this pain

To rid yourself of pain
drink holy water plain

What have they to gain
by causing you all this pain

What have you to gain
by causing all this pain

Why do they remain
both hunger and pain

You have nothing to gain
from a neck without pain

Painful

Must have painful toe
he who chooses woe

Obscurity forever
painful but clever

Put them in a painful bind
and confuse the mind

The invisible scar
painful by far

The most painful part of the hour
waiting for her at the tower

Under lock and key
matters painful and murky

Painfully

How to right this feeling
on one knee painfully kneeling

Joints that squeek
painfully they speak

Pains

How can I suffer their pains
when there are no gains

New boot
pains the foot

Not much gains
and little for his pains

Some pains can hone
into muscle and bone

What have they to gain
these aches and pains

Paint

Does it need paint
a lilly that is so quaint

Painted

He said he is not he
as he painted himself to be

He was not as tainted
as others had him painted

Pair

Circle and square
cannot be a pair

Ecstasy and despair
they function as a pair

Paired

Each other they snared
before being paired

Palate

To put food on the palate
open up your wallet

Pale

He came to the sale
and went away pale

The crocodile turned pale
at the sight of a whale

Palm

Soft winds and the palm
better than any balm

Panic

Once she sensed my panic
she too became manic

Panic when it struck
he quickly passed the buck

Pant

The working ant
never seems to pant

Pantaloon

There was a place for a spoon
in his pantaloon

Panther

The horse said to the panther
let's go out to canter

Parade

> Pretty girl's parade
> in the sunshine and the shade

Paradise

> A paradise for fools
> who don't go to schools

> All ice and nice
> the distant paradise

> Follow me to paradise
> so we both can become wise

> I wish to go there twice
> to visit your garden in paradise

> In paradise I can see
> both you and me

> Let us go skating on ice
> all the way to paradise

> Let us go to paradise
> and skate on thin ice

> Like to go there twice
> once you taste paradise

> No such thing as rule
> in the paradise of a fool

> Once there is frost
> paradise is lost

> Paradise for the wise
> not once but twice

> Paradise is nice
> they serve pickles and rice

> Paradise lost
> at what cost

> Paradise was gained
> by those who remained

> Take me back to paradise
> wherein lies all the vice

> To paradise once ushered
> into times greatly treasured

> To reclaim is nice
> the Idea of paradise

> What is the cost
> of paradise lost

> What use is a tool
> in a paradise of the fool

> When I see her around
> paradise is found

> Without spice
> no paradise

> There is no dearth
> of paradises on earth

Paradox

> Paradox abounds
> between foxes and hounds

Paranoid

> Don't annoy
> the paranoid

> His daily tonic
> for the paranoid is panic

*How to be annoyed
without getting paranoid*

Paranoids

*When two paranoids meet
they touch each others feet*

Parasite

*A parasite will fight
for his parasitic right*

*The host can tell
when the parasite is well*

Parasites

*Parasites get praise
when the host gets malaise*

Parasites

*Plants that kill the host
are parasites at their most*

*When parasites need picking
and wounds need licking*

Park

*Boulders in the park
for shoulders to park*

Parrot

*Red beak of the parrot
from eating peeled carrot*

Parrots

*Parrots they speak
with tongue in beak*

Part

*He made himself a part
of the table full of tart*

Partridge

*Chased by the hound
the partridge fell to the ground*

Pass

*All things must pass
becoming from is to was*

Pass

*Snake in the grass
don't let it pass*

Passing

*There is no one there
of passing interest where*

Passion

*A well dressed passion
is life's best cushion*

*Aflame with passion
they slept in the mansion*

*Does it need passion
great compassion*

*Each careless passion
without any ration*

*Every passion browsed
can have you aroused*

*Every passion must rest
after it reaches the crest*

Rhyming English Couplets

*Every passion will blossom
into something quite awesome*

*Good writing is passion
bad writing is fashion*

*Hard to be doused
passion once aroused*

*He didn't know how to ration
the strength of his passion*

*High and passion
for to-morrows fashion*

*How to ration
every stupid passion*

*I write for passion
not just for fashion*

*It is not in fashion
to govern his passion*

*Many a private passion
mostly after a fashion*

*No one can ration
free floating passion*

*Passion brings a strain
on the happenings in the brain*

*Passion escalates in stages
when you read these pages*

*Passion I trust
will someday turn to rust*

*Passion turns cold
when fashion turns old*

*Passion undressed
and slowly caressed*

*Passion when it sweeps
is never for keeps*

*Some find that passion
not so easy to ration*

*Spots are in fashion
for butterflies in passion*

*The passion fruit
invited the loot*

*The passion he served
had him unnerved*

*There is a passion in the air
for a new style of hair*

*They played up to passion
after a fashion*

*When passion is in season
don't hold back your reason*

*With passion they were drunk
both man and the skunk*

Passionate

*In a single passionate fit
he went after it*

*In one passionate seizure
they spent time in leisure*

P

Passionately

>Passionately he woos
>for love to pay its dues

Passions

>All of life's passions
>dictated by fashions

>Easily progressed
>passions well dressed

>Fire it burns slowly
>for passions that are lowly

>Give free reign to passions
>in your own mansions

>God gave us passions
>in slow steady rations

>He couldn't even speak
>when his passions became weak

>It is good to be schooled
>how passions are ruled

>Passions have a greed
>like a well nourished seed

>Passions have fears
>until the mind clears

>Passions keep burning
>and the stomach keeps churning

>Passions need to be quieted
>as if you have dieted

>Passions of the mind
>put them through the grind

>Small mansions
>large passions

Past

>At what cost
>must we remember the past

>Deep in the past
>where memories were lost

>How can I recover it fast
>my long forgotten past

>How to let go of the past
>once the die is cast

>Past actions buried
>and new ones queried

>Past is past
>and the future is vast

>Past is past
>future is vast

>Past lives they thrives
>like the bees in their hives

>So much of the past
>buried in the oceans vast

>The ghosts from the past
>formed a formidable cast

>The past continues to give
>memories from the past that live

>The past with all its flaws
>returns with its claws

---

*The present future and past
add up to be very vast*

Patch

*It will rain through the patch
that has no thatch*

*Many a hand
for the same patch of land*

Path

*Follow a gentle path
where there is no wrath*

*In order to avoid wrath
he took the better path*

*Straight and narrow path
where there is less wrath*

*The right path to choose
when you have nothing to lose*

Path

*There will be no wrath
if you follow the gentle path*

Patience

*For many things for sure
patience is the cure*

*Patience is better
when dealing with clutter*

*Patience is hoping
we both will be eloping*

*Patience is kind
to the restless mind*

*Patience must have length
to slowly gain in strength*

Patient

*How patient is your love
when you push and shove*

*To ease the patients strife
is the purpose of life*

Pause

*He who speaks with a pause
doesn't have to say because*

Pauses

*Too many pauses
supporting causes*

Pawn

*A single pawn it took
to knock out the rook*

Pay

*Don't pay your wages
by the number of pages*

*Make no bones
pay off your loans*

*Someday you will pay
looking at life this way*

*What should I say
to make them pay*

*Write and make them pay
when you have something to say*

Pays

> He who pays the piper
> cannot defang the viper

Pea

> It is pea green
> until it is seen

Peace

> Gives me peace of mind
> which nowhere else I find

> He is in perfect peace
> after feeding mouse with cheese

> Hold your peace
> on a tight leash

> How to give it birth
> total peace on earth

> How to seek peace
> in the midst of these geese

> I am at peace
> with myself if you please

> I have made peace
> I will not eat cheese

> I signed a lease
> for permanent peace

> I will not have peace
> until I have the golden fleece

> If peace is this
> so is bliss

> Make peace with self
> giant or elf

> Peace has appeal
> and a better feel

> Peace has its prize
> so say the wise

> Peace is here
> where death is near

> Peace it came upon us
> putting an end to fuss

> Peace it can
> start in the mind of man

> Peace you will find
> hidden deep in the mind

> Sense of peace
> when love meets cheese

> The stars must have colluded
> when peace became denuded

> There is war and peace
> between the bees

> What better diet
> than peace and quiet

Peacefully

> Peacefully why
> they won't let me lie

Peaches

> Peaches and leeches
> not found on the beaches

Peacock
> The peacock said to the quail
> where is your tail

Peak
> Himalayan peak
> not for the meek

> The waves when they speak
> have froth at their peak

Pearl
> A pearl does its duty
> by showing off its beauty

> A suitable girl
> better than a pearl

> A suitable girl
> is mother of pearl

> Pearl in the oyster
> sweetly they cloister

> She is more than a girl
> a perfect little pearl

> There is more to the pearl
> known only to the girl

Pearls
> Her neck full of pearls
> envy of the girls

> Necklace long
> pearls strong

> With teeth like pearls
> who needs curls

Peer
> Has no peer
> William Shakespeare

> I don't like my peer
> all they do is jeer

> Let's have a beer
> we have no peer

Peeves
> They had their peeves
> the forty thieves

Peg
> It starts with a peg
> and ends up in a keg

> To make the square peg round
> a lathe must be found

Penetrate
> The printed word must train
> to penetrate the brain

Pennies
> If you squabble over pennies
> you will lose big monies

Penny
> A penny as such
> is never too much

> Known to many
> things can turn on a penny

> The penny it stuck
> when he ran out of luck

People

*All the seasons they want
people who are ready to plant*

*Don't go and tangle
with people who wrangle*

*For people of a certain kind
providence is never blind*

*From people I hid
somethings I did*

*Give people their space
so they can make their case*

*High profile people
perched on top of steeple*

*I know why people cough
but why do they laugh*

*I only chatter
with people who matter*

*I would like to wander
out there where the people are fonder*

*In hell there is a dearth
of people full of mirth*

*It may take long
to prove people wrong*

*Left to their own devices
people acquire new vices*

*Like minded people
contemplate the steeple*

*Many a shadow was cast
by people who were lost*

*Most cares are found
in people who are earthbound*

*No two people are alike
in the way they ride a bike*

*Not without merit
people who get the credit*

*People and their sins
like a pair of twins*

*People are always running
to where the sun is sunning*

*People are divided broadly
into those who are remembered fondly*

*People are in a rush
to paint with a broad brush*

*People are loud in laughter
but the jackass does it softer*

*People become engaging
when hormones they are raging*

*People become naughty
once they hit forty*

*People begin to snicker
when your accent becomes thicker*

*People can get hurt
without a single squirt*

*People don't change their gripes
nor tigers their stripes*

People expect a treat
when you return from the beat

People get bored
who are ignored

People get stoned
for the mistakes they owned

People get to choose
what must become news

People go scampering
to where there is pampering

People have a knack
of resorting to flak

People have a leaning
to speak with double meaning

People have a leaning
to use words without meaning

People in a hurry
trying to catch up with worry

People in the city
need a lot of pity

People in the main
believe in causing pain

People in the main
relish not each others pain

People keep on hanging
to their only belonging

People look for perks
where danger lurks

People must be led
by the best thoughts in the head

People must be reminded
not to be serious minded

People of desperate plight
keep me awake at night

People of higher latitude
have a better attitude

People on their binges
moves them to the fringes

People tend to scamper
to where there is pamper

People tend to splurge
on an emotional urge

People they are wise
in every shape or size

People they don't give their name
lest they get the blame

People they go gunning
for things absolutely stunning

People they go hunting
pigs that are grunting

People they have a right
to get things in their sight

People they holler
at the soaring dollar

People they reverted
to the village once deserted

*People they throng
to hear a love song*

*People they throng
to where nostalgia is strong*

*People they voted
for the daring and devoted*

*People watching
can be eye-catching*

*People who are mean
not to be seen*

*People who are strong
can make right into wrong*

*People who crow
stoop so low*

*People who make you happy
when the sea is choppy*

*People who take risk
can have a slipped disc*

*People will scamper
to where there is no tamper*

*People will swarm
to where the drinks make them warm*

*People will throng
to the singer not the song*

*People with painted feet
pray at the temple down the street*

*People without a voice
aren't given a choice*

*People without feeling
they hit the ceiling*

*Some people are born
to simply mow the lawn*

*Some people get older
without getting any bolder*

*Some people they ask
for the slow easy task*

*Some people they knew
smooth words how to spew*

*The people they swim
the ocean on a whim*

*The round eyed people
on top of the steeple*

*The wrath of the people
can reach of tallest steeple*

*There are people to appease
with red wine and cheese*

*They climb many a steeple
in their minds the people*

*They more or less loathed
people fully clothed*

*They will someday surely squirt
people who they dig dirt*

*Things are said to unflatter
about people who really matter*

*Troubles they stare
at people everywhere*

Two people in a garden
makes work for the warden

Two people they meet
with a destructive streak

Two people they tire
of each others attire

Up to their gills
old people with pills

Whatever their stripe
people love to gripe

When two people fight
which one is right

Where people are strong
others will throng

Why do people go
always to and fro

Why do people write
is it out of spite

Why do you go picking
at people who are frolicking

Without ever flinching
people they go lynching

Perceived

Not always received
what ever was perceived

Perfect

Let the perfect catch
be a perfect match

She struck a perfect pose
holding on to a rose

Though bad the weather
we are perfect together

Perfection

Perfection is a quest
best laid to rest

Perfection we must strive
as long as we are alive

Perfection you can reach
if you learn how to teach

Will become sublime
perfection in its time

Perfectly

Perfectly in tune
with the floral bloom

Performance

Performance and desire
they wear a different attire

Performing

How can I kneel
asked the performing seal

The performing seals
they have no wheels

They sipped tea
watching the performing flea

Wherever he may be
he is a performing flea

Perfume
> She didn't need perfume
> with jasmine on her plume

Perils
> There are perils in the sea
> but the anemone is free

Perk
> How can it be a perk
> death where it may lurk

> How to conduct your work
> without your morning perk

> Whatever your line of work
> make sure you have enough perk

Perks
> Give them perks
> whose advice works

> Give them their perks
> whenever it works

Perky
> He gets all perky
> doing things murky

Permanence
> Little for him to gain
> from the permanence of pain

> Permanence is never
> as portrayed forever

Permanent
> Permanent it is said
> once we are dead

Permission
> All he said he wanted
> was for permission to be granted

> He raved and ranted
> and permission he granted

> In case it is required
> permission must be acquired

Permit
> Can't see the hermit
> without a signed permit

> He doesn't need a permit
> who wants to be a hermit

Perplexity
> In a new city
> Perplexity

Persistence
> Persistence pays
> in untold ways

Persistent
> Like a persistent rumour
> from a branch there hung a lemur

Person
> A person of high girth
> is the subject of mirth

> He can never be all seeing
> this person the human being

> How to make your case
> to a person without face

Rhyming English Couplets

Many a person he long
for wine women and song

Many a person was hung
by the looseness of his tongue

May not be so nice
the person without vice

My elbow is put to the test
by the person in the seat next

Who should he thank
But the person of rank

Personal

There was a squeak in his voice
by a personal choice

Personality

He was so easily charmed
his personality was harmed

Persons

Every persons beak
has a destructive streak

Petals

Petals in the gardens they stand
waiting for dew drops to land

Phantom

It takes a leap quantum
to meet up with this phantom

Memory is a kind
of phantom of the mind

Philosopher

Philosopher and fool
found in the same school

The philosophers stone
for the dog becomes a bone

Phrase

He who is able
must make phrase and fable

The phrase when it turns
to ease my heart burns

Physical

Don't get ever physical
when love it gets musical

Piano

Like a piano out of tune
the heavy rains in June

Pick

Pick and choose
the right booze

Pick your own pod
once you get the nod

Take your pick
of candles with a wick

Pickering

My name is pickering
I am prone to bickering

Pickle

He was quite fickle
about his taste for pickle

When you're in a pickle
doesn't pay to be fickle

Picture

A dragonfly on a pitcher
paints a pretty picture

A picture with a thousand birds
can't be explained in words

Even a hangdog picture
it needs a structure

He who paints a picture
dips his brush in a tincture

I'll be a fixture
you take my picture

Pigeon

Said the pigeon to the cat
It's me or the rat

How to keep it clean
where the pigeons have been

The pigeons find their perch
on top of the gothic church

Pilgrimage

Pilgrimage is a rage
of the inveterate sage

Pill

If you are not in the will
go for the pill

Keep your tongue still
when you pop the pill

Many a pill is swallowed
thinking it is hallowed

Many a to-days ill
corrected by a pill

Pillow

Rest a pillow under your head
before you go to bed

Pills

There are no pills
to make you old as the hills

They popped their pills
and headed for the hills

Pinches

Nothing less will do
than a shoe that pinches too

Pinching

Pinching is a thing
the queen does to a king

Pirate

Where do we stash
asked the pirate of the cash

Pirates

The pirates they hoard
from the ships that they board

Pistol

No one carries a pistol
in the city of Bristol

Rhyming English Couplets

Pit
When you fall into a pit
get out of it

Pitch
Like a walk in the park
when it is pitch dark

Pity
Don't shed your pity
on absurdity

Gets no pity
stupidity

Placate
Don't placate
just re-locate

Place
All things have a place
including arsenic and lace

Just find the right place
to make your case

No place for the goat
with three men in a boat

Place to hob-nob
is at the desk job

With the place in turmoil
the average persons they toil

Placid
When you sail the placid waters
wear your tight garters

Plague
Avoid it like the plague
whose cause is very vague

Plague had a mission
ruled by transmission

The great English plague
the cause was no more vague

The plague blamed the rat
rat blamed the cat

Plain
Just explain
and make it plain

Make it so plain
you don't need to explain

The autumn it remains plain
until the first drop of rain

Plan
Don't leave the clan
without a proper plan

Don't plan your feast
before you kill the beast

Every well laid plan
eventually hits the fan

Has his own plan
even the primitive man

Have a proper plan
then grab hold of your man

He worked according to a plan
unlike the everyday man

If you fall for their plan
you will get an unwanted tan

Man for man
god has a plan

Planet

Do you have a clue
why our planet is blue

Don't go to a planet
where there is no gannet

How to measure the girth
of the planet earth

Someday the planet
will only be for the gannet

There is room for the gannet
in this crowded planet

Between the planets
flight of the gannets

Planning

Planning and cunning
results can be stunning

Planning to have you hung
who speak with a forked tongue

Plans

Once he made the catch
the plans began to hatch

Well laid clams
have shut out their plans

Planted

They only planted
trees that they wanted

Play

Go find the chaps
that can play the gaps

He could play ball
who towers above them all

How can it play a part
the bullock without the cart

How to play chess
when there is a pawn less

On a clear arctic day
the reindeer are out to play

On a cold and windy day
the polar bear cubs they play

Play hard
with trump card

Play to a plan
man for man

Play too much skittle
mind becomes brittle

Sweet things to say
while you work and play

The ball doesn't say
to play or to flay

Rhyming English Couplets

The hounds when they sleep
go and play the sheep

The pianist he play
in the street café

They play the blame game
without giving it a name

They play their part
in the name of art

To fill the cup
just play it up

When the eagles they came to play
the fish they flew away

You'll end up on the moon
if you play the right tune

Played

Whenever he played against slobs
he resorted to lobs

Playing

It's easy to tell
if they are playing spin well

Playing with words
like the pecking birds

Plays

He is meek
who plays hide and seek

He plays the fiddle
resting on his middle

The apple in your cart
plays a big part

Plea

Don't bite me flea
I'll make you a plea

No need to plea
for the pardon of the flea

To her repeatedly
he made his plea

Plead

All he did was plead
for a decent book to read

Pleading

No amount of reading
can add upto pleading

The begger he cries
with large pleading eyes

With open beaks pleading
to mother who is feeding

Pleasant

Dinner would be pleasant
that served a Scottish pheasant

From simply being pleasant
he turned incandescent

Prince or peasant
say things always pleasant

The work is rather pleasant
when you are convalescent

With a feather in his cap
the pleasant weather chap

Please

Along the rest of the way
please with me just stay

At my better half
please don't scoff

Don't please lament
if this is no tenant

Everyone falls for cheese
with added wine to please

Folks who have no vices
please tell me your devices

He said in a mutter
please pass the butter

I have mice to please
let me buy some cheese

Please pull out the spigot
and stop being a bigot

Please say please
to put me at ease

Sweet butterfly
will you please flutterby

Pleased

He is easily pleased
who happily sneezed

Impulse unleashed
as and when he pleased

In order to be appeased
first be pleased

Pleases

He does what he pleases
with a variety of cheeses

Pleasing

Pleasing to the ear
the sound of jingles I hear

Pleasing to the ear
when the meaning is clear

Pleasing to the ear
will make things clear

The meaning may not be clear
but it is pleasing to the ear

While you are here pleasing
let me do my reading

Pleasure

Allow oneself the pleasure
of looking for the treasure

Books we must treasure
for their healing pleasure

Busy folks have pleasure
when they look for treasure

Ceases to be a treasure
the lifelong pursuit of pleasure

Cold beer with ice
is a pleasure so nice

Discover in leisure
double your pleasure

Don't give him the pleasure
of a slice of your leisure

Double your pleasure
with half the treasure

Each other they train
both pleasure and pain

Every little pleasure
let it add to your treasure

Half of poetry's pleasure
is in figuring out its treasure

He was singled
to be with pleasure mingled

How can we go refusing
a pleasure that is so soothing

How to lose the treasure
of unremitting pleasure

However small the treasure
we seek it for pleasure

If the honour gives you pleasure
enjoy it in leisure

Many a great pleasure
has been lost to treasure

Many a human pleasure
cannot be acquired in leisure

Men who hold pleasure
as a closely held treasure

My most exalted pleasure
is the loves that I treasure

Pain to pleasure
at your own leisure

Pen paper and leisure
seeds of love and pleasure

Pleasure and pain though fleeting
people got to them greeting

Pleasure and pain
are twins in the main

Pleasure and perk
if you love your work

Pleasure in all it's shades
eventually it fades

Pleasure in the morrow
follows the evening sorrow

Pleasure it seeks out some
who have guitar strings to strum

Poetry will give pleasure
if you read it at your leisure

Pursuit of pleasure
life's best treasure

Reading is a pleasure
with thoughts to treasure

Seek your treasure
from pain to pleasure

Self control is a pleasure
one must learn to treasure

Self denial has pleasure
beyond the greatest treasure

The pleasure of maternity
known for as long as eternity

There is more pleasure to gain
after recovering from the pain

Tortoise gets its pleasure
by crawling slowly and in leisure

Use cheap pleasure
to fill your leisure

Pleasures

All pleasures are nice
if you treasure every vice

Better to re-train
how from pleasures to refrain

Celibacy has pleasures
more than all the treasures

Fleeting pleasures will remain
the cause of all your pain

Forbidden pleasures
are short term treasures

He will find treasures
who renounces his pleasures

His pleasures became worried
when he did things as he hurried

Meaningful pleasures
from life's little treasures

Men of great treasures
seek out new pleasures

Of all the pleasures that we choose
there is nothing like the booze

Panicky measures
to unlock pleasures

Pleasures once they come
the heart begins to hum

Pleasures there are some
that never seem to come

Pleasures we must crave
until we go to the grave

Purchase your pleasures
and consume your treasures

Small pleasures
hidden treasures

So many pleasures
only some are treasures

Some of our treasures
from careless pleasures

Tears are the treasures
of love and its pleasures

The pleasures of gratitude
lie in your attitude

The pleasures of life denied
leaves everyone else satisfied

The pleasures of verse
from the rhymes we nurse

*To pleasures they are dead
once they are wed*

Pledge

*He broke a pledge
by driving a wedge*

*I will pledge you my time
if you will stop your whine*

Plenty

*Cricket can be plenty
even in twenty- twenty*

*Plenty fish in the sea
where the salt water is free*

*Pockets once with plenty
now upturned and empty*

*There is plenty of fish in the sea
and more that we cannot see*

Plight

*Alone at night
is a pitiful plight*

*Contemplate tonight
tomorrows plight*

*Day and night
each in its plight*

*For each new plight
we need a new light*

*Get it right
after the plight*

*He wakes up to his plight
in the dead of the night*

*He woke up to his plight
in full sight of the night*

*How good is your plight
are you wholesome tonight*

*In the dark hours of the night
when skeletons discuss their plight*

*It can seal your plight
if you don't get it right*

*It's better to get it right
to avoid unsavory plight*

*It's the child's plight
when parents fight*

*Let us discuss our plight
it is such a fine night*

*Non stop plight
in the middle of the night*

*On a cold and windy night
we contemplate our plight*

*Out of my plight
through her guiding light*

*Star spangled night
when hearts poured out their plight*

*The endless plight
of people in a fight*

*The Insomnics plight
always at night*

The melting ice don't care
about the plight of the polar bear

The sun contemplates his plight
in the still of the night

The tenable plight
of love at first sight

They discussed their plight
in the still of the night

They discussed their plight
on a moonlit night

They discussed their plight
on a soft moonlit night

They landed in a plight
from love at first sight

They shared their plight
in the moonlit night

They surrendered to the night
and woke up to their plight

What better plight
than dancing in the moonlight

What could be our plight
with clothes worn so tight

What is the plight
of the birds at night

What is your plight
if you miss the flight

Whatever your plight
look for delight

Plights

In search of sacred rites
and ancestors plights

Ploughing

The ploughing can't be shallow
where the earth is fallow

Plucked

A duck is ducked
once a feather is plucked

The rose plucked from the thorn
in the buttonhole to be worn

Plumage

The current rage
was to wear plumage

Plutocrat

He is a rat
the plutocrat

Poach

If you know how to poach
you are no cockroach

Poem

Poem is a feeling
needs no explaining

Poems

Poems of passion
no need to ration

Poet

A poet needs no training
for words they come raining

*A poet thinks of clay
when words are there to play*

*He can't sing a duet
though he is a poet*

*He sings his duet
like a lovelorn poet*

*Poet of the masses
survives on molasses*

*Poet will keep on writing
while his heart and soul are in fighting*

*The poet off the street
whom people stop to greet*

Poetic

*Every songbird
has a poetic word*

*He spends time inking
his poetic thinking*

*Poetic forms
that defy all norms*

*She gave it a start
his poetic part*

Poetically

*The way the words are laced
they were poetically placed*

Poetry

*A visceral part of me
poetry will ever be*

*Back in favour
poetry is there to savour*

*Even for the eel
poetry has a feel*

*Forgetting is hard
poetry for the bard*

*He can cast a spell
who reads poetry well*

*How high can it reach
poetry and speech*

*If only you knew
there is poetry in you*

*If you can read it twice
the poetry must be nice*

*Let me make it clear
poetry is for the ear*

*Like the bikes throttle
poetry will startle*

*Man it is found
to poetry he is bound*

*Meshing of sound and sense
makes poetry immense*

*Once out of the gates
poetry resonates*

*Only in poetry found
the mesmerizing sound*

*Poetry and smirks
from a brain that works*

Poetry can be found
in both rhythm and sound

Poetry can be
as loving as the bee

Poetry can glow
from the couplets that flow

Poetry causes fear
because the meaning isn't clear

Poetry does it best
when put to the test

Poetry expresses feeling
to give it extra meaning

Poetry gets a chance
to do music and dance

Poetry gets a start
with a song in my heart

Poetry gets its glow
from words in seamless flow

Poetry gets the nod
as a message from god

Poetry gives you a glimmer
of the thoughts that slowly simmer

Poetry has a history
of being in the realm of mystery

Poetry has a new feel
different with each peel

Poetry has appeal
because it has a feel

Poetry has leaning
for many layered meaning

Poetry has leanings
to rake powerful feelings

Poetry has might
to instantly delight

Poetry has the gift
to spiritually uplift

Poetry he wrote
to make the heart float

Poetry in motion
is about emotion

Poetry in part
is a laugauge of the heart

Poetry is a craft
like a slow going raft

Poetry is a feel
fresh with each peel

Poetry is a feel
that improves with each peel

Poetry is a feeling
that has no ceiling

Poetry is a mood
for some it is food

Poetry is a mood
for the heart it is food

Poetry is a mood
the hearts best food

Poetry is a rose
that can pose with any prose

Poetry is a tree
that bears fruits for free

Poetry is clever
can be remembered forever

Poetry is found
in both Rhythm and sound

Poetry is free
under the banyan tree

Poetry is just a notion
of two hearts is secret motion

Poetry is known
to come from the twilight zone

Poetry is like art
an expression of the heart

Poetry is meant
to be read with her in the tent

Poetry is the pulse
of the human impulse

Poetry it reminds
of incredible minds

Poetry knows
it is not prose

Poetry leaks
when a painting speaks

Poetry makes it clear
love is more than a tear

Poetry must seem
like a smooth sailing dream

Poetry opens the door
to get you closer to the core

Poetry that is clear
can bring forth a tear

Poetry will sink
without words that link

Poetry with a tear
marks it very clear

Poetry writes itself
said the giant to the elf

Running through his veins
poetry without reigns

There is poetry in song
when we singalong

What it tells the nose
separates poetry from prose

Whether or not blind
poetry is a state of mind

Poets

Poets have a choice
of words with many a voice

Poets live for
irony and metaphor

Poets they will teeter
trying to make rhyme and meter

Point

    Don't point the rifle
    at things small and trifle

Pointed

    She pointed her finger
    then let it linger

Poison

    Don't speak ill
    of the poison pill

    Only a frog can dwell
    in the poison well

    Poison comes free
    with a drinking spree

    Poison in its wake
    he left the snake

    The long winter road
    drained the poison off the toad

    The poison pill floats
    down peoples' throats

    The poison pill
    was also in the will

    There was poison in the dish
    of the edible jelly fish

    Who gets to sup
    the poison in the cup

Polish

    How to polish your craft
    from a sinking raft

    How to polish your craft
    while sailing on a raft

    You cannot polish your craft
    by floating on a raft

Polishes

    She polishes her tusk
    all day till dusk

Polishing

    The horse got angry at the goats
    for polishing off his oats

Polite

    He was so polite
    he offered me a light

    Polite veneer
    ruined by beer

    Things got polite
    on the return flight

    Though polite and powdered
    his manner it floundered

Political

    How to measure
    political pressure

Poor

    One is never sure
    how long we will be poor

    The poor in their plight
    have no more left of fight

*The poor tell their tale
as they slide down the scale*

Popcorn

*Popcorn can
bounce out of the pan*

*Popcorn can
pop in the pan*

Popping

*They went all quiet and still
popping a white round pill*

Porridge

*Porridge before eleven
gateway to heaven*

*We can share a carriage
but not the morning porridge*

Portends

*Portends disaster why
the storm in the sky*

Portrait

*Portrait of a friend
will lose him in the end*

*The lady in the portrait
looks at us very straight*

Pose

*For me only she did pose
nothing since has even come close*

*You can never pose
without the groove beneath your nose*

Position

*Don't make your position
into an imposition*

*His position he stated
though rather belated*

Possessed

*Of all sense dispossessed
when he was possessed*

Possible

*All things possible
cooked in a crucible*

*Everything is possible
once you drink from the crucible*

*Not possible to fend
your solitude in the end*

*Put it in a crucible
if it is possible*

*To make something possible
put it in a crucible*

Postman

*Before the bell he rings
the postman he sings*

Potboiler

*When not a potboiler
he was a toiler*

Potion

*Find me a potion
to ease this commotion*

More than a notion
this healing potion

Right now only a notion
soon it will be potion

The potion in this chalice
can rid you of malice

What better potion
than infatuation

So many notions
about pills and potions

Pound

Pound for pound
he should win every round

Pour

Pour out your woes
to people who are close

Poverty

Look around the bend
where poverty may end

Poverty has voices
but impossible choices

Poverty in a sense
is a life sentence

Poverty is a hand
in the parched land

The poverty crusade
is in need of shade

There is poverty in wealth
that is obtained in stealth

Powdered

A well powdered face
before you make your case

Power

Accolade will shower
for whom knowledge is power

At the turn of the mid – night hour
comes with it new power

Best to appeal
to those with power to heal

Every thing has power
to reach the mid-night hour

Has the power to overwhelm
every flowering elm

He built a tower
where profit is power

He picked the fairest flower
to give love its power

Let it not lie still
the power of the will

On each other they shower
their money and their power

Pollen gets its power
after butterfly sits on flower

Power is bland
if it is not in your hand

Rhyming English Couplets

Power is when
the sword replaces the pen

Power to cause pain
love it has in the main

Purple has power
especially in the flower

She has the power to sway
and to make me feel this way

Still within my power
to reach the top of the tower

The power of an open mind
welcomes even the blind

The power of her scent
for him it was meant

The power of two
known to me and you

The power of two
known to none but you

The power to heal
has a special feel

They are partners in power
who above all they tower

To get power over men
just hover over them

Powerful

Got to act faster
when you have a powerful master

Powers

Mind gets its powers
from head under the showers

The powers of the ocean
sets the waves in motion

Practice

Choose your own device
to practice your vice

In the village or in the city
the practice of humility

Make winning an art
with practice from the start

Practice it pays
to strengthen your ways

Practice what joys preach
even if it is out of reach

Practice what you preach
said one to the other leech

There were places to canter
to practice our daily banter

They practice their speech
little birds on the beach

Those who practice deceit
never give a receipt

To practice what you preach
could be out of reach

To put theory to practice
you need an artist

Practiced

*A well practiced mind
will never fall behind*

*He had the practiced air
of a man in despair*

*How can it hurt you
who practiced virtue*

Praise

*How to write sonnets
in praise of the gannets*

*In a clutch
praise them much*

*No praise is enough
for your kind of stuff*

*Praise must be sought
and soon forgot*

*Praise unsaid
take it to bed*

*Praise you must heap
even in your sleep*

*Singled out for praise
before the raise*

*They don't give you a raise
just a little praise*

*To rid me of malaise
let me sing thy praise*

Praised

*Many a child was raised
without being praised*

Praising

*Children need praising
when you are raising*

Prankster

*The prankster in him
made him a victim*

Pray

*All day I will pray
please don't go away*

*Behind their backs they say
things that will make you pray*

*Early morning pray
stay out of harms way*

*For light we must pray
on our darkest day*

*For my long lost love I pray
that she come down to greet me to day*

*How much ever you pray
you will turn grey*

*Kneel down and pray
a curse is on its way*

*Kneel down and pray
when things go your way*

*Pray tell me oh sage
how softly you age*

Pray tell me why
so eager to cry

She went her own way
and left him along to pray

The horses when they bray
stand on hindlegs to pray

The skies turned dark and gray
for the rains we kneel and pray

There will come a day
when together we sit and pray

What was it I pray
that led me astray

When trouble comes your way
just kneel down to pray

Prayed

The whole country prayed
that they not be betrayed

Wives simply prayed
husbands when they strayed

Prayer

Before he went to hang
he pulled out a prayer and sang

I come to grips
with a prayer in my lips

Prayer gets its birth
from desires of this earth

Prayer is well
if you hear the bell

Prayer it pays
in so many ways

Prayers

Daily prayers were chanted
to get what they wanted

Preach

How can I preach
for blood banking said the leech

No way to preach
to the blood sucking leech

Preached

The islanders preached
at the whale that had breached

Preaches

All that he preaches
are away from our reaches

When he walks the beaches
to the wind and wave he preaches

Preamble

Just as a preamble
cobwebs to unscramble

Precede

If you precede me to heaven
I'll go there to you is a given

Precious

Precious as beads
some of our deeds

Precious moments will be thine
if you just mark time

To the outside hurled
my precious inner world

Precise

It is so precise
don't have to read it twice

Precision

Precision is at stake
from the decisions we make

Predicament

Every predicament
needs a medicament

Predict

How to predict their fate
great affairs of the state

Predictions

I don't have predictions
about human addictions

Prejudice

Prejudice and desire
are his daily attire

Prejudice has a shape
in the form of an ape

Prejudice revealed
once unsealed

With prejudice endowed
he spoke out loud

Prejudiced

He is prejudiced but whole
in the support of the soul

Prescription

Groundless prescription
based on conviction

Presence

His presence had reminded
her to be absent minded

Present

Profoundly at odds
with present day gods

To live in the present
go hunting pheasant

Preserve

Preserve it as a duty
every dream with beauty

Preserved

Though well preserved
he was quite reserved

Pressure

When he saw the treasure
his blood picked up pressure

Pretended

Some of us pretended
more than we intended

Pretender

He is no drone
the pretender to the throne

Pretender

Many of her suitors were a pretender
with hearts less than tender

Pretending
> Fruit bats they just squeak
> pretending to speak

Pretends
> He is usually a slob
> who pretends to be a snob

> What can I do with this
> that pretends to be bliss

Pretense
> Eloquence makes sense
> when not in pretense

Pretenses
> No pretenses
> we are a bag full of senses

Pretext
> What pretext
> will it be next

Pretty
> Beyond the vale she sat
> wearing a pretty hat

> Pretty girls make me sigh
> don't know why

> Pretty girls
> with springly curls

> She makes her case
> wearing pretty lace

Prevention
> Prevention is for sure
> better than the cure

Preventive
> Preventive measures
> can bring you treasures

Prey
> Foxes and hounds
> the prey they surrounds

> Once she bags her prey
> the cheetah will not stray

> Predator and prey
> who do you think should pray

> The Reindeer they play
> where there are no prey

Preys
> Let me count the ways
> in which the tiger preys

Price
> Don't go laffin
> at the price of the coffin

> Everything has a price
> including the grain of rice

> The price he pays
> for his wayward ways

Priceless
> How to measure
> this priceless treasure

Prices
> He paid his prices
> for surrendering to his vices

Pride

A past filled with pride
opens its doors wide

Don't let yourself slide
into actions that hurt your pride

Hero tells his story
of his pride and glory

I can turn back the tide
said he with pride

I walk by her side
with an element of pride

Pride is swallowed
when love is followed

Pride it is twice
the baddest of vice

With you on my side
to enhance my pride

Prince

Both prince and page
he was also a sage

From prince to a toad
not a well trodden road

Never the same since
the frog turned into a prince

Said the pauper to the prince
where have you been since

The frog said smugly
to the prince you are ugly

The prince was painted green
like the toad he had just been

There is a prince in this toad
he said as he rode

Printing

Coins are made by minting
and notes made by printing

Privacy

Once privacy is gone
just wait for the dawn

Private

For your private affair
build a castle in the air

Many a private joke
between her and the bloke

They share forks and knives
in their private lives

Privately

Speak privately of your hurt
without having to blurt

Privileges

Privileges are due
to a select few

Privileges

Privileges of health
beats everything and wealth

Prize

I want my daily prize
of the golden sun to rise

Never mind the prize
the wallet must have size

No need to look twice
at so glittering a prize

Problem

A problem brought home
must be sent out to roam

Every problem has a heart
discovering it is an art

Every problem has a nub
emanating from the hub

Get out of it faster
problem that you cannot master

He has a problem dealing
with this macho feeling

If you don't ease the pain
the problem will remain

Problem is surmounted
once the money is counted

Problem when lugging
hamstrings get tugging

From the poor side of the fence
where the problems are immense

If you make their problems your own
they wont pick your bone

In the book shop we met
with problems to forget

Just dismount
when problems they mount

Leave problems behind
best way to unwind

Once you have resolved
many problems solved

Problems can't be cured
until the truth is lured

Problems cannot be voided
nor simply avoided

Problems get voided
when argument is avoided

Problems take up flight
when you see the light

Problems they heap
upon me in my sleep

Problems they will amplify
if you don't try to simplify

Problems will heal
once you learn to deal

She became teary
when problems made her weary

To make problems softer
that's what people are after

When problems come to roost
give them a critical boost

Professional

His writing though confessional
was also very professional

Profile

High profile coach
teaches you how to poach

Profit

Profit is none
from work half done

Who is there to cough it
writing for money and profit

Progress

Progress isn't ever still
when it is down the hill

Prominent

He had a prominent droop
and wore a shawl in one loop

Promise

A promise once made
cannot be re-laid

A promise that is kept
will be exempt

All those years of chats
I promise to keep under my hats

Even a buffoon
can promise you the moon

They promise you the moon
and deliver a baboon

You will end up with the spoon
if they promise you the moon

Promised

He promised her the moon
and a secret lagoon

He promised her the moon
just before the swoon

The promised land
is close at hand

Promises

Awake or sleeping
promises need keeping

By the river he sleep
with broken promises to keep

Her promises were meant
to cause him lament

Hidden in the shade
promises once made

How well they slept
after promises were kept

I have promises to keep
to meet mermaids in my sleep

I was quickly drawn
to the promises of dawn

Many a person has wept
from promises not kept

Promises are meant to be broken
even if they are token

*Promises are usually token
meant to be always broken*

*Promises of rapture
her friendly gesture*

*Promises once made
to rest they were laid*

*Promises reneging
that needed egging*

*Promises that I cannot keep
wake me up from my sleep*

*Promises that lure
don't constitute cure*

*Promises they heap
with no plans to keep*

*Promises they keep
angels in my sleep*

*Promises to keep
when love is asleep*

*Promises were made
before the tables were laid*

*Promises were made
holding hands in the shade*

*Promises were made
in the shade*

*Promises were made
then hidden in the shade*

*Promises were meant
to be totally bent*

*Some of us are gullible
to promises that are soluble*

*Why bother
if it promises no lather*

Prompt

*She always was prompt
in returning his warmth*

Prone

*He was prone to rage
as he read page after page*

*Though he was a snob
he was easily prone to sob*

Pronouncement

*He made his renouncement
by a public pronouncement*

Proof

*Don't be a goof
just provide the proof*

*Proof is food
to make us look good*

Prop

*First they prop you up
and let you drink from the cup*

Proper

*Prim and proper
she was a show stopper*

*There is no drape
without a proper cape*

*They came to their senses
with proper sentences*

Properly

*Every taste that I own
was properly home grown*

*They roll off the tongue
to be properly hung*

Property

*We were both fated
to live in a property gated*

Prophet

*Give him room
the prophet of doom*

Prophets

*Every where they loom
these prophets of doom*

Prose

*Cadences of her prose
makes proud each and every rose*

*Some they have a nose
for the eloquent prose*

Prospects

*Prospects are bleak
from the unending leak*

*Prospects are bleak
if you don't mend the leak*

*Prospects bleak
in a house with a leak*

Prosperity

*Prosperity is nice
if it is without vice*

*Prosperity shared
must not be snared*

Protect

*He must protect his wig
after he takes a swig*

*More than their flak
protect your back*

*Protect your throat
where the crocodiles float*

*To protect your ticker
stay away from liquor*

Protected

*He has a watch in his pocket
protected by a locket*

Protective

*The good often suffer
with no protective buffer*

*Grow it from within
a protective thick skin*

Prove

*As if something to prove
she makes her every move*

*Don't prove you are a man
just because you can*

*Every move
has something to prove*

*He had things to prove
when he made his move*

*Her every move
has nothing to prove*

*How to prove in the end
other than with a new trend*

*Many things to prove
once you make a move*

*Nothing left to prove
that others must approve*

*One last move
with something to prove*

*She doesn't have to prove
her each and every move*

*Some they have to prove
each and every move*

*Some think it is strong
to prove people wrong*

*Somethings that move
have things to prove*

*To prove everyone wrong
he has to be strong*

*When he had things to prove
he made his move*

*Why do we have to prove
every little move*

*Why improve
when I have nothing to prove*

Proven
*The story that is woven
need not be fully proven*

Proverbs
*Proverbs will rattle
as contents of a bottle*

Provocation
*Make it their vocation
some their provocation*

Provocative
*Provocative and prim
she looked to the brim*

Provoke
*How to provoke sneers
from your peers*

Prune
*Don't eat prune
in the month of June*

Psychiatrist
*Psychiatrist hired
brain re-wired*

Psychic
*Answer all your whys
through psychic eyes*

*Will it remain
this psychic pain*

Public
*To become a republic
first go public*

*Your work must be food
for the public good*

Publicly
> How can secrets be kept
> when publicly she wept

Puffed
> He was all puffed up
> as he sipped from the cup

Puffins
> The puffins they don't rest
> when far from their nest

Pulse
> Followed by a pulse
> every impulse

> His pulse was no more
> nor was his snore

Pulses
> Go on a diet of pulses
> to restrain your impulses

> One of my nobler pulses
> was to yield to my impulses

Punctuations
> Punctuations get caught
> in mid thought

Punishment
> Is it enough punishment
> crime and admonishment

> Once the punishment is meted
> will it ever be repeated

Purchased
> He purchased a steed
> but had no oats to feed

Purely
> I have now found my voice
> purely out of choice

Purify
> To prayer you must bind
> to purify the mind

Purity
> Many they are blind
> to the purity of the mind

Pursue
> Boys will be boys
> they will pursue their joys

> Men will pursue
> without any clue

Pursued
> Pursued to the depth
> where oysters were kept

Pussy
> What is that
> asked the pussy cat

Puzzle
> Don't muzzle
> the pieces of the puzzle

Puzzled
> He looked a bit puzzled
> when she held the gun by the muzzle

Pyaar
> They feel like achaar
> both paise and pyaar

Q

Quality

> The best single quality
> is punctuality

> What kind of quality
> have mirage and reality

Quarrel

> Don't pick a quarrel
> with the front teeth of the squirrel

> Every quarrel has a face
> that has shades of disgrace

> I have no quarrel
> with what's in the barrel

> One never feels better
> if you quarrel about a letter

> Quarrel not with life
> if it is laden with strife

> The quarrel was decided
> by being one sided

> When you brace up for a quarrel
> don't look for gun or barrel

> Talk about your laurels
> not about your quarrels

> They kept their quarrels
> at the bottom of the barrels

Queen

> Where have you been
> my white collar queen

Query

> Every day comes a query
> what will I become very

Question

> Can he better hear
> with his question mark ear

> Some will question why
> should we see eye to eye

> How to deal with questions
> without genuflections

> Many questions will father
> answers that much bother

> Questions him why
> her seeing eye

Quick

    The questions get tougher
    as we begin to suffer

    Find a pocket to pick
    and do it very quick

    The oil slick
    can make you quick

    Whatever it is he had
    he was quick to be glad

Quicker

    He doesn't have the ticker
    or he would be quicker

Quickly

    Can become very sickly
    fast and very quickly

Quiet

    A quiet abode
    for the meditative mode

    Keep it quiet
    if you're on a diet

    Keep quiet when you must
    before you go bust

    On the window sill they pose
    roses in quiet repose

    Quiet it will not sit
    the finger once having writ

Quietly

    He was quietly debating
    about the lie in waiting

    Quietly it won't sit
    a fire once lit

Quietness

    Up and down he would roam
    in the quietness of his home

Quips

    He has his quips
    at his finger tips

Quit

    Why do we have to quit
    once we get the hang of it

Quite

    His vitriolic murmur
    was quite a squirmer

    It is quite in keeping
    for your belly to come out leaping

Q

R

Rabbits
>*I want this and that
>and rabbits out of a hat*

Race
>*He left without a trace
>he was of a different race*

>*How to keep pace
>with the human race*

Racier
>*Nothing can be racier
>than climbing the glacier*

Radiates
>*He who radiates guilt
>never seems to wilt*

Raft
>*Is there a raft
>to get out of witchcraft*

Rage
>*He stopped being a sage
>in a fit of rage*

>*In a fit of rage
>he tore the page*

>*In a fit of rage
>he turned into a sage*

Raging
>*A raging bull
>angered to the full*

Rain
>*It takes a shower of rain
>for the green grass to remain*

>*Lightning and thunder
>with rain down under*

>*Once she missed the train
>down it came the rain*

>*Rain feels well
>after a dry spell*

>*Rain or fog
>limelight he hog*

>*Rain showers through the cloud
>thunder and lightning loud*

The cockerel takes a shower
from the rain at the noon hour

Umbrellas have much to gain
when there is pouring rain

Rainbow

Like a rainbow without colour
love without a lover

Rainbows make their call
at the morning waterfall

Where the waters fall
rainbows make a call

Raindrops

The roof once it was shed
there were raindrops in my bed

Rains

Pitter patter
the rains do matter

The rains made it green
and brought back the sheen

Rank

A man of high rank
he had reason to thank

For so high a rank
he had god to thank

High up in rank
the childs piggy bank

Low in rank
many a think tank

Rankled

Once you have them ankled
they can easily be rankled

Rapturous

The rapturous flight
of the eagle in delight

Rare

commonsense is rare
said the tortoise to the hare

Pigeons are not rare
at Trafalgar square

Rat

A rat never quibbles
at the cheese when he nibbles

Rate

They rate him first
who runs without thirst

Rather

I would rather be a toad
on grand trunk road

Rattle

To hear the beans rattle
feed them to the cattle

Ravages

Save us from the ravages
of weapon wielding savages

Raved

Raved and ranted
but nothing was granted

Raved

    Raved and ranted
    but permission granted

Reach

    Always out of reach
    the right words to preach

    He grabbed a peach
    that was within arms reach

    The telescope tries
    to reach the distant skies

Read

    As and when you read
    words they pick up speed

    As I read the fable
    I like food upon my table

    Read between the lines
    and find the gold mines

    Read between the lines
    to exercise the minds

Reader

    Every reader must handle
    the flicker in the candle

    The reader keeps searching
    for the meaning where lurking

Readers

    How many readers will gain
    from the outpourings of his pain

    The readers must huddle
    to stop their minds from muddle

Reading

    After the first reading
    his heart began bleeding

Ready

    No need to hold your tongue
    when you are ready to be hung

Reality

    All the clarity
    in ground reality

    Face reality
    in totality

    Man is out of touch
    with reality as such

    People mess with quality
    that is the ground reality

    Reality and myth
    which one are you with

    Though reality it may seem
    dream is still a dream

    Unsupported by reality
    and lacking in quality

    Virtual reality
    no less in quality

Really

    You don't have to travel far
    to find out who you really are

Realms

    To the realms all alone
    where there is no phone

Reason

A man for all reason
will he last the season

A reason to be best
is to pass the test

Even reason doesn't know why
it keeps on giving it a try

Everybody has a reason
whatever the season

Fish has a reason
to weigh in at the season

Happens for a reason
whatever the season

He who cannot see reason
will not with the change of season

How to keep your reason
this holiday season

How to nail it down
the reason for her frown

Is that the reason
we share the same season

It is the turn of reason
hot or cold the season

No reason to cry
once the tears run dry

Only one reason
for the gaming season

Pick the right season
to lose your reason

Reason came to school
in the mind of the fool

Reason it speaks loud
even through the cloud

Reason to be living
is about giving

There must be a reason
for the changing season

Triumph of reason
make it his season

Whatever the season
choose your own reason

Why oh why
reason is so shy

Reasoning's

Reasoning's of the sage
from page to page

Reasons

A man has his reasons
what he does in the seasons

Knows her reasons well
the speeding gazelle

Reasons there were none
for our seasons in the sun

She had good reasons
to go for the man for all seasons

Rebel
*Every rebel must pause
and re-think his cause*

*Rebel without a pause
looking for a cause*

*Rebel without a pause
went from is to was*

*When the rebel has a cause
it is always because*

Reborn
*With each passing of the flesh
the soul be reborn fresh*

Receding
*Far and wide
went the receding tide*

Receipt
*Self deceit
is a bad receipt*

Reception
*He kept his best reception
for his self deception*

Reckless
*Even a reckless speaker
must drink from a beaker*

*He hides behind
a reckless mind*

*In a moment that was reckless
he was rather feckless*

Reclusive
*He became reclusive
just to be elusive*

*He was reclusive
and equally elusive*

Recollections
*Recollections from the past
the only things that last*

Record
*With eyes firmly locked
world record he clocked*

Recover
*Better to recover
than to run for cover*

Recreation
*Every recreation
can act as a potion*

Reduced
*Once you are seduced
easy to be reduced*

Reel
*Reel them in
if they have a fin*

Refined
*Refined at great cost
the wines they must last*

Reflected
*Change is in the main
reflected in the brain*

Reflection

    Couldn't be his reflection
    when you see perfection

    How to see beyond
    reflections in the pond

    In old age reflections
    of erotic deflections

    Reflections are by far
    about what you are

    Reflections of the moon
    by the lagoon

    Reflections were seen
    of the garden green

    Vague reflections
    of unanswered questions

Reform

    Slow reform
    to get to the norm

    To get back to form
    just reform

Reformed

    A habit once formed
    can never be reformed

    He is well armed
    who is reformed

Reforms

    Against all norms
    many reforms

Refrain

    How to refrain
    from causing them pain

Refuse

    Repose is of use
    so don't refuse

    The only room I own
    I refuse to disown

    The tongue never refuse
    to sharpen with use

    Use it or lose it
    but just don't refuse it

Refuses

    I have yet to see a boat
    that refuses to float

    To sail a leaking boat
    that refuses to float

Regret

    Don't fret
    just regret

    My only regret
    is a burning cigarette

    One egret to the other
    don't fret or regret brother

    Show it without fret
    your proof of regret

Regrets

    Regrets I have some
    to re-live them is not fun

Reign
Reign in your senses
without any pretenses

Reigned
Mind must be trained
to be reigned

Rejoice
How I rejoice
at the sound of her voice

My ear drums they rejoice
at the sound of her voice

Rejoice and be well
you have vices to quell

Relationships
His behaviour by far
why relationships sour

Relationships collapse
as a result of a lapse

Relationships
need survival tips

Relatively
Relatively speaking
costly upkeeping

Relax
How to relax
when facing the axe

Relaxed
He is very relaxed
never seems to be taxed

Relentless
The relentless greed
of mouths to feed

Relief
Every tender leaf
Brings the caterpillar relief

Her agony got relief
but not quite the grief

I look for relief
for my every private grief

Relief
Self belief
brings relief

Such a relief
to wake up from grief

Temporary relief
if your sorrow is brief

The way to get relief
is to forget the past belief

To mothers of grief
where is relief

Relies
For eloquence she relies
on her spanish eyes

Wasp is a thing
that relies on it's sting

Relieve
To relieve your gout
watch the leaves sprout

Religion

  Even the pigeon
  has its religion

There isn't a single pigeon
that doesn't worship a religion

Relish

  All day he would relish
  the incursions of his fetish

Reluctance

  My reluctance to sleep
  forever for her to keep

Rely

  Even the gunslinger
  has to rely on a finger

Remain

  Misbegotten gain
  will so remain

Remained

  He remained tight lipped
  his friends as they quipped

  They remained tight lipped
  until their wings were clipped

Remedies

  Old remedies why
  in new illnesses try

Remember

  Always remember
  the music with timbre

  Her voice had a timbre
  forever to remember

  Just remember this
  all my joy is his

Remembered

  He was remembered
  by the way he lumbered

  I woke up from slumber
  and remembered your number

  If you're late and don't tell
  it will be remembered well

  Music made for song
  remembered very long

  Of all the things remembered
  only some were numbered

  She remembered it well
  her love where it fell

  Those dismembered
  are long remembered

Remembering

  Remembering is long
  when love is strong

Remembrance

  Remembrance is never
  brief forever

Remind

  Must I remind
  you are one of the kind

Rhyming English Couplets

Remiss
I would be remiss
if I didn't read this

Remorse
Remorse from the source
it takes it's own course

Remorse on course
is a potent force

Things done off course
without any remorse

Remove
Remove the chaff
and give it to the staff

Rendering
A very modern rendering
without much meandering

Renew
My garden it renew
from the morning dew

The rainbow has a hue
that can easily renew

Renovate
Eat rice from the bowl
to renovate your soul

Renown
How can he let you down
the four legged friend of renown

Repair
Comb through the hair
when it needs repair

How to repair the damage
of all this carnage

How to repair
this love affair

Jeans are worn in pairs
needing many repairs

Repaired
He repaired his phrase
when she gave chase

Repeat
Many a drum must beat
a sound that will repeat

Repeating
It is worth repeating
that the corn is ripe for reaping

Repentance
Doesn't make sense
repentance

Don't ruin your gait
by making repentance wait

No repentance
when I write a good sentence

Repentance is a part
of a change of heart

Repentance is in
in overcoming sin

*Repentance it came
through the hidden shame*

*Repentance wears thin
against the desire to sin*

*With a well prepared repentance
he enunciated his sentence*

*He said it without repentance
the well prepared sentence*

Replace

*She looked him in the face
an said him she will replace*

Reprieve

*No reprieve
for what adam gave to eve*

Reproachful

*A reproachful sting
is a poisonous thing*

Reprove

*Make sure it is just
when reprove is a must*

Republic

*Part of the republic
are the press and the public*

*Pick the right republic
when you wish to go public*

Reputation

*All reputation is false
can fade away like a waltz*

*Can easily wilt
a reputation well built*

*Can fade away fast
for reputation is false*

*His reputation needed painting
after all the tainting*

*Reputation becomes nice
if you do it not once but twice*

*Reputation can be a factor
when you are a stage actor*

*Reputation hung by a thread
though he was well bred*

*Reputation is best
when it withstands a test*

*Reputation is far
from what we really are*

*Reputation is served
by the deserved*

*Reputation must be got
before it gets too hot*

*Reputation once spilled
cannot be refilled*

*Though undeserved
reputation has been served*

*To recoup it is in your power
when reputation it goes sour*

*Upon a strong foundation
is built a good reputation*

*What was the cost
of reputation lost*

Request

*Every small request
she put me to the test*

Resembles

*His acquiline nose
resembles his prose*

Resentment

*Resentment and rage
took center stage*

*Resentment is a stage
that can lead to a rage*

Resist

*Don't resist
when temptations persist*

*Resist it long
if you know it is wrong*

Resistance

*Your enemies will win
when resistance is thin*

Resisted

*A vice once resisted
returns to be tempted*

Resolution

*New year resolution
is no delusion*

*New year resolution
was a delusion*

Resolve

*So many things to solve
not enough resolve*

Resonance

*A resonance that is lasting
can it lose its frosting*

*Resonance to the voice
rids it of the noise*

Resorting

*Between us was much
without resorting to touch*

Resorts

*He who resorts to threat
has lots of time to regret*

Resources

*Failed resources
made them join forces*

*Inner resources
to conquer all forces*

*Rake things from the past
where resources are vast*

Respects

*He respects himself
both giant and elf*

Resplendent

*His resplendent robes
couldn't hide his frontal lobes*

Responsibility

> *Responsibility*
> *begets ability*

Rest

> *Hospice is best*
> *before you finally rest*

> *Last one to rest*
> *the mother in her nest*

> *Old men must rest*
> *and give up their quest*

> *Why should it rest*
> *on the tea bag test*

Restless

> *The winter wind*
> *a restless thing*

> *We've had our fights*
> *and restless nights*

> *Young and the restless*
> *ever so relentless*

Restrain

> *Has much to gain*
> *the mind in restrain*

> *How to restrain*
> *the worm in my brain*

> *How to restrain*
> *this runaway brain*

> *How to restrain*
> *who works against the grain*

> *Unable to retrain*
> *nor to restrain*

> *What colour of paint*
> *will cause self restraint*

Restrict

> *To drink is no sin*
> *if you restrict it to gin*

Restrictions

> *Too many restrictions*
> *are bad prescriptions*

Result

> *All things putrid*
> *result of hatred*

> *Nothing to fill the cup*
> *when results they dried up*

Retreat

> *They take you to the brink*
> *and retreat with a wink*

Retriever

> *His pet retriever*
> *was actually a beaver*

Return

> *When it is your turn*
> *expect no return*

Returning

> *Keep the fires burning*
> *the men will be returning*

Reveal

> Doesn't fully reveal
> for poetry is a feel

> Much more to conceal
> than to reveal

> Eventually revealed
> what was concealed

> Failings concealed
> never to be revealed

Revealing

> Don't go revealing
> each bit of your feeling

Revealing

> She was up to the ceiling
> from his inner revealing

Revealing

> Undercurrents of feeling
> can be most revealing

Reveals

> A writer reveals himself
> whether giant or elf

> How quietly the morn
> reveals itself at dawn

> He revels in flanking
> the rich and high ranking

Revenge

> Revenge though sweet
> is hard on the feet

Reverence

> Reverence we must bring
> to every living thing

Reverse

> I am very much averse
> to going in reverse

Review

> Within the purview
> of peer review

Revise

> He was made to revise
> until it puffed his eyes

Revised

> Once revised
> Marginalized

Revolving

> The revolving cast
> can never last

Reward

> Misers end reward
> is also a hospital ward

Rewarding

> Marriage can be rewarding
> if both stop talking

Rewards

> Always on the cards
> life's sweet rewards

Rhyme

  For a thought to chime
  say it with a rhyme

   Go ask peter
  about rhyme and metre

  No rhyme no reason
  for the changing season

   Rhyme and Reason
  couplets are in season

Rhyme and rhythm to the fore
until no one can keep score

   Rhyme and rhythm
  seen through the prism

  Rhyme is like a hammer
can make the woodpecker stammer

   Rhyme is the pleasure
  we must cherish in leisure

   Rhyme makes it clear
  they are things that endear

She helped him pass the time
with music and songs of rhyme

  Though well past his prime
  he could construct a rhyme

  When I say it without rhyme
   the fault is all mine

  And then there were times
  of graciousness and rhymes

  Many countless times
  we sang the rhymes

  Those were heady times
when love came up with rhymes

 Earliest evidence of rhyming
 was based on pure timing

  An independent rhythm
 like light through a prism

  Birds keep to their wing
 with rhythm and swing

 Cryptic messages are found
 in both rhythm and sound

   Have good time
  with rhythm and rhyme

  No rhythm or rhyme
  don't waste my time

  Once I fall into rhythm
I feel like light through a prism

   Rhythm and rhyme
   for a good time

   Rhythm is bound
  by a pleasant sound

  Through lens or prism
 her movements have rhythm

Rhythmic

  The gentle ocean swell
  both rhythmic and well

Rich

He has a good ramus
who is rich and famous

Live rich
die without hitch

No need to toil
if you get rich with oil

Take your pick
be rich or be sick

The rich will get richer
but the poor won't see the glitter

To give up there is a hitch
especially if you are rich

Riches

In spite of all the riches
so many hitches

Once she fell upon riches
she came across many hitches

Riches said the bard
is not the way to god

Riches without hitches
had me in stitches

Richness

Richness can last
if you know the cost

Rid

Rid yourself of wrinkles
but keep your twinkles

The guitar he will strum
to get rid of hum drum

Riddle

Come up with a riddle
while you look for the fiddle

Ride

How to ride
the high and low tide

Rides

On this book it rides
much else besides

Ridiculous

Ridiculous pose
where to put the rose

Riding

Everything it lay riding
on her letter with good tiding

Rifle

For you a rifle
for me a trifle

Right

If half a dozen is six
how to get the right mix

Hold on to your rights
through thick thin and fights

Ring

Even a brass ring
is a coveted thing

Ringing
I find it hard to shed
this ringing in my head

Ringside
From the ringside
where the view is wide

Ripe
Wait for the berries to ripe
lest you suffer with gripe

Rise
A man of proper girth
can give rise to birth

Can't have happened too soon
the rise of the evening moon

They all stood up to rise
temped by a bigger prize

Rising
The rising sun
to welcome is fun

With temperatures rising
there was an uprising

Risk
At the slightest hint of risk
his pace became brisk

Business may be brisk
but never without risk

He was rewarded for risk
with a broken disc

Make it brisk
when you take risk

No slipped disc
if you don't take risk

Roll the dice
and risk it twice

Wired to detect risk
in a manner that is brisk

Risks
Of all the risks that I did take
the biggest was staying awake

Risky
Risky ventures
lose your dentures

Ritual
The ritual of sipping
can do with a bit of lipping

Rivalry
No need for chivalry
just sibling rivalry

Rivalry is best
when put to the test

There is no chivalry
in quibbling rivalry

River
Many a river can see
way down to the sea

The river finds its way
whether it is April June or May

Road

> He can see the road ahead
> although nearly dead

> How to goad
> the toad off the road

> Just to goad
> she sang on a road

> Where there is no road
> stop and ask the toad

Roads

> When the roads all seem narrow
> even for a flying sparrow

Roadways

> Roadways, trains
> and proper drains

Roam

> After I roam
> I come to feelings in the home

> Someday I will be home
> we will then hold hands and roam

> The crows stop to roam
> when the cows come home

Rocking

> She filled a rocking chair
> as she combed her hair

Role

> Suddenly put in a role
> that made her person whole

Roles

> our roles though defined
> must be refined

Romance

> Before she blinked
> romance was inked

> Chance I give to thee
> to spark the romance in me

> Comb your hair
> romance is in the air

> Couplets give us a chance
> to explore the grand romance

> Don't ruin your chance
> of a happy romance

> Every passing glance
> can cause a romance

> For romance to tick
> be romantic

> Give it a chance
> romance at the dance

> Give it a chance
> the new found romance

> Give love a chance
> with a sizzling romance

> Given half a chance
> they would opt for romance

> Here is our chance
> to sit and romance

How to enhance
this tentative romance

If you give fiction a chance
you will get love and romance

Instant romance
is a play of chance

Let us both share
the romance in the air

Let's go and dance
he said to romance

Romance and passion
how to fashion

Romance can be fun
in the mid-day sun

Romance full of hisses
are not made for kisses

Romance has a way
of paving the way

Romance is divine
with wine before you dine

Romance is in the offing
when they greet each other laughing

Romance when it is looming
needs a bit of grooming

She brushed her hair
when romance was in the air

Stick a comb in your hair
when romance is in the air

The men did their dance
hoping for romance

When will it be spilled
romance unfulfilled

Romances

Her dancing feet
for romances to greet

Hidden romances
at the dances

Island romances
and hula dances

Romances need feeding
even when you are speeding

Unforgettable romances
from the slyest of glances

Romancing

He resorts to dancing
as means of romancing

How to go romancing
without singing or dancing

Romantic

Let's go face to face
to some romantic place

Soon she will miss
the romantic bliss

Romantically

The semantically gifted
can be romantically lifted

Root

    The walrus has a tooth
    that has a deep root

    Even the grass roots
    must start as shoots

    Wear proper boots
    when you look for your roots

Rose

    Anything goes
    after smelling the rose

    Every rose she chose
    was close to her pose

    Follow your nose
    and smell the rose

    He described the rose
    with tangled prose

He gave her a rose with a stalk
during table talk

He is like a person without the nose
who cannot smell the rose

    It took purple prose
    to describe the rose

    Like a rose that adorns
    the sharpest of thorns

    Many a good prose
    can compete with the rose

    Neither poetry nor prose
    but does it match the rose

Pink rose to her nose
in a conciliatory pose

Prose
is rose

Rose is a rose
is every repose

Rose petals it is said
filled their honeymoon bed

She blushes when she speaks
with rose coloured cheeks

She has a quick nose
when he gives her a rose

The rose it can talk
to you when you walk

To put under his nose
he chose a pink rose

Whenever she pose
a rose is a rose

Roses

Bed of roses
attract all the noses

Days of wine and roses
good for both our noses

Has the smell of roses
the writing what it poses

His role was to bring roses
all the way to their noses

I have roses in my bed
and thorns in my head

In all reposes
it was wine and roses

In the early spring
I have roses to bring

Let me smell the roses
while my nose has its poses

Paper roses
don't love noses

Roses make you think
of the colour pink

Roses red and white
to make love a delight

Where have the roses gone
it is already a new dawn

Rotten

He is a rotten apple
who knows how to grapple

Rough

When times are rough
resort to bluff

It is just the sound
that makes the meaning round

Round after round
he got closer to the ground

Round after round
they yield further ground

The earth may be round
but where is it bound

Early morning sounds
of the birds making rounds

Royalty

Royalty is a kind
of a stable mind

Royalty
has loyalty

Ruby

He would gift a ruby
to every blue footed boobie

Rude

Better to be hung
than to hear a rude tongue

Rudeness

He slowly lets it float
the rudeness from his throat

If you give rudeness a voice
let it not be by choice

Ruin
can do you in

They ruin your pose
the flies on the nose

Ruined

Exorbitant shots
ruined the plots

Rule

Don't lose your cool
is a simple rule

Rule of thumb
don't let it go numb

Rule of thumb
made the mule numb

Some anointed hands
they rule many lands

There is no school
that teaches how to rule

There is no school
that teaches the golden rule

They use it like a tool
the one sided rule

Ruled

Some are schooled
not to be ruled

Ruler and the ruled
both need to be schooled

The ruler and the ruled
were differently schooled

Rulers

The rulers and the rules
each other they schooled

Rules

Games have their rules
and proper tools

He rules the crease
without so much as sneeze

He who writes the rules
corners all the tools

Poor get the rules
rich get the tools

Rules of a new game
can be without a name

They have a new name
the rules of the game

They think we are fools
those who make the rules

We feel less taxed
once the rules are relaxed

What you say and do
rules over you

Ruling

The ruling class
have their own looking glass

Rum

He told her here I come
with a bottle of rum

How can I hum
without my evening rum

The place it could hum
without a drop of rum

Rumination

All the rumination
was just hallucination

Rumour

Don't let it spill
on to the rumour mill

He is a traveling rumour
with occasional spew of humour

Only a rumour
about the paramour

Rumour is flying
and I am not lying

Rumour it leaks
from the tongue as its speaks

Rumour mills
sold as pills

Some think it is humour
to spread malicious rumour

The knight in shining armour
was just a rumour

The paramour spread a rumour
as apart of his humour

Rumoured

It has been rumoured
that he needs to be humoured

Rumours

Slow growing rumours
are they just tumours

These are not tumours
just ugly rumours

Run

He had them on the run
until he was done

Run of the mill
does it bode ill

Sheep they run helter
and the fox it runs skelter

The sheep keep him on the run
until the day is done

Rush

The sun to its morning blush
some days it must rush

Rushed

His fingers he rushed
to the hospital when crushed

Rust

To get out of his rust
the golfer must swing first

Rustic

Those who are rustic
can also be caustic

Rustle

The rustle of the leaves
couldn't stop the thieves

Ruthless

Every ruthless mile
trudge with a toothless smile

S

Sacred

    No sacred routine
manning the guillotine

Sacrifice

    If your sacrifice it twice
it will cease to be a vice

    Sacrifice great
can change your fate

    Sacrifice is a choice
made by the inner voice

    Sacrifice is nice
when to love it adds spice

    They sacrifice their heads
to the pillows in their beds

Sacrificial

    Sacrificial lamb
cannot become ham

Sad

    It is quite sad
when you don't know you've been had

Saddest

    My phantom limb
the saddest thing

    The saddest ending possible
put it in the crucible

Sadness

    A sadness came upon her face
as he tried to make his case

    A sadness once buried
can return all hurried

    Collective sadness
redeemed by gladness

    Her sadness had a tinge
of love lost after a binge

    Out of ordinary sadness
sprouts extraordinary gladness

    Sadness it shows
down to his toes

    Sadness turned to gladness
when I came home to madness

Safely
> A thing well said
> you can safely take to bed

> I'll take a bet
> there is no safety net

Sage
> If you give your daughter to a sage
> he will make her turn the page

Sail
> As they set sail
> she undid her veil

> The beached whale
> who forgot to sail

> The ship set sail
> at the pace of a snail

Sailed
> Before we could get to the quay
> the ship sailed out to sea

Sailor
> A sailor needs to sail
> like a coffin needs a nail

Sailors
> The sailors yearn
> waiting for their turn

Sails
> When the wind fails
> there is a droop in the sails

Saint
> Don't call him a saint
> he might just faint

> He told them not to paint
> him as an unholy saint

> Just because you are a saint
> don't think you cannot faint

> Oh patron saint
> relieve him of his taint

Saints
> All the saints in heaven
> can be counted in fingers seven

> In a world full of saints
> how can anyone faint

Salad
> Many a ballad
> about the leafy salad

Salesman
> Snake oil salesman
> is a good gamesman

Same
> All in the same boat
> the tiger and the goat

> Would not be the same
> the sun by another name

> Wouldn't be the same
> a rose by any other name

Sample
> Every good example
> must give out a sample

Sanctioned
> Sanctioned code
> on the road

Sanctity
> Sanctity of worlds
> is for the birds

Sandal
> He reads by the candle
> with book and a sandal

Sandals
> She walks around in sandals
> lighting little candles

Sang
> He sang his ballad
> while munching at salad

Sanity
> How to keep your sanity
> and your amity

> No sanity
> without amity

> Take a page
> from the sanity sage

Santa
> Santa put his foot
> into a chimney full of soot

Sapling
> A sapling once planted
> grows quite undaunted

Sardines
> With sardines in a tin
> and a bottle of gin

Sarong
> He wore his sarong
> two feet too long

Satanic
> Even the satanic
> can be platonic

Satire
> Not every satire
> can set your heart on fire

> People will never tire
> of aphorism and satire

> With all irons in the fire
> he narrated a satire

> Words they await his call
> writing couplets and satire till the fall

Satisfaction
> Satisfaction is lasting
> if you come to dinner fasting

Satisfactory
> He is satisfactory
> my husband at the factory

Save

*Douse the house
but save the mouse*

*Save the brinjal
and give it to us all*

*You will save yourself some ink
if you first stop and think*

Saves

*The dog comes and saves
the child under the waves*

Saviour

*Many time a saviour
her gracious behaviour*

Savory

*Savory details
have long trails*

Savour

*Make them savour
each little favour*

*Savour the feat
stare down defeat*

*There were days he could savour
when he was in favour*

Say

*Say it ain't so
before they come to know*

*Say it in a few
words that you knew*

Saying

*Keep saying things
so their heart sings*

*Some are given to saying
that to cheat can be paying*

Scale

*Couldn't get on the scale
the beached whale*

*How to weigh the whale
without proper scale*

*Not enough for the whale
both pans of the scale*

Scandal

*No need to be a vandal
to unearth a juicy scandal*

*Yet to hear of a vandal
worry about a scandal*

*Put all scandals to sleep
before it becomes a heap*

Scanner

*Being under the scanner
there was a change in his manner*

Scar

*The earth was filled with scar
from months of raining war*

Scare

*A scarecrow of a man
scare he can*

*Barbers will scare
the straightest of hair*

*He uses words
that don't even scare the birds*

*Who next to scare
who has teeth to bare*

Scared

*He was so scared
that he never dared*

*Many an apple was spared
from adam being too scared*

*Men who bellow
scared and yellow*

*The hunting dog
scared the hog*

*Too scared to jeer
people who we fear*

*Who is not scared
if love life is bared*

Scares

*He has a way with words
which scares away the birds*

*Scares the toad
when rubber meets road*

Scars

*He wore his scars well
making it hard to tell*

*Men would have no scars
if there were no wars*

Scary

*Very scary
obituary*

Scenes

*For his daily beans
he works behind the scenes*

*He was all beans
behind the scenes*

Scent

*Every sweet scent
for her it was meant*

*He waited all bent
and picked up his scent*

*It is only a scent
for the nose only meant*

*Look for his scent
to know what he meant*

*The scent from her hair
filled the evening air*

*The scent of a rose
tells poetry from prose*

Scentry

*Need many a scentry
the landed and the gentry*

Scheme

*All things have a scheme
or so it may seem*

*In the grand scheme of things
my thoughts take to wings*

*It all begins to seem
like a well intended scheme*

*It is a scheme
that has no theme*

*Men it seems
hatch up schemes*

*The writer he schemes
around popular themes*

Scholar

*Each and every scholar
thinks he is the one who is taller*

Scholarship

*Cannot keep friends
once scholarship ends*

School

*She went to school on a bicycle
the weather outside all icicle*

Scoff

*Don't scoff
at what was left off*

*Don't scoff
just laugh it off*

*Nothing to do but scoff
once the bid is off*

*They brush you off
and then they scoff*

*They cannot scoff
if you pull it off*

Scoop

*A generous scoop of salt
he added to his malt*

*To get all the scoop
you must jump through the hoop*

Score

*He made a big score
studded with four*

*If you settle an old score
there will be many more*

*Whatever the score
tea will be at four*

Scores

*Once he settles scores
they say sorry on all fours*

Scorpion

*Don't let it flail
at you the scorpion tail*

*How to rattle
the scorpion in the bottle*

*It can also flail
the scorpion tail*

*The scorpion has no wing
but its tail has a sting*

*What does the scorpion bring
other than a tail with a sting*

Scrap
> He fell into the trap
> of picking up a scrap

Scratched
> With a simian pose
> he scratched his nose

Scream
> Wake up to scream
> as you talk back to your dream

Screaming
> Screaming commerce
> attacking my purse

Sea
> Far out at sea
> hurricanes are meant to be

> For the whale it is norm
> the sea and the storm

> How to drink tea
> on a ship in the heavy sea

> It was between me
> and the swell of the sea

> Let us live by the sea
> both you and me

> No beehive nor bee
> at the bottom of the sea

> There is peril in the sea
> where the sail boats have to be

> They lay inches off the sea
> and sipped Darjeeling tea

> They sat and sipped tea
> in many a heavy sea

Seagull
> He could be seagull
> who is too frugal

> Seagulls they go lull
> when things get dull

Sealed
> Eyes peeled
> lips sealed

> Keep your lips sealed
> and eyes always peeled

> Post card under the lamp
> she sealed it with a stamp

> The path I have chosen
> is sealed completely frozen

Seamers
> Only the seamers
> they bowl the beamers

Search
> Round after round
> search for common ground

Searching
> Don't go searching the seas
> looking for biting bees

> Searching for the morning light
> chirping in delight

Season

Dress up for the season
when you find a good reason

Open season
beyond reason

Seasonal

Snow is not a blunder
but just a seasonal wonder

Seasons

Seasons in the sun
make the winters fun

Seasons in the sun
until the work was done

Seasons take their toll
life on the Atoll

Seat

He raves and rants
by the seat of his pants

Seated

I was simply seated
when she slowly visited

Seaweed

Seaweed has a smell
that can make sickness well

Seclusion

Sublime seclusion
is an inclusion

Secrecy

Secrecy in love
feels like the heaven above

Secret

A secret once told
quickly takes hold

A secret small or tall
just tell it to the wall

A secret to unload
about the prince and the toad

A secret well kept
was lost when he slept

Deep and dark secret
he shared with the egret

He becomes bold
to whom a secret is told

He is a secret friend
who is an enemy till the end

He spoke to the elf
about his secret self

His secrets they leap
when he talks in his sleep

It's the good things that follow
our deep and secret sorrow

Keep your anguish secret
until you meet a white egret

Many a secret held by the sea
told to the sailor whoever he may be

*Many a secret locked
must someday be unlocked*

*Oh so nice
my secret vice*

*Only for the egret
your darkest secret*

*Our secret lives
take nose dives*

*Secret deals are best
quickly laid to rest*

*Secret lives
of husbands and wives*

*Secret vice
do it twice*

*She had a secret doubt
that she could do without*

*She whispered to the egret
her every little secret*

*The long beak of the egret
quick to pick up your secret*

*The secret abode
of the lovesick toad*

*Their secret abode
unlocked with a code*

*There is a secret in every heart
with which they never part*

*They had a secret code
that would lead to their abode*

Secretly

*Secretly she is drawn
to brain more than brawn*

Secrets

*Don't ever fall asleep
if you have secrets to keep*

*I am totally blind
to the secrets in her mind*

*In my memory is locked
secrets that are stocked*

*Put secrets on hold
until they become cold*

*Secrets are clever
they don't keep forever*

*Secrets are kept
by the adept*

*Secrets have leapt
from where they were kept*

*Secrets never keep
for the strong or the meek*

*Secrets such as this
must be sealed with a kiss*

*Secrets that delight
of love through the night*

*Secrets that lay in this picture
cannot be covered in a lecture*

*Secrets they flutter
when two people mutter*

Secrets they heap
in the deep levels of sleep

Secrets told in a whisper
with words that are crisper

The owners were seethed
when their secrets were breathed

Unspoken secrets
by two lonely egrets

Secure

To keep the world in order
have a secure border

Seduce

Fries and shrimp
will seduce any chimp

See

I have yet to see a Sagittarian
turn into a vegetarian

Something's happen to me
that no one else can see

Seed

From seed to the fruit
a plant with a root

His words we must heed
and plant them like a seed

It all depends on the seed
how we end up as a breed

Like a seed that becomes a tree
so it is with me

Look for a seed
to give you the lead

Many it can feed
the harvest from a single seed

Once the seed is planted
many a wish is granted

This is chicken feed
said greed to the seed

Where does it lead
the once planted seed

Will not recede
hate and its seed

Seeding

Good seeding
leads to good breeding

Every little seedling
needs a bit of needling

Seeds

All seeds planted
don't grow slanted

Apprehension
from seeds of tension

How many seeds
for better breeds

Plant them as seeds
all your good deeds

Plant your seeds
with very good deeds

*Seeds can then
become deeds of men*

*Sow your seeds
for big deeds*

*Sowing the seeds
of to-morrows breeds*

Seeing

*Seeing eye dog
can't be a frog*

Seek

*Pipe they go and seek
to smoke while they speak*

*To serve and to seek
not for the meek*

Seeking

*How to get gnana
before seeking nirvana*

Seems

*Upside down it seems
like a bat hanging from beams*

Seen

*What might have been
not always seen*

Selection

*Make your selection
based on visceral connection*

Self

*Both giant and elf
need conquest of self*

*His invidious self
in the body of an elf*

*My each different self
sometimes giant sometimes elf*

*Need to study their self
both giant and the elf*

*Though he was an elf
he found his higher self*

Selfish

*Selfish and mean
where have you been*

Sell

*The book should do well
if only it would sell*

*What will sell
the press will tell*

Semantic

*Semantic guile
was meant to rile*

Semblance

*To face the ocean
without a semblance of motion*

Send

*It was a god send
but it all had to end*

Sense

*Common sense is good
when it comes to food*

*Forbearance makes sense
in present or past tense*

*He built walls
when common sense calls*

*He tries to make sense
with a finer shade of lens*

*How to make sense
out of exuberance*

*If it doesn't make sense
it can make you tense*

*Says the sound to the sense
why are you intense*

*Sense can be made
if you sit in the shade*

*Sense must be made
before the meanings fade*

*Sense of timing
when it comes to rhyming*

*Sense of wonder
with each new thunder*

*We have to work harder
for a sense of order*

*When common sense stands tall
it can prevent many a fall*

*Words don't make sense
when you are tense*

Senseless

*The most senseless part
is it the head or the heart*

Senses

*Coffee has a blend
to the senses is a friend*

*Common sense can be brewed
only by the shrewd*

*Dull without the senses
present and past tenses*

*Dullened by the senses
she lost her defences*

*He made up pretenses
when he lost his senses*

*He who conquers his senses
needs no more defences*

*Senses once put to sleep
but conscious thoughts they weep*

*She touched his senses
and ruined his defences*

*Smells for the senses
that make no pretenses*

*There are no pretenses
in all the five senses*

*There are no pretenses
when it comes to our senses*

*Your senses they will pounce
if you don't renounce*

Sensors

*From flower to flower she flitted
with sensors properly fitted*

Sensually
> The shape he gave to feeling
> was sensually appealing

Sensuous
> Sensuous joys
> leave it to the boys

Sentence
> A sentence too long
> that didn't put a foot wrong

> To make a sentence whole
> words they play a role

> Sentences from the tongue
> can have us hung

> Sentences were so old
> that the letter turned to gold

Sentimental
> Sentimental till the end
> when I meet an old friend

Sentiments
> Sentiments they pile
> mile after mile

> Without proper condiments
> what will happen to sentiments

Separation
> Separation takes longer
> if you do it in anger

Sequel
> There won't be a sequel
> if we both are unequal

Serenade
> My guitar and me
> to serenade thee

Serendipity
> Meet me in the city
> I told serendipity

Serene
> All serene
> the birds when they preen

Serenely
> Let them serenely float
> your thoughts on a rudderless boat

Serenity
> How can they be mean
> when there is serenity in the scene

> Serenity in war
> can take you very far

Serious
> Every serious cause
> fuelled by because

> Serious thinking people
> have heads shaped like a steeple

> The sailor needs to brave
> every serious wave

Serpent
> Only a serpent
> will have no repent

Servant

> I plead to you in fervent
> don't treat me like a servant

> Servant and master
> one of them is faster

Serve

> Go there to serve
> the road beyond the curve

> How to serve your master
> without getting any faster

> They also serve grub
> at the newly opened pub

> Whenever it was deuce
> his serve came of use

> The finest blend of tea
> was served for you and me

Serves

> To the lady be good
> who serves you your food

Settle

> Every flower has a petal
> on which the butterfly it settle

> Men of mettle
> they don't easily settle

Shade

> He is a jack of all shade
> that's how he was made

> Holding hands in the shade
> for which the tree was made

> Holding hands in the shade
> promises were made

> It's a choice I made
> sitting in the shade

> Many a day I wade
> through to a summer shade

> No light without the shade
> that's how things are made

> Under the shade of the banyan tree
> I lit a cigarette for me

Shades

> Look through your shades
> when the bid is seven spades

Shadow

> Every shadow will try
> to follow me why

> Just sit and eat pork
> under the shadow of your porch

> Shadow boxing
> is very taxing

> Shadow boxing
> very taxing

> Shadow dancing
> is a part of romancing

> Shadow of suspicion
> is on a mission

Shadows

> Eye shadows in the night
> makes love a delight

Rhyming English Couplets

Shadows from the past
can make you downcast

Shadows in the dark
could it be the shark

Shadows in the fog
many miles to log

Shadows in the sun
they follow me in fun

When the days work is done
to the shadows of the evening sun

Shaken

The pig was all shaken
when he heard the word bacon

Shame

He sullies anothers name
to cover up his own shame

He bears a wounded name
that cannot cover his shame

He came up lame
with a sense of shame

He went past his fame
into a world of shame

His walk is never the same
once engulfed in shame

Name of the game
envy and shame

No big shame
to lose ball game

Shame has a new name
that's the modern game

Shame makes it plain
it is a deadly pain

Such a shame
all men are the same

They are all just the same
they have to look up the meaning of shame

They cry in shame
who have lost the game

Shamed

Shall remain unnamed
he who has been shamed

Shamed into gloom
flower hesitant to bloom

Shameful

Shameful pandering
leads to wandering

Shameless

Conduct shameless
not entirely blameless

Shamelessly

Shamelessly they cheat
to accomplish any feat

Shaped

Why is the nose
shaped like a hose

Shapes
>All shapes and sizes
>they come the vices

Share
>Both they share
>jet black hair

>Children and old folks
>they share their jokes

>Forever I will be thine
>if you share with me a glass of wine

>How can we share
>the music in the air

>If you are a good doer
>share it with the poor

>Let us share
>the crisp cold air

>Share your pie
>with me not why

>Someone to share my wine
>at the table when we sit and dine

>The only thing they share
>is silvery grey hair

Shared
>Many have shared their blood
>fighting both fire and flood

>Must be shared with the gannet
>resources of the planet

>Shared with her some wine
>under the stars where they shine

Sharing
>He is not prone to sharing
>when he catches a large herring

Shark
>Hark!
>How white is the shark

>Has not yet learned to bark
>the great white shark

Sharks
>Sharks had to be fed
>by the living or the dead

Sharp
>He has only nine
>but they are sharp as canine

>Sharp as a claw
>the language of the law

Shattered
>Glass ceilings were shattered
>when it most mattered

>He lay there all shattered
>when it really mattered

>Only thing that mattered
>our vase was all shattered

Shattering
>In a wave shattering move
>the ship hit a groove

She
    She tip toes
    wherever she goes

Shear
    Shear your sheep
    when they sleep

Shed
If you have lines to shed
just use your head

Leave no room for lament
shed the confining garment

    Shed your pretenses
    to improve your senses

Sheen
    Where had you been
    to get all this sheen

    Where have you been
you haven't lost your sheen

Shelf
    I put it on the shelf
    after it wrote itself

    Take it out of the shelf
    that part of your self

Shelter
All day we must swelter
and in the evening seek shelter

    Helter skelter
    his food and shelter

    Helter skelter
    no food no shelter

Shepherd
The shepherd he must roam
until the cows come home

    The shepherd went to sleep
between the cows and the sheep

The shepherd who herds his flock
doesn't have need for a clock

    The shepherd will not sleep
    without counting sheep

Shield
    Man he must shield
his investments in the field

Shifted
    He scores who is gifted
though the goal posts have been shifted

The goalpost has been shifted
by the cunning and the gifted

Shifty
    Fifty fifty
    can make you shifty

Shine
He got rid of blues
with shine on his shoes

Let our love shine
as if soaked in wine

The shine it can mellow
from the polished halo

Shines

All that shines isn't gold
and all that smells isn't mould

Shining

A shining pearl
just like my girl

A shining single star
sparkles though very far

Better to gift him a crystal
than a shining pistol

She lit up all our faces
with bright shining teeth and laces

Shiny

Could it pass for a ring
this shiny round thing

The oyster unfurls
shiny white pearls

Ship

You will not get your mail
once the ship it sets sail

Shiver

At the mountain top they shiver
drinking oil of cod liver

It sent him a shiver
the bend in the river

Sends up your spine a shiver
when I think of my failing liver

The wildebeest shiver
as they swim across the river

To rid himself of shiver
he warmed up to her liver

Shoe

They go out and loot
both shoe laces and boot

Shoot

Some they shoot from the hip
and others from the lip

Shooting

Every shooting star
has to travel very far

Shoots

He shoots his mouth off
when he wishes to scoff

Shopping

Out of the morning mist
out came her shopping list

Shoulder

Put shoulder to the boulder
before you get older

Shout

A child will shout and fling
until she has a song to sing

Show

All of work is a show
to which we get up and go

He can only show the path
to where you can have a bath

If you don't show up
we will drink from your cup

Prim and proper
she is a show stopper

Some nights it will show
the moon in full glow

Thanks
but don't show your fangs

They who know
just run the show

Who's running the show
and who is kneading the dough

Shower

After your finest hour
go jump in the shower

Good for a shower
the early morning hour

Shrillness

We must make our choices
with shrillness in our voices

Shrine

I will go to the shrine
where god is totally mine

Shrugs

Shrugs are a way
of shrugging him away

Shut

Think with your gut
with your mouth shut

Siblings

Don't count on your siblings
to laugh at your quippings

Raucous quibblings
with her siblings

Sick

Don't ever fall sick
in the high arctic

Side

Though side by side
gulf between us wide

Sidewalk

Peanuts from the sidewalk
as they walk the talk

Sideways

On the highways and byways
crab walks always sideways

Sieves

September leaves
do they have sieves

Sight

A sight to be seen
when the ocean is blue green

Brown or white
bear is a sight

No end in sight
for the cranes in their flight

Read everything in sight
that you think is always right

Sight

We contemplate the sight
of every moonlit night

Significant

He is a significant pawn
not to be treated with a yawn

My significant other
like cap and feather

Signing

Keep signing up
for a full cup

Signs

Tell tale signs
speak of good times

Silence

A period of silence
does not require a license

Day or night
silence is might

In the silence of the grave
how to be brave

Pig became ham
from the silence of the ram

Silence and sound
makes the world go round

Silence becomes strong
that lasts a minute too long

Silence brings clarity
soon with alacrity

Silence can speak
words that we seek

Silence has treasures
and unique pleasures

Silence I behest
in my final days of rest

Silence is a part
of happiness from the start

Silence is a shelter
before helter skelter

Silence is born
of a brewing scorn

Silence is sweet
when past memories I greet

Silence makes it clear
there is a hidden fear

Silence prevails
when speech it fails

Silence starts talking
when death it comes stalking

*Silence them with a whistle
before they wake up and bristle*

*Silence too
can speak a word or two*

*The silence of the sages
lasts through the ages*

*There was a silence in the camp
once they put out the lamp*

*When silence needed a break
he went after plumb cake*

Silent

*By the silent hand
through oceans and the land*

*Even the silent sage
awoke in a rage*

*Many a silent hand
behind the big brand*

*Silent hand must guide
sailors on the oceans wide*

*Silent hand that guides
me through daily strides*

*They held hands and climbed the hill
on a night all silent and still*

*They make their choices
with silent voices*

*Some say good – bye
so silently why*

Silkworm

*The silkworm wakes up at dawn
weaving itself into form*

*Don't dilly dally
with silly sally*

*She didn't think it silly
when he proposed holding a lilly*

Simple

*It's pure and simple
why youth get pimple*

*Just a simple boy
who tries to make joy*

*Words simple
feelings ample*

Simplify

*Best way to imply
is to simplify*

*Even if he try
he cannot simplify*

Simply

*He simply lives
for his olives*

*The cause though noble
simply broke the cable*

Sin

*A bait to draw you in
into the fold of sin*

*A little bit of gin
is a prelude to sin*

Sin

All the sin
in bottled gin

Both thick and very thin
they pin on them every sin

Bottled sin
labelled as gin

Can it be sin
when forgiveness becomes thin

Every sin is a blot
worse than a blood clot

Go commit a sin
when patience wears thin

He became very thin
being robbed of his sin

He favoured sin
to a pain in the shin

He has made a pact
with sin it is fact

He has taste for sin
after bottle of gin

He poured from a bottle of gin
before he committed sin

He who is not without sin
give him a bottle of gin

Many a sin is in the main
tied to each other like a chain

Meaning of sin
bottle of gin

My only sin
is the gin within

No way to sin
without bottled gin

Sin is ugly
said he smugly

Sin once tasted
must not be feted

Sin while it is hot
not when it is not

Tea infused gin
the mornings first sin

The devil he win
when you commit sin

The enemy takes to sin
mostly the one within

The skunk he gets in
to the inner reaches of sin

There is a burning within
to commit every sin

There is a sense within
that we are victims of sin

Very much in
confessing to sin

When shall we begin
to wallow in all this sin

Rhyming English Couplets

Where have you been
the seventh sin

Why is it in
the colour of sin

Why isn't it wearing thin
that which caused the sin

Your whole world will win
when you choose virtue over sin

Since

When is it since
the frog praised the prince

Sincere

They were quite sincere
calling each other dear

Sinful

Do it with tact
every sinful act

Sing

Birds they sing to me
and I to the speaking tree

He began to sing
and threw his hat in the ring

Mosquitoes will sing
at any bloody thing

The mynah could still sing
though broken was her wing

The ocean waves they sing
against the rising wind

They sing to us their call
the parrots in the fall

To hear a bird sing
and the flutter of her wing

Singapore

Too much of a good thing
the Singapore sling

Singer

It's not the song
it's the singer who is wrong

Many a song will linger
because of who is the singer

The singer can't be wrong
about the message in the song

The singer not the song
the bell not the gong

Singing

The mosquito why
goes singing by

A single guy
can go awry

Do not mingle
with the almost single

Pockets he can pick
with a single quip

Singlehood

Nothing is as good
as singlehood

Sings

Into eardrums they sings
insects with wings

Oh sage who sings
don't clip my wings

The cuckoo it sings
to the pendulum swings

Singular

He is an elitist
with a singular twist

Singularly

They don't pine
who are singularly supine

Sinister

Tell your minister
all that is sinister

Sink

A quiet room to think
where thought is made to sink

Don't open your lips
lest it sink ships

He will one day sink
who has had too much to drink

Into the bottle he must sink
to paint his nib with ink

Sinkable

It was unthinkable
that the ship was sinkable

Sinking

How to skip
the sinking ship

She has no qualms
about sinking into his arms

The sinking globe
sheds his golden robe

Sinner

The line gets thinner
between saint and sinner

The saint in this sinner
shows up at dinner

Though I am a sinner
she invited me to dinner

There are no winners
when both harbour sinners

They all relish their dinners
both saints and sinners

Sinning

He who is caught sinning
showed up with face all grinning

Sinning comes with ease
when you stop to sneeze

With each new sinning
the head keeps spinning

Sins

Act out your sins
let's see who wins

*All our sins
need dustbins*

*Beauty is there to keep
your sins very deep*

*Better to change our sins
before one of them wins*

*Could it be from sins
the hurt in my shins*

*Eventually they find a home
sins after all day they roam*

*For the married man begins
trouble from his sins*

*He hid his sins
with bottled gins*

*He pays for his gins
also for his sins*

*He wears his sins well
from his demeanor they can tell*

*How to atone
for the sins of the drone*

*How to atone
sins of the drone*

*In hell for his sins
on needles and pins*

*Mirror held to sins
to ruffle their fins*

*Multiplied by gins
our secret sins*

*Past sins must be omitted
before new sins are committed*

*Seven deadly sins
some are just whims*

*The test it begins
when you hold back your sins*

*Thick skins
cover up sins*

*To sins I would rather
not be a father*

*Who protect their sins
rarely if ever wins*

Sip

*A sip from the cup
as you go from the ground up*

*Sip from the cup
when it doesn't add up*

*With each sip of coffee
the brain it felt sloppy*

Sipped

*His talk was all polish
as he sipped off the chalice*

Sipping

*Sipping tea in may
on a fine summer day*

*They sat there sipping
the soup that was dripping*

Sips

There are sips to be fed
from teacups in bed

Turnips and sips
of wine through the lips

Sit

They sit next to each other
like birds of a feather

Situation

Save the situation
with imagination

Sizzle

We sat by the lake
watching the sizzle in the steak

Skating

Skating on ice
for a glimpse of paradise

Skeletons

Old mother Hubbard
skeletons in the cupboard

Skeletons by the tons
mostly of the living ones

Skies

To the starlit skies
they turn their eyes

Skill

A bee must have skill
to sip from a daffodil

How to develop skill
who chooses to lie still

In the morning he took a pill
to improve his narrative skill

Man he needs skill
when he has a big beast to kill

Practiced skill
can be used at will

The devil and his skill
can be tempted by your will

The snake it needs skill
to get into the ant hill

With skill and pluck
he made his own luck

Words when they spill
need a lot of skill

Skilled

First you must have the build
then you must be skilled

For days to be filled
be specially skilled

Skills

Children get skills
without taking pills

Don't trudge the hills
with your deceptive skills

Little girl fills
her time learning skills

Skills

    Many social skills
can be learned popping pills

    People skills
need people pills

    There are no pills
for mothering skills

    They seek new thrills
to sharpen their skills

Skim

    It must have been him
who is so good at skim

Skin

    Down to his shin
he has thick skin

    The way to win
is to be thick of skin

Skip

    Some of us will trip
not knowing how to skip

Sky

    They dropped from the sky
men with beaks why

    Why oh why
the blue of the sky

Slander

    Even in slander
he couldn't be more blander

    The goose became a gander
from words spoken in slander

Slate

    Somethings of late
can't be written on a slate

Slated

    Some things are slated
never to be legislated

Slave

    A slave of the mind
we are one of a kind

    From slave to master
get there faster

    How can he behave
to whose senses who is a slave

    Who will die faster
the slave or the master

Sledding

    After their wedding
they went dog sledding

Sleep

    A sleep in the park
on a whim and a lark

    Be careful when you sleep
you have my heart to keep

    Before you sleep
climb every peak

*Can't do without
sleep after a bout*

*Don't move your feet
once put to sleep*

*From tree to tree it can leap
the squirrel in his sleep*

*In sleep she posed
with eyes gently closed*

*Once you sleep with doom
you can never become a groom*

Sleeping

*I am the sleeping thrush
who needs a bit of hush*

*Sleeping logs
abode of the frogs*

Sleepless

*After a fight
sleepless night*

Slept

*He slept over a drink
and woke up to a blink*

*The baby as she slept
her mothers heart it wept*

*When the lion got bored
it slept and snored*

Slick

*Whose tongue is very slick
rarely makes a slip*

Slightest

*Without the slightest pause
he answers to every cause*

Slip

*All his quips slip
through the lip*

*He made a slip
at a fast clip*

*Only quips
slip through her lips*

Slipped

*The golden goose
it slipped through the noose*

Slippery

*He had a slippery tongue
that fell back into his lung*

*Many a man was hung
by his slippery tongue*

*Slippery as a eel
is love's main appeal*

*Some say hope
is as slippery as soap*

*The banana peel
has a slippery feel*

Sloppy

*Don't be sloppy
make it snappy*

*Don't need a copy
of him who is sloppy*

Rhyming English Couplets

Not for the seas choppy
a sailor who is sloppy

Sloth

The larger the sloth
there is more to loathe

Slumber

He wakes up from his slumber
when he sees the right number

Slurp

We went there as a group
to slurp hot and sour soup

Smacking

Lip smacking good
not necessarily food

Smart

Cunningness is the art
practiced by the smart

Good terms are a part
of being totally smart

To deal is an art
at which some are smart

Smarter

Between you and me
I am smarter than thee

He has a smarter pen than mine
after a jug of wine

I say it with glee
I am smarter than thee

In order to be smarter
be a self starter

The medicines get smarter
after pestle and mortar

Smear

Smear causes pain
in a campaign

Smell

Every animal is well
who hasn't lost his smell

He could not smell the rose
that was too far from his nose

Smell of the earth
remembered at birth

The seeing eye dog
can smell through the fog

The smell of coriander
made her head meander

Smelling

How to better the pose
of her smelling the rose

If it isn't a fact
you're smelling a rat

Is it not a fact
you are smelling a rat

Smile

A smile once raised
cannot be erased

*A well crafted smile
shortens many a mile*

*All I can do is smile
now that I am senile*

*Can make you smile with ease
when you taste wine with cheese*

*Could be seen from a distant mile
their secret smile*

*Deep into sleep
I have a smile to keep*

*Every once in a while
I think of her and smile*

*He held out his hand
with a smile that was bland*

*He was so full of bile
he couldn't break into smile*

*Her bewitching smile
left no room for rile*

*Her prim and proper smile
hid many a guile*

*Her seductive smile
stayed with me awhile*

*How gentle is her smile
the wily crocodile*

*How to explain a smile
that lasts more than a while*

*I run a mile
when I see the crocodile smile*

*I will travel many a mile
to make people smile*

*It took a little while
to get the baby to smile*

*Last inch or mile
tread it with a smile*

*Let it be your style
to walk away with a smile*

*Let it last awhile
her expectant smile*

*Make it linger awhile
when you part with a smile*

*No need to make your case
with that smile on your face*

*No room for rile
seeing her bewitching smile*

*Red wine in a jug
brought a smile to his mug*

*She gifted me her smile
to last me many a mile*

*She turned her head to smile
at me that lasted awhile*

*She will beguile
you with her smile*

*Smile away your cares
eating Ice-cream in silverwares*

*Smile is a must
for a face that I can trust*

Smile is not a smile
that doesn't last awhile

Stayed with me awhile
her fading smile

The baby you must teach
a smile within reach

The gladness in her smile
turned to sadness for a while

The picture of her smile
that lasted a little while

The smile in her face it show
wherever she go

The sweet glow of her smile
stayed in my heart awhile

Though it may take awhile
treat it with a smile

To smile away her dimples
she waited for pimples

Up I was woken
from her smile that was broken

Where is thy guile
is it hidden in thy smile

With a pondering smile
he thought of her for a while

With a smile on her face
she is a monument to grace

With a smile on his face
he makes his case

Smiled
He smiled ear to ear
and asked god for one more year

Smiles
Two smiles when they meet
in the middle of the street

Smiling
Only a republic can
put up a smiling man

The smiling face of doll
waiting for a childs call

The way he was smiling
had opponents all riling

They have learned to bask
in a smiling mask

When you see a smiling tiger
wonder what's inside her

Smoke
He is a tough bloke
who handles the cigar and the smoke

He puffed a cigar smoke
blowing rings as he went broke

Smoke filled bars
from the smoking cigars

The zebra will lose his stripe
if you smoke that in your pipe

Smoking
For smoking it becomes ripe
once you put it in your pipe

Smoking is nice
our only lasting vice

The smoking fuse
was not much use

Smooth

Words that are smooth
only meant to soothe

Snail

Said the fox to the snail
I like your tail

Snake

What kind of snake is this
that doesn't know how to hiss

Sneaks

Why is it the rose
sneaks up the nose

Sneeze

Images such as these
starts me on a sneeze

Pollen it brings sneeze
followed by the wheeze

So easy to sneeze
in the soft summer breeze

The mouse will sneeze
at the size of the cheese

Snickering

With each snickering bit
it became a hit

Snort

He can talk to a dog
and snort with the hog

Snowbirds

Snowbirds they run
to seasons in the sun

Snowflakes

The snowflakes as they come
shining in the winter sun

Snuff

He is not upto snuff
who is all puffed up

Snuffed

Almost he was snuffed
as he huffed and puffed

Once snuffed out
no pain from the gout

Snuggled

She snuggled into the nook
between me and the book

Sobbed

After the ball was lobbed
it went out and she sobbed

Sober

He is sober and glum
when he misses his rum

He is sober and mum
when his jaw works the gum

Sobriety
> So much variety
> in sobriety

Societies
> Societies wrath
> in many a path

Society
> All the gaiety
> of high society

Socks
> Got to comb your locks
> and wash your socks

Soften
> Don't soften your stand
> you might lose your land

Softer
> Much sought after
> whose words are softer

Softly
> Speak softly into his ear
> until things become clear

Softness
> He gave up his moan
> to the softness in her tone

Soil
> Sons of the soil
> have their daily toil

Solace
> Solace it ranks
> high on the river banks

Soldier
> Soldier stands erect
> and stares at you direct

Solemn
> To give your heart a lift
> I give you this solemn gift

Solitude
> Bout of solitude
> will improve your attitude

> Cannot describe solitude
> without any platitude

> I give it amplitude
> my daily solitude

> I need the solitude
> to give my love latitude

> If solitude had a name
> would you play the game

> Into solitude I wander
> so many things to ponder

> She built up her fortitude
> in silent solitude

> Solitude and thinking
> when thought needs inking

> Solitude I will not miss
> for it is full of bliss

Solitude is a treasure
beyond all measure

Solitude is freedom
in gods kingdom

Solitude is sweet
when she comes home to greet

Solitude makes clear
there is so much to cheer

Solve

How to solve
the eyes of resolve

Somebody

Somebody up there
knows I am where

Someone

Before he went to bed
there is someone else she said

Tell them he is making dolls
if someone they calls

Something

I might have something to say
in the month of May

Sometimes

Sometimes I feel glad
that people I met were bad

Song

A song is better than a yawn
when the bird thinks it is dawn

A song without words
is music from the birds

All night long
they played our song

As I entered the door
there was a song from before

At the sound of the gong
they broke into song

Can play a good song
the fiddle for very long

Chili pepper strong
told in a song

Croak of the toad
is a song for the road

He who can weave a song
hope he lives very long

Heaven sings its song
to the stars where they belong

How can he be wrong
who goes for wine and song

It's the song not the singer
that will always linger

Many a song is sung
by the parrot and its tongue

Right or wrong
he is on song

The rowing must be strong
to sing the boating song

The song in my head
needs to be said
———
The song it dies
without music in her eyes
———
The writer does no wrong
like the singer on the song
———
They sing their song
for generations long
———
We played along
while she sang her song
———
What song to pick
for my inner music
———
When they went hunting
they heard the songs of the bunting
———
You have been for long
the only one in my song
———

Songs

Perceived wrongs
woven into songs
———
Songs get their sheen
being played on the silver screen
———
Songs he has sung
with his nimble footed tongue
———
Songs of the sea
to soothe you and me
———
Songs that are rendering
all so surrendering
———
Songs that are sung
for the old and the young
———
The songs he sings
about indelible things
———

Sonnet

When I saw her bonnet
out came a sonnet
———

Sonorous

All it will bring
is a sonorous ring
———
Hard to be amorous
when you are sonorous
———
Not only was he sonorous
he was also very onerous
———

Sooner

Sooner or later it will slip
your pants from a weak hip
———
Sooner or later
we all will teeter
———
Sooner rather than later
it is better to cater
———
The sooner you find your tongue
less chance of being hung
———

Soothing

A voice rich and soothing
when feelings need smoothing
———

Sorrow

    Will it last till the morrow
    this pang of sorrow

    A sorrow that is shared
    is properly snared

    Couldn't wait for the morrow
    my heartfelt sorrow

From each other they borrow
both joy and sorrow

    How can I borrow
    to-morrow's sorrow

I have tears till the morrow
from other peoples sorrow

    I wish I could borrow
to help you with your sorrow

Many a sorrow it will bring
a special kind of sting

    Most of our sorrow
    we wittingly borrow

    Not easy to scoff
    at sorrow or to laugh

    Short lived sorrow
    good for the marrow

    Sorrow sets in motion
    deep deep emotion

    Sorrow when it occurs
    time to use your spurs

The amount of her sorrow
could fill a wheel barrow

The door will open in the morrow
to let go of your sorrow

To rid you of your sorrow
call your neighbour in the morrow

Why can't it wait till the morrow
long shadows cast by the sorrow

    With sorrow in full flow
there was a fading in her glow

In all the future to-morrows
may the roads be free of sorrows

In multitudes they come the sorrows
causing foreheads full of furrows

    Sorrows that lie in secret
    known to him and the egret

    They listen to my sorrows
    when I speak to the sparrows

    With no sorrows to greet
    joy becomes neat

Sorry

    When sorry is enough
    is it just bluff

Sought

    Fish is sought after
    by the baby otter

Soul

A foot soldier on the whole
is a hardened soul

A part of me has soul
with her to make it whole

After the carminative mixture
his soul lost its texture

At the watering hole
where elephants bare their soul

Cannot understand it whole
the workings of the soul

Dancing on the whole
is good for the soul

Dip your soul
into the finger bowl

Don't sell your soul
partly or in whole

Each of us must make it whole
so it lives forever the soul

Every soul can
change another man

Every soul must vie
to see eye to eye

Every soul needs a balm
to keep things all calm

Every watering hole
has a pathetic soul

Fires of the burning coal
fuels the workings of the soul

Fish on the plate
is my soul mate

Foxhole has a soul
where little foxes roll

From the mare to the foal
passes the energy of the soul

He forgot his goal
the well meaning soul

He is a restless soul
who is without a goal

Head east
where your soul can feast

Her face gets its soul
from the magic in the mole

Her voice on the whole
is ravishing to the soul

How can a soul rest
when love puts it to the test

How to make him whole
the troubled soul

Inner workings of the soul
trying to make men whole

It follows me my soul
playing a passive role

Key hole has a soul
if you look through the hole

Let god read
the soul that is in need

Man with no soul
how can he be whole

Manhole has a soul
to get out of it is the goal

Mans only goal
to be a refined soul

Many a soul was saved
by being simply well behaved

Mind body and soul
each plays a role

Music can make whole
the agitations of the soul

Mutterings of the soul
couplets they make them whole

Not many a soul
beyond the pole

On the whole he can
fill the soul of man

Once the soul is saved
the path to heaven gets paved

Our main role
is to elevate the soul

Pain on the whole
good for the soul

Pearls have a role
in touching her soul

Poetry makes it whole
the window to my soul

Put together the soul
to make a greater whole

Ready to roll
body and soul

Sell your soul
and become a mole

She can make it whole
the crack in your soul

She makes it whole
my body and soul

She was my soul mate
lent to me by fate

Society is never whole
until we add to its soul

Soul in its endless flight
retires into the dark of night

Soul you must not frighten
when you try to enlighten

Take a stroll
with the workings of the soul

The effect on the soul
like a cancerous mole

The purpose of the soul
must be intact and whole

The soul makes its choice
by speaking through your voice

The soul must go far
like the pole star

The soul will never rust
while the body turns to dust

The tadpole becomes whole
becoming a frog with a soul

The unfortunate soul
at the watering hole

There is a hunger in my soul
that the mare she bears a foal

To be captured by the soul
to make them both whole

To make healthy my goal
mind body and soul

To pour out his soul
is the authors goal

To the watering hole
goes the tottering soul

Toddy without a bowl
is like a body without a soul

Unsuspecting soul
behind the peep hole

Unworthy on the whole
to be part of her soul

What kind of role
does it plan for the soul

Where the soul lurks
is where the mind works

Within us it lies
a soul that never dies

Words that make them whole
the Inner workings of the soul

Soulmate

My soulmate
who sealed my fate

Souls

Men with ravaged souls
have distorted goals

Pot holes have souls
and their own goals

Two souls that meet as one
before the day is done

Two souls that meet as one
until love for each other is done

Sound

A method must be found
to make a better sound

Breaking new ground
without a hint of sound

From the sound I can tell
all is very well

From the sound I could tell
it was the distant bell

His masters sound
heard by the hound

S

*How beautiful the sound
of the earth moving around*

*How can there be sound
if no one is around*

*How to decipher
the sound of the sand piper*

*In the ocean of sound
where the waves abound*

*Not much sound
too few boots on the ground*

*Sight sound and smell
how can you quell*

*Sound and sight
they both delight*

*The clouds they blustered into sound
and the rains found their way to the ground*

*The musical sound
of worlds hitting the ground*

*The sweetest sound he could hear
was her voice in his ear*

*Where is it found
the meaning of this sound*

Sounded

*The hounds they hounded
once the trumpets they sounded*

Sounds

*Engraved in the brain
the sounds of the rain*

*He let his shoes do the speaking
with sounds made of creaking*

*Riding to the hounds
as the bugle sounds*

*Sitting in the train
sounds of the rain*

*They respond the hounds
to words and the sounds*

*Why is it a whisper
sounds so much crisper*

Soup

*Without salt in his soup
he went on a loop*

Sour

*By the minutes and the hour
the conversation turned sour*

Source

*Waterfall at its source
has very little force*

Sources

*Well known sources
provide us with resources*

Sow

*Sow and you shall reap
what you can easily keep*

Sown

*For every seed sown
another the wind has blown*

Space
How to make my case
within a two week space

Spaces
Spaces open wide
for the journey inside

Spaghetti
There is more to yeti
than eating spaghetti

Spare
She asked me for a spare
with a pencil in her hair

When will we get there
with time to spare

Spared
He was spared
of being snared

He will be spared
who is well prepared

Not much was spared
by intention declared

Spark
All it takes is a spark
for the little pup to bark

Along the road they bark
dogs at the faintest spark

Fireflies provide the spark
when the night is dark

He is off the mark
who is without spark

It took a leap in the dark
to give their love a spark

Light a match
for a spark to hatch

Light bulb with a spark
lights up the dark

Sparkle
The sparkle in the evening star
shines brightly though far

Why have you lost why
the sparkle in your eye

Will sparkle soon
the bright side of the moon

Sparkling
He wore sparkling white
and a belt fully tight

Improve family ties
with sparkling eyes

Sparks
Sparks will hatch
from a striking match

Spat
It was just another spat
about the world being flat

Speak

Ads speak
to the moneyed and the meek

Birds when they speak
do it through their beak

Don't let it speak
your destructive streak

Every island will speak
to only those who seek

Fly home to me
when they speak ill of thee

How can I speak for you
about things that you only knew

How can I speak
to the soul who is weak

Oh wandering cloud
why do you speak so loud

Shoes that speak
with an intermittent squeak

Some would still speak
if they were born with a beak

Speak no wrong
to be strong

Speak your truth mainly
to say things plainly

The mango has a beak
that is trained not to speak

The pelicans they speak
with fish in their beak

When forced to speak
just polish your beak

When the loose tongues speak
prospects are bleak

Words that evil speak
leaks out of his beak

Words they slowly speak
from the parrots beak

You will say something wrong
if you speak enough long

Speaker

Many a speaker I have found
is much more than the sound

Speaking

The speaking tree
on a talking spree

Speaks

He speaks very candid
once you unmask the bandit

He speaks with his upper lip
at a fast clip

Himalayan peaks
have a language that speaks

Speaks for itself
truth said the elf

*The parrot he speaks
with bulging beaks*

Special

*A very special feeling
towards me when she is leaning*

*Has a special hue
the sun in the morning dew*

*Her every special move
had something to prove*

*Something special to see
she who believes in me*

*Special interest groups
have their own troops*

*Special something in the air
she got up from the chair*

*That special someone
who makes my life fun*

*Wear a special hat
just to be looked at*

Spectators

*Spectators hopes
lie beyond the ropes*

Speculation

*Speculation is a potion
sets the mind in motion*

Speech

*Halts with a screech
freedom of speech*

*I can trust the leech
to stop my flow of speech*

Speech

*It must be clear
that speech is just veneer*

*Let your speech make symphony
in polite company*

*No one can teach
the ornaments of speech*

*She said things in her speech
that were less delicate than a leech*

*Speech becomes mangled
when words get tangled*

*The tree makes a speech
by producing a peach*

*What's beyond our reach
can't be got by a speech*

Speeches

*Don't discuss leeches
in after dinner speeches*

*They don't go to beaches
to listen to long speeches*

Speed

*Crocs are known for speed
when they wish to feed*

*Motor bikes have a speed
beyond ordinary need*

Speed must not diminish
while racing to the finish

Spell

A city casts its spell
on the people in it who dwell

All things will quell
under her spell

Frog in the well
must learn to spell

He could cast his spell
by speaking very well

If it doesn't cast a spell
you haven't read it well

Once she cast her spell
impossible to quell

She cast her spell stronger
to make it last longer

Spend

Two birds in flight
how they spend the night

Spice

Salt and pepper
Also spice for the leper

Spice up your weeks
until the heart speaks

Spices

As good as spices
our familiar vices

Familiar vices
like being fond of spices

Some of them are spices
among a mountain of vices

Spices get a look
from the bold cook

Why do you need spices
if you have enough vices

Spider

Every web has a spider
that weaves a net wider

Hanging by a thread
the spider it is said

Spreads its legs wider
the arachnid spider

There is a rider
to the web of the spider

Spill

A well inked quill
has words to spill

I have a goose quill
but no ink to spill

Many a man from the hill
has a fairy tale to spill

The bile lest it spill
once you've had your fill

Spilled

    Rosy cheeks that spilled
        down to his gills

    Things that were spilled
    by even the strong willed

Spin

The batsman's understanding is slim
    faced with an alluring spin

Spinach

    Where the spinach is green
        not many have been

Spinning

Tell me all the things you can
    under a spinning fan

Spirit

        Happy spirit
        without limit

    In the right spirit
    take all the merit

Mind body and spirit
they each have their limit

      Spirit uncorked
      but he got yorked

There is a higher joy
that can make the spirit buoy

      There is no limit
for sanctuary of the spirit

There was a kind of spirit
that had crossed the basic limit

Spirits

    A bottle is smashed
when two spirits clashed

    Don't let it hamper
your good spirits in the camper

He who picks his spirits
must know his limits

    Spirits they buoy
from happiness and joy

    Spirits will buoy
when you spread joy

Follow the spiritual path
and avoid gods wrath

    Spiritual nuances
wedded to romances

Who said it is proper
our spiritual stupor

Spiritually

    Made them both pensive
when it became spiritually expensive

Splendid

So splendid in his ways
    with him she stays

Splendour

Splendour in the grass
when we turn and toss

Splurging
> Some they don't need urging
> to go on daily splurging

Splutter
> The rain it falls in a splutter
> to fill up every gutter

Spoken
> Not just token
> he is plainly spoken

Spontaneous
> Spontaneous renderings
> of the minds meanderings

Spoonful
> Ants will become bigger
> from a spoonful of sugar

Sports
> He sports a new angle
> when he is in a tangle

Spots
> The leopard has spots
> and the potter has pots

Spotted
> The tiger makes it clear
> to the spotted deer

Spouse
> Don't let him in the house
> your cheating spouse

> He turned into a mouse
> once he became spouse

> Some have a spouse
> just like Mickey mouse

Spree
> Leaves to a tree
> in a growing spree

Spring
> Spring is irate
> with summer right at the gate

> The coming of spring
> has many things to bring

Sprout
> Trees that suddenly sprout
> flowers to clear all doubt

Sprouts
> Sprouts and gravy
> fed the men of the navy

Spun
> He spun his daily yarn
> all through night to the morn

Spunk
> Takes a lot of spunk
> to become a reclusive monk

Squabble
> Don't get into a squabble
> if your health is in a wobble

Squished
> Victor to the vanquished
> how easily you were squished

Stadium
>The stadium was full
>to see the red rag and the bull

Stag
>The stag shed his horn
>when it became a thorn

Stage
>Don't let your rage
>take center stage

Stains
>Sin it retains
>many of its stains

Staircase
>The staircase to the stars
>can't be climbed without any scars

Stairs
>Have to take the stairs
>holding hands in pairs

>To heaven, up the stairs
>for our final repairs

Stalactites
>Stalactites and mites
>what do they do nights

Stale
>Drink the ale
>before it goes stale

>Never gets stale
>a child's fairy tale

Stall
>How to stall
>the wake up call

Stalling
>Don't go stalling
>faced with an honest calling

Stallion
>Every battalion
>needs more than a stallion

Stalls
>Some of the stalls
>sell only moth balls

Stand
>He who takes a stand
>defines his own brand

>If they don't understand
>just let it stand

>If you stand in one place
>you cannot make your case

>One day they stand tall
>the next ready to fall

Star
>He was a fallen star
>visited many a bar

>How far is far
>for a shooting star

>I knew she was a star
>seeing her from afar

Many a fallen star
ended up in a bar

She was a wandering star
her love was distant and far

She was by far
the best looking star

Starching

He doesn't need starching
he who is overarching

Stare

Vehicles come and stare
at you from nowhere

Stares

The rock it stares
at the ocean waves

Staring

Staring at the clock
his jaw went into a lock

Staring at the table
she contemplated a fable

Stars

Don't go and malign
the stars that align

Of all the stars in the sky
you are the brightest one why

Stars that lie in a cluster
improve their shine and luster

There was a twinkle in her eye
like the stars in the sky

Start

A good place to start
horse before the cart

Give it a start
and add pep to a part

He played his part
of husband from the start

It was meant from the start
that we must drift apart

Plague is a part
of the rat from the start

Playthings are a part
of a child from the start

The doctor gives a start
with a thump on the babys beart

To look the part
make a start

Where do I start
to teach them my art

Started

Many a thing big
started after a swig

Starter

Just as a starter
let us coffee for tea barter

Starters
> Just for starters
> they wade into your waters

Starts
> Sum of two parts
> is it enough for starts

> The whole it starts
> with a sum of its parts

Starved
> He was so starved
> the beef had to be carved

States
> The swing states
> have opened their gates

Staunch
> Men who are staunch
> develop a paunch

Stay
> Don't come to stay
> only to betray

> Old he will stay
> who has nothing to say

> The snow is here to stay
> on this white winter day

> They stay aloof
> under a thatched roof

> You never went away
> after you came to stay

Steadily
> Steer steadily onward
> to go slowly forward

Steak
> The steak it burned
> while the tables were turned

Stealing
> Stealing a run
> makes cricket fun

Steam
> Out came the steam
> with a hiss and a scream

> Steam and sauna
> without which you are a goner

Steamer
> He looked in the steamer
> for his redeemer

Steel
> The steel beneath the suit
> way down to his boot

Steeple
> He stood atop the steeple
> to watch the day to day people

Step
> Step on his toe
> who is a foe

Sternly
> She looked sternly in the eye
> at him and made him cry

Stick

How to pick
a name that will stick

Two carrots and a stick
and the mule will kick

Still

Be still
when you take pill

Lighthouse on the hill
where the ocean waters are still

Men who have a will
can simply lie still

Sting

Just beyond our grasp
the sting in the wasp

Mosquitoes with wing
and perilous sting

Reproach is a thing
that carries a sting

Some pieces of mail
like a sting in the tail

The best thing that happened to me
was not the sting of the bee

The scorpion is pale
without the sting in its tale

The sting in the wasp
was from a single clasp

What came in the mail
had a sting in the tail

You wouldn't want a thing
after her sting

Stirring

The cat said to him purring
your tea it needs stirring

Stitch

The cobblers last stitch
went without a hitch

Stitches

My muscle still twitches
after all those stitches

Stock

Stock market
case basket

Stock options
have their own captions

The cuckoo takes stock
of the tick in the clock

They all came in a flock
to examine the stock

Stocking

Gift in a stocking
came without knocking

Stocking

What's in your stocking
when Christmas comes knocking

Stolen

> Is more of a norm
> to be stolen from

> Stolen by thee
> the honey from the bee

Stomach

> The stomach weeps
> for the fox that sleeps

Stone

> Two birds they hone
> upon a single stone

Stood

> When the horse he felt good
> on his hindlegs he stood

Stop

> Don't ever stop
> your climb to the top

> The wolf howling at the moon
> must stop sometime soon

> There is a place to stop
> and pick up a prop

> When will the bus stop
> so into it I can hop

> The kangaroo it hops
> in between two stops

Store

> Need I say more
> at the toy store

Stories

> Stories about the ghost
> children they love most

> Stories are planted
> appropriately slanted

> Stories are weaved
> until they are peeved

> Stories they were woven
> though completely unproven

> Stories unravel
> about the guys who travel

> Stories with a middle
> end in a riddle

> There are many stories
> about the beginning of the fairies

> What is the use
> if your stories lack juice

Storm

> Eye of a storm
> begins to take form

> Eye of the storm
> is quite the norm

> For a sailor it is the norm
> to run into a storm

> Gathering storm
> when will it calm

> How to keep warm
> in a snow storm

Many a storm must pass
moving from is to was

Seagulls in the storm
float as if it is norm

Teacup has the form
to put lid on the storm

There is a storm in the sea
where the ships have to be

To quiet this raging storm
before it finally takes form

To weather the storm
is often the norm

Story

A story by the cat
about how he became a rat

A story is best told
while hot and not cold

A story once begun
gets a long run

A story was told
about the gulls very old

And so the story goes
about how they step on toes

Be wary
of cock and bull story

Every best seller
from a good story teller

Every seagull
has a story to mull

His face told the story
of primetime glory

His story has a nose
though limited in prose

Many a story they cooks
just to sell their books

Spend your words well
when you have story to tell

Story telling
do it without yelling

The morning tells the story
of the sun in all its glory

The story behind the scenes
of kings and the queens

The story that is knit
for the reader must be fit

To reclaim your glory
tell a long story

When god gives you glory
don't make up a story

Stout

From too much stout
he devleped the gout

Straight

Seek the straight path
where there is no wrath

Rhyming English Couplets

> The things that were said
> went straight to his head

> Walk the walk
> with straight talk

Straighten

> Straighten your fin
> when you're in a tailspin

Straightens

> Out in the morning air
> where the cold it straightens the hair

Straighter

> When he couldn't shoot any straighter
> he became a traitor

Strange

> He who is strange
> must make room for change

> I find it rather strange
> nobody seems to have change

> It is very strange
> to not like orange

> Someday you will understand
> this strange and beautiful land

> Why is it strange
> that feelings must not change

> I am a stranger in her eye
> if it's me if so why

> Stranger in my bed
> who I haven't even wed

> The stranger in the mirror
> gives me the shiver

> There is a stranger in my bed
> is he the one I wed

> Don't let books land
> in a strangers hand

> Like strangers intruding
> where people are brooding

> We feel so much better
> as strangers to the last letter

Strategic

> Clothing it sits
> on strategic bits

Strawberries

> Strawberries and cream
> my Wimbledon dream

Stray

> Many a potter will stray
> while watching her walk away

Strays

> Back to his old ways
> like the canine that strays

> Don't act like strays
> just mend your ways

Streaking

> Barking dogs
> at streaking hogs

499

Street

All the people greet
as she walks down the street

Street

Not hard on the feet
to walk on easy street

Walking down the street
little stomping feet

When shall we meet
on thread needle street

Strength

Go to any length
from a position of strength

Go to any length
to improve your strength

Go to any length
to test its strength

It is a sign of strength
that we should go to any length

She went to great length
to show her mental strength

The day he lost his plume
for his strength it spelled doom

They go to any length
to test their strength

Stress

Dress up your best
for the stress test

How to address
days filled with stress

How to deal with stress
in the midst of distress

No words can stress
love in distress

Stress is a test
meant to do your best

Stress makes its points
as pain in the joints

Strife

Strife upon strife
must be cut with a knife

Strike

Cannot strike a pose
when you are led by the nose

Strike when the iron is hot
not when it is not

Let us go there when
the clock it strikes ten

String

This is only a string
not a finger with a ring

Strings

Give away your things
with no attached strings

Guitar strings they strum
to muffle the ear drum

*The strings and their strums
and the slow muffle of the drums*

*Zig Zag things
held together by strings*

Stripe

*Don't take a swipe
at the zebra and it's stripe*

*Zebras have gripes
that they didn't earn their stripes*

Striving

*While they are striving
they also are conniving*

Stroke

*The stroke it couldn't hide
his gait that had become wide*

Strong

*A wired brain that is wrong
needs a re-wiring that is strong*

*Be strong
prove them wrong*

*Got to be strong
to pick right from wrong*

*Have to be strong
when things go wrong*

*He becomes strong
who can see what is wrong*

*He who is strong
just proves them wrong*

*How can it last long
this will to live very strong*

*How to be strong
after being wrong*

*How to be strong
when things go wrong*

*How to right a wrong
by just being strong*

*If you own up when wrong
you can get up to be strong*

*Once tethered to a wrong
the message becomes strong*

*Right or wrong
don't push too strong*

*She will be strong
who does no wrong*

*The reader cannot be wrong
that the words are too strong*

*They can do me no wrong
if I am strong*

*Though he was strong
he was done by wrong*

*Though the road is long
let your will be strong*

*Weak and the strong
both can do wrong*

When the will is strong
nothing can go wrong

Stronger

Don't make them stronger
the gossip monger

He thinks he is stronger
the war monger

Put up with it longer
it will make you stronger

Struggle

He was just an old muggle
who went through daily struggle

How to wriggle
out of the struggle

Old age is a struggle
like walking on rubble

To struggle is wise
without chasing the prize

Work your way through struggle
till the burst of the bubble

Man dog and sheep
wife struggles to keep

Struggling

Struggling to float
on a sinking boat

Stubborn

Unwilling to learn
from being too stubborn

Stuck

They are stuck to each other
till the end of their tether

Study

Only a dog can
do a proper study of man

Stuff

A lot can hinge
on the stuff you binge

Better to climb
when there is stuff to imbibe

Stunning

The tiger looked stunning
hides it well his cunning

Why do they go sunning
people who are stunning

Stunt

They know many a stunt
to live by the hunt

Stupid

Can he be called stupid
if he falls for cupid

He is a stupid rat
who says hello to a cat

He may be considered stupid
who doesn't watch his lipid

Some think it is stupid
to worry much about lipid

*With no one to fret
stupid you can get*

Stupidity

*There is no stupidity
worse than cupidity*

Stutters

*Though he stutters
he is a man of letters*

Style

*She will beguile
you with her style*

*With a smooth and flowing style
her cleverness will beguile*

Subconscious

*How to find
my subconscious mind*

*Subconscious is a kind
of corner of the mind*

*Subconscious is a place
where love gives chase*

*Subconscious order
has its own border*

*The subconscious speaks
to unscaled peaks*

*We are mostly blind
to the subconscious mind*

*When the subconscious speak
inner thoughts they leak*

Submission

*At the end of every mission
nothing left but submission*

Substance

*He always made sense
full of substance*

Succeed

*Beyond us they exceed
children who succeed*

*Children must exceed
or just succeed*

*To succeed is to stumble
said the bee to the bumble*

*To succeed with zeal
has a different feel*

Succeeded

*Wherever he pleaded
he succeeded*

Success

*No limit to excess
in the story of success*

*Small success have wings
and they lead to greater things*

*Success I must concede
depends on the planted seed*

Success

*Success is a fashion
for those without passion*

*Success may go to your head
but don't take it to bed*

―――

*Success will remain
with those who go against the grain*

Suffer

*He is a bluffer
who says he doesn't suffer*

―――

*Open your coffer
when you see someone suffer*

―――

*Those who suffer very long
end up being very strong*

Suffering

*Suffering is not wrong
if it makes you strong*

Suffers

*He suffers through his fears
until his mind it clears*

Suffice

*For the crop it is nice
if a shower will suffice*

Suicidal

*It happened in his sleep
the suicidal leap*

Sullible

*He was easily sullible
also very gullible*

Sum

*Why have you now come
just as I am doing the sum*

Summer

*The rainstorm was a bummer
in the middle of summer*

―――

*The summer does his duty
and the winters are draped in beauty*

―――

*On a languid afternoon in May
it was a long summers day*

Summit

*Even at the summit
you haven't reached the limit*

Sun

*Don't run
from a duel in the sun*

―――

*Every setting sun
proves the day is done*

―――

*First rays of the rising sun
and the night is finally done*

―――

*For a place in the sun
get your work done*

―――

*Here comes the setting sun
and my days work is done*

―――

*How to run
from the shadow in the sun*

―――

*Let us go to yonder land
where the sun meets the sand*

―――

*Made me open my mouth
when the sun came out of the south*

Rhyming English Couplets

No place in the sun
whose work is never done

On the beaches they run
of the island in the sun

Once lit by the sun
the night is done

One day the page will turn
as sure as the sun must burn

Sun wind and waves
how can they reach the caves

The dolphins they skip
as the sun takes a dip

The rising sun
makes the morning fun

The sun becomes frantic
setting into the Atlantic

The sun can make you pay
if you let it have its say

The sun it is gone
from twilight to the dawn

The sun makes it loud
the silver in the cloud

The sun shows its grace
with a warm embrace

The sun will not see her soon
though the moon she visit him at noon

The sun woke up and knew
that the petals were laden with dew

To the eyes it is a feast
the rising sun from the east

To their homes they run
with the setting evening sun

When the days work is done
here comes the setting sun

Where has the sun gone
asked the twilight to the dawn

Sunday

Sunday must be around
churchbells when they sound

Sunlight

Behind the mountain it hid
the sunlight making its bid

My choice was made
in the sunlight and the shade

Sunlight made it glow
the whiteness in the snow

The cloud can make it night
by covering the sunlight

The sunlight it beams
through the palm trees

They both opened the door
to watch the sunlight on the moor

Sunrise

The full moon I spy
against the sunrise in the sky

Sunset

Sunset looks all golden
like the lava that is molten

Sunset never fails
nor the wind against the sails

The sunset it will spawn
singing & dancing till the dawn

There is a sunset beyond the sail
which hardly ever fail

Two gunmen meet
at sunset street

Sunshine

In the sunshine she wore her bonnet
when she went to look for the gannet

Sunshine or shade
mistakes are made

Sunshine sober and soft
to keep your love aloft

Sunshine through the leaves
made patterns with sieves

The sunshine in a flood
warms my morning blood

The sunshine it speaks
to the snow covered peaks

Superstition

Every superstition
becomes a daily mission

Sure

Before I am cremated
make sure everyone is elated

Begging alms for sure
doesn't mean you are poor

Whatever you preach
make sure it has reach

Surely

Surely there must be more
to this than just furore

They take a bet
that the sun will surely set

Surfaces

It surfaces the whale
in the moonlight pale

Surprise

Element of surprise
in what they speak the wise

Every surprise
can it be a prize

Make amends
surprise your friends

Surprise is a food
that can alter your mood

Surprise surprise
I am the prize

There is a surprise in this gift
through which I must sift

*I am not surprised
that love is so prized*

*All my surmises
ended up as surprises*

Surprising

*Not surprising
she was mesmerizing*

Surrender

*Abject surrender
was it a blunder*

*Don't surrender to folly
just to be jolly*

*I am ready to render
my full surrender*

*Why must we surrender
to the day to day calendar*

Surrounded

*Before they are hounded
they are first surrounded*

Survival

*Constant revival
of our instinct for survival*

Survive

*First to arrive
last to survive*

*How to revive
the will to survive*

*Relentless drive
just to survive*

*To survive on sea holly
is just plain folly*

*To survive we must be brave
from the cradle to the grave*

*To survive we need food
thought and good mood*

Survived

*Once revived
he survived*

*Seafarming folk
survived on seagull yolk*

*To have survived
until our time had arrived*

Susceptible

*He was susceptible
to all things contemptible*

Suspenders

*He lost his suspenders
to the offenders*

Suspense

*Suspense is killing
even for the willing*

Suspicion

*Suspicion dies
when you close your eyes*

They circle with a mission
on the flimsiest suspicion

Suspicious

Always be suspicious
of the inauspicious

Anything that is specious
can be suspicious

Don't be suspicious
the moment is auspicious

Swallowed

He doesn't have a leg
the viper who swallowed the egg

There was a boy from goa
who was swallowed by a boa

Swapping

Don't go swapping
your penny for a farthing

Swarm

Birds in a swarm they flies
across the blue skies

Sweat

It is no easy read
when all your sweat turns to bead

Let the pot boil
while you sweat and toil

Sweat has a need
to drip like a bead

Under the mid-day sun
sweat dribbles to a run

Sweet

Can go to your head
the sweet nothings said

Every sweet spot
that pretends it is not

He had a sweet tooth
and a palate to boot

He held his own
with the sweet tongue of a drone

Her sweet fragrance will greet
me down to my feet

Her voice so sweet
and words discreet

How sweet is the shower
though dust settles on the flower

How to decipher
a sweet nothing whisper

It is a major feat
for the fruit to turn sweet

Round after round
he plays sweet sound

She gave me a muffin
that had sweet stuff in

Sing your sweet song
little bird very long

*Sipping sweet milk in tea
just you and me*

*Slipped under my feet
a moment so sweet*

*Stolen chatter is sweet
better than well cooked meat*

*Sweet to the ear
her words when I hear*

*Sweet words are felt
like Ice-cream that doesn't melt*

*The sweet smell of the rain
can ease many a pain*

*Where have you been
sweet morphine*

*Would it taste as sweet
if sugar it was called meat*

Sweeter

*What is sweeter than wine
when we both sit and dine*

Sweetie

*They call each other sweetie
as if it is a duty*

Sweetness

*All her sweetness lies
in her heart through my eyes*

*The sweetness of her smile
in my memory stays awhile*

Swift

*Once you get the drift
get out of there swift*

*They have positions that shift
so justice must be swift*

*With the sword he is swift
with the pen he has gift*

Swiftly

*The sheep has a knack
of swiftly turning black*

Swim

*A swim with the school
of fish in the pool*

*Gannets are things
that can swim with their wings*

*They swim the ducks
with approving clucks*

Swing

*Swing and a miss
was just a swish*

Swish

*The fish eagle will swish
at the flying fish*

Switch

*How to switch
from being poor to rich*

Switched

*To her eye he switched
completely bewitched*

Sword
> Better to use a word
> than the point of a sword

Sycophant
> A sycophant
> must learn to chant

Symphony
> A man by his company
> and orchestra by its symphony

> From sound bite to Symphony
> they kept each other company

> Pick your company
> before you go to the symphony

> Sweet symphony
> is epiphany

> Three will be symphony
> in better company

> When the company is wrong
> symphony won't be strong

Symptoms
> Though the symptoms are vague
> every paradise has its plague

T

Tackle

*How to tackle
when love becomes a debacle*

*How you tackle
day to day obstacle*

Tact

*Once you are willing to act
they will react with tact*

Tactic

*It is a good tactic
to be syntactic*

Tactical

*A tactical retreat
to avoid the heat*

Tail

*Has nothing to flail
the dog without a tail*

*Many a dog will wail
at the cutting of his tail*

Tale

*How to spin a tale
about harpooning the whale*

*Many a tale
about the hearty and the hale*

*Many a tale
over a bottle of ale*

*Tale about a whale
that wouldn't fit on a scale*

*The tale is in the telling
and not in the yelling*

*They construct a tale
that the fish was a whale*

Talent

*His talent pristine
at times very mean*

*His talent was latent
because he wasn't blantant*

*To-days mantrum
is about talent and tantrum*

Tales

*Fairy tales
about nightingales*

He tells tall tales
about harpoons and whales

Tales they weaves
who are thick as thieves

They tell tall tales
both elephants and whales

Talk

I shared her walk
and her talk

Talking

Talking is for the tongue
and walking is for the lung

Tall

Even the tall
cannot see the writing on the wall

He is tall
who can make sense of it all

He who stands tall
usually gets the call

Until the rains they fall
the grass will not grow tall

Tame

Nothing stays the same
always things to tame

Tampering

The new ball needs pampering
without a hint of tampering

Tangle

How to tangle
with someone without an angle

Tangled

The spider it dangled
from a web all tangled

Tangles

The fish it dangles
in a net full of tangles

Tap

Her tap on his shoulder
made him a bit bolder

Target

I have so much girth
I am the target of mirth

The target must be shielded
against the power being wielded

With all this girth
I am a target for mirth

Task

One way to take them to task
is to just remove their mask

Take him to task
the man behind the mask

What is his task
the man behind the mask

Taste

Don't read it in haste
it's all a matter of taste

He was respected by his peers
for his taste in beers

If salt it loses a grain
the taste will still remain

Some they can tell
music has taste and smell

Taste of things to come
sweetened by a sip of rum

The taste it lingers
after fish fingers

The wine bottle in haste
uncorked to taste

Tasted

Better ways to be tasted
time that was wasted

Tastes

Whatever tastes good
need not only be food

Taught

Hemophilia has taught
that blood will never clot

I learned a lot
more than I was taught

Many a potter has taught
others how to make pot

Not taught in schools
that common sense rules

Of all the things I was taught
the first thing was naught

Some people are taught
to see things as they are not

Somethings he taught her
even the giant otter

Sooner or later caught
why isn't it taught

The first thing he taught her
how to use the blotter

What has it taught
this gut in a knot

Taunt

All day it will taunt
our each and every want

What do they really want
that they all day have to taunt

Taunted

When a person feels unwanted
he doesn't mind even being taunted

Tax

Just relax
tax is just tax

They are never lax
who collect your tax

Taxes

>Before your income waxes
>better pay your taxes

>First he pays his taxes
>then he goes home and relaxes

Tea

>Cups of tepid tea
>I shall with her and me

>Over a cup of tea
>just you and me

Teach

>Once you teach them to sneer
>they will have nothing left to cheer

Team

>A team will do well
>who dream but don't dwell

Tear

>A tear drop fell on the page
>he instantly became a sage

>A tear in each eye
>for all those who die

>A tear makes it clear
>she is far and not near

>A tear makes it clear
>that love is very near

>Both laughter and tear
>happen between the ear

>Couldn't keep pace
>with tear drops down her face

>Distances become clear
>after the drop of a tear

>Ecstasy I fear
>ends up with a tear

>Every drop of tear
>a symptom of fear

>Every eye has a tear
>not usually from beer

>Hard to tear it apart
>this niggle in my heart

>How to explain a tear
>except by drinking beer

>How to explain a tear
>that doesn't make things clear

>How to explain a tear
>to friend, foe or peer

>How to explain a tear
>when it so plain and clear

>How to tear it apart
>the words of a broken heart

>I never fail to hear
>the dripping of a tear

>In moments they are cast
>tear drops from the past

>Many a tear
>has been cured by beer

>Many a tender tear
>that made her eyes a blear

Once the tear did drop
her writing came to a stop

Poetry is like a tear
explains itself very clear

She can drop a tear
to make her feelings clear

Spare her a tear
when she is near

Tear drop in the march of time
where the heart beats to a rhyme

Tear makes it clear
love is very near

The more I explain a tear
the less it becomes clear

The writing made it clear
that hard work is full of tear

We are full of parts
that tear us apart

We exchanged a tear
and drank pints of beer

When will it tear
if it is worse for the wear

Why explain a tear
drown your sorrow with beer

Why explain a tear
when it makes itself clear

With a pillow under her head
a droplet of tear was shed

Teardrops

In a background of chime
teardrops sublime

Tearing

Where does it get a start
tearing each other apart

Tears

A friend who wipes your tears
share with him a few beers

All my future tears
drown them in to-days beers

As fast as she cried
her tears they dried

Be prepared to shed
tears before we are wed

Brings out the tears
her voice in my ears

Credit card goes swiping
when the tears need wiping

Dripping tears
speak of her fears

He is sober behind the ears
and drunk from too many beers

He spent many years
reforming through the tears

Her tears were meant
for his heart to melt

T

His tears they ran dry
from the malice in his eye

How to fend off tears
in your autumn years

I have counted enough years
to begin to shed tears

I have enough tears to slosh
and faces to wash

I know the tears will dry
so why not cry and cry

In a valley full of tears
her throat she constantly clears

Into uncharted waters swept
where tears rolled down as she wept

It must have been an issue
if tears filled the tissue

It tears you asunder
when love it becomes a blunder

Many drops of tears
through the turbulent years

No reason to cry
once the tears they run dry

Nothing left in the cup
once the tears have dried up

Once the mind clears
so do the tears

She explained her fears
with droplets of tears

She whispered in my ears
with her eye dripping tears

So many tears were shed
with her back turned to my head

Sunset years
shut out the tears

Tears and laughter
make each other softer

Tears are a part
of the inconsolable heart

Tears can fill a drain
more than any rain

Tears from her eyes
when baby elephant dies

Tears give relief
when overcome with grief

Tears of a young heart
from being torn apart

Tears once they crop
must eventually drop

Tears ran dry
once there was trust in her eye

Tears that last awhile
finally break into smile

Tears they fell like the dew
in my search for you

Tears us apart
our wandering heart

Tears when they came
reflected their shame

Tears will buoy
a heart filled with joy

Tears you apart
anger from the start

The demon he fills my ears
to the point of falling tears

The eye it spills tears
until the mind it clears

The knots were tied
after the tears they dried

The mind it clears
after pouring out tears

The tears in my eyes
from family ties

The tears they trickle
to love that is fickle

There was blood in her tears
as the deadline nears

Throat ran dry
no tears to cry

Until the mind clears
the heart drops many tears

We must say cheers
when the eye is without tears

When the laughter clears
making way for tears

Whenever I am reduced to tears
I seek solace with bottled beers

Why do we cry
till the tears run dry

Why it slowly dries
the tears in her eyes

Tease

Right from wrong to tease
can never be done with ease

Teasing

A form of mind teasing
that is also amusing

Technical

In not so technical a term
a worm is still a worm

Technique

The technique must be learned
for temper to be spurned

Teeth

With false teeth you must pay
for ever tooth decay

Temper

A well kept temper
sounds like a whimper

He was a man of high temper
except when he wore his jumper

Ill temper has a cost
that can never be lost

>Whose temper is at a loss
>he easily gets cross

Temperament
>Temperament and will
>all add up to skill

Tempered
>Short tempered guy
>so stubborn why

Tempest
>Tempest gets a spot
>in the teapot that is hot

>The teapot is no best
>place for a tempest

Temples
>They built it with their hands
>temples from many lands

Temporarily
>Temporarily blind
>when he spoke his mind

Tempt
>Him she tried to tempt
>though he was unkempt

Temptation
>Needs condemnation
>the last temptation

>Temptation has a source
>that can take you off course

>Temptation is when
>you are lured into the den

>Temptation it must be stressed
>must be addressed

>Temptation once fed
>doesn't need to be dead

>There is a temptation
>to re-work the interpretation

>Better to insist
>when temptations persist

>Have a day on the field
>with temptations to yield

>People never tire
>of temptations that fire

>Temptations at best
>surrender to your quest

>Temptations come to the fore
>if you don't keep score

>Temptations must be fed
>before we are dead

>Temptations of the nest
>known to the birds best

>Temptations we must stall
>before it causes downfall

>Temptations will flicker
>with a little bit of liquor

>Temptations will last
>if you don't ignore it fast

>When temptations tug
>just pull the plug

Tempted

It is better to be pre-empted
when we are tempted

Many things are not attempted
though we are fully tempted

Sins that have tempted
must never be attempted

Some things are attempted
just because we are tempted

When tempted he was twice
he gave up being wise

Tendency

Donkeys that bray
have tendency to stray

Tendency to gloat
over the ego afloat

There is a tendency to fall
in love with alcohol

Well practiced deceit
tendency to repeat

Tendrils

The tendrils they seek the sun
who always is on the run

Tense

Don't be tense
if it doesn't make sense

When the sound makes sense
I become less tense

Tension

How to attract attention
without building up tension

Keeps up the tension
and your attention

Tent

Do it in the tent
if you have spleen to vent

Tentacles

Gently removing his spectacles
he slowly raised his tentacles

When tentacles alight
review your plight

Termites

The termites attack
behind my back

Terms

Even the worms
live on their terms

Every garden has its worms
which live according to their terms

Fish and worms
must come to terms

He who sets the terms
makes the listener squirm

They set their own terms
the garden filled with worms

Territory

Let it be known
that this territory is our own

They both parted
into territory uncharted

Terror

A simple human error
can hold many a terror

Every imagined terror
usually a mental error

Human error
holds many a terror

Human error
it holds no terror

In trying to hold off terror
he killed himself in error

Not without error
the war on terror

The face of terror
he sees in the mirror

Terrors

The strong they hold no terrors
for they make simple errors

Test

Being born is not the best
way to put man to the test

Fishing is best
when the worm is put to test

He gave off his best
when put to the test

His vocal best
was enough for the test

How to test
him who is honest

I get to finally rest
without daily being put to the test

In ways that I know best
I put it to the test

Is there no place to rest
after life's grueling test

It was a token test
but he was at his best

Just when you have to rest
you will be put to the test

Once put to the test
the mind needs a rest

Once you withstand the test
you have given it your best

Put him to the test
the demon in your breast

Put it to the test
and give it some rest

Put it to the test
what you do best

Put it to the test
what you know best

Rhyming English Couplets

She put him to the test
in quiet ernest

Systems are best
put to the test

They put you to the test
though it may be in jest

They test each others might
two elephants when they fight

Things though said in jest
can put your nerves to the test

What you know best
put it to the test

Whatever the test
you are simply the best

When man is put to the test
nature knows best

When mother is put to the test
she doesn't even rest

Test

When put to the test
give off your best

Whenever put to the test
they were a cut above the rest

Who knows himself best
can stand up to the test

Your mettle you must test
when you are at your best

Tested

I always detested
forever being tested

Testing

Never get a testing
from unruly jesting

Text

He became all vexed
when he saw the text

Thank

Whom should I thank
for a mind all blank

Theme

Behind every theme
is an untold scheme

Each endearing theme
must keep its sheen

Every endearing theme
must have a scheme

Themes and schemes
add up to reams

Themselves

They make it into a tool
calling themselves old school

To rid themselves of frown
they did the town

Thief

Doesn't take a thief
to bring you grief

T

*If you partner with a thief
you will have no relief*

Thieves

*Even the thieves
have their pet peeves*

*Thick as thieves
sharing betel leaves*

Thin

*Thin as wafers
to-days news papers*

Things

*Little things they come asking
when I lay in the sun basking*

*Once you say things
the words take to wings*

*Things change in a day
doesn't have to be may*

*Things may be few
that all of us can do*

Think

*A quiet room to think
and a pen full of ink*

*A quiet room to think
till the face turns pink*

*By looking at his tail
don't think the tiger is frail*

*Everyday I think
of her when I blink*

*He settled into pen and ink
to improve how to think*

*How big can you think
how quick can you blink*

*How can I think
when eyelids they blink*

*How to make him think
asked the couch to the shrink*

*How to put into ink
what we really think*

*How to think
during a blink*

*I close my eyes and think
of the things we could do in a blink*

*I don't know what I think
until I see it in ink*

*I like to think
my eyes never will blink*

*It's not what you ink
it's what they think*

*Made me stop to think
why this blotch of ink*

*Once they are made to think
the eyes stop their blink*

*Some think it is prized
to be always despised*

Rhyming English Couplets

They think it fun
to have you on the run

Those who think well
of you you can tell

To see and to think
and put it down with ink

To think big
wear a wig

When I close my eyes and think
she shows up in a blink

Wherever you may be
don't forget to think of me

Thinking

Clear thinking
comes with blinking

Coffee drinking
helps my thinking

Do your thinking in lectures
that have a lot of pictures

Find a new way of linking
past and present thinking

He is less given to thinking
about his daily drinking

He who is given to drinking
wakes up next day thinking

If you ask them to do your thinking
your ship will soon be sinking

Much too much thinking
held back the blinking

No worse wrong
than thinking you are strong

Slow down your thinking
without ever blinking

So much wishful thinking
without any inkling

The bear he ate cherries
thinking they were berries

The light got him thinking
should he really be drinking

There is so much thinking
I do without blinking

Thinking has become quicker
from the ferment in this liquor

Thinking makes him foe
from head to toe

Unaccustomed to thinking
how much he was drinking

We cannot go inking
all that we are thinking

Writing is thinking
even when you are blinking

Zen thinking
done without blinking

T

Thinks

    A soldier who thinks
    is liable to blink

The owl thinks it is too soon
as the wolf howls at the moon

Thinner

    How can I be thinner
    after a big dinner

Thirst

    Shall we quench our thirst
    in one single burst

Thorn

    How to adorn
both the rose and the thorn

Many a thorn will pose
for the hand that plucks the rose

    Not yet born
a rose without a thorn

Stem though full of thorn
is where the rose is born

The thorn is the warden
    of the rose garden

The thorn it chose
to stay close to the rose

The thorn it not poses
a threat to the roses

The thorn it poses
by the flowering roses

To every rose is born
a neighbour who is a thorn

Thorns

    Dilemma has horns
    like the rose has thorns

Thought

A good deed from a thought
    must be carefully sought

A thought becomes a word
    waiting to be heard

    A thought conceived
    never deceived

A thought is best revealed
by the world that is concealed

A thought once hatched
    cannot be matched

A thought once held
can never be felled

A thought once planted
never grows up slanted

    A thought sneaks in
when resistance is thin

A thought that is bland
leaves the pencil in the hand

A thought that is old
    must be re-told

A thought well conceived
    is well received

A thought well dressed
is easily addressed

All human thought I am told
is lined with silver and gold

Bring it unto your fold
human thought that is old

Can it be bought
your so called thought

Clarity is sought
in every human thought

Day behind in thought
will someday get you caught

Defies all logic
this thought meteoric

Don't get caught
in unsavoury thought

Don't get caught
between word and thought

Don't get caught
sinning with your thought

Don't get caught
thinking their thought

Eventually you will be caught
holding an unchased thought

Every speeding thought
in memory it is caught

Every thought has a reason
depending on the season

Every thought once peeled
the meaning gets revealed

Every thought process
needs a good recess

Every thought she kept
filed away as she wept

Every waking thought
is about her and me a lot

Experience teaches a lot
about many an ancient thought

For poet it is the norm
to put thought into perfect form

For thought it is food
when you say something good

He lets the thought ride
who has things to hide

He needs to be caring
about the thought he is wearing

He stole it blind
a thought from my mind

He thought he was straight
until he came to chapter eight

He thought he was winning
when his hair resorted to thinning

He took some thought to the grave
the ones that caused a close shave

He woke up to the thought
that love had him caught

*Her thought fixed on a star
that twinkled very far*

*How can it be not
a free flow of thought*

*How can the mind speak
when the thought is too weak*

*How to put it to bed
the thought that enters your head*

*I might later rue
what I thought to be true*

*I will wake up not
caught in deep thought*

*If writing is not
close to your thought*

*If you know it is not my thought
prove that it is not*

*In a world of thought
often we are caught*

*In between caught
between two streams of thought*

*In my thought it stayed awhile
her slow but fading smile*

*Inside thought
need not be taught*

*It starts as a simple thought
that is waiting to be caught*

*Just a passing thought
in it I am caught*

*Just when he thought
that he couldn't get caught*

*Lovers they were caught
in Pensive thought*

*Many a fanciful thought
poetry it has caught*

*Many a serious thought
halfway became taught*

*Many a thought is fashioned
by words that are rationed*

*Many a thought will leak
if you think less and speak*

*Many a thought
is in hiding a lot*

*Many an old thought
must be experienced a lot*

*Many have been taught
by a good mans thought*

*More than a foolish risk
to make thought and words brisk*

*Music does a lot
to quiet your thought*

*My experience has caught
many an ancient thought*

*My thought kept its wrinkle
through the bell and its tinkle*

*New things are taught
by the frontiers of thought*

Rhyming English Couplets

Once you experience a thought
memories become a lot

Once you speak your thought
with danger it is fraught

Permanence is assured
for the thought once secured

Pieces of thought
together when they are brought

Poetry has caught
both emotion and thought

Rain it is not
just my train of thought

Savour your thought
when it is hot

She poured a cup of tea
which I thought was just for me

So many streams
of thought it seems

Some people are caught
in preposterous thought

Teacher has a thought
and students get caught

The anatomy of thought
says forget me not

The mind has been taught
to get lost in thought

The thinking lot
they hold down their thought

Thought and feeling
that sets the mind reeling

Thought and flight
through Arabian night

Thought for me is food
it must be understood

Thought for the day
will pave your way

Thought has attraction
when put into action

Thought is a bubble
that can burst into trouble

Thought is a part
of feelings of the heart

Thought made laconic
is concentrated tonic

Thought needs a seed
from which it is freed

Thought of food
can alter your mood

Thought they take turn
when they return

Thought when it appears
is accompanied by fears

To put thought into words
like the chirping of the birds

Until the thought has gelled
it must be withheld

Waiting to be caught
many a frivolous thought

What has it taught
this unending thought

What have they taught
these lines of thought

When the first thought is hot
the second thought is not

When thought becomes strange
one is in need of change

Where's the doubt
that it was not thought out

Whose thought is kind
is of a generous mind

Why can't I hear
the thought in my ear

Thoughtful

Put them to use
your thoughtful muse

Thoughts

All thoughts efface
at the sight of a pretty face

All thoughts forgotten
when I think something rotten

All thoughts lead to action
including its every fraction

All tied in knots
people by their thoughts

Around her little finger
were thoughts that linger

Channel your thoughts
with forget me nots

Evil thoughts can win
if you commit them to sin

For thoughts to be plastic
be enthusiastic

Good thoughts must be raked
before they are forsaked

Guiding light
for thoughts in flight

Happy thoughts
make them lots

Have their special slots
my collected thoughts

He hangs his thoughts on a peg
which happens to be his leg

He nods his head
when he has thoughts to shed

He put his thoughts in a bottle
and threw it so the fish would startle

He treated it as a whim
thoughts that occurred to him

He tried in vain
but the thoughts remain

He was all tied in knots
after renouncing his thoughts

He woke up to his thoughts
that tied him up in knots

His thoughts couldn't have been blunter
the happy hunter

How to remember
thoughts during slumber

I couldn't have been dumber
than to put my thoughts into slumber

I have thoughts to think
and beers to sink

I put words on to paper
as my thoughts began to taper

If it makes you feel well
let your thoughts dwell

If you let them fortify
thoughts they might mortify

In my thoughts when she came
I gave her many a name

In the middle of the night
thoughts that take to flight

In your eye they show
thoughts that come and go

Lamp with a soft yellow glow
to make your thoughts flow

Leave them to their thoughts
that are filled with faults

Let us gloat
over thoughts that are afloat

Like the flowers in the wild
the thoughts of a child

Man he talks
through hidden thoughts

My pen began its revolt
when my thoughts began to bolt

My phantom thoughts
about her lots

My thoughts take to flight
like a bird in delight

My thoughts they take me far
without a motor car

Negative thoughts
like black ink spots

No need for words
thoughts that are for the birds

No thoughts of sleep
with a love so deep

Old thoughts once burned
cannot be re-learned

Once you are jaded
your thoughts need to be upgraded

Parents are in our thoughts
in the abode of the gods

People when they speak
let their thoughts leak

Private thoughts
can say things lots

Random thoughts
forget me nots

Rid your mind of thoughts
that tie you up in knots

Sharing my thoughts
with the people outside lots

She had thoughts to chew
when he said my heart belongs to you

She was privy to his thoughts
and other what nots

She would make my head go spinning
while slowly my thoughts they go sinning

Smile lasts a short while
but thoughts can travel a mile

Some thoughts that were planted
they grew up all slanted

Storage space in the mind
where thoughts are left behind

The mind is a stable
where thoughts are able

The tiger he has lots
of prey in his waking thoughts

They come in lots
these amorous thoughts

They come in lots
these floating thoughts

They tie us up in knots
some of our thoughts

Think positive thoughts
make them into forget me nots

Thoughts become blurred
by the use of too many word

Thoughts came reeling
from this mysterious feeling

Thoughts can fall apart
if they are not from the heart

Thoughts get cluttered
before they are muttered

Thoughts get their latitude
best in quiet solitude

Thoughts half dressed
can't be expressed

Thoughts hidden they leak
the subconscious when it speak

Thoughts I must own
while words I disown

Thoughts I must pick
to play with sweet music

Thoughts must be fed
to the living from the dead

Thoughts must be mastered
before you get plastered

Thoughts need to be chased
and others to be faced

Thoughts of a certain kind
keep simmering in my mind

Thoughts replayed
and demons slayed

Thoughts that delight
as they take to flight

Thoughts that kindle
like thread from spindle

Thoughts that make you cringe
make you go on a binge

Thoughts that rattle
even the cattle

Thoughts that were bred
from the thinking in his head

Thoughts that were unsaid
how can they be fed

Thoughts that you think
put paper to ink

Thoughts they abound
that make the meaning round

Thoughts they come in jumping
then they go out limping

Thoughts they feed
upon your every deed

Thoughts to nurse
through my verse

Thoughts to treasure
for your reading pleasure

Thoughts unravel
during honeymoon travel

Thoughts unspoken
were anyway token

Thoughts will flow
with a magical glow

Thoughts with a special glow
to make the words really flow

Ties us up in knots
some of our thoughts

Two thoughts that feel as one
until love is done

Unchased thoughts
say forget me nots

Unsaid thoughts
forget me nots

Until they develop feet
thoughts they will stay too deep

Unwanted thoughts
add up to naughts

Unwanted thoughts
forget me nots

We must all be glad
all thoughts are not bad

We people our head
with thoughts unsaid

When the subconscious mind speaks
hidden thoughts they leaks

When thoughts they bungle
feelings will tumble

Wild flowers like thought
by anyone can be caught

Words are the link
that make thoughts think

Words enter the brain
to make thoughts that remain

Words they fuel
thoughts that duel

Thread

Hangs on to a thread
the spider it is said

They all did dread
his deceptive thread

They will be well bred
who use a fine thread

Thread your soul
through the loop hole

With thread that is very thin
we weave a tapestry of sin

Threads

How to pick up the threads
of wrongs done to their heads

Threat

Don't fret
the present is under threat

How to forget
the imagined threat

Threat of any kind
will clear the mind

Threat thinly veiled
easily derailed

Throat

In her throat a niggle
interrupted by a giggle

In the throat it stuck
the quack of the duck

On each other they dote
while being at each others throat

She gave me goose bumps
and a throat full of lumps

They show off their throat
crocodiles when they float

To get to each others throat
first you must cross the moat

Throne

Don't stick to your throne
said the bee to the drone

Moan and groan
your way to the throne

Throng

The bees they will throng
to where you do wrong

Through

Just hold your nerve
through many a curve

She can see through the sieves
of the tea leaves

Through Africa and Asia
they push panacea

Throw

Throw the dog a bone
and two birds with a stone

Thumb

Keep them under your thumb
until your finger goes numb

The rule of thumb
made it numb

Thunder

A scientific blunder
that stole the thunder

Eardrums torn asunder
from lightning and thunder

It's not just the thunder
that fills me with wonder

June without a cloud
or thunder that isn't loud

Like thunder his voice
was more than just noise

No it wasn't the thunder
it was all in the blunder

Thundering

Thundering loud
the passing cloud

Tibetan

Tibetan tea
for you and me

Tickle

His intellect is fickle
and it responds to a tickle

Tiddly

After a bite of Idly
he felt all tiddly

Tide

Much to gain
once you tide over the pain

The boatmen they ride
against the ocean tide

Tie

They till the soil
with faith and toil

Tie your boot laces
let's go to unknown places

Tied

Whenever he lied
he was tongue tied

Tiger

To wake a sleeping tiger
is not really like her

Tight

Let your focus be tight
when you do things right

*To sleep well at night
hold her very tight*

*When money is tight
go to the isle of wight*

Tighten

*If we don't tighten our belt
the ice cap it will melt*

*Tighten your belt
he said as he knelt*

Tighter

*The gifted writer
who sits the words tighter*

Tightly

*Don't take it lightly
life must be lived tightly*

Tights

*Wear your tights
for the last rites*

Time

*A long time it took
to get the fish to the hook*

*A time for reflection
and genuflexion*

*A time it was then
when word meant more than the pen*

*A time to rejoice
at the sound of her voice*

*About time we cared
for the good times we shared*

*All he could was mime
man when he go back in time*

*All I have is time
to make my couplets rhyme*

*All the rest will come later
if you have time to cater*

*All those years of writing
no time for nail biting*

*All we want in the end
is time together to spend*

*Before you put pen to ink
make sure you have time to think*

*By the time it was told
the story it turned cold*

*Doesn't cost a dime
to go back in time*

*Don't go there
if you have time to spare*

*Don't have time for games
or for calling names*

*Don't tinker
with the time you give the thinker*

*Each time there is thunder
I begin to wonder*

*Easy to mark time
when thoughts they rhyme*

Every time he forgets
he has no regrets

Every time they flatter
she took them to the altar

Fables of our time
are so sublime

Fun wait's there
who have time to spare

Get rid of gripe
when the time is ripe

Give it enough time
and all things will rhyme

Give them a bit of time
to turn juice into lime

Given enough time
he forgets every crime

Grown men blink
with no time to think

Have good time
when rhythm meets rhyme

Have time to spare
build castles in the air

Have time to spare
for compassion and care

He didn't have time to weep
for he died in his sleep

He has blundered
whose time he has plundered

He has time to gloat
for he is a swing vote

He is half way there
with time to spare

He spends time in the gym
singing his daily hymn

He spent so much time reading
that his hair started receding

He waits for me all day
for tonight we have time to play

He was bang on time
and could turn on a dime

He who creates a stink
hasn't had time to think

He will not spare the time
to do things sublime

His mind it wandered
while time he squandered

His only crime
he was a thief of your time

How can it be wasted
if time hasn't been tasted

How to bide time
with this lonely heart of mine

How to mark time
to music and rhyme

I have no time to waste
on words lacking in taste

I took time to rest
at the doctors behest

I wouldn't waste time
if this thought were not mine

If I could go back in time
when lemon was just lime

If you give it enough time
you can say things with rhyme

If you have the time to spare
sin it is everywhere

If you have time to spare
let's play doubles as a pair

If you have time to spare
seek solace elsewhere

In due time
things fall in line

It is time for some to pray
and for others to bray

It is time to cheer
for solitude has no fear

It must be a good rhyme
to stand the test of time

It was a marathon day
it is now time to pray

It's time to let loose
on our sunset cruise

It's time to say cheers
to a full stomach with beers

It's about time to falter
on your trips to the altar

It's about time you knew
to get what is due

It's about time
we take pleasure in Rhyme

It's no time to gloat
when there is a leak in your boat

It's not the time for hello
to the wounded buffalo

It's time to address
the causes of stress

It's time to be merry
with bottle of sherry

It's time to be sober
it is the first of October

It's time to be sober
romancing days are over

It's time to be stronger
in a moment of anger

It's time to go far
chewing my cigar

It's time to launch
your support that is staunch

It's time to share the corn
once romantic love is born

It's time to think
when pen meets ink

It's time to wander
like the geese and the gander

Jobs take time
both yours and mine

Keeping time
with music and rhyme

Less time to weep
if I sing you to sleep

Let us go back in time
when a dime was still a dime

Let us listen to the bands
we have time on our hands

Look back to the time
when a dime was just a dime

Meanings to unlock
if there is time on the clock

My mind let it wander
I have time to squander

No better thing called time
to make our love sublime

No time for batters
to discuss ugly matters

No time to cry
for her woe begotten eye

No time to falter
when you're alone at the altar

No time to fret
over past regret

Nothing else will do
than time spent with you

Now is the time
to speak a good rhyme

On borrowed time
till we run out of dime

Once upon a time
through the grape vine

One step at a time
slow and sublime

Others will cry
when its time to die

Over time they mount
the mystical account

Pick and choose
your time to snooze

Sailors life becomes bland
if he spends much time on land

Sample the example
when time is ample

So much time is wasted
from love not being tasted

Some they spend time hating
instead of on dating

Something special in the air
do you have time to spare

Springtime sublime
will appear on time

Take time into your fold
is one way to get old

Take your time to pick
work ethic that is thick

The fly on the lions nose
had time enough to pose

The gap became wide
with time and tide

The goose with a golden leg
at a time laid a golden egg

The only time for behaving
is when I am daily shaving

The ravages of time
can be made sublime

The sailor needs lime
in the course of time

The time added will stay
to my age every day

The time is due
for a bloodless coup

The time it took
for the death of a book

The time that was spent
trying to be a gent

The time we did waste
and the elixir we didn't taste

The twins must be fed
before it's time for bed

There is a time and a place
to make your case

There is a time and a place
to wear your best lace

There is a time of brewing
every wrong doing

There was a time when speech
was out of mans reach

There was nothing left to experiment
after spending their time in merriment

They spent their time
with tulips and wine

They spent time
over Arabian wine

This nest is mine
where I take my time

This side of the grave
best time to be brave

Though I have time to spare
she is no longer there

Time and distance
for love is a nuisance

Time and tide defies
adventure through our eyes

Time and tide
keep them on your side

Time and time again
the devil he must be slain

Time has a hand
writing letters in the sand

Time has chose
to slip under my nose

Time has reminded
it cannot be re-winded

Time is fleeting
and fast retreating

Time is never found
to do things that are sound

Time is not meant to be wasted
it's ticking to be always tasted

Time is very clever
for it can last forever

Time isn't enough
to get in all the stuff

Time it causes droops
of both eyelids and stoops

Time keeps passing by
without having to try

Time tends to age
the piper and the sage

Time to take stock
when the clock says tick-tock

Time to write a letter
before I go where it is better

Time well spent
for love it is meant

To get your juice of lime
get there on time

To go back in time
when love was divine

Too much regard for time
chasing every dime

Under the deluge of time
many a forgotten crime

Usually found
next time around

Way back in time
when things were spoken in rhyme

We can get you there
if you have time to spare

What was the cost
of time that was lost

When a young man speaks with rhyme
give him plenty of time

When junior has a moment
he finds time for lament

When things are going your way
take time to sit and pray

Will have time to think
and put it down in ink

Won't be the first time
dime is not worth a dime

Work is able
to fill the time table

Timeless

A timeless eastern rhyme
that simply bides its time

A timeless tryst
through haze and mist

I have the number
of a timeless slumber

Times

At times it seems
it's about Ice creams

He fell into the rough
when times were tough

He interweaves the lines
to tell the story of the times

In times of good health
all we need is wealth

Learned his lesson well
after many times he fell

Many times it has been said
go early to bed

Need more dimes
for changing times

Nine times out of ten
there is a bear in the den

Read between the lines
and find the good times

So fast why
times gone by

The goat has remained a goat
from times very remote

Timid

When he is livid
his voice is less timid

Timing

End up shining
with luck and timing

Tip

Don't do this or that
just tip your hat

The iceberg has a tip
where the penguins sit and quip

Tired

Don't ever get tired
about being re-wired

Once you are tired
it's time to get re-wired

Some of us are wired
to be always tired

We are tired
of the way society is wired

Tireless

Sleep in the end
is a tireless friend

Tires

He never tires
of his burning fires

Tiresome
> Every tiresome slumber
> was an easy way to numb her

Tissue
> He picked up a tissue
> faced with a hot button issue

Tit
> Tit for tat
> this for that

Titanic
> All dressed and gowned
> as the titanic it drowned

Toad
> How to goad
> the croak out of the toad

Tobacco
> Tobacco he poked
> into the pipe as he smoked

> Tobacco he tucked
> into his pipe as he sucked

Toes
> Down to his toes
> he was full of woes

> He who comes and goes
> has pointed toes

Together
> All together the grafters
> they fill up to the rafters

> Bind it in leather
> once you put it together

> Both master and pupil
> together up the steeple

> Come home to me
> and together we will see

> Joy and pain
> together they train

> Like birds of a feather
> they jostle together

> Squint of the eye is clever
> looking both ways together

> That which holds us together
> will not last through the winter weather

> The petals together they pose
> in the form of a fragrant rose

> They bind together
> like birds of a feather

> Together some day
> god willing we may

> Together they become whole
> my life and my soul

> Together they come faster
> both magic and disaster

> Together why they pose
> both thorn and the rose

> We must get together
> we have the same feather

We're in this together
in all kinds of weather

We're in this together
this hunt for leather

Toil

The batsmen toil
on foreign soil

Token

Even though token
keep one eye open

Told

How can it take hold
without being told

Told each other fables
sitting on separate tables

Tolerance

Tolerance is seen
as part of being queen

Tolerant

She put up a tolerant ear
everytime he appear

Tomorrow

If there were no to-morrow
how much would you borrow

Tonic

For the best tonic
just go organic

Gin and tonic
can make you pranic

Go for the tonic
at the first sign of panic

No better tonic
than platonic

No better tonic
than to become manic

What better tonic
than her singing that was euphonic

What better tonic
than her voice all euphonic

Tools

Pick up your tools
when you fall between the stools

Top

Even the top brass
say things that are crass

He didn't know how to stop
once he got to the top

Tops

The fog it hops
over mountain tops

Topsy

Topsy turvy
made him nervy

Tortuous

He thinks it pays
his tortuous ways

Touch

> He drank from a tall glass
> with a touch of class

> Much of the land
> needs the touch of hand

> Not easily as such
> comes the midas touch

> They bless you with a touch
> that means so much

> Touch your feelings
> with love and appealings

> Without ever having to touch
> between us there was much

Tough

> Some tough issues
> cannot be cleansed with tissues

Tourist

> The tourist must earn
> his every sunburn

Tower

> In a mans darkest hour
> he jumps from the tower

Town

> When he goes to town
> his tail let it be down

Toys

> Let them keep their toys
> the men and the boys

Trace

> He left without a trace
> after winning the race

Traces

> Leaves traces of meaning
> and an evanescent feeling

Track

> He began to pack
> with his syntax on track

> To the track he lumbers
> to play his numbers

Trademark

> How to nurse
> the trademark curse

Tradition

> No oral tradition
> without rendition

> Oral tradition
> best for rendition

> Oral tradition
> for all rendition

Tragedy

> Every tragedy has eyes
> way up to the skies

> How to get ready
> to face a tragedy

Trail

> The thief had a tail
> and he left no trail

Trails

There is always a trail
even if it sets sail

A serpent never fails
to leave behind its trails

Train

How to pull the chain
of the oncoming train

How to train
the phantom in my brain

Trained

Easily gained
by the well trained

Some are trained
to be hare brained

Training

Training would be silly
for the beautiful black filly

Traits

Long forgotten traits
were remembered in the straits

Tranquility

Tranquility more than pity
is needed in the city

Transformed

Be transformed
and reformed

Transmitted

Many a disease
transmitted by the breeze

Transparent

Make it apparent
you are transparent

Transparent through her eyes
there is fear say the wise

Transplanted

I thank the giver
of my transplanted liver

Trap

Trap shuts when
you're inside the den

Traps

So many traps
where character can lapse

Trash

Don't call it trash
can get you hard cash

Travel

Travel a mile
in comfort and style

With pen in hand
I travel many a land

Traveled

They traveled many a land
holding each others hand

*With well manicured hands
she traveled distant lands*

Traveling

*The traveling woodpecker
uses the double decker*

Travelled

*Travelled the world over
only to find her in Dover*

Tray

*Everything I have to say
I put it on a tray*

Treacherous

*Down the treacherous road
it leapfrogged the toad*

Treason

*Treason will remain treason
once you venture into reason*

Treasure

*How can we measure
a mind without treasure*

*How can we treasure
something that has no measure*

*How do we measure
a book full of treasure*

*How to measure
a national treasure*

*In about equal measure
I share with her my treasure*

*Science is a treasure
brings misery in good measure*

*Thank him for the treasure
that was beyond all measure*

Treasure

*There is no measure
for thought that is treasure*

*These moments I treasure
of love and its pleasure*

*Where is the need to measure
when you discover a treasure*

Treasured

*If it can be measured
it can be treasured*

Treasures

*All treasures must dwindle
for victims of a swindle*

*Deterrent measures
are our best treasures*

*Elusive since birth
the treasures of the earth*

*Hidden treasures
for your pleasures*

*My treasures will not be whole
without you in my soul*

Treasures

*The treasures of metre and Rhyme
It's about time*

There are treasures in the heap
of the mountain that is steep

Treasures in the pan
are measures of the man

Treasures they are vast
glimpses from the past

Under the ocean deep
many treasures they sleep

Treasury

Filled up treasury
will ease your misery

Treat

They went for a treat
to their country retreat

Treat everyday like a prize
that is a big surprise

Treat with disdain
bruises in the main

You're in for a treat
from the dancing feet

To end up is a trend
with a love without no end

Trendy

He had trendy blue eyes
like the colour of the skies

Trials

Trials and tribs
pain in the ribs

Tribe

They all belong to a tribe
whose currency is all bribe

Tribute

Best place to pay tribute
is on carpets made of jute

By remaining mute
comes the best tribute

Is it tribute
a smile from the brute

They pay tributes
to those with attitudes

Trick

All the rhetoric
was just a trick

Trickle

Don't rely on trickle
it can be very fickle

The trickle in her tear
made it all clear

They trickle the tears
from unknown fears

Where is my trickle
why is it so fickle

Trickles

The melting snow from the mountains
trickles down into the fountains

Tricks

A dog he sticks
to his bag of tricks

An old fox he picks
his own little tricks

Bricks become sticks
when the mind plays tricks

No bag of tricks
without pinpricks

They play their tricks
with semantics

Tried

They tried to pull away
when things didn't go their way

Tries

He always tries to better
the way he writes a letter

Trigger

Nothing is bigger
than the finger on the trigger

Trimming

Trimming the hedge
to give it a clean edge

Trip

A trip of the tongue
had him hung

I am in the grip
of an exciting trip

The opening line has a grip
that can easily make you trip

Triplets

She ate too many cutlets
and bore him a bunch of triplets

Triumph

In every triumph of the mind
there was one eye that was blind

Trivial

It may be a trivial thing
but it can fracture my wing

Nothing is trivial
not even convivial

Trivialities

Back and forth they walk
with trivialities that pass for talk

Trolley

The overflowing trolley
was filled with mans folly

Trouble

A wound once peeled
has trouble to be healed

After a late night snuggle
he got into trouble

Flirt with trouble
will burst the bubble

Great ambitions cause trouble
when they end up as rubble

He keeps working
where trouble is lurking

How to deal with trouble
and make it into rubble

In times of trouble
blow soap bubble

It burst and caused trouble
love that was just a bubble

It will trouble your nose
if you read it like prose

No trouble to float
the properly manned boat

Oil and water
trouble for a starter

Some day your virtue
into trouble it will get you

Such a delicate bubble
a life that is courting trouble

The soap in the bubble
was the cause of trouble

Trouble in paradise
could still be quite nice

Trouble it breeds
unwholesome deeds

Waiting for trouble
bursting bubble

Troubled

A troubled and distant land
without its own ocean or sand

He was troubled by
a single blind eye

In troubled waters
don't fish for starters

Troubles

Champagne bubbles
can drown your troubles

How to make bubbles
out of your troubles

Many of my troubles
before they became bubbles

Surface bubbles
portend troubles

Though troubles may be few
they show up when they are due

Troubles abound
where you skirt around

Troubles they have taught
that danger is usually sought

Troubles they start when
you stop using the pen

Troubles told to the letter
can make you feel better

Troubles up to the ears
can last many long years

Troublesome
> Many a person would wilt
> wearing a troublesome kilt

Trout
> Eating a lot of trout
> was it the cause of gout

> How to be without
> watching the leap of the trout

Truculence
> Truculence is best
> put to rest

True
> How true is your joy
> depends on what you see in the boy

> Out of the blue
> the meaning comes true

> The cobbler made a shoe
> that was creaky and true

> True to his attire
> he would quench his desire

> What might be true
> came out of the blue

> You know it is true
> when your face turns blue

Truly
> Was truly earned
> what I have learned

> How to trust him twice
> who proclaims no vice

> It turned to rust
> their mutual trust

> Misplaced trust
> tends to rust

> Put your trust
> in money you must

> Restore trust
> first you must

> Rid of it first
> this lack of trust

> She said she would trust
> his heart filled with lust

> Some place their trust
> where it is bound to rust

> Trust is portrayed
> as a thing to be betrayed

> Verify must
> before of trust

> When it comes to money
> I trust my own penny

Trusted
> Can be trusted
> who says it is done and dusted

> Old friends can be trusted
> once they are dusted

Trusting
> He was simple and trusting
> and did his daily dusting

Trusting

*If you give them a trusting eye
they will cheat you till you die*

Truth

*All things look fine
until truth gets out of line*

*An old truth re-told
to bring it out of the cold*

*Battles have to be fought
when truth it is sought*

*Discussion bears fruit
and uncovers the truth*

*Don't spend your youth
with light regard for the truth*

*Don't tell the truth
about your wayward youth*

*His truth has a side
that is a lie gaping wide*

*How to mull
over truth when it is dull*

*I forget to mention
that the truth is in question*

*If you pray inside a booth
you will realize the truth*

*Let the truth be told
and not put on hold*

*Many a truth is told
to hide the lies untold*

*Many a truth was denied
just because he lied*

*Old age is about the truth
that there is no fountain of youth*

*Once a theory takes shape
the truth it will gape*

*Once corrupted
truth gets interrupted*

*Peel off the layers
to find the truth from the players*

*Rather uncouth
to lie about the truth*

*The truth about you
known to very few*

*The truth began to dawn
when she replied with a yawn*

*The truth can in the main
cause all the pain*

*The truth it lay dormant
waiting for a comment*

*The truth was muttered
once the lie was discovered*

*There is a kind of truth
that regularly bears fruit*

*There wasn't even a frown
when truth turned upside down*

*They can tell truth from the lies
if you advertise to the wise*

Truth and illusion
will there be collusion

Truth and lies
have family ties

Truth and lies
only for his eyes

Truth be bared
and the lies be snared

Truth be told
words incisive and cold

Truth can get comical
when it is economical

Truth comes in grains
not in goods trains

Truth gets a scorn
though lie from it is shorn

Truth has a duty
to appreciate its beauty

Truth has no name
when he loses all shame

Truth is not far
if you don't know who you are

Truth is undivided
when honestly provided

Truth it gets stretched
only by the wretched

Truth known will last
while lies disappear fast

Truth like the sloth
move slowly they both

Truth we must nudge
out said the judge

Truth will set you free
when you climb up the tree

When truth and fiction tangle
gives it a new angle

When truth wakes up from sleep
mouth shut you must keep

Wine is a lotion
to bring out truth and it's portion

Great truths
bear fruits

Truths

Old truths re-told
to firmly take hold

Try

He is wily and wry
without having to try

If you don't try
the well will run dry

Try to be alone
when you wish upon a bone

Without having to try
some people they lie

Trying
He became pale
trying to turn the scale

Tryst
He had a tryst to keep
the wolf dressed as the sheep

Tulips
Foot hills will bring
out the tulips in the spring

Tumbling
Many a flower will see
the tumbling bumble bee

Tumour
Huge hidden tumour
bigger than the rumour

The tumour was benign
let us share some wine

Tune
Easy to stay in tune
if it is mid-June

Turbulence
There is turbulence in the east
let's call off the feast

Turbulence is a part
of blood flow to the heart

Turbulent
Babies they lay curled
in this turbulent world

Boats he charters
for the turbulent waters

From where does it spring
this turbulent thing

Turbulent times
need grape wines

Turkey
Like a turkey they cluck
is it a wild duck

The turkey feels bad
for the christmases she could have had

What has the turkey done
to be treated like one

Turn
Colour of paint I am told
can turn silver into gold

Every good turn
ends up in the urn

He took a turn
at every tavern

She waited her turn
for his safe return

Turn your eyeballs in
to find out where you have been

Turning
Tide is slowly turning
when my aches turn to burning

Turtle
Once there was a turtle
who detested his name called myrtle

Twice
A word from the wise
is never told twice

It came up twice
the issue of price

She came back twice
once we broke the ice

Twice would be jolly
both vice and folly

Valour is nice
when it comes twice

Will it look nice
if you do it twice

Twilight
Many things unknown
lie in the twilight zone

Twinkle
The stars have lost their twinkle
so he said to tinkle

Twinkling
The night sky though far
there lies a twinkling star

Twist
Each and every twist
known to the fatalist

Many have been hung
from a false twist of the tongue

Once you get the gist
hard to miss the twist

Twister
He ran into a twister
ended up with a blister

Twit
Bit by bit
two half wits make a twit

Type
He was the type
who could all day snipe

U

Umbilical
> Object of mirth
> his umbilical girth

Unassuming
> Make it your banner
> your unassuming manner

Unawares
> Caught unawares
> without any spares

Uncap
> Uncap your pen
> when the bear comes out of the den

Uncaring
> Uncaring world
> at which things are hurled

Uncensored
> Uncensored act
> broke the pact

Uncertain
> His eyes they look certain
> when all else seems uncertain

> How to erase
> the uncertain phase

Uncivilized
> Reasons are devised
> by the uncivilized

Uncoil
> The mongoose must toil
> to make the snake uncoil

Unconcerned
> With unconcerned beauty
> they simply did their duty

Unconscious
> Unconscious sources
> are my hidden forces

Uncontrolled
> Uncontrolled surges
> of latent urges

Underdog
> When the underdog
> became a hog

Understood
It must be understood
it all happens for the good

They understood one another
and stood for each other

Undeterred
How much ever he erred
he was undeterred

Undone
He was forever undone
by the duel in the sun

Whatever they do the pros
will be undone by the cons

Uneasy
Uneasy truce
between the gander and the goose

Unending
Seems to be unending
against the fast ball fending

Unequal
We were all born unequal
so we wait for a sequel

Unexplored
Mind unexplored
must be deplored

Unfaithful
Don't climb the ladder
with an unfaithful bladder

Unforgettable
Unforgettable it will remain
love and its pain

Unfulfilled
Ego gets spilled
from things unfulfilled

Unguarded
Unguarded moment
life of lament

Unhappy
Unhappy in his skin
too afraid to win

Unhelpful
Unhelpful and resentful
they are always full

Unhinged
He was unhinged
by the things that he binged

Unkempt
The porcupine was meant
to be always unkempt

Unkind
All things unkind
in the recesses of the mind

Don't be unkind
though you speak your mind

Don't be unkind
to the ravages of the mind

They start being unkind
those who read your mind

Unknown
Unknown to the weak
that they have a sharp beak

Unless
Be soft when you spar
unless you are in a bar

Unlike
They want to be
unlike me

Unlocked
When he unlocked the door
he found vice on the floor

Unloved
The unloved in the end
will have god as a friend

Unlucky
He is an unlucky fellow
whose head goes through his halo

Unmistakable
Her unmistakable voice
on the phone line by choice

Unraveled
Travel unraveled
on the road less traveled

Unrealistic
He seems to pick
the unrealistic

Unreasonable
Every unreasonable plan
starts from the unreasonable man

Unreasonable folk
can't handle a joke

Unrest
Cycle of unrest
reaches its rest

Unsaid
They both went to bed
with things left unsaid

Words that are unsaid
must remain in the head

Unsavoury
How to erase
the unsavoury phrase

Unsavoury things spill
from the rumour mill

Unscathed
Came back unscathed
and fully bathed

Unscrupulous
Many a man was hung
by the unscrupulous tongue

Unseasonable
Unseasonable times
when good becomes a crime

Unsolicited
> Put it on ice
> your unsolicited advice

Unspeakable
> Can the unspeakable
> be made seekable

> He who is able
> does the unspeakable

> Unspeakable joys
> in the company of boys

Unsuited
> Though suited and booted
> to each other unsuited

Unsure
> She wrote letters in the sand
> with an unsure trembling hand

Unveiled
> They unveiled their plot
> with a single warning shot

Unwanted
> Not severely daunted
> by being unwanted

> The coconut tree grew slanted
> as if it was unwanted

> The unwanted few
> force themselves on you

> They are undaunted
> those who are unwanted

> Unwanted inches
> easy for pinches

Unwelcome
> Unwelcome tangles
> of legal wrangles

Unwilling
> Their demeanor was chilling
> against the unwilling

Unwise
> Don't get caught
> in unwise thought

Unyielding
> He told them their fielding
> must be unyielding

Upheavals
> Upheavals they have taught
> that with danger they are fraught

Uplift
> A gift for sure
> will uplift the poor

Uplifted
> Some people are gifted
> at making others feel uplifted

Uplifting
> As they were squeaking
> with their tails uplifting

> Gifting
> is uplifting

*Uplifting hands
needed in shifting sands*

Upright

*Upright was her nose
even in repose*

Uprising

*Learn the way of rising
above every uprising*

Upside

*Like upside down rats
they hang the bats*

Urban

*From village to urban
the man in a turban*

*How can you be urban
without a draped turban*

Urge

*Every primitive urge
ends up being a scourge*

*When man gets the urge
nothing to stop the surge*

Urges

*Urges that were nice
must be felt twice*

Useful

*It's a useful tool
to pretend and be fool*

Utility

*Futility
has no utility*

V

Valentine
> *Valentine valentine*
> *where shall we got to dine*

> *Love on valentines day*
> *is a little more than play*

Valentines
> *To make more than hay*
> *on valentines day*

> *Valentines day is near*
> *her voice I wait to hear*

Validation
> *Whatever their station*
> *they seek validation*

Value
> *If gold loses a grain*
> *the value is never the same*

Valued
> *Valued much*
> *the midas touch*

Values
> *Their values must leap*
> *the things you buy cheap*

Vampires
> *Vampires in the night*
> *blood curdling sight*

Vanishing
> *His vanishing plume*
> *refuses to bloom*

Vanities
> *All the little vanities*
> *as if they were calamities*

Vanity
> *A man without vanity*
> *too close to calamity*

> *Can't keep your sanity*
> *interrupted by vanity*

> *It was vanity by a nose*
> *when both stood up to pose*

> *Pursuit of vanity*
> *is it always sanity*

> *Vanity is cherished*
> *and also embellished*

Variety
> Variety it must savour
> for life to get its flavour

Vaulted
> He vaulted himself whole
> with the newly minted pole

Vegetation
> The vegetation is dense
> on one side of the fence

Veil
> The veil must be lifted
> to unlock the gifted

> The veil once lifted
> tells us who is gifted

> The veil when it drops
> hides the mountain and its tops

Vengeance
> They made a pact
> to vengeance react

> Vengeance is no bluffer
> always meant to suffer

Venomous
> Venomous ink
> will make you think

Venture
> Two sets of denture
> in their first joint venture

Ventures
> He will lose his ventures
> without proper dentures

Verbal
> He was so verbal
> I went for the herbal

> With a verbal attack
> they broke his back

Verse
> A verse once crafted
> has to be properly grafted

Verses
> His verses were unending
> and defied all rendering

Version
> Events have a version
> known only to the sturgeon

> New version of the tale
> makes the old one look pale

Versus
> Holes in the head
> versus nails in the bed

Vertical
> Can be stiff
> the vertical cliff

Vices
> He has vices
> as many as spices

Vicious

> Even the vicious raptor
> shows kindness to the captor

> How to tide
> over my vicious side

Victim

> Victim of a scandal
> he became a vandal

Victory

> Victory to defeat
> try not to repeat

Vigilant

> He sits on his throne
> the ever vigilant drone

Village

> Grasshopper mostly seen
> on the village green

> I sat and pondered by the quay
> in the village of Torquay

> Out of the woods he came
> into the village without a name

Violence

> I am mortified
> when violence is justified

> People play a part
> in violence from the start

> The violence of culture
> unbecoming of the vulture

> Violence pays
> in violent ways

Violent

> Every violent pose
> must end in repose

Virtual

> Virtual reality
> brings out the clarity

Virtue

> A school where they teach you
> each and every virtue

> Don't think twice
> between virtue and vice

> Everything is a virtue
> that cannot hurt you

> Follow the path of virtue
> or else it might hurt you

> He who is blessed with virtue
> can also sometimes hurt you

> He who shows no virtue
> can really hurt you

> How can it haunt you
> all his virtue

> How to chew
> on easy virtue

> Paragons of virtue
> how can they hurt you

> The road to virtue is long
> but that is where we belong

*Vice and virtue
both can hurt you*

*Vice and virtue
both have taught you*

*Vice and virtue
which one can hurt you*

*Virtue adds spice
to every little vice*

*Virtue and vice
change places twice*

*Virtue and vice
do each of them twice*

*Virtue and vice
they both love spice*

*Virtue and vice
twins for a single price*

*Virtue and vice
when they roll over is nice*

*Virtue has a price
not once but twice*

*Virtue in the end
may not make a friend*

*Virtue is nice
if it is camouflaged in vice*

*Virtue is nice
if it is without a price*

*Virtue is not the only food
for him who thinks he is good*

*Virtue it flees
in slow degrees*

*Virtue looks nice
when laced with vice*

Virtues

*He takes his cues
from peoples virtues*

*Her virtues I adore
and wish for more*

*How hard it is to choose
between two virtues*

*Let virtues be twice
that of each vice*

*No one was offended
of virtues upended*

*To ignore is hard
the virtues of the bard*

*Virtues exaggerated
always exonerated*

*Virtues have a limit
even in sporting spirit*

*Virtues must be oiled
to stop from being soiled*

Virtuous

*His path was very tortuous
until he became virtuous*

*No better giving
than virtuous living*

Virus
The virus of fear
can cost your dear

Visible
She was from afar
like the morning star

Vision
A task with a vision
make it your mission

Lack of vision
failure of mission

Lack of vision
leads to superstition

Vision for the blind
the inner reaches of the mind

Vision unclear
when paralysed by fear

Vocabulary
Clean up your vocabulary
when you go to the constabulary

Vocabulary
Don't be in a hurry
to use your vocabulary

Vocation
Some choose a vocation
that has to do with excavation

Voice
A voice to blurt
until the eyeballs hurt

Don't raise your voice
always make your choice

I lost my voice
when death made its choice

I miss the ringing tone
and her voice on the phone

Say it with a single voice
if you're the wrong choice

Who gives it voice
the background noise

Voices
What more can be said
about voices in the head

Void
A void completely filled
had her fulfilled

Volcano
The volcano was wide
with an open ended side

Vote
One man one goat
better than one vote

Vulnerable
Though he is able
he is vulnerable

V

W

Waddle
> So many places to waddle
> If I could get me a paddle

Wage
> I'm no sage
> I need my wage

> He serves good wages
> for all his pages

> Minimum wages
> upped in stages

Wait
> I just can't wait
> to unload the freight

Waited
> On a late evening in June
> they waited for the man on the moon

> With her back gently curved
> she waited for tea to be served

Waiting
> All it did was rain
> while waiting for the train

> Don't go baiting
> him when he is waiting

> Polar bear stands tall
> waiting for the winter to call

> Waiting to be full soon
> many a half moon

Wake up
> As soon as I wake up
> I go for my makeup

> I wake up from sleep
> and go riding in a jeep

Wake
> I wake up every day
> to think of you and pray

Wakefulness
> Wakefulness and sleep
> have boundaries to keep

Wakes up
> Is he half right
> who wakes up at night

Waking
>Waking up it lit
>his mind with words that fit

Walk
>How to talk
>during tightrope walk

>Let's take a walk
>and resort to serious talk

>When I take a walk
>I hear the trees talk

Walking
>Boots are made for walking
>tongue made for wagging

Wallet
>Many a kith and kin
>have made your wallet thin

Wand
>The fairy has a wand
>of which she is fond

Wander
>Don't think beyond her
>when you start to wander

>Goose to the gander
>where shall we wander

>How shall I wander
>asked the goose to the gander

Wandering
>Next to him was a seat
>for her wandering feet

>Oh wandering tongue
>why did you have me hung

>The windmills go squandering
>the winds that come wandering

Want
>They want the big yard
>both lord and the bard

>Whatever you want to do
>is up to you

>Whatever you want
>just ask the aunt

Wanted
>Of all the things that are wanted
>only some of them are granted

War
>A country can go far
>with the utensils of war

>Can it take you far
>beating drums of war

>Can't get you far
>life's tug of war

>Don't be forgetting
>we're on a war footing

>It may be near or far
>but always prepare for war

>Only so far
>can get you this war

>Start a war with ease
>becomes impossible to cease

*The day is not far
when the world will be at war*

*The war it made him lame
and things were never the same*

*The war machine is fed
so the prople may be bled*

*The weapons of war
cannot take you far*

*Through thick and thin
there is a war within*

*War best to fight
middle of the night*

*War is no stranger
to men who seek danger*

*War is senseless
especially against the defenseless*

*War they wage
like birds in a cage*

*When two dogs go to war
they end up with a scar*

*Will it get you far
a new bold war*

*Won't get you far
this turf war*

W

Warm

*He would cease to be warm
without any qualm*

*Teacup warm
brewing a storm*

Warmth

*Children they roam
where there is warmth in the home*

*Every ray of the sun
where warmth has begun*

*My blues get undone
by the warmth of the winter sun*

*The warmth of her glow
will forever show*

*Warmth is at hand
in my motherland*

Warn

*They warn you at night
the dogs before they bite*

Warning

*I'll give you a warning
it's shoe horning and darning*

*Make your warning shot
both red and hot*

Warns

*The snow it warns
the landing swans*

Wars

*They don't make wars
who go to Many bars*

Rhyming English Couplets

> Wars must beget peace
> piece by piece
>
> Wars they begin
> at the drop of a pin
>
> Why is it a must
> that all wars are just

Warts

> Way off the charts
> his wayward warts

Waste

> Don't waste your dime
> nor your precious time
>
> Each has his taste
> some of which is waste
>
> Some consider it a waste
> unsuitable to their taste

Wasted

> No trip is wasted
> until the journey is tasted
>
> Nothing must be wasted
> without first being tasted

Wastes

> He who wastes time
> doesn't think it a crime

Watch

> It's good for a chuckle
> so watch your buckle

> Watch your hemmings
> when you swim with the lemmings

Water

> Drinking water with lime
> the sailor passed his time
>
> Hot water river
> to soothe every quiver
>
> How can it spill
> the water uphill
>
> How much water it takes
> to fill up the lakes
>
> It must be a fish
> that caused the water to swish
>
> It was water he could tell
> that she drew from the well
>
> Like water through the sands
> once through your hands
>
> Need water to douse
> when fire hits the house
>
> No stone can stop her
> the little drops of water
>
> Water that slowly drips
> through many a stone it rips
>
> When the sharks begin to circle
> the water begins to gurgle

Watering

> Make it mouth watering
> when you go bartering

Waters

Floating lilies they are fond
waters of the golden pond

In deep waters they sleep
big fish in the deep

It plowed into calmer waters
escaping the Icebergs for starters

Watertight

Who is right
is not watertight

Wave

With each ocean wave
he had a close shave

Waved

He waved his wand
and created a pond

Waves

Close shaves
when we ride the waves

Don't make any waves
when you are inside the caves

He waves his fist
the alarmist

Spend your days
making waves

The gulls they are flapping
their wings at the waves slapping

Way

All the way upto the gate
the river is in full spate

How did we get this way
without me having a say

If you have things to say
let it find it's way

Keep the mosquitos at bay
when fever comes your way

They will find a way
to say it every which way

Waylaid

For his salty tongue he was paid
and was quickly waylaid

Ways

He spends his days
with his gypsy ways

High handed ways
with him it stays

Men they had their ways
back in the good old days

The fish have their ways
in the inland bays

To return there are ways
to the good old days

With him it stays
his errant ways

Wayward

> The wayward brain
> like a chugging train

Weak

> Double speak
> meant for the weak

> For the weak and the strong
> wrong is wrong

> Help is there to seek
> for the strong and the weak

> No voice to speak
> once you become weak

> Weak or strong
> wrong is wrong

Weakness

> A horse that shows weakness
> don't let it run at preakness

> God rid me of this weakness
> to go weekly to preakness

> The only human weakness
> is to spend time at preakness

> To gamble at preakness
> is an annual weakness

Weaknesses

> Apparent weaknesses are meant
> to shield inordinate strength

Wealth

> Awe inspiring wealth
> not as good as health

> He is wise to the ways of wealth
> foolish to the ways of health

> In sickness and in health
> preserve your wealth

> Is it really wealth
> when you're in pink of health

> Some are improved by health
> and others by a bit of wealth

> They charged him out of his wealth
> having noticed his failing health

> They nursed him back to health
> so that he could distribute his wealth

> Wealth and fame
> to seek is a game

> Wealth has need
> and a greed to feed

> Wealth laid bare
> can act as a snare

> Wealth of information
> led to confirmation

> Why think of death
> when health is your only wealth

Wealthy

> The wealthy may get it
> without their own merit

Weapons

> Weapons in many lands
> are just bare hands

Wears

> Can't sit on a boat
> he who wears a tailcoat

> Everything wears thin
> except bottle of gin

> He wears it in June
> the loose pantaloon

Weary

> He made them so weary
> they all became teary

Weather

> A floating white feather
> foretells the weather

> All meet in rough weather
> they sit and clean their feather

> Birds clean their feather
> in the warm weather

> Both wind and weather
> can ruffle many a feather

> Can it stand the weather
> the cap made of feather

> He hung like a feather
> on the mountain top weather

> In all kinds of weather
> shoes made of leather

> In all kinds of weather
> cricketers hunt leather

> One way or the other
> we must wait for fair weather

> Ruffle not her feather
> he told the wind and the weather

> The weather as it warmed
> the rice fields they farmed

> The weather hot and seething
> made for heavy breathing

> They peck at their feather
> when there is lull in the weather

> They sail in all weather
> without a ruffled feather

> We had enough of each other
> so we changed like the weather

> We seek from each other
> in all kinds of weather

Web

> The spider in it's web
> hanging by a thread

> After they were wed
> things happened in their head

> Before they were wed
> they jumped into bed

> Must I wed
> this stranger in my head

Wedding

> She coaxed him into giving
> a wedding ring

Wedlock

> The clock struck one
> and wedlock was done

Weed

> Demonic speed
> it grows like a weed

> Doesn't become a weed
> every planted seed

> It is just a common weed
> doesn't serve much as feed

> Many a shallow weed
> makes the river gain speed

> The flower and the weed
> both from the seed

> They all start as a seed
> good deed and the weed

Weeds

> Good deeds are seeds
> not replaced by weeds

> Too many weeds
> between the words and the deeds

> Wear your beads
> and inhale weeds

Week

> The whole week knows
> how your Monday goes

Weekends

> Spice up your weekends
> with deep knee bends

Weeping

> One weeping eye
> the other to the sky

Weight

> Many a ship will hold
> more than its weight of gold

Welcome

> Welcome tomorrow
> is a good phrase to borrow

> You are welcome to this bottle
> to cure your throat of the rattle

Well

> Don't dwell
> live well

> He who gives up his bone
> will not do well as a drone

> If you think you are well
> don't ask don't tell

> No need to dwell
> just speak well

Whale

> A cock and bull tale
> about fishing for a whale

> The Beluga whale
> has her own fairy tale

Yet to see a whale
grow fat on ale

Whatever
Whatever I have done
was something under the sun

Whatever it takes
I want an Eden without snakes

Whatever you say
can go the other way

Why did it get this way
whatever they may say

Whim
On a whim
she altered him

Whims
He shapes his fins
according to his whims

Whirl
Boy meets girl
they go on a whirl

Whisky
Once the whisky comes to dine
out goes the wine

Whisky down your throat
and the head begins to float

Whisper
Couldn't have been brisker
when he escaped by a whisper

Hand in hand they walked
in a whisper they talked

The winter air is crisper
down to the last whisper

When you carry a whisper
repeat it more crisper

Why is it always crisper
words told in a whisper

Whispered
What the neighbours heard
was whispered to the bird

Whispering
They sat and tasted the wines
among the whispering pines

Whispers
Nothing much they yield
whispers off the field

Whistle
Many a trains whistle
makes you want to listen

Yet to see a bird
whistle a four letter word

Whiteness
With whiteness why
the clouds they paint the sky

Whole
Each fish of the shoal
is part of the whole

Rhyming English Couplets

Flags on the whole
take a toll on the pole

To get the whole picture
listen to the lecture

Why

Why it pays
to mend your ways

Wicked

With him it stays
his wicked ways

Wicket

He can't be a sleeper
the gloved wicket keeper

Wet and sticky wicket
let's stick to cricket

Wide

Eyes were wide open
but not a word was spoken

Open the gates wide
before you step aside

Who will decide
when the gap is wide

Wider

She spread her net wider
the long legged spider

Wild

No room for bungle
in the wild jungle

Wildness

Wildness they say
was moulded by the clay

Will

Against his will
she went up the hill

For greater exertions of the will
where do I find the pill

He wrote his will
with a goose quill

I will not lie still
until I am in your will

Lentils can fill
my hunger at will

Many an ill will
has an unsavoury spill

Mosquito has the will
and the ability to kill

Not against his will
he stand still

Take a pill
and swallow the will

Takes a bit of will
to lie perfectly still

Technology used at will
is neither potion nor pill

The midnight will
into the morning spill

To be buried by the daffodil
was written into his will

Willed

Be strong willed
to be fulfilled

Willing

Are you willing to spend
money till the end

Every single shilling
to spend must be willing

The author must be willing
to do some bean spilling

There isn't a single drone
willing to give up his throne

Willing to live
willing give

Willow

He held on to his willow
with his face buried in a pillow

Win

All it took to win
was a sock on the chin

Always trying to win
my unabashed twin

Don't let him win
the monster within

Must atonement win
against all sin

Nothing could be brisker
if you win by a whisker

The win was so slender
it needed a blender

To win he tries
by the weight of his lies

Under your skin
the mites they win

Wind

All the way to sindh
the straws in the wind

As the wind blows
so the cloud flows

Don't bend
to every change in the end

In and out of the caves
the wind and the waves

Like leaves in the wind
from Mumbai to sindh

The leaves rustle in the wind
from serendip to sindh

The wind and the rain
didn't stop the train

Where the wind takes
I sail across the lakes

Wind, wave and song
made their love strong

Window
>Upon the window pane
>pitter patter said the rain

Winds
>They relied on trade winds
>to take tea to the sindhs

>Trade winds to find
>for the nautical mind

>Winds of change
>have a long range

>Winds of the ocean
>set the sails in motion

Wine
>After a bottle of wine
>he became sanguine

>It must have been the wine
>that made him cross the line

Wined
>He wined and dined
>and pocket he lined

Wings
>Why do they take to wings
>these foolish things

Wink
>He turned all pink
>when she gave him a wink

Winked
>Again and again she winked
>at him until he blinked

>She winked at him why
>when he caught her eye

Winner
>Candlelight dinner
>made him a winner

>If we have dinner
>both will be winner

>The winner at the post
>gets all the toast

>Though he is a winner
>part of him is a sinner

>Weight is the winner
>if you eat a big dinner

>Who is the winner
>between the sin and the sinner

>Sinners and winners
>they both come to the dinners

Winning
>On the road to winning
>when you stop all sinning

>You're on the way to winning
>by stopping all sinning

Wins
>He who wins
>drops all the pins

>No one wins
>if you bottle up your sins

>Until it wins
>he attends to his sins

Winter

Winter is here
and Christmas is near

With winter on the brink
the penguin begins to blink

Winterland

She must have had a hand
in our winterland

Winters

Even the white swan
to where the winters have gone

What is there to say
on a cold winters day

Wired

A brain hard wired
is newly attired

Wisdom

Ancient wisdom will come
handed from mum to mum

He does not have enough wisdom
to hang on to his kingdom

How to be without
both wisdom and doubt

If wisdom cost a penny
It would be a part of many

In wisdom you will find
words simple and kind

The price of wisdom
varies with the kingdom

To squeeze wisdom out of sorrow
don't wait till the morrow

Wisdom and wealth
can it buy health

Wisdom bottled in drink
how can it make us think

Wisdom comes twice
but only once for the wise

Wisdom endures
and provides all the cures

Wisdom gives strength
to life's breath and length

Wisdom has a way
of being wiser to-day

Wisdom is a grain
we need to train

Wisdom of the ages
acquired in stages

Wisdom once found
better be sound

Wisdom you will find
if you re-position the mind

Wise

A person who is wise
will never leave his vice

A serpent is wise
puts his tongue out twice

*Are we wise
to modernize*

*Even the wise
can easily capsize*

*He doesn't think twice
who thinks folly is wise*

*He was wise beyond his years
by conquering his fears*

*How can he be wise
the fool behind his eyes*

*How can he be wise
with those careless eyes*

*I am wise
I don't agonize*

*If you hold your tongue twice
you will appear to be wise*

*It would be nice
to always be wise*

*Not always wise
to go clockwise*

*Stay away if you are wise
from prying eyes*

*Think twice
before you call yourself wise*

*Those who are wise
they come in a pocket size*

*To laugh at someone twice
is not for the very wise*

*Too late to be wise
after you pay the price*

*Wise head is dead
once you get to bed*

*Wise men have a den
where they keep their hen*

Wisely

*He who lived wisely
will he die nicely*

Wiser

*He became wiser
after being a miser*

*On many a yesterday
I was wiser than to-day*

Wises

*He quickly wises
upto his disguises*

*He who wises
upto shapes and sizes*

Wish

*Be a little slick
if you wish to click*

*Every child has a wish
to catch a big fish*

*Every shark has a wish
that his jaw could hold many fish*

*Hire the undertaker
if you wish to meet your maker*

His wish when it came true
he uncorked a special brew

I don't wish to live far
from the martinis at the bar

I only wish
I was a mermaid and not a fish

I wish he were kinder
than to bowl me a blinder

I wish I lived then
no cell phones when

I wish I only knew
all the things about you

I wish my destiny
keeps me company

I wish she knew
no one else will do

I wish some were dead
the people in my head

I wish we have the means
to buy our daily store of beans

I wish you knew
I am fed up of you

I wish you would heed
what daily I plead

If you wish to be liked
the price must not be hiked

If you wish to be tripped
go beyond the script

If you wish to grow
learn to say no

If you wish to reach parity
don't be a minority

Keep it latent
when you wish to be blatant

Little silver fish
granted a Childs wish

Make a wish
and drink like a fish

One last wish
let me eat fish

Sharks they don't chew
I wish I already knew

Sometimes I wish
my neighbour was a fish

The big fish have a wish
to have little ones on a dish

The fungus has a wish
for a tasty petri dish

The gold fish made a wish
I don't want to end up as dish

The wish in my bone
turned into stone

There is a wish in me
to catch all the fish in the sea

There is this person in me
who I don't wish to be

What is true is not new
I wish I knew

When you wish to appease
use a chunk of cheese

When you wish to be a thinker
hide behind a blinker

When you wish to quip
shoot from the lip

When you wish to trim
don't do it on a whim

Whenever you wish to beg
just stand on a single leg

Wish it would forever stay
the love we had in May

Wishes

A stylish English rose
with her he wishes to pose

Go do the dishes
fulfill my wishes

He must speak with forked tongue
who wishes to be hung

He who wishes to win
quickly jumps out of sin

How can I resent the rose
with scent who wishes to pose

Our wishes last forever
fulfilled sometimes never

To fulfill your wishes
just do the dishes

With wishes as big as a mountain
they threw coins into the fountain

Wishful

Wishful thinking
doesn't need blinking

Wishful thinking
happens without blinking

Wishful thinking
not without blinking

Wishful thinking
without once blinking

Wishing

So many years wishing
that we could go fishing

Wishing upon a bone
reminiscing alone

Wit

He is not fit
who is without wit

Within

To see what's within
that's where I've been

Without

Without you how
on the dhow

Witnessed
> The man in the moon
> witnessed them swoon

Wobble
> His legs they wobble
> and mouth it babble

Woe
> Cup of woe
> down to the toe

Woes
> Mosquito has its woes
> spreads malaria to its foes

> Rid yourself of woes
> put paint on your toes

> Wherever she goes
> so do my woes

Woke
> She woke me up from my stupor
> and I felt super duper

Wolverine
> Where have you been
> my sweet wolverine

Woman
> Woman she can
> be smarter than man

Won
> He is a cowboy with a saddle
> that won many a battle

Wonder
> As I sit and wonder
> at the rain and the thunder

> No sense of wonder
> until she heard the thunder

> Product is wonder
> after each blunder

> She was left to wonder
> at her choices of blunder

> Some days I wonder
> why did we blunder

> Some days I wonder
> why the sun goes under

> Sometimes I wonder
> how we avoid blunder

> The world is full of wonder
> down to the last thunder

> To make huge blunder
> and then sit and wonder

> Will always remain a wonder
> how we go from blunder to blunder

Wondered
> Have you ever wondered
> at all the things squandered

Wonderful
> He was a wonderful wit
> that's where he planned to sit

Into it we are hurled
this wide and wonderful world

Wonderful thing
pearls on a string

Wonderful thing
surprise when they spring

Wonderful things
these offerings

Wondering

They kept wondering
why all this pondering

Wonderland

Children must have a hand
in building their wonderland

He who has a hand
in this winter wonderland

Wonders

How to make blunders
into seven wonders

I've seen all the wonders
of life and its blunders

The earths wonders best told
In letters written in gold

Wonders of their craft
were hatched in a raft

Woodpecker

To the tree he talks
the woodpecker when he knocks

Word

A word it is said
just pops into the head

A word once it is said
is perpetually fed

Don't listen to the word
of every mockingbird

Every misplaced word
waiting to be heard

Fewer the word
easier heard

In every word I say
she is in it all the way

Listen to every word
of the mocking bird

Many a word it slips
through her aching lips

Master of the written word
reads out loud to be heard

Not a word I did hear
when she whispered in my ear

She gave him her word
until it was heard

She kept her word
the lady bird

Spread the word
how speech is heard

When you share a word
make sure it is heard

Words

Don't be high strung
as words roll over from the tongue

Each other they cause friction
words arranged without diction

He was prone to mince
words with a wince

His words became all splintered
soon after being uttered

Words

His words were engaging
though in mind he was aging

How the words they tether
to each other

I think of her every day
searching for words to say

I'll give you words to shuffle
so that feathers you can ruffle

Just like the birds
he can think without words

More than I could pen
words were uttered then

Never short of words
describing the birds

Not enough words it is said
to describe the way he bled

Reading glass was tinted
to read words that are printed

Say it with less
words to caress

She curled her lip
and let the words slip

Soars like the birds
sentence with few words

The words fall into rhythms
like the spectrum runs through prisms

The words may not be clear
but the music is what they hear

They mouth the right words
that are mostly for the birds

Thinking without words
not just for the birds

What words should I say
if you decide to go away

When two words have leanings
for opposite meanings

When words were new
and known to few

Words are simply token
so easily broken

Words can charm
and also harm

Words come and sit
to make the best fit

Words fall into place
like they were knitted into lace

Words from the pen and tongue
had him nearly hung

Words from the wise
listen to them twice

Words given a chance
can become song and dance

Words given a chance
can make love and romance

Words have a friend
in him no end

Words he can speak
the parrot with a beak

Words in proper company
result in the best symphony

Words just like lace
with all the holes in place

Words keep their glow
when the creative juices flow

Words need preening
before they go off careening

Words of a feather
to each other they tether

Words so deceptive
how to make them receptive

Words spoken in jest
to bring out the best

Words spoken out of turn
caused many a heart to burn

Words take on meaning
that can be demeaning

Words that cast a spell
have many a story to tell

Words that cast a spell
in lingering memory dwell

Words that keep company
to produce wonderful symphony

Words that make you think
and the lights that make you blink

Words they fall
to beck and call

Words they sit in pairs
like in musical chairs

Words were meant to hide
thoughts that lay inside

Words woven together
in never ending tether

Words you must refrain
that are loaded with pain

Written on every page
the words of a sage

Wore

He wore his clogs
while playing with the dogs

Work

Here comes the setting sun
when the days work is done

His work it has shown
is in a league all its own

Must not be frittered away
things learned in work and play

He works with a light hand
who builds castles in the sand

World

A new world is waiting
where death is awaiting

All the world over
he searched for tasty clover

At us unhurled
the big bad world

Beyond the bend
is a world without end

Caused a world wide trance
as they watched the dance

Find a way of leaving
this world without bereaving

For all the world on a platter
I would not miss her chatter

Half the world is in tatters
from unsolved money matters

He pulled out his performing flea
for all the world to see

He went looking for clover
all the world over

If the world were a kinder place
men would boldly wear lace

In the womb all curled
in a perfect world

Not enough fodder
for a new world order

Once world gets around
people they hound

Once you hit your stride
the world is open wide

The whole world I roam
to finally end up home

The world is a better place
when she wears tunic and lace

The world is full of wonder
until the last blunder

The world is replete
with people who cheat

The world is so mean
where have you been

The world is unforgiving
when it comes to make a living

The world will someday know
the meaning of inferno

There is a better world
where brickbats are not hurled

*There is a part of me
the world will never see*

*They make their home the bugs
in a world full of rugs*

*What a wonderful world
where the centipedes lay curled*

*While we engage with the world
so many things are hurled*

Worm

*One worm to the other
I wish I was covered in feather*

*The chick once he hatch
must have a worm to catch*

Worms

*He opens and squirms
at the can of worms*

Worried

*Worried about swindles
he put his money in bundles*

Worries

*Bears feed on berries
to get rid of worries*

*He who hurries
has no worries*

Worry

*To worry about your attire
when the house is on fire*

*Tons of curry
to rid you of worry*

*Why worry about attire
in a circle of fire*

*Worry is the need
of the worry bead*

Worrying

*Leave the worrying to me
said the honey bee*

*Too much quarrying
is also worrying*

Worse

*For the better or worse
just fill your purse*

*From bad to worse
without money in the purse*

*What can be worse
than a Fridays curse*

*Worse with each drink
to the point where he couldn't think*

Worship

*Object of worship
try not to skip*

Worshipping

*Forever I will be
worshipping thee*

Worst

*The worst is yet to be
in place we cannot see*

*Tyranny comes first
from bad to the worst*

Worth
>Worth going a mile
>to see her elusive smile

Worthy
>From the head to his toe
>he was a worthy foe

>He is no worthy foe
>he has whitlow in his toe

Wound
>A wound can be cured with malt
>not by rubbing to it salt

>Best redress
>is a wound addressed

>How will the pain halt
>if wound is bathed in salt

>Many a wound it gapes
>in the land of the apes

>Wound that is festering
>constantly pestering

Wounded
>With a frown she sounded
>him that she was wounded

Wounds
>Don't stop leading
>when old wounds are bleeding

>Wounds that last
>they don't cure fast

>Wounds will fester
>said the court jester

Wrangle
>Don't tangle
>with all the wrangle

Wrath
>Don't let your wrath
>put hurdles in your path

>Down the primrose path
>engendered all her wrath

>Make sure there is no wrath
>in your chosen path

>To rid you of wrath
>check into hot bath

>When will it come
>this wrath to some

Writer
>Every writer must choose
>how to put words to use

>The making of a writer
>who fits in the words tighter

Writers
>Writers have a wanting
>to receive a bit of prompting

>He writes with his left
>with plenty of deft

Writing
>Good writing
>must be rather inviting

>Writing brings it sheen
>what is said to be seen

    Writing it reminds
    us of the best minds

The waves they lend a hand
to the writings on the sand

Written

    Once it is well written
    it has them all smitten

    Once smitten
    the sonnet is written

    She was smitten
    by the way it was written

    Written all over
    on leaves of clover

Wrong

Better to right a wrong
though the road may be long

If I knew why I was wrong
I could end up quite strong

It is usually the strong
who get it all wrong

Nothing is wrong
it's the singer not the song

Things could go wrong
when the waves and wind are strong

    Why do we long
    for things that are wrong

    Wrong or right
    don't pick a fight

You will say something wrong
if you speak enough long

Wrongdoing

    No need to be suing
    each and every wrongdoing

Y

Yahoo

> Don't look for bahoo
> in a portal called yahoo

Yawn

> A yawn is a feeling
> that can be very revealing

> He stretched into a yawn
> at the break of dawn

> Once the sword is drawn
> don't just stand there and yawn

> Some day it will dawn
> that a yawn is just a yawn

> Wake up to a dawn
> with nothing but a yawn

Yawning

> See you in the morning
> before you start yawning

Yearn

> Many things to yearn
> but no where to turn

Yearning

> This loss of yearning
> how to keep it burning

Years

> In his autumn years
> he goes for beers

Yesterday

> A new day must come
> once yesterday is done

Yield

> Awaiting their yield
> from the poppy field

> For crops to yield
> we must till the field

> Runs you will yield
> if you misfield

> Some they will yield
> to problems on the field

> Survey the field
> to assess the yield

*The blade of grass will yield
to the winds that blow through the field*

*There will be no yield
if you don't plow the field*

Yorker

*Bowl a yorker
at the nosey parker*

Young

*The young and the restless
are so relentless*

*Young and the restless
also very relentless*

*Young lady wore a bonnet
where eggs were laid by the gannet*

Younger

*I have no hunger
to go back to being younger*

Yourself

*All by yourself
cleaning out the shelf*

*At least laugh yourself silly
if you don't have fire in your belly*

*Giant or elf
examine yourself*

*In the company of yourself
you can be a giant or an elf*

*To keep yourself going
got to keep on rowing*

Youth

*They have a long plume
the youth when they bloom*

*What use is youth
spent in a telephone booth*

*Youth aspires
for fancy attires*

*Youth is full of follies
and also some jollies*

Youthful

*The youthful smile
has its own guile*

*The youthful smile
has its own style*

Z

Zeal

*Untold zeal
when tiger sees meal*

HISTORY OF THE COUPLET

ANTIQUITY

"**Shi Jing**" Chinese 10th Century B.C. early evidence of Rhyme
↓

"**Ramayana**" 500 to 100 B.C. by Valmiki 24000 couplets in Sanskrit
↓

"**Mahabharata**" 200 B.C. to 200 A.D. by Vyasa 100,000 couplets in Sanskrit
↓

"**Thirukkural**" Tamil Couplets (Kurals) 200 B.C. to 800 A.D. by Thiruvalluvar 1,330 couplets
↓

"**Shahnameh**" (Persian) 10th Century A.D. by Ferdowsi 50,000 couplets
↓

"**Masnavi-ye-Manavi**" (Persian) by Rumi (1207-1273 A.D) 30,000 couplets
↓

"**Canterbury Tales**" (Old English) couplets by Chaucer (1343- 1400 A.D)
↓

John Gower (1330 – 1408 AD) 34,000 English Couplets
↓

John Dryden (1631 – 1700 A.D) English Couplets
↓

Wali Deccani (1667 – 1707 A.D) Urdu Couplets
↓
Jonathan Swift (1667 – 1745 A.D) English Couplets
↓
Isaac Watts (1674 – 1748 A.D) English Couplets
↓
Alexander Pope (1688 – 1744 A.D) English Couplets
↓
Ghalib (1797 – 1869 A.D) Urdu Couplets
↓
Lewis Carroll (1832 – 1898 A.D) English Couplets
↓
M.R. Shetty (1940) English Couplets 60,000 in 60 months published 2005-2009
"Encylopaedia of Quotable Couplets" (2005)
"Quotable English Couplets"(2007)
"English Couplets" (2007)
Rhyming English Couplets (2009)Volume 4

Index

A

Abandon, 1
Abide, 1
Ability, 1
Able, 1
Abode, 1
Absconded, 1
Absence, 1
Absolutely, 2
Absorbed, 2
Abstinence, 2
Abstruse, 2
Abuse, 2
Accent, 2
Acceptance, 2
Accidents, 2
Acclaim, 2
Accomplished, 2
Accumulate, 2
Accuracy, 2
Accusations, 2
Accused, 2
Accusing, 3
Ace, 3
Acerbic, 3
Aces, 3
Acquainting, 3
Acres, 3
Across, 3
Act, 3
Action, 3
Active, 3
Acumen, 3
Adam, 3

Addiction, 3
Addition, 4
Adept, 4
Adjust, 4
Adjusted, 4
Admire, 4
Admiring, 4
Admonishment, 4
Adorable, 4
Adoration, 4
Adrenal, 4
Adult, 4
Adultery, 4
Adventure, 4
Adversity, 5
Advice, 5
Affable, 5
Affair, 5
Affection, 5
Affinity, 6
Affluent, 6
Afford, 6
Afloat, 6
Afraid, 6
Afternoon, 6
Afterthought, 6
Against, 6
Age, 6
Aged, 8
Aged, 8
Ageing, 8
Agent, 8
Ages, 8
Aggression, 8
Aging, 8

Agony, 8
Agreeing, 8
Agreement, 8
Aided, 8
Ailing, 9
Aim, 9
Aims, 9
Air, 9
Alarming, 9
Alcoholic, 9
Alien, 9
Aligned, 9
Alive, 9
Alley, 9
Aloft, 9
Alone, 9
Alpha, 10
Alphabet, 10
Already, 10
Alter, 10
Always, 10
Amaze, 10
Amazed, 11
Amazing, 11
Ambition, 11
Ambitious, 11
Amends, 11
Amiable, 11
Amuse, 11
Anaconda, 11
Ancestors, 11
Anchor, 11
Anchored, 11
Anew, 11
Angel, 11

Angelic, 12
Anger, 12
Angles, 12
Angry, 12
Annoyance, 12
Answer, 12
Answering, 12
Anxiety, 12
Anything, 12
Anytime, 13
Ape, 13
Appeal, 13
Appeal, 13
Appealing, 13
Appease, 13
Appetite, 13
Applause, 14
Apple, 14
Appliance, 14
Appreciate, 14
Approach, 14
Approval, 14
Approve, 14
Aptitude, 14
Arabia, 14
Arabian, 14
Arched, 14
Arctic, 15
Argument, 15
Army, 15
Aroma, 15
Arrange, 15
Arrival, 15
Arrived, 15
Arrogance, 15

Index

Arrogant, 15
Arrow, 15
Arteries, 15
Ashamed, 15
Ashore, 16
Ask, 16
Asked, 16
Asleep, 16
Asphalt, 16
Assault, 16
Assess, 16
Assurances, 16
Astray, 16
Ate, 16
Atonement, 16
Attached, 16
Attachment, 16
Attack, 16
Attention, 17
Attentive, 17
Attire, 17
Attired, 17
Attitude, 17
Attracted, 18
Attraction, 18
Attracts, 18
Attributes, 18
Audience, 18
Author, 18
Authority, 18
Autocrat, 18
Autumn, 18
Avenge, 19
Averse, 19
Avid, 19
Avoiding, 19
Awake, 19
Awaken, 19
Aware, 19
Awareness, 19
Away, 19
Awe, 19
Awesome, 19
Awful, 19
Awhile, 19
Awkward, 19

B

Babies, 20
Baby, 20
Bachelor, 20
Back, 20
Backed, 20
Backroom, 20
Bad, 20
Badly, 20
Baiting, 20
Baked, 21
Bakes, 21
Balance, 21
Balanced, 21
Balancing, 21
Bald, 21
Ball, 21
Ballot, 21
Ban, 21
Banana, 21
Band, 21
Bandit, 21
Banished, 21
Bank, 21
Barber, 21
Bare, 21
Barefoot, 21
Bargain, 21
Bark, 21
Barn, 22
Barter, 22
Bash, 22
Bats, 22
Batsmen, 22
Battle, 22
Battlefields, 22
Battles, 22
Bay, 22
Beached, 22
Beaks, 22
Beamer, 22
Beaming, 22
Beans, 22
Beard, 23
Bearded, 23
Beast, 23

Beat, 23
Beats, 23
Beautiful, 23
Beauty, 24
Bed, 24
Bee, 24
Bee-hive, 24
Beer, 24
Before, 24
Beginning, 25
Begs, 25
Behave, 25
Behaved, 25
Behaves, 25
Behaving, 25
Behaviour, 25
Behind, 26
Behold, 26
Beholden, 26
Beholder, 26
Belief, 26
Believe, 26
Belittle, 26
Belong, 26
Belonging, 26
Bend, 26
Bended, 27
Beneath, 27
Benefits, 27
Berated, 27
Beside, 27
Best, 27
Bet, 28
Betray, 28
Betrayal, 28
Betrayed, 28
Better, 28
Between, 29
Beware, 29
Beyond, 29
Bidding, 29
Big, 29
Binding, 29
Biography, 29
Bird, 29
Birth, 30
Birthday, 30

Bit, 30
Bites, 30
Biting, 30
Bitter, 30
Bitterness, 30
Blackboard, 30
Blame, 31
Bland, 31
Blank, 31
Bleach, 31
Bleary, 31
Bled, 31
Bleed, 31
Blend, 31
Blending, 32
Bless, 32
Blessed, 32
Blessing, 32
Blind, 32
Blinded, 33
Blindfold, 33
Blinding, 33
Blindness, 33
Blinds, 33
Blink, 33
Blinking, 34
Bliss, 34
Blood, 34
Blooded, 34
Bloodshed, 35
Bloody, 35
Bloom, 35
Blossom, 35
Blossomed, 35
Blot, 35
Blow, 35
Blows, 35
Blue, 35
Bluff, 36
Blunder, 36
Blurred, 36
Body, 36
Bold, 36
Bolder, 37
Bolt, 37
Bonding, 37
Bone, 37

Book, 37
Boom, 37
Border, 38
Bore, 38
Bored, 38
Boredom, 38
Boring, 38
Born, 38
Borrow, 39
Borrowed, 39
Borrower, 39
Bother, 39
Bottom, 39
Bought, 39
Boulder, 39
Bouncer, 39
Bound, 39
Boundless, 39
Bowler, 39
Brain, 39
Brand, 40
Brandish, 41
Brands, 41
Brave, 41
Bravely, 41
Bravery, 41
Braves, 41
Bread, 41
Break, 41
Breakdown, 41
Breath, 41
Breathe, 41
Breaths, 41
Breed, 42
Breeder, 42
Breeding, 42
Breeds, 42
Breeze, 42
Brevity, 42
Brew, 42
Brewed, 42
Bribes, 42
Bride, 42
Bridge, 42
Brief, 43
Briefcase, 43

Bright, 43
Brighten, 43
Brightened, 43
Brightest, 43
Brightness, 43
Brilliant, 43
Brisker, 44
Brittle, 44
Broke, 44
Broken, 44
Brook, 44
Broom, 44
Brother, 44
Brought, 44
Browser, 44
Brunch, 44
Brunette, 44
Brute, 44
Bubbles, 44
Buck, 44
Bud, 44
Buddies, 45
Budding, 45
Buddy, 45
Budged, 45
Build, 45
Bullet, 45
Bully, 45
Bumper, 45
Bumpy, 45
Bungle, 45
Burden, 45
Buried, 45
Burn, 45
Burning, 46
Burst, 46
Business, 46
Busters, 46
Busy, 46
Butterflies, 46
Butterfly, 46
Buy, 46
Buzz, 46
Bye, 46

C

Cage, 47
Caged, 47
Calamity, 47
Calcium, 47
Calendar, 47
Calling, 47
Callous, 47
Calm, 47
Calmer, 48
Camp, 48
Campfire, 48
Campus, 48
Can, 48
Candle, 48
Canister, 48
Canoe, 48
Cantering, 48
Capacious, 48
Capacity, 48
Captivating, 48
Capture, 48
Care, 48
Career, 49
Careful, 49
Carefully, 49
Careless, 49
Carelessly, 50
Cares, 50
Caress, 50
Caressings, 50
Caring, 50
Carnival, 50
Carousers, 50
Carry, 50
Cars, 50
Case, 50
Cash, 50
Castle, 50
Casual, 51
Cat, 51
Catch up, 51
Cattle, 51
Caught, 51
Cause, 51
Caves, 51

Cease, 51
Ceases, 52
Celebrate, 52
Celebration, 52
Cement, 52
Center, 52
Century, 52
Certain, 52
Chalice, 52
Champagne, 52
Chance, 52
Change, 53
Changing, 53
Channels, 53
Character, 53
Charge, 53
Charger, 53
Charitable, 53
Charity, 53
Charm, 53
Charmed, 54
Charmer, 54
Charming, 54
Charms, 54
Chase, 54
Chasing, 55
Chat, 55
Chatter, 55
Chattering, 55
Chatting, 55
Cheap, 55
Cheat, 55
Cheating, 55
Cheats, 55
Checking, 55
Cheeks, 55
Cheer, 56
Cheerful, 56
Cheers, 56
Chest, 56
Chew, 56
Chicken, 56
Chicks, 56
Chide, 56
Chiding, 56
Child, 56
Childhood, 56

Index

Children, 56
Chilli, 56
China, 57
Chip, 57
Chirp, 57
Chocolates, 57
Choice, 57
Cholera, 58
Choose, 58
Choosing, 58
Chords, 58
Chore, 58
Chose, 58
Chosen, 58
Church, 58
Churning, 58
Cigarette, 58
Circumspect, 58
Circumstances, 58
City, 58
Civilization, 59
Civilized, 59
Claimed, 59
Clairvoyant, 59
Clarity, 59
Clash, 59
Class, 59
Classes, 59
Clause, 59
Clawed, 59
Clean, 59
Cleanliness, 60
Clear, 60
Cleft, 60
Clever, 60
Cleverly, 60
Cleverness, 60
Clients, 60
Climbs, 60
Clock, 61
Clockface, 61
Cloistered, 61
Clone, 61
Close, 61
Closer, 61
Closet, 61
Cloud, 61

Cloven, 61
Clover, 61
Clown, 61
Cluck, 61
Clucked, 61
Clue, 61
Clutch, 62
Coalfires, 62
Coffin, 62
Coherence, 62
Coiled, 62
Coin, 62
Cold, 62
Collection, 62
Collusion, 62
Colour, 62
Colourful, 62
Columbus, 62
Combines, 63
Come, 63
Comedy, 63
Comfort, 63
Comfortable, 63
Comical, 63
Command, 63
Commander, 63
Commas, 63
Comment, 63
Commit, 63
Common, 63
Commotion, 63
Company, 63
Compared, 64
Compassion, 64
Compassionate, 64
Competent, 64
Competition, 64
Complain, 64
Complaint, 64
Complicated, 64
Compliment, 64
Composed, 64
Composition, 64
Composure, 64
Compromise, 64
Compulsion, 65
Compulsive, 65

Conceal, 65
Conceit, 65
Concentrated, 65
Concept, 65
Concerns, 65
Concessions, 65
Conclusion, 65
Concrete, 65
Conditions, 65
Confess, 65
Confession, 65
Confessional, 66
Confidence, 66
Confident, 66
Confines, 66
Conflict, 66
Conform, 66
Confront, 66
Confronted, 66
Confronting, 66
Confused, 66
Confusion, 66
Conical, 66
Conquer, 67
Conquest, 67
Conscience, 67
Conscious, 68
Consciousness, 68
Consequences, 68
Considerable, 68
Considers, 68
Consoling, 68
Constantly, 68
Constitution, 68
Consume, 68
Consumption, 68
Contact, 68
Contagious, 69
Contemplate, 69
Contemplation, 69
Contender, 69
Contentment, 69
Contracts, 69
Control, 69
Controlled, 69
Controversy, 69
Convenient, 69

Convention, 69
Converging, 69
Convert, 69
Conveys, 69
Convictions, 69
Convincing, 69
Cook, 70
Cooking, 70
Cool, 70
Corals, 70
Cordials, 70
Cornered, 70
Corporate, 70
Correction, 70
Corridors, 70
Corrosion, 70
Corruption, 70
Cosmetic, 70
Cost, 70
Cosy, 70
Cottage, 70
Couch, 70
Counted, 70
Counting, 71
Country, 71
Couple, 71
Couplets, 71
Courage, 71
Courier, 71
Course, 71
Coverage, 72
Coward, 72
Cowardice, 72
Cowboy, 72
Cozy, 72
Crab, 72
Cracked, 72
Craft, 72
Cranes, 72
Crawl, 72
Creaking, 72
Creaky, 72
Crease, 72
Creative, 72
Creatively, 73
Creativity, 73
Creature, 73

595

Credit, 73
Cricket, 73
Cried, 73
Cries, 73
Crime, 73
Crimes, 73
Crisp, 73
Crisper, 73
Critically, 73
Critics, 74
Crocodile, 74
Crossroads, 74
Crowd, 74
Crown, 74
Cruel, 74
Cruelty, 74
Cruise, 74
Crushes, 74
Crutch, 74
Cry, 75
Crying, 75
Cryptic, 75
Crystal, 75
Cue, 75
Cultivate, 75
Cultivates, 75
Cultivation, 75
Culture, 75
Cunning, 75
Cunningness, 76
Cure, 76
Cured, 76
Cures, 76
Curiosity, 77
Curl, 77
Currency, 77
Current, 77
Curse, 77
Cursed, 77
Curses, 77
Curtain, 77
Curve, 78
Custom, 78
Customer, 78
Cute, 78
Cynical, 78

D

Dad, 79
Dagger, 79
Daily, 79
Dame, 79
Dance, 79
Dancing, 80
Danger, 80
Dangerous, 80
Dangers, 80
Dare, 80
Dares, 80
Daring, 80
Dark, 80
Darker, 80
Darkest, 81
Darkness, 81
Darling, 81
Date, 81
Daughter, 81
Dawn, 81
Day, 81
Daydreams, 82
Daylight, 82
Days, 82
Daytime, 82
Dead, 82
Deadliest, 83
Deadline, 83
Deadlines, 83
Deadly, 83
Deaf, 83
Deal, 83
Dealing, 84
Dealt, 84
Dear, 84
Death, 84
Deathbed, 87
Deathly, 87
Deaths, 87
Debate, 87
Debt, 88
Debts, 88
Decaffeinated, 88
Deceit, 88
Deceive, 88

December, 88
Deception, 88
Decided, 88
Decision, 88
Declined, 89
Declining, 89
Decorate, 89
Decry, 89
Dedication, 89
Deed, 89
Deeds, 89
Deep, 89
Deeper, 90
Defanged, 90
Defeat, 90
Defeated, 90
Defeating, 90
Defeatist, 90
Defence, 90
Defend, 91
Defensive, 91
Defies, 91
Defined, 91
Defy, 91
Degenerate, 91
Delicate, 91
Delight, 91
Delightful, 92
Delightfully, 92
Delighting, 92
Delights, 92
Deluded, 92
Delving, 92
Demand, 92
Demanding, 92
Demon, 93
Den, 93
Denial, 93
Deny, 93
Denying, 93
Depending, 93
Depends, 93
Deployed, 93
Depressed, 93
Depression, 93
Depths, 94
Derail, 94

Describe, 94
Desert, 94
Deserve, 94
Deserving, 94
Designer, 94
Designs, 94
Designs, 94
Desire, 94
Desired, 96
Desires, 96
Desolation, 97
Despair, 97
Desperation, 97
Despise, 97
Despite, 97
Destinies, 97
Destiny, 97
Destroy, 97
Destruction, 97
Destructive, 98
Detached, 98
Detached, 98
Detail, 98
Detest, 98
Develop, 98
Developed, 98
Devices, 98
Devil, 98
Devoted, 99
Devotion, 99
Devour, 99
Devouring, 99
Dew, 99
Dialogue, 99
Diamond, 99
Dictatorships, 100
Die, 100
Died, 101
Dies, 102
Diet, 102
Differences, 102
Different, 102
Difficult, 102
Dignity, 102
Digression, 102
Dim, 102
Dine, 102

Diner, 102
Dinner, 102
Dinosaurs, 103
Diplomacy, 103
Dire, 103
Dirty, 103
Disagreements, 103
Disappear, 103
Disappointingly, 103
Disarray, 103
Disaster, 103
Discard, 103
Discipline, 103
Discomfort, 104
Discontent, 104
Discounted, 104
Discoveries, 104
Discreet, 104
Discrete, 104
Disease, 104
Disgrace, 104
Disgrace, 104
Disguise, 104
Disgust, 104
Dish, 104
Dishonesty, 104
Dismount, 104
Disorder, 105
Disown, 105
Dispelling, 105
Display, 105
Dissensions, 105
Dissent, 105
Dissenting, 105
Dissolve, 105
Distance, 105
Distant, 105
Distinct, 106
Distortions, 106
Distraction, 106
Distress, 106
Distressed, 107
Distribute, 107
Disturbed, 107
Disturbing, 107
Divergent, 107

Diverted, 107
Divide, 107
Dividends, 107
Divine, 107
Divorce, 107
Dog, 108
Domain, 108
Donate, 108
Donations, 108
Done, 108
Doubt, 108
Doubted, 109
Down, 109
Down, 109
Down, 109
Dragon, 110
Drain, 110
Drained, 110
Drank, 110
Drawn, 110
Dreads, 110
Dream, 110
Dreamer, 112
Dreamless, 112
Dreams, 112
Dreamt, 114
Dreamy, 114
Dressed, 114
Dried, 114
Drink, 114
Drinking, 115
Drive, 115
Drone, 115
Drooped, 115
Drop, 115
Droplets, 115
Dropped, 115
Drought, 115
Drowned, 115
Drum, 115
Drumsticks, 115
Drunk, 116
Drunkard, 116
Drunken, 116
Dry, 116
Ducklings, 116
Due, 116

Dull, 116
Dumb, 116
Dust, 116
Dutiful, 116
Duty, 116
Dwell, 117
Dweller, 117
Dying, 117

E

Eager, 118
Eagle, 118
Eagles, 118
Early, 118
Ears, 118
Earth, 118
Earthly, 119
Ease, 119
Easier, 119
Easy, 119
Eat, 119
Eating, 119
Eats, 119
Eavesdropping, 119
Echo, 119
Economic, 119
Economies, 119
Economy, 120
Ecstasy, 120
Ecstatic, 120
Eden, 120
Effective, 120
Efforts, 120
Egg, 120
Ego, 120
Egret, 120
Elaborate, 120
Elegance, 120
Elegant, 120
Elegantly, 120
Elephant, 120
Elf, 121
Elope, 121
Eloquence, 121
Else, 121

Emotion, 121
Emotional, 122
Emotionally, 122
Emotions, 122
Emperor, 122
Empire, 122
Empires, 122
Employ, 122
Emptily, 122
Empty, 123
Enchanting, 123
Encouraged, 123
Encumbrance, 123
End, 123
Endearing, 123
Ending, 123
Endless, 123
Ends, 124
Endurance, 124
Endure, 124
Enemies, 124
Enemy, 124
Energetic, 124
Energies, 124
Energy, 124
Engagement, 124
Engaging, 124
Enjoy, 124
Enraptured, 125
Enslave, 125
Entail, 125
Entertained, 125
Entertaining, 125
Entice, 125
Enticing, 125
Entrusted, 125
Envious, 125
Epidemics, 125
Episode, 125
Equality, 125
Equations, 125
Erase, 125
Erased, 125
Erotic, 125
Error, 125
Escape, 125
Escape, 125

Escaped, 126
Especially, 126
Essence, 126
Esteem, 126
Eternal, 126
Eternity, 126
Ethic, 126
Eve, 126
Even, 126
Evening, 126
Everlasting, 127
Everyone, 127
Everything, 127
Everytime, 127
Evidence, 127
Evil, 127
Evolution, 128
Examine, 128
Example, 128
Exchange, 128
Exchanging, 128
Excited, 128
Excitement, 128
Exciting, 128
Excursions, 128
Excuse, 128
Exercise, 129
Expanses, 129
Expect, 129
Expectation, 129
Expendable, 129
Expended, 129
Expensive, 129
Experience, 130
Experiment, 130
Experimentation, 130
Explain, 130
Explaining, 131
Expression, 131
Extinct, 131
Extravagant, 131
Extreme, 131
Eye, 131
Eyelids, 131
Eyes, 131
Eylids, 131

F

Fable, 132
Fabric, 132
Face, 132
Facial, 133
Facility, 133
Fact, 133
Fade, 133
Faded, 133
Fading, 133
Fail, 134
Failed, 134
Failing, 134
Fails, 134
Failure, 134
Faint, 134
Fainted, 134
Faintest, 135
Faintly, 135
Fair, 135
Fairies, 135
Fairy, 135
Faith, 135
Faithful, 135
Faithfully, 135
Fake, 135
Fall, 135
Fallen, 136
Falling, 136
False, 136
Faltered, 136
Fame, 136
Familiar, 136
Family, 136
Famine, 136
Famous, 136
Fanciful, 137
Fancy, 137
Fans, 137
Fantasies, 137
Fantasy, 137
Far, 137
Fare, 137
Farewell, 137
Farm, 137
Fashion, 137

Fast, 137
Faster, 138
Fatal, 138
Fatal, 138
Fate, 138
Fateful, 139
Fates, 139
Fault, 139
Favour, 140
Fear, 140
Feared, 143
Fearful, 143
Fearless, 143
Fears, 144
Fearsome, 145
Feast, 145
Feasting, 145
Feather, 145
Fed, 145
Feed, 146
Feeding, 146
Feel, 146
Feeling, 147
Feels, 149
Feet, 149
Feline, 149
Fell, 149
Felt, 149
Fence, 149
Fences, 149
Ferocious, 149
Fetching, 150
Feted, 150
Fever, 150
Few, 150
Fickle, 150
Fiction, 150
Fidelity, 150
Fidelity, 150
Fierce, 150
Fight, 150
Fighting, 151
Fights, 151
Fill, 151
Filled, 151
Final, 151
Financial, 151

Financially, 151
Find, 151
Fine, 151
Finger, 151
Fingertips, 151
Finish, 151
Finishing, 152
Finite, 152
Fins, 152
Fire, 152
Fireflies, 152
Fireproof, 152
Fires, 152
Fireside, 152
Firmly, 152
First, 152
Fish, 153
Fishing, 153
Fist, 153
Fit, 153
Fitness, 153
Fitted, 153
Fix, 153
Flail, 153
Flail, 153
Flair, 153
Flak, 154
Flake, 154
Flame, 154
Flames, 154
Flamingos, 154
Flash, 154
Flashed, 154
Flatter, 154
Flattered, 154
Flattering, 154
Flaunt, 155
Flavour, 155
Flawless, 155
Flea, 155
Fleece, 155
Flicker, 155
Flickered, 155
Flight, 155
Flightless, 156
Flights, 156
Flighty, 156

Index

Flirt, 156
Flirting, 156
Float, 156
Floating, 156
Flock, 156
Flora, 156
Flounder, 156
Flourish, 156
Flower, 156
Flowering, 157
Flowers, 157
Flowing, 157
Flows, 158
Flu, 158
Fluorescent, 158
Flushing, 158
Fluster, 158
Flustered, 158
Flutter, 158
Fluttering, 158
Fly, 158
Flycatcher, 158
Flying, 158
Flytrap, 159
Focus, 159
Focused, 159
Focussing, 159
Foils, 159
Fold, 159
Folded, 159
Follow, 159
Fond, 159
Fonder, 159
Fondly, 159
Fondness, 159
Food, 159
Fooled, 160
Foolish, 160
Fools, 160
Footprints, 160
Footsteps, 160
Forbidden, 160
Force, 160
Forced, 161
Forecast, 161
Forest, 161
Foretelling, 161

Forever, 161
Forfeited, 161
Forget, 161
Forgetting, 162
Forgive, 162
Forgiveness, 162
Forgiving, 162
Forgot, 162
Forgotten, 162
Fork, 163
Formal, 163
Fortitude, 163
Fortunate, 163
Fortune, 163
Forward, 163
Foul, 163
Found, 164
Fountain, 164
Fours, 164
Fox, 164
Fragile, 164
Fragrance, 164
Fragrant, 165
Frail, 165
Frame, 165
Frangrance, 165
Fraudulent, 165
Freak, 165
Freckled, 165
Freckles, 165
Free, 165
Freedom, 167
Freely, 168
Freeze, 168
French, 168
Frenetic, 168
Frequently, 168
Fresh, 168
Friction, 168
Friend, 169
Friendless, 169
Friendly, 169
Friends, 170
Friendship, 170
Fright, 171
Frightened, 171
Frisky, 171

Frolicking, 171
Front, 171
Frosting, 171
Frown, 171
Frozen, 171
Frugal, 171
Frugality, 172
Fruit, 172
Frustration, 172
Fulfilled, 172
Fun, 172
Function, 174
Funeral, 174
Funny, 174
Furious, 174
Furniture, 174
Fury, 174
Fuse, 174
Fuss, 174
Future, 175

G

Gadfly, 177
Gain, 177
Gallop, 177
Gambling, 177
Game, 177
Gander, 178
Gangrene, 178
Gasping, 178
Gather, 178
Gathering, 178
Gaze, 178
Gears, 178
Gender, 178
Generally, 178
Generosity, 178
Generosity, 178
Gentle, 178
Germinate, 178
Germination, 179
Germs, 179
Gesture, 179
Get, 179
Ghost, 179
Giant, 179

Gift, 179
Gifted, 180
Giggle, 180
Gin, 180
Girl, 180
Girth, 180
Glad, 180
Gladder, 180
Glamour, 180
Glance, 180
Glancing, 180
Gland, 180
Glare, 180
Glides, 181
Glitter, 181
Glitter, 181
Glittering, 181
Globe, 181
Gloom, 181
Glories, 181
Glorious, 181
Glory, 182
Glossies, 182
Glow, 182
Glowing, 182
Goal, 182
God, 182
Goddess, 185
Godforsaken, 185
Godless, 185
Gods, 185
Godsend, 186
Gold, 186
Golden, 186
Good, 186
Goodness, 186
Goodwill, 186
Gorilla, 186
Gorillas, 186
Gossip, 186
Gossips, 186
Governess, 186
Grab, 187
Grace, 187
Graces, 187
Gracious, 187
Graduated, 187

Graduation, 187
Grammar, 187
Grand, 188
Grandiose, 188
Granted, 188
Grasp, 188
Gratitude, 188
Grave, 188
Gravel, 188
Graveled, 188
Gravestone, 188
Gray, 188
Grease, 189
Greasy, 189
Great, 189
Greed, 189
Greedy, 189
Greek, 189
Green, 190
Greet, 190
Greeting, 191
Greetings, 191
Greets, 191
Grew, 191
Grey, 191
Grief, 191
Grieves, 191
Grieving, 192
Grin, 192
Grinds, 192
Grip, 192
Gripe, 192
Gritty, 192
Groom, 192
Ground, 192
Group, 192
Grouped, 192
Grow, 192
Growing, 192
Growl, 192
Grown, 192
Growth, 193
Grudge, 193
Gruel, 193
Guess, 193
Guest, 193
Guidance, 193

Guiding, 193
Guilt, 193
Guitar, 193
Gulf, 193
Gunfight, 193
Gunslingers, 194
Guts, 194
Guzzle, 194
Guzzled, 194
Guzzling, 194
Gym, 194

H

Habbit, 195
Hair, 196
Half, 196
Halfway, 196
Halves, 196
Hamlet, 196
Hand, 196
Handshake, 196
Hang, 196
Hanging, 196
Happening, 196
Happiest, 196
Happiness, 196
Happy, 198
Hard, 198
Hardest, 199
Hare, 199
Harm, 199
Harmed, 199
Harmful, 199
Harms, 199
Harried, 199
Harshness, 199
Harvest, 199
Haste, 199
Hat, 199
Hatch, 199
Hatched, 200
Hatches, 200
Hate, 200
Haul, 200
Hauling, 200
Haunt, 200

Haunting, 200
Haven, 200
Having, 200
Hawking, 200
Head, 200
Head, 200
Headache, 201
Heads, 201
Heal, 201
Healing, 201
Healing, 201
Healing, 201
Health, 201
Healthy, 201
Heap, 201
Hear, 202
Heard, 202
Hearing, 202
Hears, 202
Heart, 203
Heart, 203
Heartache, 213
Heartbeat, 213
Heartbreaks, 213
Heartburn, 214
Hearted, 214
Heartfelt, 214
Heartful, 214
Heartless, 214
Hearts, 214
Hearty, 215
Heat, 216
Heaven, 216
Heavenly, 217
Heavens, 218
Heaviest, 218
Heavily, 218
Heaviness, 218
Heavy, 218
Hefty, 218
Heights, 218
Hell, 218
Help, 218
Helpless, 218
Hermits, 219
Hesitates, 219
Hidden, 219

Hide, 219
Hiding, 219
High, 219
Himself, 219
Historical, 219
History, 219
Hitch, 220
Hitched, 220
Hitches, 220
Hold, 220
Holding, 220
Hole, 220
Holiday, 220
Holy, 220
Home, 220
Homely, 220
Homeward, 221
Honest, 221
Honesty, 221
Honey, 221
Honeydew, 221
Honeymoon, 221
Honoured, 221
Hooked, 221
Hope, 221
Hopeless, 223
Hopes, 223
Hopped, 223
Hormone, 223
Hormones, 223
Horn, 223
Horn, 223
Horns, 223
Horoscopes, 223
Horses, 223
Host, 223
Hostile, 223
Hot, 223
Hours, 223
House, 223
Housewife's, 224
Huddle, 224
Hug, 224
Hugged, 224
Human, 224
Humanised, 224
Humans, 224

Index

Humble, 225
Hummer, 225
Humming, 225
Humor, 225
Humour, 225
Hump, 225
Hunches, 225
Hundred, 225
Hung, 225
Hungry, 225
Hunt, 225
Hunted, 225
Hunter, 225
Hunting, 225
Hunts, 226
Hurricanes, 226
Hurry, 226
Hurt, 226
Hurts, 226
Husband, 226
Hush, 226
Hype, 226
Hype, 226
Hyperbole, 226
Hypocrisy, 227
Hypothetical, 227

I

Ice, 228
Iceberg, 228
Icing, 228
Idea, 228
Ideals, 228
Ideas, 228
Idiotic, 228
Idle, 228
Idling, 229
Idly, 229
Ignited, 229
Ignorance, 229
Ignorant, 229
Ignore, 229
Ignoring, 229
Ill, 229
Illness, 229
Illnesses, 230

Illusion, 230
Imagery, 230
Images, 230
Imagination, 230
Immature, 230
Immense, 231
Immortal, 231
Immortality, 231
Impatiently, 231
Impending, 231
Imperfect, 231
Imperfection, 231
Imperfections, 231
Imperious, 231
Implication, 231
Implicit, 231
Implied, 231
Impositions, 231
Impossible, 231
Imposters, 231
Impression, 232
Improbable, 232
Improper, 232
Impropriety, 232
Improve, 232
Impulse, 232
Impulsive, 232
Impulsiveness, 232
Incense, 232
Incessant, 232
Inches, 232
Income, 232
Incompetence, 232
Incomplete, 232
Incompetence, 233
Inconvenient, 233
Incorruptible, 233
Increase, 233
Increased, 233
Increases, 233
Indecision, 233
Indelible, 233
Indelible, 233
Independent, 233
Indifferent, 233
Indiscreet, 233
Indiscretions, 233

Individual, 233
Induct, 233
Indulge, 233
Indulgent, 233
Ineptitude, 234
Inevitable, 234
Infantile, 234
Infatuation, 234
Infective, 234
Infested, 234
Infidelity, 234
Infinity, 234
Inflation, 234
Information, 234
Ingratitude, 234
Inherit, 234
Inheritance, 234
Inhibition, 234
Inhumanity, 234
Initial, 235
Injury, 235
Injustice, 235
Ink, 235
Innocence, 235
Innocent, 235
Insane, 235
Insanity, 235
Insecure, 235
Insensitive, 235
Insight, 235
Inspired, 235
Instant, 235
Instead, 235
Instinct, 236
Instinctual, 236
Insults, 236
Intact, 236
Integrity, 236
Intellectual, 236
Intemperance, 236
Intemperate, 236
Intense, 236
Intensity, 236
Intentions, 236
Interact, 236
Interest, 237
Interesting, 237

Interference, 237
Interpret, 237
Interpreter, 237
Interrupts, 237
Intervention, 237
Intimacy, 237
Intimate, 237
Intoxicated, 237
Introduction, 237
Introspection, 237
Invade, 237
Invented, 237
Invention, 237
Investments, 237
Invincibility, 238
Invisible, 238
Invitation, 238
Invite, 238
Inviting, 238
Invoke, 238
Invulnerable, 238
Irate, 238
Ire, 238
Ironical, 238
Ironist, 238
Irony, 238
Irrational, 239
Irregularity, 239
Irresistible, 239
Irreverent, 239
Island, 239
Itch, 239

J

Jealous, 240
Jealousy, 240
Jellyfish, 241
Jerks, 241
Jingles, 241
Job, 241
Joke, 241
Jolly, 241
Journey, 241
Journey, 241
Joy, 242
Joys, 242

Judge, 242
Judged, 242
Judgement, 242
Judicial, 243
Juice, 243
Juices, 243
July, 243
Jumper, 243
Jumping, 243
Jumpstart, 243
Juncture, 243
Jungles, 243
Justice, 243

K

Kangaroo, 244
Keen, 244
Kept, 244
Key, 244
Kick, 244
Kill, 244
Killer, 244
Kills, 244
Kind, 245
Kinder, 245
Kindness, 245
Kinds, 246
King, 246
Kingdom, 246
Kingfisher, 246
Kings, 246
Kiss, 246
Knees, 246
Knight, 246
Knighted, 246
Knock, 246
Knots, 247
Know, 247
Knowing, 247
Knowledge, 247

L

Labour, 248
Lace, 248
Lacking, 248
Laid, 248
Lake, 248
Lame, 248
Lament, 248
Land, 248
Landscape, 248
Language, 248
Last, 249
Lasting, 249
Late, 249
Lately, 250
Latent, 250
Laughter, 250
Lavish, 250
Lavishness, 250
Law, 250
Lawsuits, 251
Lay, 251
Laying, 251
Lays, 251
Lazier, 251
Lazy, 251
Lead, 251
Leader, 251
Leaf, 252
League, 252
Leaguer, 252
Leak, 252
Leaks, 252
Lean, 252
Leaning, 252
Leap, 252
Learn, 252
Learn, 252
Learned, 253
Learning, 253
Learns, 253
Leave, 253
Left, 254
Legal, 254
Legally, 254
Legend, 254
Legend, 254
Leisure, 254
Lend, 254
Less, 254
Lessen, 254
Lesson, 254
Letter, 254
Liable, 255
Liar, 255
Liberty, 255
License, 255
Lie, 255
Lied, 255
Lies, 256
Life, 256
Lifelong, 263
Lifespan, 263
Lifestyle, 263
Lifetime, 263
Lifting, 263
Light, 263
Lighthouse, 264
Lightning, 264
Like, 264
Limit, 264
Linguistic, 264
Link, 264
Lions, 264
Lipped, 264
Liquor, 265
List, 265
Listen, 265
Listened, 265
Literature, 265
Little, 265
Live, 265
Lived, 266
Liver, 266
Lives, 266
Living, 267
Living, 267
Lizard, 267
Loan, 267
Lock, 267
Logic, 267
Loneliness, 267
Lonely, 267
Lonesome, 268
Longing, 268
Look, 268
Look, 268
Looks, 268
Loon, 269
Loopholes, 269
Looseness, 269
Loot, 269
Loots, 269
Lord, 269
Lose, 269
Loss, 269
Losses, 269
Lost, 269
Lotion, 270
Lotus, 270
Lotuses, 270
Loud, 270
Love, 270
Lovebirds, 324
Loved, 324
Loveless, 324
Loveliness, 325
Lovely, 325
Lover, 325
Loves, 325
Loving, 327
Lovingly, 327
Loyal, 327
Loyalties, 327
Loyalty, 327
Luck, 327
Luckiest, 328
Lucky, 328
Lumbers, 328
Luminous, 328
Lunatic, 328
Lunch, 328
Lure, 328
Lures, 328
Lurks, 328
Luster, 328
Lustre, 329
Lustrous, 329
Luxurious, 329
Luxury, 329
Lying, 329
Lyre, 329

M

Machine, 330

Index 603

Macon, 330
Made, 330
Madness, 330
Magic, 330
Magical, 331
Magnificent, 331
Magnify, 331
Maid, 331
Majestic, 331
Majesty, 331
Make, 331
Makeover, 331
Maker, 331
Male, 331
Malice, 331
Malicious, 331
Mammal, 331
Man, 331
Manipulate, 332
Mankind's, 332
Manner, 332
Mantelpiece, 332
March, 332
Mares, 332
Marginal, 332
Marigold, 332
Marital, 332
Market, 332
Marriage, 332
Married, 333
Marrow, 334
Marry, 334
Mask, 334
Master, 334
Mastered, 334
Mastery, 334
Matador, 334
Match, 335
Match, 335
Material, 335
Maternal, 335
Maternity, 335
Mathematical, 335
Matrimony, 335
Matter, 335
Me, 335
Meal, 335

Mean, 335
Meander, 336
Meaner, 336
Meaning, 336
Meaningful, 336
Meaningless, 336
Means, 336
Meant, 337
Measure, 337
Medal, 337
Medicine, 337
Mediocrity, 337
Medium, 337
Meek, 338
Meet, 338
Meeting, 338
Meets, 338
Mellow, 338
Melodies, 338
Memories, 338
Memory, 341
Men, 343
Mend, 343
Mendacity, 344
Mended, 344
Mending, 344
Mends, 344
Mental, 344
Mental, 344
Mention, 344
Mentor, 344
Merciful, 344
Mercifully, 344
Merciless, 344
Mercy, 344
Mermaid, 345
Merry, 345
Mesmerizing, 345
Mess, 345
Message, 345
Metal, 346
Metaphor, 346
Methods, 346
Metric, 346
Midnight, 346
Might, 346
Mighty, 346

Mild, 347
Miles, 347
Milkman, 347
Million, 347
Mind, 347
Mindedly, 351
Mindful, 351
Mindless, 351
Minds, 351
Mine, 351
Miner, 351
Mingle, 351
Mint, 351
Minute, 351
Miracle, 352
Mirror, 352
Mirthful, 352
Misadventure, 352
Misbehaves, 352
Mischief, 352
Miseries, 352
Misery, 352
Misfortune, 352
Misguided, 352
Mislead, 352
Misleading, 353
Misplaced, 353
Miss, 353
Missed, 353
Missing, 353
Mission, 353
Missionary, 353
Misspoken, 353
Mist, 353
Mistake, 353
Mistaken, 354
Mistakes, 354
Mistook, 354
Misunderstanding, 354
Misuse, 354
Moan, 355
Mob, 355
Moderation, 355
Modest, 355
Moment, 355
Momentary, 355

Moments, 355
Money, 355
Monk, 357
Monogamy, 357
Monster, 358
Mood, 358
Moon, 358
Moonlight, 358
Moral, 358
Moribund, 359
Morn, 359
Morning, 359
Morrow, 360
Mosquitoes, 360
Mother, 360
Motion, 360
Motives, 360
Mould, 360
Mountain, 360
Mountainous, 360
Mountains, 360
Mouth, 361
Move, 361
Much, 361
Multiple, 361
Multitude, 361
Mum, 361
Murmer, 361
Muscle, 361
Muscular, 361
Music, 361
Musical, 363
Must, 363
Myopic, 363
Mysteries, 363
Mysterious, 363
Mystery, 363
Mystic, 364
Mystical, 364
Myth, 364
Mythical, 364
Myths, 364

N

Name, 365
Naps, 365

Narrow, 365
Nation, 365
Nature, 365
Naughty, 366
Navigate, 366
Near, 366
Neat, 366
Necklace, 366
Nectar, 366
Need, 366
Needed, 368
Needle, 368
Needs, 368
Negotiate, 369
Negotiating, 369
Neighbour, 369
Neither, 370
Nerd, 370
Nerve, 370
Nerves, 370
Nervous, 370
Nesting, 370
Never, 370
New, 370
Newborn, 370
Newfound, 370
News, 371
Newspapers, 371
Nexus, 371
Nibble, 371
Nice, 371
Nifty, 371
Night, 371
Nightingale, 372
Nightmare, 372
Nights, 372
Noble, 372
Nod, 372
Noise, 372
Nonetheless, 372
Nonsense, 372
Nose, 373
Nothing, 373
Nourished, 373
Novice, 373
Nuclear, 373
Number, 373

O

Obedient, 374
Obese, 374
Obsessed, 374
Obsolete, 374
Obviously, 374
Occasionally, 374
Ocean, 374
Oceans, 375
Offend, 376
Offending, 376
Offer, 376
Often, 376
Old, 376
Omission, 376
Onions, 377
Opaque, 377
Open, 377
Opinion, 377
Opponents, 377
Opportunity, 377
Opposition, 377
Optimism, 377
Optimist, 377
Option, 377
Orchids, 377
Ordinary, 377
Original, 378
Ouch, 378
Ounce, 378
Outsider, 378
Over, 378
Oversell, 378
Overstepped, 378
Overtake, 378
Owes, 378
Owned, 378
Owner, 378

P

Pace, 379
Paces, 379
Pack, 379
Pact, 379
Paddle, 379

Page, 379
Paged, 380
Paid, 380
Pain, 380
Painful, 381
Painfully, 382
Pains, 382
Paint, 382
Painted, 382
Pair, 382
Paired, 382
Palate, 382
Pale, 382
Palm, 382
Panic, 382
Pant, 382
Pantaloon, 382
Panther, 382
Parade, 383
Paradise, 383
Paradox, 383
Paranoid, 383
Paranoids, 384
Parasite, 384
Parasites, 384
Parasites, 384
Park, 384
Parrot, 384
Parrots, 384
Part, 384
Partridge, 384
Pass, 384
Pass, 384
Passing, 384
Passion, 384
Passionate, 385
Passionately, 386
Passions, 386
Past, 386
Patch, 387
Path, 387
Path, 387
Patience, 387
Patient, 387
Pause, 387
Pauses, 387
Pawn, 387

Pay, 387
Pays, 388
Pea, 388
Peace, 388
Peacefully, 388
Peaches, 388
Peacock, 389
Peak, 389
Pearl, 389
Pearls, 389
Peer, 389
Peeves, 389
Peg, 389
Penetrate, 389
Pennies, 389
Penny, 389
People, 390
Perceived, 393
Perfect, 393
Perfection, 393
Perfectly, 393
Performance, 393
Performing, 393
Perfume, 394
Perils, 394
Perk, 394
Perks, 394
Perky, 394
Permanence, 394
Permanent, 394
Permission, 394
Permit, 394
Perplexity, 394
Persistence, 394
Persistent, 394
Person, 394
Personal, 395
Personality, 395
Persons, 395
Petals, 395
Phantom, 395
Philosopher, 395
Phrase, 395
Physical, 395
Piano, 395
Pick, 395
Pickering, 395

Index

Pickle, 395
Picture, 396
Pigeon, 396
Pilgrimage, 396
Pill, 396
Pillow, 396
Pills, 396
Pinches, 396
Pinching, 396
Pirate, 396
Pirates, 396
Pistol, 396
Pit, 397
Pitch, 397
Pity, 397
Placate, 397
Place, 397
Placid, 397
Plague, 397
Plain, 397
Plan, 397
Planet, 398
Planning, 398
Plans, 398
Planted, 398
Play, 398
Played, 399
Playing, 399
Plays, 399
Plea, 399
Plead, 399
Pleading, 399
Pleasant, 399
Please, 400
Pleased, 400
Pleases, 400
Pleasing, 400
Pleasure, 400
Pleasures, 402
Pledge, 403
Plenty, 403
Plight, 403
Plights, 404
Ploughing, 404
Plucked, 404
Plumage, 404
Plutocrat, 404

Poach, 404
Poem, 404
Poems, 404
Poet, 404
Poetic, 405
Poetically, 405
Poetry, 405
Poets, 407
Point, 408
Pointed, 408
Poison, 408
Polish, 408
Polishes, 408
Polishing, 408
Polite, 408
Political, 408
Poor, 408
Popcorn, 409
Popping, 409
Porridge, 409
Portends, 409
Portrait, 409
Pose, 409
Position, 409
Possessed, 409
Possible, 409
Postman, 409
Potboiler, 409
Potion, 409
Pound, 410
Pour, 410
Poverty, 410
Powdered, 410
Power, 410
Powerful, 411
Powers, 411
Practice, 411
Practiced, 412
Praise, 412
Praised, 412
Praising, 412
Prankster, 412
Pray, 412
Prayed, 413
Prayer, 413
Prayers, 413
Preach, 413

Preached, 413
Preaches, 413
Preamble, 413
Precede, 413
Precious, 413
Precise, 414
Precision, 414
Predicament, 414
Predict, 414
Predictions, 414
Prejudice, 414
Prejudiced, 414
Prescription, 414
Presence, 414
Present, 414
Preserve, 414
Preserved, 414
Pressure, 414
Pretended, 414
Pretender, 414
Pretender, 414
Pretending, 415
Pretends, 415
Pretense, 415
Pretenses, 415
Pretext, 415
Pretty, 415
Prevention, 415
Preventive, 415
Prey, 415
Preys, 415
Price, 415
Priceless, 415
Prices, 415
Pride, 416
Prince, 416
Printing, 416
Privacy, 416
Private, 416
Privately, 416
Privileges, 416
Privileges, 416
Prize, 416
Problem, 417
Professional, 418
Profile, 418
Profit, 418

Progress, 418
Prominent, 418
Promise, 418
Promised, 418
Promises, 418
Prompt, 419
Prone, 419
Pronouncement, 419
Proof, 419
Prop, 419
Proper, 419
Properly, 420
Property, 420
Prophet, 420
Prophets, 420
Prose, 420
Prospects, 420
Prosperity, 420
Protect, 420
Protected, 420
Protective, 420
Prove, 420
Proven, 421
Proverbs, 421
Provocation, 421
Provocative, 421
Provoke, 421
Prune, 421
Psychiatrist, 421
Psychic, 421
Public, 421
Publicly, 422
Puffed, 422
Puffins, 422
Pulse, 422
Pulses, 422
Punctuations, 422
Punishment, 422
Purchased, 422
Purely, 422
Purify, 422
Purity, 422
Pursue, 422
Pursued, 422
Pussy, 422
Puzzle, 422

Puzzled, 422
Pyaar, 422

Q

Quality, 423
Quarrel, 423
Queen, 423
Query, 423
Question, 423
Quick, 424
Quicker, 424
Quickly, 424
Quiet, 424
Quietly, 424
Quietness, 424
Quips, 424
Quit, 424
Quite, 424

R

Rabbits, 425
Race, 425
Racier, 425
Radiates, 425
Raft, 425
Rage, 425
Raging, 425
Rain, 425
Rainbow, 426
Raindrops, 426
Rains, 426
Rank, 426
Rankled, 426
Rapturous, 426
Rare, 426
Rat, 426
Rate, 426
Rather, 426
Rattle, 426
Ravages, 426
Raved, 426
Raved, 427
Reach, 427
Read, 427
Reader, 427
Readers, 427
Reading, 427
Ready, 427
Reality, 427
Really, 427
Realms, 427
Reason, 428
Reasoning's, 428
Reasons, 428
Rebel, 429
Reborn, 429
Receding, 429
Receipt, 429
Reception, 429
Reckless, 429
Reclusive, 429
Recollections, 429
Record, 429
Recover, 429
Recreation, 429
Reduced, 429
Reel, 429
Refined, 429
Reflected, 429
Reflection, 430
Reform, 430
Reformed, 430
Reforms, 430
Refrain, 430
Refuse, 430
Refuses, 430
Regret, 430
Regrets, 430
Reign, 431
Reigned, 431
Rejoice, 431
Relationships, 431
Relatively, 431
Relax, 431
Relaxed, 431
Relentless, 431
Relief, 431
Relief, 431
Relies, 431
Relieve, 431
Religion, 432
Relish, 432
Reluctance, 432
Rely, 432
Remain, 432
Remained, 432
Remedies, 432
Remember, 432
Remembered, 432
Remembering, 432
Remembrance, 432
Remind, 432
Remiss, 433
Remorse, 433
Remove, 433
Rendering, 433
Renew, 433
Renovate, 433
Renown, 433
Repair, 433
Repaired, 433
Repeat, 433
Repeating, 433
Repentance, 433
Replace, 434
Reprieve, 434
Reproachful, 434
Reprove, 434
Republic, 434
Reputation, 434
Request, 435
Resembles, 435
Resentment, 435
Resist, 435
Resistance, 435
Resisted, 435
Resolution, 435
Resolve, 435
Resonance, 435
Resorting, 435
Resorts, 435
Resources, 435
Respects, 435
Resplendent, 435
Responsibility, 436
Rest, 436
Restless, 436
Restrain, 436
Restrict, 436
Restrictions, 436
Result, 436
Retreat, 436
Retriever, 436
Return, 436
Returning, 436
Reveal, 437
Revealing, 437
Revealing, 437
Revealing, 437
Reveals, 437
Revenge, 437
Reverence, 437
Reverse, 437
Review, 437
Revise, 437
Revised, 437
Revolving, 437
Reward, 437
Rewarding, 437
Rewards, 437
Rhyme, 438
Rhythmic, 438
Rich, 439
Riches, 439
Richness, 439
Rid, 439
Riddle, 439
Ride, 439
Rides, 439
Ridiculous, 439
Riding, 439
Rifle, 439
Right, 439
Ring, 439
Ringing, 440
Ringside, 440
Ripe, 440
Rise, 440
Rising, 440
Risk, 440
Risks, 440
Risky, 440
Ritual, 440
Rivalry, 440
River, 440
Road, 441
Roads, 441

Index

Roadways, 441
Roam, 441
Rocking, 441
Role, 441
Roles, 441
Romance, 441
Romances, 442
Romancing, 442
Romantic, 442
Romantically, 442
Root, 443
Rose, 443
Roses, 443
Rotten, 444
Rough, 444
Royalty, 444
Ruby, 444
Rude, 444
Rudeness, 444
Ruined, 444
Rule, 445
Ruled, 445
Rulers, 445
Rules, 445
Ruling, 445
Rum, 445
Rumination, 445
Rumour, 446
Rumoured, 446
Rumours, 446
Run, 446
Rush, 446
Rushed, 446
Rust, 446
Rustic, 446
Rustle, 446
Ruthless, 446

S

Sacred, 447
Sacrifice, 447
Sacrificial, 447
Sad, 447
Saddest, 447
Sadness, 447
Safely, 448

Sage, 448
Sail, 448
Sailed, 448
Sailor, 448
Sailors, 448
Sails, 448
Saint, 448
Saints, 448
Salad, 448
Salesman, 448
Same, 448
Sample, 449
Sanctioned, 449
Sanctity, 449
Sandal, 449
Sandals, 449
Sang, 449
Sanity, 449
Santa, 449
Sapling, 449
Sardines, 449
Sarong, 449
Satanic, 449
Satire, 449
Satisfaction, 449
Satisfactory, 449
Save, 450
Saves, 450
Saviour, 450
Savory, 450
Savour, 450
Say, 450
Saying, 450
Scale, 450
Scandal, 450
Scanner, 450
Scar, 450
Scare, 450
Scared, 451
Scares, 451
Scars, 451
Scary, 451
Scenes, 451
Scent, 451
Scentry, 451
Scheme, 451
Scholar, 452

Scholarship, 452
School, 452
Scoff, 452
Scoop, 452
Score, 452
Scores, 452
Scorpion, 452
Scrap, 453
Scratched, 453
Scream, 453
Screaming, 453
Sea, 453
Seagull, 453
Sealed, 453
Seamers, 453
Search, 453
Searching, 453
Season, 454
Seasonal, 454
Seasons, 454
Seat, 454
Seated, 454
Seaweed, 454
Seclusion, 454
Secrecy, 454
Secret, 454
Secretly, 455
Secrets, 455
Secure, 456
Seduce, 456
See, 456
Seed, 456
Seeding, 456
Seeds, 456
Seeing, 457
Seek, 457
Seeking, 457
Seems, 457
Seen, 457
Selection, 457
Self, 457
Selfish, 457
Sell, 457
Semantic, 457
Semblance, 457
Send, 457
Sense, 457

Senseless, 458
Senses, 458
Sensors, 458
Sensually, 459
Sensuous, 459
Sentence, 459
Sentimental, 459
Sentiments, 459
Separation, 459
Sequel, 459
Serenade, 459
Serendipity, 459
Serene, 459
Serenely, 459
Serenity, 459
Serious, 459
Serpent, 459
Servant, 460
Serve, 460
Serves, 460
Settle, 460
Shade, 460
Shades, 460
Shadow, 460
Shadows, 460
Shaken, 461
Shame, 461
Shamed, 461
Shameful, 461
Shameless, 461
Shamelessly, 461
Shaped, 461
Shapes, 462
Share, 462
Shared, 462
Sharing, 462
Shark, 462
Sharks, 462
Sharp, 462
Shattered, 462
Shattering, 462
She, 463
Shear, 463
Shed, 463
Sheen, 463
Shelf, 463
Shelter, 463

Shepherd, 463
Shield, 463
Shifted, 463
Shifty, 463
Shine, 463
Shines, 464
Shining, 464
Shiny, 464
Ship, 464
Shiver, 464
Shoe, 464
Shoot, 464
Shooting, 464
Shoots, 464
Shopping, 464
Shoulder, 464
Shout, 464
Show, 465
Shower, 465
Shrillness, 465
Shrine, 465
Shrugs, 465
Shut, 465
Siblings, 465
Sick, 465
Side, 465
Sidewalk, 465
Sideways, 465
Sieves, 465
Sight, 465
Sight, 466
Significant, 466
Signing, 466
Signs, 466
Silence, 466
Silent, 467
Silkworm, 467
Simple, 467
Simplify, 467
Simply, 467
Sin, 467
Sin, 468
Since, 469
Sincere, 469
Sinful, 469
Sing, 469
Singapore, 469

Singer, 469
Singing, 469
Singlehood, 469
Sings, 470
Singular, 470
Singularly, 470
Sinister, 470
Sink, 470
Sinkable, 470
Sinking, 470
Sinner, 470
Sinning, 470
Sins, 470
Sip, 471
Sipped, 471
Sipping, 471
Sips, 472
Sit, 472
Situation, 472
Sizzle, 472
Skating, 472
Skeletons, 472
Skies, 472
Skill, 472
Skilled, 472
Skills, 472
Skills, 473
Skim, 473
Skin, 473
Skip, 473
Sky, 473
Slander, 473
Slate, 473
Slated, 473
Slave, 473
Sledding, 473
Sleep, 473
Sleeping, 474
Sleepless, 474
Slept, 474
Slick, 474
Slightest, 474
Slip, 474
Slipped, 474
Slippery, 474
Sloppy, 474
Sloth, 475

Slumber, 475
Slurp, 475
Smacking, 475
Smart, 475
Smarter, 475
Smear, 475
Smell, 475
Smelling, 475
Smile, 475
Smiled, 477
Smiles, 477
Smiling, 477
Smoke, 477
Smoking, 477
Smooth, 478
Snail, 478
Snake, 478
Sneaks, 478
Sneeze, 478
Snickering, 478
Snort, 478
Snowbirds, 478
Snowflakes, 478
Snuff, 478
Snuffed, 478
Snuggled, 478
Sobbed, 478
Sober, 478
Sobriety, 479
Societies, 479
Society, 479
Socks, 479
Soften, 479
Softer, 479
Softly, 479
Softness, 479
Soil, 479
Solace, 479
Soldier, 479
Solemn, 479
Solitude, 479
Solve, 480
Somebody, 480
Someone, 480
Something, 480
Sometimes, 480
Song, 480

Songs, 481
Sonnet, 481
Sonorous, 481
Sooner, 481
Soothing, 481
Sorrow, 482
Sorry, 482
Sought, 482
Soul, 483
Soulmate, 485
Souls, 485
Sound, 485
Sounded, 486
Sounds, 486
Soup, 486
Sour, 486
Source, 486
Sources, 486
Sow, 486
Sown, 486
Space, 487
Spaces, 487
Spaghetti, 487
Spare, 487
Spared, 487
Spark, 487
Sparkle, 487
Sparkling, 487
Sparks, 487
Spat, 487
Speak, 488
Speaker, 488
Speaking, 488
Speaks, 488
Special, 489
Spectators, 489
Speculation, 489
Speech, 489
Speech, 489
Speeches, 489
Speed, 489
Spell, 490
Spend, 490
Spice, 490
Spices, 490
Spider, 490
Spill, 490

Index

Spilled, 491
Spin, 491
Spinach, 491
Spinning, 491
Spirit, 491
Spirits, 491
Spiritually, 491
Splendid, 491
Splendour, 491
Splurging, 491
Splutter, 492
Spoken, 492
Spontaneous, 492
Spoonful, 492
Sports, 492
Spots, 492
Spotted, 492
Spouse, 492
Spree, 492
Spring, 492
Sprout, 492
Sprouts, 492
Spun, 492
Spunk, 492
Squabble, 492
Squished, 492
Stadium, 493
Stag, 493
Stage, 493
Stains, 493
Staircase, 493
Stairs, 493
Stalactites, 493
Stale, 493
Stall, 493
Stalling, 493
Stallion, 493
Stalls, 493
Stand, 493
Star, 493
Starching, 494
Stare, 494
Stares, 494
Staring, 494
Stars, 494
Start, 494
Started, 494

Starter, 494
Starters, 495
Starts, 495
Starved, 495
States, 495
Staunch, 495
Stay, 495
Steadily, 495
Steak, 495
Stealing, 495
Steam, 495
Steamer, 495
Steel, 495
Steeple, 495
Step, 495
Sternly, 495
Stick, 496
Still, 496
Sting, 496
Stirring, 496
Stitch, 496
Stitches, 496
Stock, 496
Stocking, 496
Stocking, 496
Stolen, 497
Stomach, 497
Stone, 497
Stood, 497
Stop, 497
Store, 497
Stories, 497
Storm, 497
Story, 498
Stout, 498
Straight, 498
Straighten, 499
Straightens, 499
Straighter, 499
Strange, 499
Strategic, 499
Strawberries, 499
Stray, 499
Strays, 499
Streaking, 499
Street, 500
Street, 500

Strength, 500
Stress, 500
Strife, 500
Strike, 500
String, 500
Strings, 500
Stripe, 501
Striving, 501
Stroke, 501
Strong, 501
Stronger, 502
Struggle, 502
Struggling, 502
Stubborn, 502
Stuck, 502
Study, 502
Stuff, 502
Stunning, 502
Stunt, 502
Stupid, 502
Stupidity, 503
Stutters, 503
Style, 503
Subconscious, 503
Submission, 503
Substance, 503
Succeed, 503
Succeeded, 503
Success, 503
Success, 503
Suffer, 504
Suffering, 504
Suffers, 504
Suffice, 504
Suicidal, 504
Sullible, 504
Sum, 504
Summer, 504
Summit, 504
Sun, 504
Sunday, 505
Sunlight, 505
Sunrise, 505
Sunset, 506
Sunshine, 506
Superstition, 506
Sure, 506

Surely, 506
Surfaces, 506
Surprise, 506
Surprising, 507
Surrender, 507
Surrounded, 507
Survival, 507
Survive, 507
Survived, 507
Susceptible, 507
Suspenders, 507
Suspense, 507
Suspicion, 507
Suspicious, 508
Swallowed, 508
Swapping, 508
Swarm, 508
Sweat, 508
Sweet, 508
Sweeter, 509
Sweetie, 509
Sweetness, 509
Swift, 509
Swiftly, 509
Swim, 509
Swing, 509
Swish, 509
Switch, 509
Switched, 509
Sword, 510
Sycophant, 510
Symphony, 510
Symptoms, 510

T

Tackle, 511
Tact, 511
Tactic, 511
Tactical, 511
Tail, 511
Tale, 511
Talent, 511
Tales, 511
Talk, 512
Talking, 512
Tall, 512

Tame, 512
Tampering, 512
Tangle, 512
Tangled, 512
Tangles, 512
Tap, 512
Target, 512
Task, 512
Taste, 513
Tasted, 513
Tastes, 513
Taught, 513
Taunt, 513
Taunted, 513
Tax, 513
Taxes, 514
Tea, 514
Teach, 514
Team, 514
Tear, 514
Teardrops, 515
Tearing, 515
Tears, 515
Tease, 517
Teasing, 517
Technical, 517
Technique, 517
Teeth, 517
Temper, 517
Temperament, 518
Tempered, 518
Tempest, 518
Temples, 518
Temporarily, 518
Tempt, 518
Temptation, 518
Tempted, 519
Tendency, 519
Tendrils, 519
Tense, 519
Tension, 519
Tent, 519
Tentacles, 519
Termites, 519
Terms, 519
Territory, 520
Terror, 520

Terrors, 520
Test, 520
Test, 521
Tested, 521
Testing, 521
Text, 521
Thank, 521
Theme, 521
Themselves, 521
Thief, 521
Thieves, 522
Thin, 522
Things, 522
Think, 522
Thinking, 523
Thinks, 524
Thinner, 524
Thirst, 524
Thorn, 524
Thorns, 524
Thought, 524
Thoughtful, 528
Thoughts, 528
Thread, 532
Threads, 532
Threat, 532
Throat, 532
Throne, 532
Throng, 532
Through, 532
Throw, 533
Thumb, 533
Thunder, 533
Thundering, 533
Tibetan, 533
Tickle, 533
Tiddly, 533
Tide, 533
Tie, 533
Tied, 533
Tiger, 533
Tight, 533
Tighten, 534
Tighter, 534
Tightly, 534
Tights, 534
Time, 534

Timeless, 540
Times, 540
Timid, 540
Timing, 540
Tip, 540
Tired, 540
Tireless, 540
Tires, 540
Tiresome, 541
Tissue, 541
Tit, 541
Titanic, 541
Toad, 541
Tobacco, 541
Toes, 541
Together, 541
Toil, 542
Token, 542
Told, 542
Tolerance, 542
Tolerant, 542
Tomorrow, 542
Tonic, 542
Tools, 542
Top, 542
Tops, 542
Topsy, 542
Tortuous, 542
Touch, 543
Tough, 543
Tourist, 543
Tower, 543
Town, 543
Toys, 543
Trace, 543
Traces, 543
Track, 543
Trademark, 543
Tradition, 543
Tragedy, 543
Trail, 543
Trails, 544
Train, 544
Trained, 544
Training, 544
Traits, 544
Tranquility, 544

Transformed, 544
Transmitted, 544
Transparent, 544
Transplanted, 544
Trap, 544
Traps, 544
Trash, 544
Travel, 544
Traveled, 544
Traveling, 545
Travelled, 545
Tray, 545
Treacherous, 545
Treason, 545
Treasure, 545
Treasure, 545
Treasured, 545
Treasures, 545
Treasures, 545
Treasury, 546
Treat, 546
Trendy, 546
Trials, 546
Tribe, 546
Tribute, 546
Trick, 546
Trickle, 546
Trickles, 546
Tricks, 547
Tried, 547
Tries, 547
Trigger, 547
trimming, 547
Trip, 547
Triplets, 547
Triumph, 547
Trivial, 547
Trivialities, 547
Trolley, 547
Trouble, 547
Troubled, 548
Troubles, 548
Troublesome, 549
Trout, 549
Truculence, 549
True, 549
Truly, 549

Index

Trusted, 549
Trusting, 549
Trusting, 550
Truth, 550
Truths, 551
Try, 551
Trying, 552
Tryst, 552
Tulips, 552
Tumbling, 552
Tumour, 552
Tune, 552
Turbulence, 552
Turbulent, 552
Turkey, 552
Turn, 552
Turning, 552
Turtle, 553
Twice, 553
Twilight, 553
Twinkle, 553
Twinkling, 553
Twist, 553
Twister, 553
Twit, 553
Type, 553

U

Umbilical, 554
Unassuming, 554
Unawares, 554
Uncap, 554
Uncaring, 554
Uncensored, 554
Uncertain, 554
Uncivilized, 554
Uncoil, 554
Unconcerned, 554
Unconscious, 554
Uncontrolled, 554
Underdog, 554
Understood, 555
Undeterred, 555
Undone, 555
Uneasy, 555
Unending, 555

Unequal, 555
Unexplored, 555
Unfaithful, 555
Unforgettable, 555
Unfulfilled, 555
Unguarded, 555
Unhappy, 555
Unhelpful, 555
Unhinged, 555
Unkempt, 555
Unkind, 555
Unknown, 556
Unless, 556
Unlike, 556
Unlocked, 556
Unloved, 556
Unlucky, 556
Unmistakable, 556
Unraveled, 556
Unrealistic, 556
Unreasonable, 556
Unrest, 556
Unsaid, 556
Unsavoury, 556
Unscathed, 556
Unscrupulous, 556
Unseasonable, 556
Unsolicited, 557
Unspeakable, 557
Unsuited, 557
Unsure, 557
Unveiled, 557
Unwanted, 557
Unwelcome, 557
Unwilling, 557
Unwise, 557
Unyielding, 557
Upheavals, 557
Uplift, 557
Uplifted, 557
Uplifting, 557
Upright, 558
Uprising, 558
Upside, 558
Urban, 558
Urge, 558
Urges, 558

Useful, 558
Utility, 558

V

Valentine, 559
Valentines, 559
Validation, 559
Value, 559
Valued, 559
Values, 559
Vampires, 559
Vanishing, 559
Vanities, 559
Vanity, 559
Variety, 560
Vaulted, 560
Vegetation, 560
Veil, 560
Vengeance, 560
Venomous, 560
Venture, 560
Ventures, 560
Verbal, 560
Verse, 560
Verses, 560
Version, 560
Versus, 560
Vertical, 560
Vices, 560
Vicious, 561
Victim, 561
Victory, 561
Vigilant, 561
Village, 561
Violence, 561
Violent, 561
Virtual, 561
Virtue, 561
Virtues, 562
Virtuous, 562
Virus, 563
Visible, 563
Vision, 563
Vocabulary, 563
Vocabulary, 563
Vocation, 563

Voice, 563
Voices, 563
Void, 563
Volcano, 563
Vote, 563
Vulnerable, 563

W

Waddle, 564
Wage, 564
Wait, 564
Waited, 564
Waiting, 564
Wake up, 564
Wake, 564
Wakefulness, 564
Wakes up, 564
Waking, 565
Walk, 565
Walking, 565
Wallet, 565
Wand, 565
Wander, 565
Wandering, 565
Want, 565
Wanted, 565
War, 565
Warm, 566
Warmth, 566
Warn, 566
Warning, 566
Warns, 566
Wars, 566
Warts, 567
Waste, 567
Wasted, 567
Wastes, 567
Watch, 567
Water, 567
Watering, 567
Waters, 568
Watertight, 568
Wave, 568
Waved, 568
Waves, 568
Way, 568

Waylaid, 568
Ways, 568
Wayward, 569
Weak, 569
Weakness, 569
Weaknesses, 569
Wealth, 569
Wealthy, 569
Weapons, 570
Wears, 570
Weary, 570
Weather, 570
Web, 570
Wedding, 571
Wedlock, 571
Weed, 571
Weeds, 571
Week, 571
Weekends, 571
Weeping, 571
Weight, 571
Welcome, 571
Well, 571
Whale, 571
Whatever, 572
Whim, 572
Whims, 572
Whirl, 572
Whisky, 572
Whisper, 572
Whispered, 572
Whispering, 572
Whispers, 572
Whistle, 572
Whiteness, 572
Whole, 572
Why, 573
Wicked, 573
Wicket, 573
Wide, 573
Wider, 573
Wild, 573
Wildness, 573
Will, 573
Willed, 574
Willing, 574
Willow, 574

Win, 574
Wind, 574
Window, 575
Winds, 575
Wine, 575
Wined, 575
Wings, 575
Wink, 575
Winked, 575
Winner, 575
Winning, 575
Wins, 575
Winter, 576
Winterland, 576
Winters, 576
Wired, 576
Wisdom, 576
Wise, 576
Wisely, 577
Wiser, 577
Wises, 577
Wish, 577
Wishes, 579
Wishful, 579
Wishing, 579
Wit, 579
Within, 579
Without, 579
Witnessed, 580
Wobble, 580
Woe, 580
Woes, 580
Woke, 580
Wolverine, 580
Woman, 580
Won, 580
Wonder, 580
Wondered, 580
Wonderful, 580
Wondering, 581
Wonderland, 581
Wonders, 581
Woodpecker, 581
Word, 581
Words, 582
Words, 582
Wore, 583

Work, 584
World, 584
Worm, 585
Worms, 585
Worried, 585
Worries, 585
Worry, 585
Worrying, 585
Worse, 585
Worship, 585
Worshipping, 585
Worst, 585
Worth, 586
Worthy, 586
Wound, 586
Wounded, 586
Wounds, 586
Wrangle, 586
Wrath, 586
Writer, 586
Writers, 586
Writing, 586
Written, 587
Wrong, 587
Wrongdoing, 587

Y

Yahoo, 588
Yawn, 588
Yawning, 588
Yearn, 588
Yearning, 588
Years, 588
Yesterday, 588
Yield, 588
Yorker, 589
Young, 589
Younger, 589
Yourself, 589
Youth, 589
Youthful, 589

Z

Zeal, 589